2010Boston: The Changing Contours of
World Mission and Christianity

2010Boston: The Changing Contours of World Mission and Christianity

Edited by
Todd M. Johnson,
Rodney L. Petersen,
Gina A. Bellofatto,
and Travis L. Myers

PICKWICK *Publications* • Eugene, Oregon

2010BOSTON: THE CHANGING CONTOURS OF WORLD MISSION AND CHRISTIANITY

Copyright © 2012 Wipf & Stock. All rights reserved. Except for brief quotations in critical publications or reviews, no part of this book may be reproduced in any manner without prior written permission from the publisher. Write: Permissions, Wipf and Stock Publishers, 199 W. 8th Ave., Suite 3, Eugene, OR 97401.

Pickwick Publications
An Imprint of Wipf and Stock Publishers
199 W. 8th Ave., Suite 3
Eugene, OR 97401

www.wipfandstock.com

ISBN 13: 978-1-61097-265-9

Cataloging-in-Publication data:

2010Boston : the changing contours of world mission and christianity / edited by Todd M. Johnson, Rodney L. Petersen, Gina A. Bellofatto, and Travis L. Myers.

xxvi + 358 p. ; 23 cm. Includes bibliographical references and index.

ISBN 13: 978-1-61097-265-9

1. Missions. 2. Missions—Congresses. 3. World Missionary Conference (1910: Edinburgh, Scotland). 4. Missions—Developing countries—Case studies. I. Johnson, Todd M. (Todd Michael), 1958–. II. Petersen, Rodney L. III. Bellofatto, Gina. IV. Myers, Travis L. V. Title.

BV2060 J64 2012

Manufactured in the U.S.A.

Contents

Preface / vii
Contributors / xi
An Introduction to 2010Boston: The Changing Contours of World Mission and Christianity / xvii

Part I: The World Christian Movement

1 The Demographics of World Mission and Christianity, 1910–2010
 —*Todd M. Johnson* / 3

2 Boston, Students, and Missions from 1810 to 2010
 —*Dana L. Robert* / 13

3 From Boston to the Whole World: Twentieth-Century North American Roman Catholic Missions and the "Antioch Agenda"
 —*Angelyn Dries, O.S.F.* / 28

4 Discerning the Future of World Christianity: Vision and Blindness at the World Missionary Conference, Edinburgh 1910
 —*Brian Stanley* / 47

Part II: Mission in the Twenty-first Century

5 Journey to the Center of Gravity: Christian Mission One Century after Edinburgh 1910—*Athanasios Papathanasiou* / 67

6 Mission and Interreligious Dialogue: Edinburgh, Vatican II, and Beyond—*Peter C. Phan* / 84

7 Wooden Boxes and Latticed Windows: Christian Confession and Post-colonizing Mission—*Ruth Padilla DeBorst* / 110

8 Finding the Seventh Story—*Brian D. McLaren* / 124

vi Contents

   9 Theological Education and Mission in Euro-American Institutions of Higher Learning: A Non-Western Reflection
—*Daniel Jeyaraj* / 132

Part III: Student Perspectives

10 The Student Paper Workshops of 2010Boston
—*Travis L. Myers* / 155

11 "From Among Her Own Children": African-Americans and the Evangelization of Africa in the Nineteenth Century
—*Mary Cloutier* / 163

12 Disciples in Mission: Evangelization, Liberation, and a "Theology of Neighbor"—*Marcus C. Mescher* / 180

13 Do-It-Yourself Missions: The Rise of Independent Faith-Based Organizations and the Changing Contours of Missions
—*Eva Pascal* / 193

14 Methodist Border Friendship Commission: A Case Study
—*Lisa Beth White* / 213

15 A Preliminary Study of Symbiotic Mission through Floral Beauty
—*Megumi Yoshida* / 228

Part IV: Reports and Conclusion

16 2010Boston from the Student Perspective—*Gina Bellofatto* / 245

Introduction to the Three Conference Reports / 254

17 Tokyo 2010: Global Mission Consultation—*Allen Yeh* / 256

18 Lausanne III: A Success?—*LouAnn Stropoli* / 261

19 Witnessing for Christ Today: Christian Mission Beyond Edinburgh 2010—*Kapya John Koama* / 267

20 The Eight Themes of 2010Boston—*Rodney L. Petersen* / 273

Appendix I: 2010Boston Schedule / 303
Appendix II: 2010Boston Worship Guide / 312
Index / 337

Preface

NUMEROUS BOOKS ON CHRISTIANITY and world mission have been published in the past three decades. Nearly all recognize a massive shift in the demographic center of global Christianity from North to South, yet there are still major areas of inquiry related to this shift that have received little attention. One of these is the contrast between Western missionary-led conferences of one hundred years ago and truly global Christian gatherings in the twenty-first century. This volume is one attempt at filling in this gap in scholarship.

Most chapters in this volume were originally given as papers at a conference in Boston in November 2010. The conference was organized by the International Mission and Ecumenism (IME) faculty committee of the Boston Theological Institute (BTI). As the fourth and final international conference in 2010 to mark the 100th anniversary of the 1910 Edinburgh World Missionary Conference, it afforded the opportunity to reflect on the ensuing 100 years post-Edinburgh, on the state of the world Christian movement in 2010, as well as on the previous three centennial celebrations. While Edinburgh 1910 was primarily a Protestant conference, in 2010 a broad range of Christian traditions reflected on the anniversary. Many of these traditions were represented by the keynote speakers and other participants at 2010Boston.

Gratitude is due first to the faculty, deans, and presidents of the nine (now ten) schools of the BTI. The conference was built on over forty years of teaching, research, and publications of these individuals. The BTI faculty participating in the planning of this conference included Daniel Jeyaraj and Nimi Wariboko (Andover Newton Theological School), Fr. Raymond Helmick, S.J. and Catherine Cornille (Boston College Department of Theology), Margaret Guider, O.S.F. (Boston College School of Theology and Ministry), Dana Robert and Elizabeth

Parsons (Boston University School of Theology), Ian Douglas and Christopher Duraisingh (Episcopal Divinity School), Todd Johnson and Peter Kuzmič (Gordon-Conwell Theological Seminary), Susan Abraham (Harvard Divinity School), and Fr. Luke Veronis (Holy Cross Greek Orthodox School of Theology).

We are grateful to our sponsors, the DeFreitas Foundation of Eastern Bank and the Day Foundation. We are also thankful for support from the Massachusetts Council of Churches (Jack Johnson, Executive Director), the Overseas Ministries Study Center (Jonathan Bonk, Director), the American Society of Missiology (Eastern Fellowship), and the American Academy of Religion (New England-Maritimes region, with assistance from Rebecca Norris). We acknowledge the rich contributions of OMSC scholars in residence who attended, especially OMSC artist in residence Emmanuel Garibay, who generously loaned a special exhibition of his artwork and spoke in a workshop about it during the conference. Independent film producer Christopher Gilbert and Andover Newton videographer Robert Craigue made their own special contributions.

Special thanks to the Walker Center for Ecumenical Exchange for housing many of our conference participants from out of state and other countries. Our memories and also our thanks extend to the late Rev. Peter J. Gomes, Plummer Professor of Christian Morals and Pusey Minister in The Memorial Church, and to Jan Randolph, who together made possible our closing assembly at The Memorial Church, Harvard University.

Travis Myers was the conference organizer and Br. Lawrence Whitney, LC+ was the student secretary of the BTI IME committee and conference registrar. Tracy Howe Wispelwey was the 2010Boston worship coordinator and contributed to graphic design and web development. These three worked tirelessly throughout the planning and implementation of the conference. Special thanks to Jesudas Athyal, Kirsten Borror, Debbie Brubaker, John Chung, Christopher Gilbert, Hillary Greer, Mangyang Imsong, Kara Jackman, Jack Johnson, Chaoluan Kao, Septemmy Lakawa, Donna LaRue, Grace Man, Dorsey McConnell, Daniel Nicholas, Chris Nichols, Emma O'Donnell, Eva Pascal, Clifford Putney, Mugur Roz, Stephanos Ritsi, Isaac Seelam, Sam Sigg, Marian Simion, Joyce Simon and the Andover Newton Bookstore,

Charles "Chuck" Wynder and a host of others who made the conference a success.

The unique feature of 2010Boston was its students and this volume is dedicated to the students of the BTI. In particular, we'd like to thank all of the student paper presenters who catalyzed enriching dialogue throughout the conference. We also could not have brought this present volume to print without the skillful efforts of Gina Bellofatto and Travis Myers in editing these chapters.

Todd M. Johnson
Director
Center for the Study of Global Christianity
Gordon-Conwell Theological Seminary

Rodney L. Petersen
Director
Boston Theological Institute

June 2011

Contributors

Gina A. Bellofatto (MA in religion) is a Research Associate at the Center for the Study of Global Christianity at Gordon-Conwell Theological Seminary. Her research interests include Christian mission, world religions, and evangelicals and interfaith dialogue. She was the Senior Editorial Assistant for the *Atlas of Global Christianity* (Edinburgh University Press, 2009).

Mary Cloutier served for ten years as a missionary in Gabon, Africa with the Christian and Missionary Alliance. She is currently professor of Intercultural Studies at Nyack College (Nyack, NY) and pursuing a PhD in Intercultural Studies through Trinity Evangelical Divinity School in Deerfield, IL.

Ruth Padilla DeBorst has been involved in leadership training, campus ministry, and community development with Christian Reformed World Missions. She is general secretary of the Latin American Theological Fraternity, on the board of International Justice Mission, and director of Ediciones Certeza Unida, the publishing house of Spanish-speaking movements of the International Fellowship of Evangelical Students (IFES). Padilla DeBorst was a speaker at the triennial Urbana student missions conference in 2009 and a keynote Bible expositor at Cape Town 2010 (Third Lausanne Congress on World Evangelization).

Angelyn Dries, O.S.F. is Danforth Chair in the Humanities in the Department of Theological Studies at Saint Louis University. Her book, *The Missionary Movement in American Catholic History* (Orbis, 1998), pioneered the field. She is completing a history of the Maryknoll Society. Dries is past president of the American Society of Missiology and has worked with Korean communities in Milwaukee and a Franciscan Sisters' congregation in Cameroon.

Daniel Jeyaraj is an Indian mission historian and leading authority on the study of the Royal Danish-Halle Mission (Tranquebar Mission), Pietism, the emergence of Protestant churches in eighteenth-century India, and Christian interactions with people of Indic religions. He is the Professor of World Christianity and Director of the Andrew Walls Center for the Study of African Christianity at Liverpool Hope University. He is a visiting lecturer at Andover Newton Theological School.

Todd M. Johnson is Associate Professor in the Study of Global Christianity and Director of the Center for the Study of Global Christianity (CSGC) at Gordon-Conwell Theological Seminary. He is also Research Fellow at Boston University's Institute on Culture, Religion and World Affairs. He is the co-editor, with Kenneth R. Ross, of the *Atlas of Global Christianity* (Edinburgh University Press, 2009).

Kapya John Kaoma received his ThD in Ecology and Mission from Boston University and is a Visiting Researcher at the Boston University Center for Global Christianity and Mission. He formerly served as dean of St. John's Cathedral, lecturer at Africa University in Mutare, Zimbabwe, and academic dean of St. John's Anglican Seminary in Kitwe, Zambia. He is currently the rector of Christ Church (Episcopal Diocese of Massachusetts), Hyde Park, MA and a project director at Political Research Associates.

Brian McLaren is an author and international speaker and activist for "emergent" Christianity. His work has been covered by *Time* (where he was noted one of America's twenty-five most influential evangelicals), *Christianity Today*, *The Christian Century*, and *The Washington Post*, among others. His best known books include *A Generous Orthodoxy* (Zondervan, 2004) and *Everything Must Change* (Thomas Nelson, 2007).

Marcus Mescher is pursuing a PhD in Theology and Education at Boston College. His current studies and concentration on Christian discipleship draw from his numerous years of ministry with high school and college students, especially through service programs and international immersion trips. Mescher is specifically interested in the practical dimensions and pedagogical implications of Catholic Social Teaching.

Travis L. Myers (MA Christian missions and intercultural studies, MDiv biblical and theological studies) is a ThD candidate in missiology (Boston University School of Theology and Gordon-Conwell Theological Seminary). He is a former faculty member of the Cameroon Baptist Theological Seminary and has been involved with ministries to children and youth, the elderly and disabled, international students and recent immigrants in Chicago, Minneapolis, Louisville, and Boston.

Athanasios N. Papathanasiou has practiced law and holds a doctorate in theology. He teaches at the Hellenic Open University, Athens, and is the editor-in-chief of the theological quarterly *Synaxis*. He is the author of *Future, the Background of History: Essays on Church Mission in an Age of Globalization* (Alexander Press, 2005).

Eva Pascal is a PhD candidate in the Division of Religious and Theological Studies in the History of World Christianity and Mission at Boston University. After receiving an MDiv from Harvard Divinity School, she was a lecturer in religion from 2006 to 2010 at McGilvary College of Divinity at Payap University in Chiang Mai, Thailand, teaching such subjects as Christianity, Buddhism, and gender. She has served as a ministerial coordinator for young adults at Boston Temple Church and as a summer term pastoral counselor for HIV/AIDS advocacy groups in Guatemala City, Guatemala.

Rodney L. Petersen is Executive Director of the Boston Theological Institute (BTI), moving to the Boston area from Switzerland in 1990. He is an ordained minister in the Presbyterian Church, U.S.A., serving on several of their committees, and served for seven years as the pastor of the Allston Congregational Church (United Church of Christ). His many publications include co-editor, *The Antioch Agenda: Essays on the Restorative Church in Honor of Orlando E. Costas* (ISPCK, 2007).

Peter C. Phan, a native of Vietnam, is the first non-Anglo to be elected President of the Catholic Theological Society of America. He holds the Ignacio Ellacuría Chair of Catholic Social Thought at Georgetown

University and is on faculty at the East Asian Pastoral Institute, Manila, and Liverpool Hope University, England. He has authored and edited numerous books, including *Christianities in Asia* (Wiley-Blackwell, 2011).

Dana L. Robert is the Truman Collins professor of World Christianity and History of Mission at Boston University School of Theology and co-director of BU's Center for Global Christianity and Mission. A leading historian of mission, she was the opening keynote speaker at Edinburgh 2010. She is the author of *American Women in Mission* (Mercer 1997), *Occupy until I Come: A. T. Pierson and the Evangelization of the World* (Eerdmans, 2003), and *Christian Mission: How Christianity became a World Religion* (Wiley-Blackwell, 2009).

Brian Stanley is Professor of World Christianity and Director of the Centre for the Study of World Christianity at the University of Edinburgh School of Divinity. He has authored histories of Protestant missions and British imperialism (Apollos, 1990), the Baptist Missionary Society (T. & T. Clark, 1992), and the Edinburgh 1910 World Missionary Conference (Eerdmans, 2009).

LouAnn Stropoli holds an MM degree from the Eastman School of Music and an MDiv and ThM from Gordon-Conwell Theological Seminary. She has taught or guest lectured at Gordon College, Newbury College, and at Perspectives classes, as well as in India and Cambodia. She is currently a Research Associate at the Center for the Study of Global Christianity, a missions conference speaker, and world religions instructor. Her ministerial license is held with the Conservative Congregational Christian Conference (CCCC).

Lisa Beth White is an elder in the United Methodist Church and a doctoral student in Practical Theology and Mission at Boston University. She has worked with youth short-term mission programs in Texas and has led adult mission teams on trips to Honduras and South Africa. Rev. White currently serves as a coordinator for teams with Partners In Mission of the Texas Annual Conference (UMC) and is the proud mother of two daughters.

Allen Yeh is a professor at Biola University in Los Angeles, California, teaching World Christianity and the history of missions in the School of Intercultural Studies. He founded and chaired the World Christianity Consultation at the 62nd annual meeting of the Evangelical Theological Society. He attended the four major 2010 conferences (Tokyo, Edinburgh, Cape Town, Boston) and has a forthcoming book about them.

Megumi Yoshida is a doctoral student at the Doshisha School of Theology in Kyoto, Japan. She has served as a researcher of East Asian mission and theology at Tomisaka Christian Center in Tokyo and has been a Visiting Scholar or Fellow at Yale, Birmingham (UK), and Hawai'i Universities. She has participated in the Programme for Theology and Cultures in Asia and the Asian Christian Art Association. Yoshida is an *ikebana* (Japanese flower arranging) master of the Misho School, and a tea ceremony master of the Urasenke School.

An Introduction to 2010Boston: The Changing Contours of World Mission and Christianity

THE "2010BOSTON" CONFERENCE TITLED, "The Changing Contours of World Mission and Christianity," was a four-day conference hosted by the schools of the Boston Theological Institute (BTI) from November 4–7, 2010. It was organized by the International Mission and Ecumenism (IME) committee of the BTI with faculty representing all of the major traditions of Christianity. Co-sponsors included the Massachusetts Council of Churches, the American Academy of Religion (New England-Maritimes region), the American Society of Missiology (Eastern Fellowship), and the Overseas Ministries Study Center (New Haven, CT).

THE BOSTON THEOLOGICAL INSTITUTE

The Boston Theological Institute is an association of ten theological schools in the Greater Boston area and one of the oldest and largest theological consortia in the world. It is composed of schools that represent a wide range of Christian churches and confessions, while also (since 2011) including Hebrew College with its Rabbinical School, making the BTI not only ecumenical, but interfaith. The IME committee is comprised of missions and world Christianity faculty from BTI schools. The BTI is known for the sharing of faculty and resources; the schools' theological libraries together contain almost two million volumes. Cross-registration allows more than 4,500 students to enjoy unparalleled access to academic courses and programming. The BTI also supports ecumenical and interfaith work in the areas of interest to its constituencies through special events like workshops, colloquia, and conferences.

CONFERENCE DIRECTION

The 2010Boston conference was both an event and a process. It was a conscious part of the centennial commemoration of the Edinburgh 1910 World Missionary Conference, coming fourth in line after conferences in Tokyo, Edinburgh, and Cape Town. It was part of a broader conversation among Christians around the world about the meaning of mission in the twenty-first century. Most notably, 2010Boston was about students. More than other centennial gatherings, this conference demonstrated the inseparability of students, theological education, and missions. Such a collaboration of piety and learning forged the North American mission movement and even today continues to shape student involvement in cross-cultural, evangelistic, dialogical, and social justice missions. 2010Boston highlighted the historic role of New Englanders in crossing geographic and cultural boundaries. This commitment to mission ranges from the translation of the Bible into Algonquin by John Eliot in 1661–63 to the founding of the American Board of Commissioners of Foreign Missions in 1810. It includes the launching of American Catholic foreign missions from Boston a century ago. More recently, in the twentieth century, one can add the inception of a neo-Evangelical movement growing out of Boston's Park Street Church.

Student movements in New England, whether Pentecostal, Evangelical, mainline Protestant, Roman Catholic, or Orthodox, continue to energize new forms of mission. Mission is now from the whole church to the whole world, and from around the world back to Boston, as seen in the vibrant ethnic churches that are re-seeding neighborhoods with hope and hospitality, and in multi-ethnic Christian fellowships on many of the area's university campuses. Mission is also a topic of global importance, as questions of religious identity loom large in today's increasingly divided and pluralistic world.

ECUMENICAL AND MISSION ORIENTATION

The 2010Boston conference was ecumenical in outlook and approach. The Ecumenical Movement developed out of concerns within and among Roman Catholic, Orthodox, Protestant, Anglican, Evangelical, and Pentecostal churches and ecclesial fellowships. Among Protestants, orientation to the World Council of Churches and the World Evangelical Alliance (or the Lausanne Movement) has often shaped patterns of relationship with other Christian traditions. An additional way to understand contemporary ecumenism is around the three primary patterns of "faith and order," "life and work," and "mission." Commissions of churches, agencies, or interests around these three areas have been determinative of the structure of the World Council of Churches (WCC), frequently seen as the "banner ship" of ecumenism. However, these areas also shape other patterns of Christian cooperation and bilateral church relationships as well as wider religious engagement. An encyclical of the Ecumenical Patriarchate (1920) called for deeper Christian dialogue structured in a parallel fashion to the new League of Nations. Eventually through the reforming council of the Roman Catholic Church, Vatican II (1962–65), there would arise fresh perspectives on the question of Christian unity with concern for issues of Faith and Order, Life and Work, and the nature of Mission.

The nature of the missionary movement became an ecumenical priority in the twentieth century. Ecumenical missionary conferences in London, England (1888), New York City, USA (1900), Madras, India (1902), and Shanghai, China (1907) were precursors of the influential Edinburgh 1910 World Missionary Conference. Affirming a commitment to make Christ known to the whole world, a movement formed out of this conference under the influence of Methodist John R. Mott to develop a unitive effort on the part of the different Protestant denominations through the formation of the International Missionary Council (IMC, 1921). The IMC conducted significant work in the ensuing years with the World Alliance of YMCAs and YWCAs, the World Student Christian Federation, and Inter-Varsity Christian Fellowship. While the post-WWII years saw the formation of numerous "faith" missions, the missionary efforts of old-line Protestant denominations—insofar as they were united in the IMC—became a third strand of the WCC from 1961–90 as the Department of World Mission and Evangelism. At the same time, Evangelical, Roman Catholic, Orthodox, Anglican,

Pentecostal, and other traditions were also building global networks and holding numerous conferences on the subject of mission.

CONFERENCE LOCATIONS

One unique feature of the 2010Boston conference is that it was held in multiple locations in Boston that represent different Christian traditions. Sessions and events were held at Andover Newton Theological School (American Baptist and United Church of Christ), Boston College (Roman Catholic), Boston University (United Methodist), The Memorial Church, Harvard University (interfaith and ecumenical), Holy Cross Greek Orthodox School of Theology (Orthodox), and Park Street Church (Evangelical Protestant). Multiple site coordinators at the various locations—among them BTI faculty, students, and friends of the host institutions—made such a ecumenical journey around the Boston area possible.

CONFERENCE THEMES

Eight themes were chosen around which the conference was developed. These were related to the themes of the Edinburgh 1910 and 2010 conferences.

1. Changing Contours of Christian Unity

The stress on the importance of cooperation at the Edinburgh Mission Conference has led to a century of ecumenical exploration. Now, in a new century of mission and church life, it is necessary to articulate a missional ecclesiology that places the church squarely as both recipient and herald of the good news offered by Jesus Christ.

2. Mission in Context

The context of the mission enterprise has shifted dramatically since 1910, perhaps most strikingly in the shift from a North-South directionality to South-North. Furthermore, mission takes place in the context of the increasingly prevalent forces of globalization. Respective movements of

Christians in mission must be able to interpret the variety of contexts they each encounter as well as their interaction with one another.

3. Disciples in Mission

If there is one thing that has been learned in the century since the 1910 Edinburgh World Missionary Conference, it is that discipleship is costly. It is necessary to recover and renew spiritual practices as the foundation of mission enterprises as well as to articulate and embody the Christian life in ways both credible and authentic.

4. Education for Mission

Who is a missionary? Who is responsible for the mission enterprise? These questions engender reflection about the catechetical formation of missionaries as well as the theological education of clergy and others responsible for them. Special attention should be given to the role of theological students and ministerial candidates, who are in the process of being educated while also serving as educators for others.

5. Mission and Post-Colonialism

With the demise of colonial models of mission since 1910, contextual theologians have launched a strong critique of Christian mission. A post-colonial mission paradigm must be developed that addresses these critiques while still holding true to the universality of the gospel.

6. Mission in a Pluralist World

One of the major changes in the past century is a greater prevalence and cognizance of religious plurality. A twenty-first century mission theology must grapple with the diversity of religious beliefs, the increasing interaction of adherents of different faiths, and the violence that sometimes accompanies it.

7. Mission and Post-Modernity

Apart from intra-Christian and inter-religious critiques of mission, the rise of secular postmodernity challenges the very relevance of Christianity and therefore its impulse to reach out. Mission paradigms of the twenty-first century must successfully answer secularism and relativism while utilizing the tools of information technology and communications that are hallmarks of our age.

8. Salvation Today

"Salvation" is a contested term in theological discourse, with differing definitions setting various trajectories and goals for ecclesial life. This might include drawing on so-called secular ways of bridging non-Christian and Christian entities. An example of this is the concept and goal of "human flourishing" and how Christian understandings of salvation might relate to the U.N.'s Millennium Development Goals.

WORSHIP

A special conference program of worship songs and prayers was compiled and led by Harvard Divinity School student Tracey Wispelwey of the Restoration Project. By leading many of the worship sessions herself, Wispelwey's voice and presence provided continuity in multiple venues and faithfulness to the commitment of conference organizers to doxological participation. Wispelwey, being attentive to the global nature of the conference purview and constituency, employed various musical styles and liturgies focused on mission and world Christianity. See Appendix II for the conference's complete worship guide.

WALKING THROUGH THE CONFERENCE[1]

Thursday Evening, November 4

The conference was prefaced with several events through the day on Thursday, including a seminar by Norman Thomas on the century since Edinburgh 1910 and a trolley tour of "Boston Mission Sites," organized by Donna LaRue, that highlighted places significant to the origin of the North American mission movement. The conference formally began with an open meeting at Park Street Church. After worship and some introductory remarks by the conference organizers, Dr. Dana Robert gave the first plenary talk titled "Boston, Students, and Missions from

---

1. See Appendix I for the complete conference schedule.

1810 to 2010." Robert utilized a series of photographs and recounted the history of student missions in and from Boston.

Friday Morning, November 5

The next morning the conference moved to Marsh Chapel at Boston University. Following a time of worship, Dr. Brian Stanley gave the second plenary talk titled "Discerning the Future of World Christianity: Vision and Blindness at the World Missionary Conference, Edinburgh 1910." Some additional time was given for questions from the audience. After a short break, a series of reports were presented from the other centennial conferences, moderated by Episcopal Bishop Dr. Ian Douglas. Dr. Allen Yeh reported on Tokyo 2010, Dr. Kapya John Kaoma on Edinburgh 2010, and Rev. LouAnn Stropoli on Cape Town 2010.

Friday Afternoon, November 5

Friday afternoon the conference moved to the Colloquium Room of the Photonics Center at Boston University, where the American Society of Missiology, Eastern Fellowship held a luncheon meeting. There the third plenary, open to all conference participants, was given by Dr. Daniel Jeyaraj titled "Theological Education and Mission in Euro-American Institutions of Higher Learning: A Non-Western Reflection." Following that message, eight concurrent sessions of student paper presentations were held in BU classrooms, facilitated by various BTI faculty. Following those in the afternoon, two additional sessions featured mission and the arts. The Overseas Ministries Study Center (OMSC) artist in residence Emmanuel Garibay, award-winning Filipino artist, discussed his craft and mission as a Christian painter working from a post-colonial perspective. An introduction to the OMSC artists in residence program in general was first given by Rev. Dr. Dwight Baker. Another session offered at the same time featured film producer Christopher Gilbert, who screened a trailer for a new documentary film "Beyond Empires," the story of Bartholomaus Ziegenbalg (1684–1719), which shows how Ziegenbalg's life and work as India's first Protestant missionary anticipated the post-colonial world.

xxiv An Introduction to 2010Boston

Friday Evening, November 5

In the evening the conference moved to Holy Cross Greek Orthodox School of Theology. Father Luke Veronis welcomed the group and led Holy Vespers in the chapel; a delight for the many non-Orthodox conference participants who had never experienced an Orthodox service. After a reception at Holy Cross's Maliotis Cultural Center, Dr. Athanasios N. Papathanasiou presented the fourth plenary, "Journey to the Center of Gravity: Christian Mission One Century after Edinburgh 1910."

Saturday Morning, November 6

In the morning, the conference moved to McGuinn Hall at Boston College where worship was followed by the fifth plenary by Rev. Ruth Padilla DeBorst, titled "Wooden Boxes and Latticed Windows: Christian Confession and Post-colonizing Mission." After a short break, Dr. Peter C. Phan presented the sixth plenary, "Mission and Interreligious Dialogue: Edinburgh, Vatican II, and Beyond." During lunch there was a reception sponsored by the New England-Maritimes region of the American Academy of Religion (NEMAAR) with brief presentations by NEMAAR President Grove Harris and AAR President Dr. Kwok Pui-Lan of Episcopal Divinity School.

Saturday Afternoon, November 6

In the afternoon, the next batch of student papers was presented in eight classrooms of McGuinn Hall, again moderated by BTI faculty members. A special session of OMSC scholars in residence, "Our stories: The World Church in Mission," was moderated by Dr. Jonathan Bonk, Executive Director of the OMSC. After a short break, Todd Johnson presented a brief overview of the *Atlas of Global Christianity*, a major new reference work covering the past 100 years of Christianity, incorporating the work of over sixty scholars from six continents. Immediately following was a special worship session led by Tracey Wispelwey—including a small band of her friends with an eclectic mix of instruments—in celebration of the world church. After worship, Dr. Angelyn Dries, O.S.F. presented the seventh plenary, "From Boston to the Whole World: Twenieth-Century North American Roman Catholic Missions and the 'Antioch Agenda.'"

Saturday Evening, November 6

Many of the conference participants attended a gala dinner sponsored by the Massachusetts Council of Churches in the Heights Room at Boston College, during which Brian McLaren shared some thoughts on the future of denominations. After this special event the conference moved to St. Ignatius Chapel, adjacent to the Boston College campus, where McLaren presented the eighth plenary, "Christian Mission and Peace-Making: Discerning our Secret Non-Weapon." This was followed by a closing liturgy led by students from the Boston University School of Theology.

Sunday Morning, November 7

At The Memorial Church, Harvard University, Anglican Archbishop of York John Sentamu presented a sermon titled "Who is Jesus and What Does He Mean to Those Who Put Their Trust in Him?" This constituted the ninth and final plenary of the 2010Boston conference.

Sunday Afternoon, November 7

After a break for lunch, the final session of the conference was held back at The Memorial Church, Harvard University, where a question on the nature of mission in the twenty-first century was posed by Harvard professor Susan Abraham. Each of the plenary speakers from the conference was given five minutes to respond to Dr. Abraham's question. After the responses, participants broke into small groups to further discuss the questions. These group discussions were led by BTI faculty who then reported back to the larger group when reconvened together. The conference closed with a prayer by acting BTI chairperson, Dr. Dennis Hollinger, President of Gordon-Conwell Theological Seminary, and a reception in the Buttrick Room.

CONCLUSION

The 2010Boston conference had as one of its major goals the involvement of students in reflecting on the past, present, and future of the world church. Leading scholars of world Christianity and mission from Boston and from around the world challenged students and others to think about the historical role of students in the changing contours of world mission and Christianity. In addition, plenary talks emphasized present and future potentialities for students in shaping Christian identities, unity, and the course of mission. Students made their own robust contributions to shared reflection on the conference themes by way of their paper presentations.

2010Boston was the fourth and final of the major conferences commemorating the 1910 World Missionary Conference in Edinburgh. It provided a truly ecumenical view *and local experience* of the remarkable transformation of Christianity worldwide throughout the past 100 years. It did so by utilizing and setting forth the resources of institutions for theological education for the ongoing reflexive process of prophetic discernment and Christian discipleship in a globalized era.

Conference co-chairs

Todd M. Johnson
Rodney L. Petersen

Part I

The World Christian Movement

1

The Demographics of World Mission and Christianity, 1910–2010

Todd M. Johnson

THE *ATLAS OF GLOBAL Christianity* is the first scholarly atlas to document the shift of Christianity to the global South. It features contextual maps of world issues and major religious traditions, including global coverage of religious freedom and religious diversity. It is the first atlas to map Christian affiliation at the provincial level. It is a unique Christian publication in the sense that it contains ecumenical and global coverage, including all Christian traditions in every country. It partners full-color maps of Christian affiliation in every United Nations region with historical essays on Christianity by sixty-four scholars *from* every region of the world to highlight the 100-year history of Christianity. Included with the atlas is an interactive presentation assistant on CD of all maps and graphics for classroom use.

To understand the status of global Christianity and world evangelization 100 years after the Edinburgh 1910 World Missionary Conference, one can consider trends both inside of global Christianity and outside of global Christianity.

4 Todd M. Johnson

TRENDS INSIDE GLOBAL CHRISTIANITY

One major trend within global Christianity is that Christianity has shifted dramatically to the South. Looking at the graph below (global Christian percentage), one can see that at first glance there has been little change in the status of global Christianity over the past 100 years. For the entire 100-year period, Christians have made up approximately one-third of the world's population. This masks dramatic changes in the geography of global Christianity—a process of both north-south and east-west movement stretching back to the earliest days of Christianity.

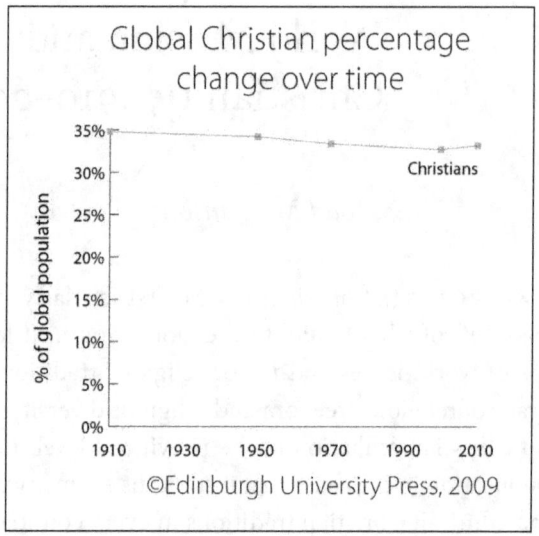

The shift in demographics by continent from 1910 to 2010 most clearly illustrates the shift of Christianity to the global South. While 66 percent of all Christians lived in Europe in 1910, by 2010 only 25.6 percent lived there. By contrast, less than 2 percent of all Christians lived in Africa in 1910, skyrocketing to almost 22 percent by 2010. The global North (defined as Europe and Northern America) contained over 80 percent of all Christians in 1910, falling to under 40 percent by 2010.

The 1910 World Missionary Conference in Edinburgh was placed directly in this Western-dominated picture of global Christianity. As recounted by Ken Ross, "the delegates were, overwhelmingly, British (500) and American (500). Representatives from continental Europe were a small minority (170). Even fewer were the delegates from the 'younger churches' of India, China and Japan (17). There were no African participants, nor were there any from Latin America. No delegate was invited from the Roman Catholic or Eastern Orthodox Churches. While the participants were struck by the diversity of participants, from a longer historical perspective it is striking how limited was their range."[1]

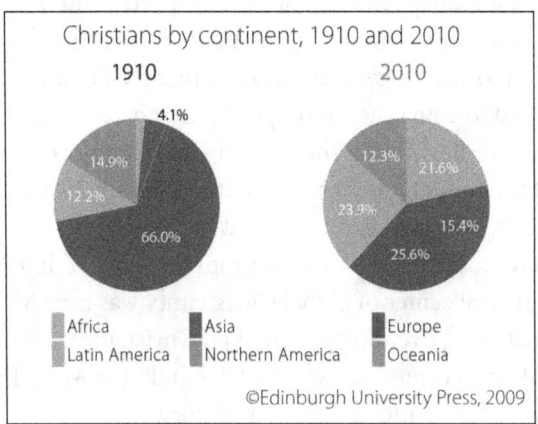

Western influence extended far beyond just the Christian world; Western overconfidence in science and technology was also a major factor throughout the twentieth century. Daniel Jeyaraj notes that "Unprecedented Western discoveries in science, technology, medicine, information communication, dissemination of knowledge, and transportation predicted not only progress and prosperity for all peoples, but also the end of poverty and other miseries. People hoped for a mutual sharing of the earth's resources. They anticipated equal access to knowledge, opportunities, just global markets and politics."[2]

Simultaneous to the shift of Christianity to the South was the decline of Christianity in the North. Moonjang Lee notes with irony, "it was through the modern missionary movement that Christianity became a worldwide phenomenon, and in that process Christianity came to acquire the image of a Western religion. The subsequent globalisation of the image of Western Christianity poses a problem for non-Western Christianity. Though we talk about a post-Christian West and a post-Western Christianity, the prevailing forms of Christianity in most parts of the non-Western world are still dominated by Western influences."[3]

1. Ross, "Edinburgh 1910," xvi.
2. Jeyaraj, "Re-emergence of Global Christianity," 54.
3. Lee, "Future of Global Christianity," 104.

The transition of Christian leadership from North to South has been anything but smooth. Daniel Jeyaraj notes that "When World War II broke out, Western missionaries had to hand over power to the native Christians, whom they had failed to train for leadership tasks, and thus these could not manage the vast landed properties, huge buildings, and money- and time-consuming administrative structures the missionaries left behind. In order to generate money, many church properties were sold. Greed led to court cases, competitions and betrayals."[4]

One way of illustrating the shift of Christianity is to map the statistical center of gravity of global Christianity over the past 2,000 years (shown below). One can readily see that in the modern period there has been a decisive southern shift. At the time of the 1910 Edinburgh conference the statistical center of global Christianity was near Madrid, Spain. In fact, at that time, over 80 percent of all Christians were European. In 2010 the statistical center was south of Timbuktu in Mali. This 100-year shift is the most dramatic in Christian history.

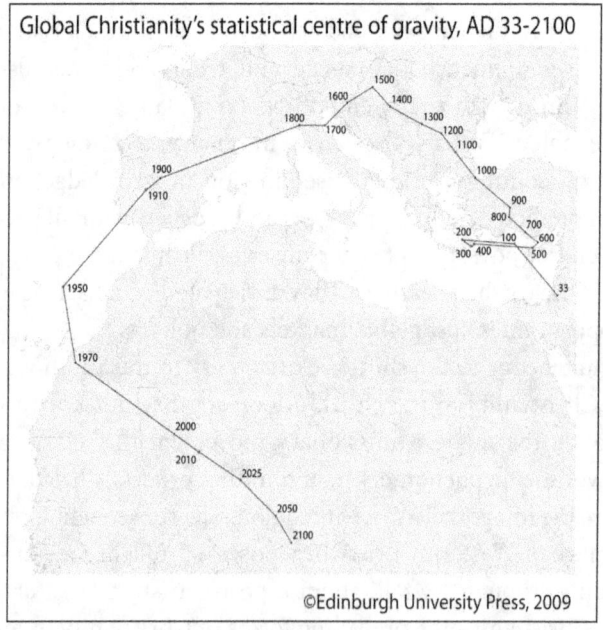

The southern shift can also be put in context of the entire history of Christianity. Christians of the global South were in the majority for the first 900 years of Christian history. European domination of global Christianity

---

4. Jeyaraj, "Re-Emergence of Global Christianity," 54.

can be seen as a recent phase of world Christianity that has now passed. Since 1981, Southern Christians are, once again, in the majority.

It is obvious to see from the various maps in the atlas that Christianity in 1910 was largely a Western phenomenon—including a strong European Roman Catholic presence in Latin America, where few church leaders were Latin Americans. By mapping the same phenomenon by province one hundred years later, it is clear that the global situation has changed. The most dramatic difference between these two dates is in Africa—less than 10 percent Christian in 1910 but nearly 50 percent Christian in 2010, with sub-Saharan Africa well over 70 percent Christian.

The top ten countries with the most Christians in 1910 and 2010 are presented below, where the southern shift can be quickly perceived. Nine of the top ten countries in 1910 were in the global North, whereas seven of the top ten in 2010 are in the global South. The fastest growth over the past one-hundred years and over the past ten years has all been in the global South (over the past one-hundred years, the top five fastest Christian growth was in Burkina Faso, Chad, Nepal, Burundi, and Rwanda. Over the past ten years, the countries include Afghanistan, Cambodia, Burkina Faso, Mongolia, and Timor). In terms of language, Spanish (the top global language with the most Christians) and Portuguese (ranked third) reflect the numerical strength of Christianity in Latin America.

Largest Population of Christians			
1910	Christians	2010	Christians
1 USA	84,800,000	USA	257,311,000
2 Russia	65,757,000	Brazil	180,932,000
3 Germany	45,755,000	Russia	115,120,000
4 France	40,894,000	China	115,009,000
5 Britain	39,298,000	Mexico	105,583,000
6 Italy	35,330,000	Philippines	83,151,000
7 Ukraine	29,904,000	Nigeria	72,302,000
8 Poland	22,102,000	DR Congo	65,803,000
9 Brazil	21,576,000	India	58,367,000
10 Spain	20,357,000	Germany	58,123,000

©Edinburgh University Press, 2009

A second trend within global Christianity is the fragmentation of the religion. Christians are now found in 41,000 denominations. These range in size from millions of members to less than one hundred members and are listed for each of the world's 238 countries in the *World Christian Database*.[5] Moonjang Lee observes that "Christianity has become too fragmented. Existing in a fragmented world, churches fail to show a united front. There are so many divisions within Christianity that it is an intriguing task to clarify a Christian identity. At the beginning of Christian history, the designation of a person as a 'Christian' was sufficient to tell about his or her social, religious and cultural identity. Today, however, we have to supply subcategories to tell about who we are as Christians, for there are many different and conflicting forms of church life."[6]

The chart below shows denominations and congregations enumerated by major tradition. Note that the vast majority is in the Independent and Protestant traditions. If current trends continue, by 2025 there will likely be 55,000 denominations.

Major traditions by denominations, 2010

	Denominations		Congregations	
	Total	Average size	Total	Average size
Anglican	169	514,000	103,200	840
Independent	27,010	14,000	2,496,100	150
Marginal	1,800	19,000	157,800	220
Orthodox	1,030	268,000	120,320	2,280
Protestant	10,840	39,000	1,404,900	300
Roman Catholic	239	409,000	568,200	2,030

©Edinburgh University Press, 2009

A third trend is the unprecedented renewal occurring globally within all Christian traditions. There are many forms of renewal within global Christianity including Evangelical movements, liturgical renewal, Bible-study fellowships, and house church movements. One of the most significant is the Pentecostal/Charismatic renewal, which coincides with the 100-year period that we have been reflecting on. A part of this Christian renewal around the world is the changing role of women in Pentecostal churches. Daniel Jeyaraj observes,

5. See the *World Christian Database*.
6. Lee, "Future of Global Christianity," 104.

Another major player in this period was Pentecostal Christianity with its modern beginnings in the USA. It promotes the ideals of Spirit-filled holy life, apostolicity and catholicity. It incorporates practical ways of leadership, training and mission that draw much inspiration not only from Western business models, but also from local socio-religious customs, hierarchies and practices. Its emphasis on tithing of financial resources and time, using personal talents in mission, and accountability to the Holy Spirit make it mostly self-sufficient and self-propagating (although its view on material wealth and good health as symbols of God's blessings is critiqued).[7]

The locus of the renewal is clearly in the global South where the majority of its practitioners live and where it is growing the fastest. The largest population of renewalists worldwide in both 1910 and 2010 were in the global South—1910 in South Africa and 2010 in China (though note that the USA remained in the #3 spot in both years). The United States is the only country on the top ten list of highest percentage of renewalists worldwide in 2010, with countries in Africa largely dominating the list. Lastly, the fastest growth of renewalists globally is also occurring in the global South: Brazil, Philippines, Laos, and Afghanistan top the 100-year and ten-year growth rate charts.

Finally, the unequal distribution of Christian resources worldwide is another trend within global Christianity. A serious aspect of suffering for Christians of the global South is the disparity in resources, especially compared to the global North. Christians in the South represent 60 percent of all Christians worldwide but receive only about 17 percent of all Christian income. This puts them at a disadvantage in many areas including health, education, communications, and overall quality of life. This imbalance is one of the great tragedies of global Christianity that could not have been easily predicted by our predecessors at the Edinburgh 1910 meeting.

TRENDS OUTSIDE GLOBAL CHRISTIANITY

A current trend affecting global Christianity is the opposing views of what Moonjang Lee has described as secularization and spiritualiza-

---

7. Jeyaraj, "Re-Emergence of Global Christianity," 54.

tion.[8] In an age of church buildings being renovated into apartment buildings, some may wonder if the Christian faith—or any religious faith—can survive at all. The post-modern era, however, is proving to be quite interested in religious adherence, evidenced by a religious revival that was thought impossible by many throughout the twentieth century. At the same time, Western intellectualism is also sprouting forth a fierce secularization that poses a serious and consistent threat to Christian faith. Lee states further, "Christianity in the West suffers from an image problem. Christianity has ceased to be an attractive religion among the younger generation."

One might have the impression today that what is needed is more evangelism to reach the world for Christ. But, in sheer quantity, there is already enough evangelism in the world today for every person to hear a one-hour presentation of the gospel every other day all year long. This amounts to over 1,136 billion hours of evangelism generated by Christians every year, ranging from personal witnessing to television and radio broadcasting. When broken down by UN region, it is easily seen that Asia and Northern Africa have the lowest amount of evangelism but the largest non-Christian populations.

The churches of the global South are notable for their dynamic nature. Daniel Jeyaraj observes,

> Yet non-Western Christianity shows signs of vitality, authenticity, and hope. It is far from perfect but moves towards better manifestations of Christian beliefs in word and action. The ethos of the Euro-American Enlightenment does not constrain non-Western Christians. They do not see Jesus Christ of the Bible reflected in Western theologies centered on God and God's rule. They constitute suffering minorities in anti-Christian settings. They carry the burden of past Euro-American political colonialism and contemporary forms of economic and military neocolonialism. They seek to interpret their Christian beliefs and practices among the peoples of other living religions and ideologies who too are engaged in purposeful missionary activities. The interventions of Christians on behalf of the poor and neglected have socio-economic repercussions. Their discipleship is often a costly affair.[9]

---

8. Lee, "Future of Global Christianity," 105.
9. Jeyaraj, "Re-Emergence of Global Christianity," 55.

Another startling reality is that most Christian outreach never reaches non-Christians—over 85 percent of all Christian evangelism is aimed at other Christians. The *Atlas of Global Christianity* graphs the deployment of the world's foreign missionaries, but close examination of virtually any Christian evangelistic activity reveals this massive imbalance. Part of the explanation is the unanticipated success of Christian missions in the twentieth century. Much missionary deployment is trying to service the growth of the churches in Africa, Asia, and Latin America. What is surprising today is how missionaries from the global South have also been drawn into missions, primarily to other Christians. Deployment studies in Nigeria and India have shown this to be the case, although there is a perceptible shift in the past decade toward work among non-Christians.

Recent research reveals that as many as 86 percent of all Muslims, Hindus, and Buddhists do not personally know a Christian. This must be judged critically in light of the strong biblical theme of incarnation that is at the heart of Christian witness. Christians should know and love their neighbors! In the twenty-first century it is important to realize that the responsibility for reaching Muslims, Hindus, and Buddhists is too large for the missionary enterprise. While missionaries will always be at the forefront of innovative strategies, the whole church needs to participate in inviting people of other faiths to consider Jesus Christ. Note that Muslims, Hindus, and Buddhists are increasingly found living in traditionally "Christian" lands.

Our analysis in the *World Christian Database* reveals that of the top one-hundred most responsive people groups over 1 million in size, twenty-two are tribal (9 percent of the total by population), thirty-one are Hindu (48 percent), thirty-one are Muslim (25 percent), and four are Buddhist (9 percent). The five most responsive of these are the Jinyu of China (Buddhist), the Khandeshi of India (tribal), the Southern Pathan of Afghanistan (Muslim), the Magadhi Bihari of India (Hindu) and the Maitili of India (Hindu). This means that the most responsive groups appear to be in the least-Christian areas.

In the past, innovation in mission was spurred by an understanding of holistic ministry, such as that of women medical missionaries in the Punjab in 1900. Over the course of the century, missionaries realized the need for a new understanding of Christian mission, much like those at the 2010Boston meeting are doing for the next century. The twentieth century raised doubts about not only missionary methods, but also doubts regarding particular "Western" theologies, approaches to personhood, and activities of governments worldwide. Mission gradually moved outside the context of colonialism, and in doing so lost the institutional support it once had.[10]

The biblical text (Rev 5:9; 7:9) leads us to a world where all peoples have access to the gospel message. The body of Christ will not reach its full stature until all peoples are worshipping at the throne of God. The cover of the *Atlas of Global Christianity* features artwork from Chinese Christian artist He Qi. Here, the resurrected Jesus is seen with the peoples of the world looking on. This is the ultimate destination of both global Christianity and its global mission. The global family is dynamic and diverse. In order for Christian faith to continue throughout the twenty-first century and beyond, it is going to have to embrace this global family for what it is, and be willing to dialogue and interact with it in new ways.

WORKS CITED

Jeyaraj, Daniel. "The Re-Emergence of Global Christianity." In *Atlas of Global Christianity*, edited by Todd M. Johnson and Kenneth R. Ross, 54–55. Edinburgh: Edinburgh University Press, 2009.

Lee, Moonjang. "Future of global Christianity." In *Atlas of Global Christianity*, edited by Todd M. Johnson and Kenneth R. Ross, 104–5. Edinburgh: Edinburgh University Press, 2009.

Robert, Dana L. "Missionaries Sent and Received, Worldwide, 1910–2010." In *Atlas of Global Christianity*, edited by Todd M. Johnson and Kenneth R. Ross, 258–59. Edinburgh: Edinburgh University Press, 2009.

Ross, Kenneth R. "Edinburgh 1910: A Defining Moment." In *Atlas of Global Christianity*, edited by Todd M. Johnson and Kenneth R. Ross, xvi–xvii. Edinburgh: Edinburgh University Press, 2009.

World Christian Database. http://worldchristiandatabase.org. Leiden, Netherlands: Brill Online, 2011.

---

10. See Robert, "Missionaries Sent and Received, Worldwide, 1910–2010," 258–59.

2

Boston, Students, and Missions from 1810 to 2010

Dana L. Robert

ONE HUNDRED YEARS AGO, 1,200 representatives of Protestant missionary societies gathered in Edinburgh at the World Missionary Conference. Through their study commissions and their ten days of worship and reflection, they charted the path for the next century of evangelical and ecumenical world missions.

Tonight we are celebrating the past century of mission theology and practice, taking stock of where we are today, and planning for the future. We at the Boston Theological Institute are holding this conference because we believe that theological students and educators, in collaboration with North American churches, have something important to contribute to the 2010 process. 2010Boston is but one node on a global network of 2010 meetings that began nearly a decade ago. Each meeting involves a different constituency of stakeholders—ecclesial, organizational, theological, denominational, or regional. Each meeting contributes to worldwide reflection on the nature of Christian mission in the twenty-first century.

This opening lecture focuses on the unique historic relationship among students, missions, and the context of Boston.[1] In this address, I will sketch some of the highlights of student missions and the Boston context in 1810, 1910, and 2010. Although this essay is suggestive and

---

1. This paper was the first keynote address of the 2010Boston conference and was accompanied by a slide presentation.

not exhaustive, it illustrates the importance of student leadership for Christian mission. Young people try to change the world. For this reason alone, it is impossible to talk about the past, present, and future of missions without reminding ourselves of the centrality of students.

THE CONNECTION BETWEEN STUDENTS AND MISSIONS

Throughout the history of Christianity, student involvement in global mission has shared common characteristics. First is the critical mass of young people gathered into one place at a life stage when they are idealistic, energetic, and figuring out God's purpose for their lives. Second is the creative intellectual stimulation provided by learning—of gaining knowledge about new ideas, deepening traditions, and encountering other cultures and peoples. Third is spiritual formation for mission, including Bible study, reading spiritual classics, and prayer. And fourth is a dynamic socio-political and cultural context that draws students outward, rather than maintains the status quo. When the disciplines of piety and study converge in the social milieu of student life, the results are movements to change the world.

The connection between students and missions has been a recurring theme since the rise of the medieval university. In 1311, the study of Arabic, Hebrew, and Chaldean were introduced into medieval universities to train students as missionaries. In 1534, Ignatius of Loyola gathered six fellow students from the University of Paris to found the Society of Jesus. Their group, the Jesuits, became the largest Catholic men's missionary order in the history of Christianity. In the late 1720s, John and Charles Wesley and George Whitefield founded the "Holy Club" at Oxford, from which flowed urban and prison ministries, and the intercontinental evangelistic movement called Methodism. In the United States, student activism has energized cross-cultural missions since the colonial Great Awakening, when Yale student David Brainerd was expelled for spiritual "enthusiasm" and became a missionary to the Indians in Stockbridge, Massachusetts.

200 YEARS AGO: THE ORGANIZATION OF AMERICAN PROTESTANT MISSIONS

The organization of American Protestant missions two hundred years ago occurred during the rise of the American republic. The early 1800s saw the solidification of the democratic republic, the elimination of slavery in the Northeast, and the Louisiana Purchase that doubled American territory and opened North America to immigrant expansion. Young New Englanders in the early 1800s felt they carried a unique message for the world—that salvation and democracy rested on the Protestant virtues of a Bible-believing republic.

In 1806 at Williams College, five students sought shelter in a haystack during a rainstorm and prayed for the conversion of the non-Christian world. The influence of the Haystack Prayer Meeting continued at Andover Seminary, founded in 1807 as the first postgraduate theological seminary in the United States. One of the Haystack students, a Congregationalist pastor's son named Samuel Mills of Torringford, Connecticut, enrolled at Andover, where he became a catalyst for missionary enthusiasm. Joined by a group of seminarians that included another Congregationalist minister's son, Adoniram Judson of Malden, Massachusetts, Mills held a regular secret prayer meeting for missions. Andover students studied the sermons and reports of Cornelius Buchanan and William Carey in India, the accounts of London Missionary Society (LMS) missionaries in the South Pacific, and the spiritual journal of David Brainerd. Despite there being no mission agency to send Americans abroad, several of the group began searching for ways to be appointed as missionaries.

In the meantime, an orphan named Henry Opukaha'ia was fleeing clan violence in Hawaii that killed his family. He boarded a ship to New England and fell in with some Yale students. They tutored him both in modern knowledge and in Christianity, and Opukaha'ia became a Christian. Before enrolling at Andover, Samuel Mills visited Yale in 1809. He met Opukaha'ia, and helped sponsor him for high school education at Bradford Academy, a school located about eight miles north of Andover. While at Bradford, Opukaha'ia lived with the family of Deacon John Hasseltine.

It so happened that Deacon Hasseltine's daughter, Ann, had also attended Bradford Academy. In 1806, the same year as the Haystack Prayer Meeting, Ann Hasseltine underwent a conversion experience while a student there. The trinitarian evangelical theology of the day taught Ann that she was spiritually equal to men, and that the success of a democratic republic required the basic education of women. Although theology was typically a male course of study in the early 1800s, after her conversion Ann put herself on a reading course of Jonathan Edwards, Samuel Hopkins, Joseph Bellamy—the same theologians that ministerial students were reading at Andover Seminary. Like Opukaha'ia, Ann Hasseltine had a tremendous thirst for theological knowledge despite having no clear path to obtain it.

In 1810, the General Association of Congregational Churches met in Bradford, and naturally the church leaders opened their homes to the visiting ministers. Several of the Andover students sent a petition to the association, requesting that it found a missionary society to send them abroad as missionaries. The leader of the petitioners, Adoniram Judson, boarded at the Hasseltine home. Perhaps he met Henry Opukaha'ia there. He definitely met Ann, or Nancy as she was called, because she waited the tables for her family's guests. Within two and a half months, Adoniram proposed. After a psychological and spiritual struggle over several months, Ann agreed to marry him, knowing full well that his life goal was to become the first U.S. foreign missionary.

Adoniram and the group of seminarians kept the pressure on the Congregational ministers to find the means for them to sail abroad. By 1812, the American Board was ready to send a group to India. Despite the historical precedent that missionaries were typically unmarried males, Adoniram insisted they be allowed to marry. And so in February of 1812, shortly after their wedding, Ann and Adoniram Judson sailed for India from Salem Harbor. The larger missionary company included three married couples and two unfortunate single men whose fiancées' parents had refused to let their daughters go on such a dangerous adventure.

In the meantime, Samuel Mills was sent by the American Board to raise funds for the new venture, and to scout locations for missions to the American Indians. In his travels through the United States, Mills witnessed the dire poverty of new Americans on the expanding frontier. He experienced the needs of urban slum dwellers and frontier migrants, including European immigrants, African slaves, and American Indians. And so in 1816 he co-founded the American Bible Society, an organization devoted to making the Bible available to everyone. In

New York City, he founded the Marine Bible Society for seamen. After travels through the Mississippi Valley, where he met African slaves, he co-founded the American Colonization Society in 1817 to repatriate slaves to Africa. He hoped that the Colonization Society would become a major missionary agency for the evangelization of Africa, with former African slaves as missionaries. In 1818, Samuel Mills died at sea from diseases contracted in Liberia, where he had gone to make arrangements for African-Americans to emigrate there.

While Samuel Mills was crisscrossing the country, founding major mission organizations to meet the needs of the expanding young republic, Adoniram and Ann Judson sailed to India on the same boat with Samuel and Harriet Newell. In addition to rotating their small cabin for conjugal relations, jumping rope for exercise, and bathing with sea water, they prayed and studied theology. Bible study led the Judsons to embrace believers' baptism. By the time the group arrived in India, the Judsons had become Baptists and were immersed by William Carey. Theological study not only deepened piety, but it caused a break in the tiny missionary community, as the Newells and Judsons had to separate. The Judsons waited for Baptists in the United States to organize support for them, and then caught a ship to Burma. After numerous hardships and heroic deeds, Ann Judson died in 1826. Adoniram lived to marry twice more, to create a Burmese dictionary, and to translate the Bible into Burmese.

Back in Massachusetts, Henry Opukaha'ia was involved in a mission venture of his own. In 1817 the Foreign Mission School in Cornwall, Connecticut was opened (led by a Yale graduate Opukaha'ia had met in New Haven). There Opukaha'ia began studying biblical languages, and translated the book of Genesis from Hebrew into Hawaiian. He wrote a Hawaiian grammar and spoke at churches to raise support for a mission to Hawaii. He planned to return to his people as a missionary, but tragically died of typhus. Opukaha'ia's vision of evangelizing his own people was fulfilled in 1819, when at Park Street Church the first group of Congregational missionaries to Hawaii were covenanted together. Around a dozen New Englanders, including two Andover graduates, and three of Opukaha'ia's Hawaiian classmates from the foreign mission training school, departed as the first missionaries to Hawaii.

This network of student relationships tells us several crucial things about the origins of American foreign missions. First, we see that missions two hundred years ago were youth movements. Of these four student leaders (Adoniram Judson, Ann Hasseltine Judson, Samuel Mills, Henry Opukaha'ia), only Adoniram Judson lived past the age of 36. Second, piety and education were friends, not enemies. Before the founding of Andover in 1807, young clergymen were mentored one at a time. But the creation of theological seminaries created a critical mass of highly educated and motivated young people eager to answer God's call. Third, Massachusetts seminarians knew of worlds beyond American shores. They were the most highly-educated men in their communities. Massachusetts was the hub of the U.S.-China trade, and young men from Bradford, Malden, and other towns studied navigation, geography, and mathematics in school. They read about the first Protestant missionaries in India, and decided to imitate them by translating the Bible into other languages. The founding of the American missionary movement harnessed the energy of youth to evangelical piety, religious certainty, and intense intellectual interest in other peoples and cultures. The work of Samuel Mills in founding the American Bible and Colonization Societies also shows the linkage between the evangelization of North America and American interests overseas. Fourth, the influence of Henry Opukaha'ia reminds us that international students have played a catalytic role in most major mission movements. Opukaha'ia was not only the first Hawaiian Christian, but he was the living bridge between the South Pacific and the students of New England. His conversion in New England was a counterpoint to the trauma he had experienced in the murder of his family in Hawaii. He wrote of his deep desire to return to Hawaii as a missionary: "My poor countrymen—who are yet living in region and shadow of death—without knowledge of the true God and ignorant of the future world—have no Bible to read—no Sabbath . . . May I live with them as a stranger and pilgrim upon the earth as long as I live: and spend and be spent in the service of the Redeemer. May the Lord teach me to live in his fear, to do his will and to live devoted to his service."[2] Finally, the life of Ann Judson reminds us that young women were a vital component of the student matrix of 1810. She was a self-educated theologian and teacher known for bringing her students to vital piety. The high level of her linguistic ability, her scripture transla-

---

2. Opukaha'ia quoted in Dwight, *Memoirs of Henry Obookiah*. For information on Henry Opukaha'ia, see the Opukaha'ia Collection at http://www.obookiah.com/Obookiah.com/Welcome.html.

tions into Thai and Burmese, her history of the Burmese mission, and her heroism in rescuing her husband from Burmese prisons, validated the cross-cultural abilities of women as equal to those of men. From Ann Judson onward, the educated missionary family was the gold standard agent of Protestant missions, rather than the celibate male. In the United States, missions became a cause embraced by women, for women.

100 YEARS AGO: STUDENT ACTIVISM WIDENS

During the 1800s, church people organized missionary societies according to theological, geographical, denominational, and gender interests. For example, women founded mission societies to raise money for China missions years before missionaries could enter. From 1810 to 1870, approximately 2,000 U.S. missionaries were sent abroad by missionary societies that emerged during the 1800s, 10 percent of whom went among the American Indians. But the work of foreign missionary societies paled in comparison to the conquest and settlement of North America. During the 1800s, the vast outpouring of missionary energy from the Northeast was largely directed to the evangelization of North America, including the building of churches, parsonages, and schools.

By the 1880s, however, Americans turned their attention abroad. The British Empire and the notable advances via telegraph, railroad, and steamship opened new vistas for the missionary imagination. In the decades prior to the Edinburgh 1910 World Missionary Conference, visions of worldwide Christian fellowship stimulated the rapid global spread of Christian youth organizations such as the Young Men's Christian Association (YMCA) for college students, and Christian Endeavor for teenagers. Christian Endeavor, for example, began in 1881 as a church youth group in Portland, Maine. Twenty-five years later, there were four million members in 67,000 societies around the world.

It was in this rapidly globalizing context that evangelist Dwight Moody held a summer conference for 250 collegiate YMCA leaders at his home in Northfield, Massachusetts. The presence of the sons of missionaries, an international student from Siam, and speeches about the needs and opportunities of the non-Christian world converged, causing one hundred young men from that conference to volunteer as foreign missionaries. The "Mt. Hermon One Hundred" marked the beginning of the Student Volunteer Movement for Foreign Missions. Within a year, 2,200 students had signed the Volunteer Pledge to give their lives to foreign missions and the cause of world evangelization. The new student volunteers filled the ranks of denominational mission boards, and overflowed into the formation of new independent faith missions. Both Christian Endeavor and the Student Volunteer Movement (SVM) held regular student mission conferences, a practice continued today by the Inter-Varsity Christian Fellowship's Urbana conferences. By 1910, around 4,500 student volunteers from the United States had reached the foreign mission fields.

Back in Boston during the 1880s and 1890s, mission prayer groups and SVM study clubs proliferated in the theological seminaries of Andover, Boston University, and Episcopal Theological School. With a missionary department chartered in 1869, the Boston University School of Theology as early as the 1870s was teaching Sanskrit and Mandarin, along with courses on missions and comparative religions. Evangelists like Bishop William Taylor, and General William Booth of the Salvation Army recruited new missionaries from among the theology students. By the time of the Edinburgh Missionary Conference of 1910, the B.U. School of Theology had sent at least 100 missionaries abroad.

Industrialization drew immigrants from abroad and migrants from the countryside into Western cities. As immigrants poured into Boston in the late 1800s, the line between home and foreign missions blurred. Seminarians from Andover opened a settlement house in the South End. Boston University students regularly conducted evangelism and outreach in the emigrant slums of the North and West Ends. In 1896, a recent Boston theology graduate, Edgar Helms, launched an innovative approach to the empowerment of the poor. Helms pioneered the model of collecting goods from the wealthy that could be fixed and sold by the poor, for their economic self support. Today his Goodwill Industries remains the largest nonprofit employer of disabled people in the United States.

In 1889, the New England Deaconess Home and Training School opened, and began training women for both urban and foreign mission work, with special focus on nurses' training that led to the founding of Deaconess Hospital. Students at the Boston theology and deaconess schools took courses together in urban evangelism, sociology, and missions.

Meanwhile across town, also in 1889, A. J. Gordon founded the Boston Missionary Training School in the basement of his Clarendon Street Baptist Church. Designed to speed up the training of missionaries urgently needed for both urban and foreign work, an advertisement for Gordon's training school in the mid-1890s described it as "A condensed and efficient course of preparation for men and women having a divine call to Christian Work. Inter-denominational, Evangelical, Spiritual, Practical."

The life of Martha Drummer illustrates how a century ago urban and foreign missions converged with a Boston education. Martha was an African-American woman from Georgia who worked her way through Clark College in Atlanta by doing house cleaning and laundry. In 1901 she entered the Boston Deaconess Training School. For two years she studied sociology, urban evangelism, and related subjects, followed by three years of nurses' training. Then Martha was appointed a missionary nurse deaconess to Angola in 1906, where she remained for twenty years.

As a nurse deaconess, Martha Drummer combined educational, medical, and evangelistic work. During the dry season, she itinerated with a helper through villages full of people suffering from tropical diseases, and she treated them for malaria, fevers, boils, and numerous medical problems. Because she was the only nurse in the vicinity, by 1911 she had treated persons of twelve different nationalities, and had delivered many babies. On her visits to villages, she preached outdoors to hundreds of people. Her "regular" work consisted of caring for and teaching orphan girls. Her mission station still exists today.

The presence of so many missionary training programs, combined with the excitement of the Student Volunteer Movement, and the urgent problems of urban poverty, created huge energy around missions in Boston at the turn of the twentieth century. This evangelistic energy also spawned competition and dissension. Mission theology became a lightning rod for theological divisions. In its early years, for example, admission to A. J. Gordon's school did not require a high school diploma; it taught from the English Bible only, and attracted mostly uneducated women. It sought to equip "eleventh hour" laborers to bring in the harvest of souls, rather than to spend years learning Greek and Hebrew. Faculty at Boston, Andover, and Newton accused Gordon of being a "short cut" path to ordained ministry and missionary preparation. Within Andover, conflicts over the damnation of the unsaved stoked the "future probation" controversy—a position widely seen to undercut the theological basis of evangelical missions. Missionary candidates from Andover indicated that the unsaved in this life might have a second chance for salvation after their deaths. The number of students plunged at Andover, and in 1908 it tried to survive by merging with its old enemy, the Unitarian Harvard Divinity School.

But even bigger than controversy among Protestants was the tension between Protestants and Catholics. Irish and Italian immigrants filled the Boston slums. They were the objects of the settlement houses, evangelistic campaigns, and YMCA night schools supported by Protestant seminarians. Thus with a sense of urgency, in 1884 the Catholic archdiocese opened St. John's Seminary to train Catholic priests. In 1886, a young Irish-American from Cambridge named James Anthony Walsh entered the seminary. He had attended Boston College, then primarily a preparatory school for priests. While at St. John's Seminary, Walsh imbibed the missionary spirit of his teachers, Sulpician missionaries from France. Although the United States was officially a Roman Catholic mission field until 1908, Walsh was consumed with the desire to awaken the missionary consciousness of American Catholics. In 1903 he was tapped to direct the regional office of the Society for the Propagation of the Faith. This society raised funds for the support of European-staffed missions.

As Walsh collected money for missions, he was constantly aware of the competition with Protestant missionaries in Boston, and the false impression abroad that the United States was a Protestant country because it lacked its own Catholic missioners. Along with other former classmates from St. John's, he envisioned founding a seminary to train American Catholics for cross-cultural missions. In the meantime, at Smith College, a young Catholic student from the Boston suburbs named Mollie Rogers was having her own awakening about the need to launch American Catholic missions. The Student Volunteer Movement was strong at Smith College. When faced with an excited group of Smith Volunteers, singing "Onward Christian Soldiers" as they prepared to leave for China, Mollie rushed into the Catholic church to pray. There she dedicated her life to God's work, whatever that might involve. By 1906, she and Fr. James Walsh were working together to produce a new illustrated popular magazine, *The Field Afar*, that laid the claims of foreign missions before American Catholics.

The hard work of Walsh and Fr. Thomas Price resulted in the founding of the Catholic Foreign Mission Society of America, and its theological seminary in Maryknoll, New York, in 1911. In 1912, Mollie Rogers became the foundress of the Maryknoll Sisters of St. Dominic. The Maryknoll Fathers and Brothers, and the Maryknoll Sisters, were the first American Catholic foreign mission sending organizations. They represented the coming of age of American Catholicism, and its transition from being a receiver to a sender of missionaries.

One hundred years ago, Boston was a hotbed of *collaborative* and *competitive* student missionary activism. The relationship among Boston, students, and missions a century ago tells us several things. First is that the cross-fertilization between competing movements actually created synergy that strengthened American missions. Despite holding different ecclesiologies, eschatologies, and theologies, taken as a whole, Boston-area students worked to bring in the kingdom of God through evangelism and social transformation. A second lesson to draw from the Boston context a century ago is that urban immigration was the crucial link between foreign and home missions. As a city of immigrants, the Boston context produced a missionary consciousness that activated multiple forms of cross-cultural missions, ranging from world evangelization to social and medical work, to the founding of numerous charitable and cultural institutions in Boston and abroad. And third, behind the Edinburgh conference a century ago was a quarter century of student activism, and countless campus study and prayer circles. The organization and leadership of the Edinburgh conference came straight from the momentum of Protestant student movements that had begun in the 1880s in Massachusetts. The chairman of the World Missionary Conference, John R. Mott, was one of Moody's "Mt. Hermon One Hundred" in 1886. Student volunteers in the United Kingdom personally intervened to convince the high church Anglicans to send representatives to the conference. The 1910 Edinburgh Conference would have been impossible without the rich history of student mission movements behind it, both in the United States and Europe. Conversely, Edinburgh 1910 itself influenced the theological seminaries in the Boston area. The teaching of world Christianity, world religions, and the social sciences received a huge boost from the conference.

TODAY: THE GLOBALIZATION OF CROSS-CULTURAL MISSIONS

And so here we are, students and teachers and pastors, gathered in the great city of Boston in 2010. How has the context changed for student missions movements from a century ago?

First, we inhabit a context of increased global interconnectivity that has a big impact on missions in our generation. But instead of the telegraph, steamship, and locomotive of a century ago, our interconnection comes through air travel, the Internet, and high levels of human migration. What we call "globalization" has collapsed time and space, with global flows of ideas and movements, both good and bad, racing around the world at an unprecedented speed. Globalization creates instant awareness of problems on the other side of the world, as well as makes feasible the rapid mobilization of resources and hands-on personal involvement in a multitude of issues such as global health, saving the planet from environmental destruction, human trafficking, and other issues important for abundant life.

Second is the shift of Christian energy and population to the global South, and to parts of Asia like Korea and China. Mission movements of a century ago were largely European and North American. Today's growing student Christian movements are Asian, African, and Latin American, with plateaued numbers in North America and decline in Europe. With the shift of Christian population, mission today is truly to and from all parts of the world. The United States, for example, is both the largest sender and the largest receiver of missionaries.

Third, new forms of collaboration shape missions today. The western denominational missionary society of a century ago is no longer the primary delivery system for cross-cultural missions. The last quarter century has seen an explosion of non-governmental organizations and other specialized international agencies that are funded, staffed by, and partner with church people. Evangelicalism and denominational groupings like the Anglican Communion are now global, multicultural, and multi-ethnic, with all the benefits and challenges this presents. A century ago, there was enmity among Catholics, Protestants, and Orthodox that, while still present, has subsided in many places. For example, in June 2010 the Pope endorsed the conference that commemorated the centennial of the Protestant World Missionary Conference of 1910. Even as Christians call persons to join them in following Jesus Christ, contextual theologies, interethnic friendships, and personal interfaith relationships are more common than was the case in missions a century ago.

Lack of time prevents me from mentioning more factors that shape the changing context for Christian missions in the twenty-first century. As in 1810 and 1910, however, in 2010 students remain at the forefront of emerging mission movements. The characteristics of a critical mass of young people gathered in one place, creative intellectual stimulation, spiritual formation for mission, and dynamic and outward looking social contexts still converge to inspire students to transform the world in their own generation. The apostolic call for faithfulness to God's mission through Jesus Christ and the Holy Spirit energizes student mission movements in Boston today, and around the world. And as the home of hundreds of thousands of college and university students, the Boston student matrix still plays a role in God's purposes.

While we cannot know what future sacrifices and contributions today's students will make, let me conclude this presentation by mentioning a few of the ways in which Boston-area students remain at the forefront of trends in cross-cultural mission.

REVIVAL OF ORTHODOX MISSIONS

Two hundred years ago, student activism helped create American Protestant missions; a century ago was the creation of Catholic foreign missions, and today we see the revival of Orthodox missions. After suffering the worst martyrdoms of the twentieth century—first under the Turkish Empire and then under Soviet communism—the fall of the iron curtain in 1989 opened the opportunity for Orthodox missions to the former communist countries. The creative interaction of Orthodox students with the Protestant missionary movement has been part of the building momentum for Orthodox missions taking place over the past thirty years. And earlier in 2010, Orthodox mission leaders established the Missions Institute of Orthodox Christianity at the Holy Cross Greek Orthodox School of Theology in Brookline, Massachusetts.

MISSION AND MINISTRY BY AND AMONG INTERNATIONAL STUDENTS

Boston remains a Mecca for international students. Today's reversal of the outward missionary flow a century ago has brought record numbers of international students to Boston. Many of these students are already Christians or become Christians in the United States. They use their Boston educational context as a launching pad for their own missionary engagements, either from the United States or back in their home countries. And like Opukaha'ia two hundred years ago, the faithfulness of international students inspires their American classmates.

MISSIOLOGICAL REFLECTION IN 2010 CONFERENCES

Boston-area students, faculty, and alumni have made significant contributions to the worldwide network of 2010 conferences that are considering the theological and missiological foundations of mission as a global movement. In fact, the only organizing meeting of the heads of all four major conferences was held in Boston. Boston-area students and faculty attended the Tokyo, Edinburgh, and Lausanne 2010 conferences. We anticipate that participation in the various 2010 conferences will stimulate fresh missiological insights for our educational work.

ADVANCED STUDENTS IN THE EMERGING FIELD OF WORLD CHRISTIANITY

Boston is home to a network of advanced students in world Christianity and missiology. With the presence of nine theological seminaries and religion departments in the Boston Theological Institute, intellectual leadership for world missions still flows from Boston, just as it did in 1810 and 1910.What is the contribution of this student generation to the *missio Dei*, the mission of God in the world? How will future generations remember the commitment of today's students to world mission? Already we see passionate student leadership in twenty-first century issues such as ecological justice and care for the earth, engagement with Islam, the new monasticism and missional solidarity with the urban poor, evangelization of the unreached, challenging the U.S. empire, relational forms of mission (such as hospitality and cross-cultural friendship), peace-building and conflict transformation, leadership of short-term mission teams, and interracial and multiethnic mission to and from all parts of the world.

As we wrestle with the meaning of mission during this conference, it is important to remember that Jesus expressed his own personal responsibility for the kingdom of God through being a student. When Jesus was twelve, he became separated from his parents on a trip to Jerusalem. After three days they found him, listening to and questioning the teachers in the temple. When his parents rebuked him, Jesus replied, "Did you not know that I must be in my Father's house?" (Luke 2:49). Following the example of Jesus, let students gathered in Boston this weekend remember that *your lives belong to God*. In 2010, Christ's mission of love and justice, of salvation and liberation, of witnessing across the boundaries that divide, rests on your shoulders.

WORKS CITED

Dwight, Edwin W. *Memoirs of Henry Obookiah, a Native of Owhyhee, and Member of the Foreign Mission School; Who Died at Cornwall, Connecticut February 17, 1818, Aged 26* (1818 version). Philadelphia: American Sunday School Union, 1830. No pages. Online: http://www.obookiah.com/Obookiah.com/Memoirs1.html.

3

From Boston to the Whole World

Twentieth-Century North American Roman Catholic Mission and the "Antioch Agenda"

Angelyn Dries, O.S.F.

WHAT WAS HAPPENING LOCALLY in 1910 within a mission group not invited to the Edinburgh Missionary Conference, the Roman Catholics? This paper will explore the experience of Roman Catholic Boston, a geographic area from which came the greatest number of U.S. Catholic missionaries, according to Richard Cardinal Cushing. The examples that will be analyzed form a microcosm of twentieth-century mission theology and practice. In the first section, we will open a family photo album of sorts, people important to Roman Catholic missions in the Boston area from the end of the nineteenth century into the 1960s. The pages will include particular Sulpician faculty at St. John's Seminary, Brighton, a succession of extraordinary directors of the Society for the Propagation of the Faith (SPF) in the Archdiocese of Boston, Mary Josephine Rogers, foundress of the Maryknoll Sisters, and Jesuit missionary anthropologist, Joseph J. Williams of Boston College. We will highlight elements of their mission theology as reflective of the mindset of the period. In the second section we will examine what happened in the development of their mission theology and practice, as that played out in new contexts of the last half of the twentieth century. That historical experience will then be related to elements of the "Antioch Agenda,"[1] with the hope of making a contribution to the ongoing questions raised in the century following the Edinburgh Missionary Conference of 1910.

AWASH IN A SEA OF PROTESTANT MISSIONS IN BOSTON

In 1798, when Roman Catholics were few and far between in New England, French émigré Bishop Jean-Louis Cheverus (1768–1836), sent a letter to the Roger Hanley family with directions for family prayer on the Sundays when priests were not available for a Eucharistic liturgy. Among the suggestions he made was that the family gather in the morning and evening to read the prayers and instructions for the Mass of that day, a chapter from *The Poor Man's Catechism*, and prayers from Richard Challoner's popular, *The Garden of the Soul*.[2] The bishop further admonished, "Have charity for all men, pray for the salvation of all, do good to everyone according to your power, whatever may be his religious persuasion, but never forget that you belong to the Roman Catholic Church, that is to say, to the true Church of Jesus Christ & that it is unlawful for you to attend the worship of any other persuasion."[3] Cheverus extended his pastoral hand to isolated Catholics to remind them they were to be civil to their Protestant neighbors. However, Catholics should not fall prey to any spiritual attraction to other Christian communities, who might extend an invitation to join them. Two years later, the Massachusetts Home Mission Society (1799) was organized and a little over a decade later, the American Board of Commissioners for Foreign Missions (1810) began what would become a significant mission funding and sending organization. By the time of the dazzling and dramatic 1911 World in Boston Exposition held in the Mechanics Building,[4]

---

1. The term is gleaned from the introduction to the edited work of Jeyaraj et al., *The Antioch Agenda*.

2. Mannock, *Poor Man's Catechism*, though there were earlier editions. Challoner, *The Garden of the Soul*.

3. "Sunday Obligation without a Priest, 1798," 12.

4. Chamberlin and Gardner, *Handbook and Guide*. The following year, the Second American Catholic Congress was held in Boston, organized by Francis C. Kelley, founder of the Catholic Church Extension Society. The Congress brought together representatives of many home and foreign mission sending and funding societies, but the event was shorter and with far less drama than the World in Boston event.

the Woman's Board for Missions, the Woman's Home Missionary Association, and the Boston Seaman's Friend Society were among the seventeen Protestant missionary organizations with headquarters in the Boston area.

Indeed, it could be said that by the beginning of the twentieth century, American Catholics in Boston were awash in a sea of Protestant mission societies, to stretch Jon Butler's use of the term.[5] So, aside from impressive Catholic evangelization aimed at strengthening the faith of masses of immigrants to the Greater Boston area throughout the nineteenth and early twentieth centuries, did Roman Catholics of Boston have any boat to row in this ocean of Protestant missions to educate clergy and laity about global mission, or "foreign missions," as it was termed at the time? We will look briefly at three sets of snapshots in the Boston Catholic mission photo album.

The first is a composite of some Sulpicians, the Society of French clergy who taught at St. John's Seminary, Brighton, from its opening in May, 1884 until 1911, when William Cardinal O'Connell replaced them, one could say, because of their differences in ecclesiology: he was a Roman trained, Roman-minded Ultramontanist and they were Gallicanists transplanted to America. John Hogan was the seminary rector and gave periodic talks about missionaries and mission life.[6] It was from him that the future founder of the Maryknoll Society, James A. Walsh, learned of the death of Hogan's seminary classmate, Theophane Vénard, martyred in southeast Asia. This hero-martyr image would enter the ethos of Maryknoll, beginning with books Walsh published on the French missionary martyrs. Walsh named the first preparatory seminary after Vénard. Gabriel André, who would be a key figure in the Americanist controversy,[7] co-supported a missionary in Japan with seminarian Walsh. Scripture professor Joseph Bruneau, while at Dunwoodie Seminary, New York, was associated with the controversial *New York Review* and had introduced his students to the "higher criticism" that he

---

5. Butler, *Awash in a Sea of Faith*.

6. For insight on seminaries of this period and Hogan's involvement in their reform, see Talar, "Seminary Reform," 1–17.

7. "Americanist" is the term given to liberal bishops and clergy who favored a progressive adaptation of Catholicism to American political and social life in the late nineteenth century. The position of some of these men was questioned by the Vatican and "Americanism" was the term given to the set of "doctrines" condemned by Pope Leo XII in *Testem Benevolentiae*, 1899.

learned from his teacher, Alfred Loisy.[8] The approach was reflected in Bruneau's, *Harmony of the Gospels*.[9]

The Sulpicians read to the seminarians moving letters from missionary friends, while visits from missionaries themselves provided first-hand glimpses of life on the missions. Professor of Dogmatics, Francis Gigot, shared a letter from a colleague, who had come from a distinguished and wealthy family in Paris and who was now a missionary in China. The seminarian who heard Gigot read the letter, remarked:

> The missionary chose, for the love of God, to renounce the brilliant prospect that tempted him to a life of ease and luxury in Paris . . . to wear out his young life, perhaps spill his blood, in apostolic service among the heathen. He was sent to one of the most dangerous districts in China, where fierce persecution has been going on for some months . . . Oh, what a living example of heroic self-sacrifice! What an elegant reproach to us Seminarians who find it hard to deny ourselves a few petty worldly pleasures and honors and who, living in peace and comfort, find it irksome at times to maintain that ardor of zeal which ought always to stir every fibre of a young ecclesiastic's heart.[10]

While there were cultural tensions between the largely Irish-American seminarians and the French Sulpicians, the Society's mission spirit touched many students and, once in parishes, priests sought them out for spiritual direction. The Sulpician element of austerity in their spirituality combined with a vision that clergy renewal occurred through Scripture study, prayer and identification with Christ's sacrifice on the cross (Jesus as martyr-witness). Clergy renewal, based on an understanding that the priesthood was essentially missionary, would redound to the revitalization of the whole church. The Sulpicians highlighted here were progressive in their ecclesiology and advocated a personal appropriation of missionary life as one of witness, even to the point of death. While mission theology or history was not part of the seminary curriculum, mission education occurred through osmosis and

---

8. The works of French Scripture exegete and theologian, Alfred Loisy (1857–1940), were considered "modernist" and were placed on the Vatican's *Index of Forbidden Books*.

9. Bruneau, *Synopse évangélique*.

10. Aiken, *Diary*, 50. Aiken taught at the Catholic University of America from 1897–1924. Known as an Orientalist, his *The Dahmma of Gotama the Buddha and the Gospel of Jesus Christ* was his best-known work. Aiken and James A. Walsh were classmates at St. John's Seminary.

was absorbed by seminarians through the lives of particular Sulpician faculty, missionary letters, Sunday afternoon mission talks, and assistance to the Paulist Fathers in their missions in the southern United States in the late 1890s.[11]

A second group in the photo album is a succession of outstanding and gifted Society for the Propagation of the Faith (SPF) directors. Each director was expected to raise money to support overseas missionaries (many of whom were European) and to send the accumulated funds to the SPF central headquarters in Paris. Even early in the twentieth century, Boston, along with New York, outpaced the financial contributions among the other archdioceses in the country. But all four directors did far more than that. Joseph V. Tracy, a Boston clergyman, taught New Testament exegesis at St. John's Seminary. In 1899, he was appointed the first diocesan director of the SPF while he continued to teach. Tracy's idea was that unless clergy were mission conscious, the people in the pews would not be wakened to missions. Toward that end, he began a mission *Academia* at the Theology House of the seminary in 1901. Seminarians delivered monthly papers "on the Christian apostolate in action and combined Church History, Historical Geography, Christian Biography, Pagan Folk-Lore, Catholic and non-Catholic Mission Methods, and Practical Means in interesting people in Mission Work."[12]

When Tracy's health became precarious, he visited James A. Walsh at St. Patrick's, Roxbury, to invite him personally to be a fulltime SPF director of the Archdiocese of Boston (1903–11). Walsh, whose home parish was St. Paul's, Cambridge, had briefly attended Harvard and graduated from Boston College before he entered St. John's, where he caught the mission ambience of the Sulpicians. Beyond raising funds for missionaries, Walsh saw the importance of mission education—as had Tracy before him—only Walsh's focus would mainly emphasize materials for laity. He published several books related to the late nineteenth-century French martyrs, whose stories he heard at the seminary and whose homes he visited in France. He set up a four-member Catholic Foreign Mission Board (1904) to assist him with

11. See Christopher Kauffman for the development of the Society. For the influence of Sulpicians on the Catholic Foreign Mission Society of America, see Dries, "The Sulpician Mission Legacy," 167–76. For a glimpse into seminary life while the Sulpicians were at St. John's, see Sullivan, "Beneficial Relations," 201–38 (especially 214–18).

12. Sexton and Riley, *History of St. John's Seminary*, 119. The mission sessions were organized in much the same way as were the Scripture groups at St. John's.

mission education, especially with the magazine, *The Field Afar*, and ultimately to prepare for a mission seminary, a purpose the group kept quiet for the moment. One of the board members was Joseph Bruneau, the Sulpician Scripture professor mentioned earlier. Walsh would later provide a copy of St. John's Rector, John Hogan's, *Daily Thoughts*, to the newly ordained Maryknollers.

Associated with Walsh when he was SPF director, Mary Josephine Rogers—Mollie, as her family called her—was from Roxbury and confirmed in Jamaica Plain. One of eight children, who attended local public schools, Mollie learned the importance of missions from her parents, who subscribed to European mission magazines and prayed and sacrificed for missionaries so that they would be successful in "teaching people about God."[13] However, her experience at Smith College as a student and zoology demonstrator there, led to a mission vocation call for Mollie. She recounted later: "the mission activities of the Protestant groups moved me deeply to an appreciation of the fact that our American Catholic girls were doing nothing for the foreign mission, chiefly because they knew nothing of them; while Protestants were sending the finest of our college girls to the fields afar, supporting them royally, and were teaching others of their work by means of organized mission classes."[14]

To gather more information about missions while she was at Smith, she wrote to SPF Director Walsh, and eventually they met. She subsequently worked part-time in the SPF office translating mission letters from French and doing editorial work for *The Field Afar*. Walsh recognized Rogers' leadership qualities and she became the head of a small group of women who left Boston for New York, as did Walsh. The women formed the Foreign Mission Sisters of St. Dominic (Maryknoll Sisters), while Walsh, along with Thomas F. Price, a missionary from North Carolina, inaugurated the Catholic Foreign Mission Society of America (Maryknoll, 1911), two groups which collectively would send several thousand men and women throughout the world in the century ahead.

---

13. Mary Josephine Rogers quoted in Hendricks, "The Legacy of Mary Josephine Rogers," 72–80. Rogers was confirmed at St. Thomas Church, Jamaica Plain, by Archbishop John J. Williams.

14. Rogers quoted in Kennedy, "Mission Spirit," 3.

When Walsh left Boston for New York to begin the Catholic Foreign Mission Seminary (Maryknoll), Joseph McGlinchey (1882–1959) was named the new SPF director. Assistant pastor at St. Paul's Cambridge at the time, McGlinchey had a keen interest in mission because his brother, Henry (a Jesuit missionary), died in Patna, India.[15] Joseph dramatically increased annual monies from $28,000 in 1911 to $2,000,000 in 1928 when he left the office. But he also contributed significantly to mission education through translation and adaptation of Paolo Manna's, *The Workers are Few* (1911) and *The Conversion of the Pagan World* (1921), both of which became standard works for American Catholic perception of the mission vocation until 1960. His books found their way onto bookshelves of Catholic high schools and colleges all across the country.[16]

The last SPF Director we will highlight is Richard James Cushing (1895–1970), chosen by McGlinchey to succeed him as Director. The South Boston priest was a perfect candidate. He had been secretary of the missionary *Academia* in 1918–19 at St. John's Seminary and the following year he became president of the organization. He and another seminarian shared their experience of the *Academia* with members of the newly founded Catholic Students Mission Crusade, when the group met in Washington, D.C. Cushing, who attributed his deep interest in the missions to the Sulpicians, cajoled and wheedled money from seminarians and friends to support missionaries, a trait he carried into his episcopacy as cardinal archbishop of Boston.

Collectively, the SPF directors not only raised money but were deeply and personally committed to mission education of clergy, laity, and seminarians. They viewed mission as central to Catholic life. Director James A. Walsh harbored an embryonic idea for an "American" foreign mission seminary, an idea which found fruition in the establishment of Maryknoll, after he moved to New York for that purpose, as did Mollie Rogers and the women in the *Field Afar* office in Boston.

Our final snapshot in this section examines the use of anthropology in mission through the work of Joseph J. Williams, SJ (1875–1940), a

---

15. Boyton, *A Yankee Xavier*.

16. McGlinchy also composed a *Catechism of the Foreign Missions* (1918) and authored *Mission Tours, India* (1925). He had the opportunity to travel widely while he was secretary to Cardinal O'Connell. McGlinchy delivered mission talks on the "Catholic Hour Radio" in Boston during his term as SPF director.

faculty member at Boston College. Williams entered the Jesuits after his freshman year at BC, completed a doctorate in ethnology at Woodstock, and was assigned to Jamaica in 1906. His interaction with the Jamaican people in the "bush," as he termed the experience, left an indelible mark on him.[17] After a short stint as editor of *America* (1910–11), he returned to Jamaica for five years before coming to teach at Boston College.

Through the years Williams collected over 10,000 books, maps, lithographs, and woodcuts related to African and Caribbean cultures and Judaism. Some of these objects and others of Asian and Native American origin became the center of a small archaeological museum at Boston College in the former Stinson mansion.[18] Williams' ethnology lectures beginning in 1932 at the Graduate School and a journal, *Anthropological Series of the Boston College Graduate School*, became the foundation of the institution's anthropology department. Williams had two major projects. One was a study of monotheism among African tribes and "Hebrewisms," both having to do with the origin of religion. The other project was an examination of the worldview of Jamaicans, based upon narratives he heard from the Afro-Creole population. The stories were associated with a spider, the *Anansi* stories. Williams also conducted retreats in Boston and his anthropological/mission perspective affected the direction of his first two books on spirituality. *Keep the Gate* and *Yearning for God* were based on the *Spiritual Exercises* of St. Ignatius, but both books contained several incidents and perspectives from his interaction with Afro-Creole life in Jamaica, thereby providing retreatants with another worldview for their spiritual consideration.[19] Thus, in Joseph Williams' view, anthropology provided a locus beyond one's religious group to obtain insight on religious questions. For Williams, mission was to permeate all of life, including the spiritual life.

---

17. For biographical details, I have relied on Stewart, "The Contributions of Joseph John Williams." See also, Stewart, *Religion and Society* (especially pages 136–38 for aspects of Williams' view on Afro-Creolization).

18. The Nicholas M. Williams special collection is now housed through the John J. Burns Library at Boston College.

19. Williams, *Keep the Gate*. Williams, *Yearning for God*.

CATHOLIC MISSIONS SAIL FROM THE BOSTON HARBOR

In the second part of this paper, we will return to a few figures identified above and inquire: What happened to mission theory and emphasis in the last half of the twentieth century, once missionaries sailed from the Boston Harbor, though, of course, many of them sailed from other piers and by the late 1950s were beginning to fly to their missions?[20]

With a strong sacramental tradition in Roman Catholicism—here is meant the use of ritual and tangible elements of water, oil, and bread as bearing the weight of the sacred and significant beyond their visual elements—it is surprising that Catholics did not collectively embrace anthropology as a vehicle for mission. Joseph Williams' anthropology journal was short-lived, apparently lasting only until World War II, though a similar journal begun in the mid-1920s at The Catholic University of America, continues to the present as *Practical Anthropology*. An ethnology emphasis came to the fore again, when J. Franklin Ewing (1905–68), Jesuit anthropologist at Fordham, placed anthropology as an important element in his Mission Institute, which continued until 1962 but ceased with Ewing's death. A more sustained anthropology influence came through the Society of the Divine Word, with its European tradition of scientific methodology. One of their missionaries, Louis Luzbetak, wrote, *The Church and Culture: Applied Anthropology for the Religious Worker* in 1963. This and his 1988 revised edition were used as textbooks for some Roman Catholic and Protestant mission training programs.[21]

By the mid-1960s the social sciences, rather than those fields allied with ethnology or cultural anthropology, became the method of choice for many American Catholic missionaries. This might have reflected the practical bent associated with Americans, as well as the influence

---

20. It is particularly fitting that the coat of arms of the Archdiocese of Boston displays two of the area's key geographic markers: the three hills (Beacon Hill in Boston, Copp Hill in Revere, and Fort Hill in Roxbury) and the waves of Massachusetts Bay, standing underneath a cross whose tips display the fleurs-de-lis, the latter touch in memory of French missionaries who kept the faith of Catholics alive in the early days of the Diocese. William Cardinal O'Connell designed the original crest with a Latin cross displayed atop the other elements noted. His successor, Cardinal Cushing, made the change to a French-influenced cross, for the reason given above. See Archdiocese of Boston, "Coat of Arms."

21. Luzbetak, *The Church and Cultures: Applied Anthropology*; Luzbetak, *The Church and Cultures: New Perspectives*.

of Belgian Joseph-Léon Cardijn's (1882–1967), "observe, judge, act" approach to mission in society. Cardijn's method was manifested in groups ranging from Young Christian Students and Catholic Action, to the use of the method as a platform for what later became liberation theology. In the 1960s, cultural anthropology provided significant underpinnings for reshaping the liturgical Rite of Christian Initiation of Adults. More recently, the word "anthropology" has tended to flow more from a theological rather than an ethnological pen, as in the term "theological anthropology," for example.

Richard Cushing continued as director of the Propagation of the Faith, even after being named a bishop in 1939 and archbishop of Boston in 1944. Mission was central to everything he did. He organized mission groups among workers in the Boston Archdiocese so that lay Catholics became knowledgeable and supportive of missions. The group leaders personally brought their collected monies to him. Cushing inaugurated the Father Jim Hennessey Mission Club, patterned after the *Academia* of the seminary, whereby laymen heard personal experiences of missionaries passing through Boston and became aware of the needs of local churches around the world. While not expressed by Cushing in his inaugural speech to the group, it was assumed that of course, once men heard the stories, they would be inspired to support the missioner financially, as well as with prayers.[22] It was through this sodality that Cushing was able to finance several Boston clergy who served in Sioux Falls, South Dakota in 1946, in a kind of lend-lease program for home missions.

Cushing welcomed religious communities of missionaries into the archdiocese and the Xaverian Brothers, for example, showed their appreciation by featuring Cushing on a stained glass window in their new chapel in the early 1960s. The Boston Cardinal authored or prefaced many pamphlets and books related to missions, including his own: *The Missions in War and in Peace*, *Multiplying the Missionary* (on the lay apostolate), *The Modern Challenge of the Missions*, and *Questions and Answers on Communism*. A brief look at the latter book provides an insight into his understanding of the role of missionaries in a Post-World War II era.

After the War, many Americans felt a palpable struggle for world order, a potential fight to the death between democracy and Communism,

22. Cushing, "The Father Jim Hennessy Mission Club Bulletin," box 10.3.

between freedom and socialism, between the free world and Soviet Russia. The anti-Communist rhetoric of Senator Joseph McCarthy in the 1950s displayed one facet. Cushing viewed the struggle to be against "godless" or "atheistic" Communism, and he noted that the United States held a unique role to work toward its defeat: "our hope today is that America may somehow do creative deeds that will help bring order out of confusion, and somehow do redemptive deeds that will help set us free from manifold tyrannies."[23] But Cushing also placed the conflict in quasi-philosophical terms in his *Questions and Answers on Communism*. He discussed the ideological premises, major books and persons connected with European Communism. Chapter 1 asked, for example, "What does Communism mean?" and "How does Communism contend that it will 'prove' that God does not exist?" Then, in Question 5, Cushing injected a neo-Thomist worldview as the major Catholic response to the premises underlying Communism. He queried, "Have the Communists ever been able to answer the five proofs of St. Thomas Aquinas for the existence of God?" The answer was, "No, they have always evaded the teachings of St. Thomas Aquinas."[24] While Catholics feared Communist Russia, it was Chinese Communism and stories of imprisoned, tortured, and exiled missionaries, that after 1949 became the public face of communist horror in books, films, and appearances at mission conferences. Cushing devoted an entire chapter of his *Questions and Answers* to "Communism and China."

American Catholic concern about Communism was beginning to spill over toward Latin America, where communist activity seemed a viable alternative for the majority of the poor. With more U.S. financial aid being sent there—partially to combat Communism—the presence of more Protestant missionaries, and urgings from the Vatican and Latin American bishops, American Catholics now had several reasons to send U.S. Catholic missionaries to the Southern Hemisphere. The Boston prelate played a significant role as representative of the U.S. bishops to oversee a re-established Latin America Bureau in 1960, an office that was the hub of information, insight, and focus for a surge of U.S. Catholic missionaries in that direction. Its director was Maryknoll Father John J. Considine, whose, *Call for Forty Thousand* (1946), was a clarion call for U.S. Catholics to send ten percent of their priests and

---

23. Cushing, untitled sermon, 1945, quoted in O'Toole, "Prelates and Politicos," 44.
24. Cushing, *Questions and Answers*, 12.

religious to serve in Latin America. About the same time as the beginning of the Bureau, Cushing founded the Missionary Society of Saint James the Apostle.[25] He viewed the Society as a "lend-lease" program of Boston priests to dioceses in Peru, Ecuador, and Bolivia for a period of five years, until the Latin American Catholic churches could build up their "apostolic forces." He also saw the Society as a "buffer" against Communism. The Boston prelate, who made at least two trips to Latin America, had wanted to resign his post as archbishop of Boston in order to serve as a missionary in Latin America.

Thus, the specter of Communism and growing numbers of Protestant missionaries in Latin America proved a challenge to U.S. Catholics. It is also worth noting, though, that the very socio-economic areas that Communism challenged were often addressed by women missionaries: medical ministrations, social work, literacy, economic self-sustenance through teaching people crafts, sewing, or later acting as agents to sell those products to U.S. markets.

We return now to the last photos from the first part of this paper, to those of James A. Walsh, who, along with Thomas F. Price, founded the Maryknoll Society in 1911. While the focus of mission activity in U.S. publications often highlighted Asia and China in particular from 1920–50, the turn toward Latin America at the half century presented the need for a quite different understanding of mission. A number of Maryknoll's seasoned China missioners, expelled from Asia, now found themselves in Chile or Peru, wondering why they were sent to a "Catholic" country that did not seem to have any "pagans."

Maryknoller John J. Considine, from New Bedford, Massachusetts, is a link between the Cushing worldview of missions in relation to Communism and the perspective that Maryknoll and other mission groups began to adopt in the 1960s and 1970s. Considine, to recall, was director of the Latin America Bureau from 1960–68 and for many years was a main force in Maryknoll's mission education programs. He was influenced by Protestant mission theorists, including J. H. Oldham (1874–1969), secretary of the Edinburgh Missionary Conference of 1910, and was a friend and visitor to mission historian, Kenneth Scott Latourette at

---

25. For the context, principles and development of the Society, see Garneau, "Commandos for Christ." Cushing's nephew, William Cushing Francis (1933–2006), was a St. James Society missionary for ten years in Cuzco, Peru and then a longtime Boston police chaplain.

Yale Divinity School.[26] Considine's consistent themes in mission education are found in his presentations to educators, his many writings and in his *World Christianity* (1945). While he, too, feared that Communism could be a dominant, destructive force in a post-war world, he stressed that people needed to know and understand the church's theological teaching on its "world-wide mission." Five emphases are notable. Catholics needed: a knowledge of and regard for all peoples of the Earth as brothers and sisters in Christ; a comprehension of socio-economic problems; a realization that Christ's life of charity should be brought to all, regardless of race, creed, or color; an appreciation of the impact of other religions and anti-religious forces on the human race; and, an embrace of justice with a responsibility to promote the welfare of all. This approach to mission education evoked a much richer texture to the goal of mission work than simply "saving souls."

One way to achieve some of the values Considine noted was found in the co-operative programs missionaries inaugurated. Many missionaries, including several men and women Maryknollers, were trained in the Antigonish Movement, a program and perspective formalized by Canadian founder, Moses M. Coady (1882–1959).[27] Antigonish emphasized the dignity of each person, as well as group action linked with economics as key elements in the process of social reform. Organizing people to establish credit unions or agricultural cooperatives was a different form of "human flourishing"[28] from the traditional work of missionary women who established clinics, hospitals, maternity centers, orphanages, and education centers.

But the theme of "human flourishing" took a new and significant turn in 1970, when Maryknoll decided to inaugurate Orbis Books with Miguel d'Escoto, MM as director. Their narrative shifted from a focus on

26. Considine found Oldham, *Christianity and the Race Problem* especially insightful and useful.

27. Coady, *Masters of Their Own Destiny*; Coady, *Social Significance*. Sister Mary Gabriella Mulherin, MM became nationally known in South Korea for the work she began in 1959 to establish what became an international credit union. See also, Dries, "Two Sides of the American Catholic Mission Coin," 23–44.

28. For U.S. Catholic involvement in human promotion in the 1980s, see "The Role of U.S. Religious in Human Promotion," a joint project of the Conference of Major Superiors of Men and the Leadership Conference of Women Religious from 1981–84. The two groups explored the major theses of the 1978 Vatican document, "Religious and Human Promotion," in the context of North America. The project took shape during the Fourth Inter-American Conference on Religious held in Santiago, Chile in 1980.

the missionary to attention to Third World voices and to values articulated decades earlier by Considine. While the 1960s had been designated as the first of what would become several United Nations' decades of development, gradually some missionaries realized that development was another form of colonialism. Gustavo Gutiérrez's *Theology of Liberation: History, Politics and Salvation,* published by Orbis in 1973, reflected that shift from development to liberation.

Missionaries, not only in Latin America but elsewhere, came face to face with oppression and human destruction and by the late 1980s their theological vocabulary changed from liberation to reconciliation and included theological viewpoints from other religions. Orbis Books identified the changing directions in titles such as Virginia Fabella and Mercy Oduyoye, *With Passion and Compassion: Third World Women Doing Theology* (1988), Robert J. Schreiter, *The Ministry of Reconciliation: Spirituality & Strategies* (1998), and D. N. Premnath, *Border Crossings: Cross-Cultural Hermeneutics* (2007).

BOSTON CATHOLIC MISSIONS AND THE ANTIOCH AGENDA

The Boston-influenced Catholic experience identified in this paper links with many elements of the "Antioch Agenda" proposed by Jeyaraj, Pazmiño, and Petersen mentioned earlier. Briefly expressed, the issues they raise include the establishment of new relationships, a surmounting of deep-seated prejudices through an alternative lifestyle that bridges the gap between insider and outsider, a need for and vision of human flourishing, a review the Millennium Development Goals of the United Nations, engagement in the demands of reconciliation, and freedom from fear.[29]

The highlighted Boston Catholics struggled with similar issues in their times with their insights. While those in the West have become more aware of the "Changing Contours of World Christianity" in relation to

---

29. The *Antioch Agenda* points also seem perfectly matched with the *Our Father*: Establish new relationships (Our Father); overcome deep seated prejudices by providing alternative lifestyle that bridges the gap between insider and outsider (Your kingdom come); need for and vision of human flourishing; Millennium Development Goals of the U.N. (Give us this day our daily bread); demands of reconciliation (Forgive us our trespasses, as we forgive those who trespass against us); freedom from fear (Deliver us from all evil).

demographic shifts of Christianity, the basic issues of the *Antioch Agenda* were the fabric of mission theory and practice of the past one hundred years. The directors of the SPF, the Jesuit anthropologist Williams, Considine, and Orbis Books emphasized the importance of knowing people beyond the borders of the United States as a basis for understanding other religious and ethnic cultures, a knowledge that would be conducive to the reduction of prejudicial attitudes. This knowledge, in turn, motivated Catholics to support mission work but further provided vicarious connections with people and issues different than one's own experience. Cushing, equipped with a neo-Thomist perspective, attempted to deal with an ideology that brought fear into the hearts of many, both within and outside of the Iron and Bamboo Curtains.

In the last century, Roman Catholics have seen published a multitude of official church documents on the *Antioch Agenda* topics related to overcoming prejudices, the need for human flourishing, the demands of reconciliation, and the establishment of new relationships, but it seems that coming together to effect change requires all of our capabilities and gifts from each of our religious traditions.

CONCLUSION

Throughout the twentieth century the Roman Catholic mission boat carried and was transformed in its theology of mission, but certain elements remained in place. Successful Protestant mission activity was a goad for Catholics to support missions financially and prayerfully. Theologically, mission could not be an after-thought for pious people, a specialization for a few, or an act of charity, but mission was to be at the heart of the baptismal call. Seminary professors, who worked in a restricted theological and philosophical curriculum in the first half of the twentieth century, the SPF directors who insisted on mission as central to Catholicism, and John Considine's efforts to educate in world Christianity all found a more developed mission theology at and following the Second Vatican Council. A stunning, simple line in *Ad Gentes*, the document on mission activity, read: "The Church on earth is by its very nature missionary since, according to the plan of the Father, it has its origin in the mission of the Son and of the Holy Spirit."[30] The state-

---

30. "*Ad Gentes Divinitus*," in Flannery, *Vatican Council II*, paragraph 2.

ment, similar to the concept of *missio Dei* some Protestants had been examining earlier, gave theological language to the assumptions, intuitions and expressions of those viewed in the Boston mission album. The idea further underlined the importance of relationship as life-giving and redemptive as the focus of mission.

As we conclude, it might be of interest to point out an impressive mural in the sanctuary of St. Paul's Church, Cambridge, a church familiar to several of the people noted in the chapter. Though painted in the mid-1920s, the mural recognized Boston area Catholic missionaries. On the right front side mural, six clergy are portrayed, among them James A. Walsh and the Jesuit Henry McGlinchey.[31] What is significant about the mural is that each preceding panel depicted one of the traditional "epochs" of mission history: the apostolic period, the "national" period of monks like Cyril, Methodius, and Boniface, and the sixteenth-century missionaries who moved from Europe to the New World and elsewhere. The addition of the Boston American panel signified that a new mission age had begun, so to speak, with American Catholic missionaries heading overseas after World War I.

Even while Boston-area Catholic missionaries went abroad, the continuing progression of migrating peoples plied the waters *into* the Boston Harbor during the century following the Edinburgh Conference.[32] Earlier immigrant populations of Irish, Germans, and French-Canadians gave way to Italians, Polish, and Lithuanians by the mid 1940s, followed later by Vietnamese, Brazilians, Cape Verdeans, Haitians, and various African groups, among others. In that time, Roman Catholic understanding of mission/missions underwent theological and practical changes, but some perennial themes remained. As we view the heritage of the highlighted Boston Catholics, who sought to make mission as central to seminary curriculum and Catholic self-understanding many questions arise including: Why does it appear that the ecclesial location of mission/mission theology hugs the margins

---

31. Other men pictured in addition to William Cardinal O'Connell, who stands in front of the altar, are Father Celestine Roddan, CP, who was from Randolph, Massachusetts and Superior of the Passionist Fathers' first mission to Hunan, China in 1921, and Fr. Paul F. Rooney, OFM, (Harvard A.B. 1898), who worked among Native Americans in Oklahoma and Baja California.

32. Law, *Solidarity in Favour of New Migrations* and *Migration at the Threshold*. The two books provide talks given at the third and fourth World Congresses sponsored by the Pontifical Council for the Pastoral care of Migrants and Itinerant People, 1999.

of the curriculum in Roman Catholic seminaries and universities in a post-Christian world?[33] Will their curricula engage the *Antioch Agenda* elements in a significant manner, particularly with the diversity of world cultures coming to Boston? What might a curriculum look like with mission at the center, particularly as the reality of the "Changing Contours of World Christianity" are in our midst?

WORKS CITED

Aiken, Charles F. *Diary, 1886–8*, p. 50 no. 46, Charles F. Aiken Papers, Large Collections, ACUA.

Archdiocese of Boston, "Coat of Arms." No pages. Online: http://bostoncatholic.org/About-The-Archdiocese/Content.aspx?id=11574.

Boyton, Neil. *A Yankee Xavier, Henry P. McGlinchey, SJ*. New York: Macmillan, 1937.

Bruneau, Joseph. *Synopse évangélique*. Paris: LeCoffre, 1901.

Butler, Jon. *Awash in a Sea of Faith: Christianizing the American People*. Cambridge, MA: Harvard University Press, 1990.

Challoner, Richard. *The Garden of the Soul: Or, A Manual of Spiritual Exercises and Instructions for Christians, Who Living in the World Aspire to Devotion*. London: Coghlan, 1793.

Chamberlin, Harrie R., and A. M. Gardner. *Handbook and Guide of the World in Boston*. Boston: The World in Boston, 1911.

Coady, Moses M. *Masters of Their Own Destiny: The Story of the Antigonish Movement of Adult Education Through Economic Cooperation*. New York: Harper, 1939.

———. *The Social Significance of the Cooperative Movement*. Antigonish, Nova Scotia: St. Francis Xavier University, 1958.

Cushing, Richard. *Questions and Answers on Communism*. Boston: Daughters of St. Paul, 1959.

———. "The Father Jim Hennessy Mission Club Bulletin." February–March, 1946. SPF Files. Record Group III.D.16. Box 10.3. Archives, Archdiocese of Boston.

———. Untitled sermon, 1945 (?), Cushing Sermons, Archives of the Archdiocese of Boston.

Dries, Angelyn, O.S.F., "The Sulpician Mission Legacy and the Foundation of Maryknoll." *Bulletin de Saint-Sulpice* 17 (1991) 167–76.

———. "Two Sides of the American Catholic Mission Coin: Mission Funding and Credit Unions." *American Catholic Studies* 117.1 (Spring 2006) 23–44.

33. The current curriculum for one Roman Catholic seminary in the United States is revealing in this regard. In the pre-theology program (college level), students take thirty-five credits of philosophy and twelve credits of theology, under the rubric of Catechism I and II, Church History I and II, Prayer I and II. On the graduate level, while there are two credits given to Mariology, none are given to mission. Given decrees from the Vatican offices regarding seminary education, over the last decade, this seminary is probably not unique in its outline of courses. To the seminary's commendation, one credit was given for Ecumenism and three credits for The Triune God and World Religions.

Flannery, OP, Austin. *Vatican Council II. The Conciliar and Post Conciliar Documents.* Northport, NY: Costello, 1992.

Garneau, James. "'Commandos for Christ'; The Foundations of the Missionary Society of St. James the Apostle and the 'Americanism' of the 1950s and 1960s." PhD diss., The Catholic University of America, 2000.

Hendricks, MM, Barbara. "The Legacy of Mary Josephine Rogers." *International Bulletin of Missionary Research* 9 (April 1997) 72–80.

Jeyaraj, Daniel, Robert W. Pazmiño, and Rodney L. Petersen, eds. *The Antioch Agenda: Essays on the Restorative Church in Honor of Orlando Costas.* New Delhi: Indian Society for the Promotion of Christian Knowledge for Andover Newton Theological School and the Boston Theological Institute, 2007.

Kennedy, MM, Camilla. "Mission Spirit of Mother Mary Joseph Rogers." Missionary Spirituality Report No. 6. *Maryknoll Formation Journal* (Spring 1982) 3.

Law, Bernard F. *Migration at the Threshold of the Third Millennium.* Vatican City: Pontifical Care of Migrants and Refugees, 1998.

———. *Solidarity in Favour of New Migrations: Proceedings of the III World Congress for the Pastoral Care of Migrants and Refugees.* Vatican City: Pontifical Council for the Pastoral Care of Migrants and Itinerant People, 1992.

Luzbetak, Louis J. *The Church and Cultures: An Applied Anthropology for the Religious Worker.* Techny, IL: Divine Word, 1963.

———. *The Church and Cultures: New Perspectives in Missiological Anthropology.* Maryknoll, NY: Orbis, 1988.

Mannock, J. *The Poor Man's Catechism: Or, The Christian Doctrine Explained.* Baltimore: Dorin, 1815.

O'Toole, James. "Prelates and Politicos." In *Catholic Boston. Studies in Religion and Community, 1870–1970*, O'Toole and Sullivan, 44. Boston: Roman Catholic Archbishop of Boston, 1985.

Oldham, J. H. *Christianity and the Race Problem.* New York: Doran, 1924.

Rogers, Mary Josephine. Letter to Miss Kathryn Maggio. File A-3, Folder 4#4. Maryknoll, NY: Maryknoll Sisters Archives.

Sexton, John R., and Arthur J. Riley. *History of St. John's Seminary.* Boston: Roman Catholic Archbishop of Boston, 1945.

Stewart, Robert J. "The Contributions of Joseph John Williams, SJ, 1875–1950 to the Study of Religion in the History of Africa and the Caribbean." A paper presented in March 1991 at the annual conference of the Association of Caribbean Historians. Joseph J. Williams folder, Reading Room desk, John J. Burns Library, Boston College.

———. *Religion and Society in Post-emancipation Jamaica.* Knoxville, TN: University of Tennessee Press, 1992.

Sullivan, Robert E. "Beneficial Relations toward a Social History of the Diocesan Priests of Boston, 1875–1944." In *Catholic Boston: Studies in Religion and Community, 1870–1970*, edited by Robert E. Sullivan and James M. O'Toole, 201–38. Boston: Roman Catholic Archdiocese of Boston, 1995.

"Sunday Obligation without a Priest, 1798." In *Prayer and Practice in the American Catholic Church*, edited by Joseph P. Chinnici, OFM and Angelyn Dries, O.S.F., 12. Maryknoll, NY: Orbis Books, 2000. Original in Cheverus Papers, Box 1/12, 1797–1835. Archives of the Archdiocese of Boston.

Talar, C. J. T. "Seminary Reform and Theological Method on the Eve of the Modernist Crisis: Transatlantic Reception of J. B. Hogan's *Clerical Studies* (1898)." *U.S. Catholic Historian* 28.3 (Summer 2010) 1–17.

Williams, SJ, Joseph J. *Keep the Gate: Guarding the Soul Against Sin*. New York: Benziger Brothers, 1923.

———. *Yearning for God: The Path to Peace of the Soul*. New York: Benziger Brothers, 1924.

4

Discerning the Future of World Christianity

Vision and Blindness at the World Missionary Conference, Edinburgh 1910

Brian Stanley

ONE HUNDRED YEARS ON, how should we remember the World Missionary Conference? Should we venerate it as the formal beginning of the institutional ecumenical movement, the first step along the road that led to the formation of the Church of South India in 1947 and, one year later in Amsterdam, to the opening assembly of the World Council of Churches? The origins of both the Church of South India and the WCC owe a great deal to the impetus supplied by the Edinburgh conference, but Protestant missionary ecumenism had already taken institutional shape in North America and in much of Europe well before 1910, while in both China and India indigenous Christian leaders and missionaries were already engaged in serious discussions about structured forms of missionary cooperation. Indeed, in China, a committee to discuss Protestant church union was formed as early as November 1902, and the Shanghai centenary missionary conference of 1907, though not yet ready to commit itself to the goal of a united church, recommended the formation of a federal union of all Protestant churches in China.[1] Nevertheless, the misconception that Edinburgh 1910 somehow

---

1. Cochrane, "Church union", 179-82; *Records: China Centenary Missionary Conference*, 689, 719.

marked the *genesis* of, rather than a major milestone in, the ecumenical movement survived tenaciously here and there throughout the centennial commemorations held in 2010. Equally it still remains necessary to reiterate the obvious point that the Edinburgh assembly was a conference of missionary society delegates convened to talk about missionary problems, not a conference of delegates of churches convened to discuss church unity. The problem for many of us, I suspect, is that the more we focus on Edinburgh 1910 as what it was, a *missionary* event, the more embarrassed we become, for it was overwhelmingly white and Protestant in its delegate composition, entirely unashamed in its acceptance of Western colonialism, and unambiguously committed to the now unfashionable view that Christianity was destined by divine fiat to the eventual conquest of all other world faiths. What I intend to do in this paper is to analyze an aspect of the conference that may yield some fruitful insights for reflection on Christian witness in today's very different world: how perceptive and accurate was the conference in its reading of the signs of the times and hence in its deduction of appropriate priorities for the world mission of the church?[2]

I propose to begin, not with the World Missionary Conference itself, but with an address given in Edinburgh nine months later by the Scottish theologian, Professor David S. Cairns. Cairns had played a crucial role in the conference, chairing Commission IV on "The Missionary Message in Relation to Non-Christian Religions," whose deeply reflective report has been more extensively, though not entirely accurately, analyzed by modern scholars than have any of the Edinburgh 1910 documents.[3] On March 23, 1911, Cairns was back in Edinburgh addressing a conference of Scottish students under the auspices of the Student Christian Movement. His advertised subject was "The vocation of Scotland in view of her religious heritage," but Cairns in fact devoted the substantial opening portion of his address to an analysis of "the condition of the world" which might equally well have come from the lips or the pen of John R. Mott, the American Methodist lay evangelist who chaired the World Missionary Conference. Indeed, the central preoccupations of Cairns's remarks in this section are almost identical

---

2. This paper thus marks a return to themes which I first explored in a paper written for the Currents in World Christianity Project in 1999, "Twentieth-century world Christianity," 52–83. Readers are recommended to read the two papers together.

3. See Stanley, *World Missionary Conference*, 205–47.

to those which characterized Mott's Commission I report on "Carrying the Gospel to all the Non-Christian World," submitted to the Edinburgh conference in the previous year. Cairns would undoubtedly have read Mott's report, and evidently endorsed its principal arguments, though it is not necessary to posit Mott as the sole or even the primary influence on Cairns's address.

Like Mott's Commission I report, Cairns rapidly homed in on what was then known as the Orient. What he termed the "Dark Continent" of Africa and the advance of Islam were mentioned on the first page, but only to be summarily dismissed in favor of India and "above all, of the Farthest East—for it is here that the interest is sharpest." He observed that a "strange tremor of unrest has suddenly spread across Asia, from Bombay to Moukden"—western India and Manchuria being two of the principal fields of Scottish Presbyterian missionary endeavor.[4] These tremors were produced by the jarring encounter of two mighty tectonic forces: on the one hand, the ancient religions and civilizations of Asia; and, on the other, the incursion of new cultural influences from the West. Christianity was one of these, but Cairns was in little doubt that the more potent disruptive influence was of a very different kind: "Wherever the new scientific knowledge comes throughout the Orient, there the ancestral faiths must wither and die. Those Eastern nations cannot assimilate the techniques of Western civilization and Western militarism without assimilating the scientific method on which these are based, and where the scientific method comes the old faiths must, sooner or later, go. The real alternative that lies before China and Japan, if they persist on their present paths, must be between Christianity and Secularism."[5]

The alarming prospect that Cairns raised in the minds of his student audience was of east Asia going over *en masse* to atheism, an outcome whose "disastrous reaction would be felt throughout Christendom." The growing irreligion that British Christians lamented to find in their own society was as nothing in comparison with what would soon be observable "if this great spiritual disaster comes to pass, if Christendom idly allows it to pass." Cairns believed that "a certain instinct and divination" of this portentous trend impelled the international student movement of which this particular meeting in 1911 was a part, and the same convic-

---

4. Cairns, *The Vocation of Scotland*, 7–8.
5. Ibid., 10–11.

tion, he noted, "certainly" lay "behind the World Missionary Conference in this city last June."[6] The vocation of Scotland in particular, and more broadly the missionary calling of the Western Protestant churches as a whole, was nothing less than to halt and even reverse the downward slide of Asia, and east Asia in particular, towards a godless future that would prove deeply damaging to the global fortunes of Christianity. Scotland, with its great missionary tradition and its Reformed theological emphasis on the absolute sovereignty of God over all areas of human activity, not excepting the turbulent waters of politics and ideology, was, according to Cairns, uniquely well-placed to discharge the task.[7]

Cairns's message was distinctively honed for a Scottish theological audience, but his identification of the essential priorities for global missionary strategy was a faithful replication of the central thrust of Mott's message to the Edinburgh conference, as expressed in the Commission I report. Three unifying premises may be identified underpinning both Cairns's address and Mott's report, although the second and third of these were less consistently made explicit than the first. I propose to examine these three assumptions in some detail, and make some reference to how far the subsequent course of world Christian expansion has either borne out or invalidated these assumptions.

THE RELIGIOUS IMPACT OF MODERNIZATION

The first premise evident in both Cairns's address and the Commission I report was the assumption that the ancient religions of Asia were losing their hold on the educated elites who were being drawn to the "modern" and "progressive" ideologies emanating from the West. Modernization of education and economy, it was assumed, would inevitably lead to the disintegration of Asia's traditional faiths. This erosion of the religious foundations of Asian civilizations and the uniquely "plastic condition" of Asian nations constituted both opportunity and threat for Christianity.[8] In China, as also in Korea, Japan, India, Turkey, and Persia, the question was whether the church would be able to channel the strengthening currents of political, educational, and religious reform in the direction of

6. Ibid., 12–13.
7. Ibid., 16–18, 41–42.
8. World Missionary Conference, 1910, *Report of Commission I*, 25, 27.

Christianity: "if the tide is not set toward Christianity during the next decade both in the Far East and the Near East, it may be turned against us in the decade following."[9]

The report noted how the ancient Confucian society of China was turning from its conservative preoccupation with the traditions of the ancestors to a focus on the future, a trend that had impressed itself on Mott during his third visit to China in 1907, when he had been struck by the hunger of China's student class to seize new educational opportunities abroad, especially in Tokyo.[10] The Commission I report observed that thousands of ambitious Chinese youths were going to study in "Japan, America, and Europe to prepare themselves for the leadership of the new China."[11] Their appetite for Western education and scientific knowledge was, Mott argued, an invitation for missions to present "the latest scientific truth along with the Gospel," thus showing the Chinese that "all truth is one," and leading them to accept the gospel sugared by a coating of Western scientism. The priority was therefore to expand greatly the Christian educational enterprise in China, following a policy that may be denominated as "Christianity plus . . . ": "It is western education that the Chinese are clamouring for, and will have. If we can give it to them, plus Christianity, they will take it; if we cannot give it to them, they will get it elsewhere, without Christianity—and that speedily."[12]

Such widening exposure to Western learning did not, however, imply that China's long-standing tradition of anti-foreignism was about to evaporate; on the contrary, Mott discerned in "the new national spirit" coursing through China's educated classes a redoubled insistence on "China for the Chinese" and a strengthening hostility to many aspects of foreign influence, a recognition that ought to have led Mott to question the assumption that education offered by the missions would inevitably lead to the acceptance of Christianity as part of the package.[13] China, the report concluded, presented the spectacle of "a great Empire in a state of flux," a mass of plastic ideological metal, lying inert in the furnace of revolutionary change, ready to be set in either a Christian or a materialist mould; the outcome would depend on what "proper plant and force

9. Ibid., 29.
10. Hopkins, *John R. Mott*, 310–13.
11. World Missionary Conference, 1910, *Report of Commission I*, 12, 26.
12. Ibid., 30.
13. Ibid., 96.

were at hand"—in other words, on whether Christian missions were willing to devote sufficient personnel and resources to the furnace of a China in the midst of revolutionary change.[14]

On one level the diagnosis offered by the report proved to be extraordinarily accurate. It was not inconceivable in 1910 that the currents of modernizing reform and nationalist politics in various parts of Asia would flow over the next two to three decades in directions broadly sympathetic to Christianity. In India, until Gandhi's very public attack in 1936–37 on Christian proselytism as a threat to Indian national identity and Hindu "tolerance," it was not wholly clear that the nationalist movement would take a predominantly Hindu form, synthesizing India's ancestral faith with modern political ideologies in a way that neither Mott nor Cairns had contemplated.[15] The mass or people movements of "untouchables" (now known as Dalits) into Christianity maintained extraordinary momentum in the two decades after 1910, increasing the Christian population of India by an estimated 40.6 percent between the 1911 and 1931 censuses, far in excess of the rate of growth of the national population.[16] However, in the wake of Gandhi's campaign against conversion, the rate of Christian expansion in India slowed. The famous declaration in 1935 of B. R. Ambedkar, spokesman for the untouchables, that, though born a Hindu, he "would not die a Hindu," did not raise widespread hopes that he might opt for Christianity. Ambedkar, followed by hundreds of thousands of his followers, finally converted—to Buddhism—exactly twenty-one years later on October 14, 1956.[17]

In China, on the other hand, Christian hopes remained buoyant for longer. Republican China under Sun Yat-sen adopted a broadly pro-Christian stance, and, through the influence of the YMCA, the new Western-educated elite gravitated for a time towards Christianity: by 1922 the YMCA could claim 24,000 student members and a further 54,000 members of city associations throughout China.[18] Sun Yat-sen's successor, Chiang Kai-shek, married devout Methodist Soon Mayling in 1927, was baptized in October 1930, and became a regular Bible-reader

14. Ibid., 107, 362.

15. See Harper, *Shadow of the Mahatma*, 315–18.

16. Webster, *A History of the Dalit Christians*, 56.

17. Harper, *Shadow of the Mahatma*, 307; Tartakov, "B. R. Ambedkar and the Navayana Diksha," 192–215.

18. Garrett, *Social Reformers*, 175.

and man of prayer after his traumatic imprisonment by two rebel warlords at X'ian in December 1936; it was not wholly foolish of missionary observers to imagine that he was "China's greatest hope at the present time."[19] Nevertheless, by 1927–28 the anti-Christian movements had confronted Christian missions with the uncomfortable fact that their promise of national self-strengthening and modernization through the medium of Christianity had been upstaged by an ideology of exactly the atheist variety of which Mott and Cairns had warned. Marxist-Leninism, despite being *more* Western in both its origins and its philosophical texture than was Christianity, appeared to offer the Chinese elite the same material benefits as did the "Christianity-plus" package marketed by the missionaries but without the need to accept foreign tutelage and informal control. Protestant missions in Republican China continued to invest heavily in higher education and to present Christianity as the foundation of scientific progress. At Shandong Christian University in Jinan, the Whitewright Institute and Museum—founded by the English Baptist missionary J. S. Whitewright in 1887—displayed the wonders of Western science in what R. E. Speer hailed as "the most effective piece of university extension work which can be found in Asia, if not in the world."[20] However, the methodology of "Christianity-plus" was fundamentally flawed. China provides the most telling example of how Mott's analysis was both uncannily prescient, but at the same time dangerously unaware of the ultimate implications of the strategic emphases that he was urging Western missions to adopt.

THE STRATEGIC AND GEOGRAPHICAL PRIORITIES OF WESTERN MISSIONS, 1910–2010

The second premise underlying the missionary strategy outlined in the Commission I report and, by implication, in Cairns's 1911 address was that missionary effort should be concentrated on those portions of non-Christian humanity that were deemed to have the greatest collective vitality and hence maximal potential to influence others, either towards

---

19. Ronald Still to his parents, December 30, 1936, in Salters, *Bound with Love*, 90. See Kyounghan, "Chiang Kai-shek and Christianity," 1–10; Taylor, *Generalissimo*, 73–74, 91–92, 108–9.

20. Middlebrook, *Memoir of H. R. Williamson*, 33; cited in Stanley, *History of the Baptist Missionary Society*, 306.

the acceptance of Christianity or its rejection. Here the influence of contemporary racial theory, strongly tinged as it was with social Darwinist connotations, was implicit, and occasionally made explicit. The Chinese, observed the report, were the opposite of "certain decaying races with which missions also have to do": their energy and endurance made them hard to win, yet also decidedly worth winning.[21] A similar verdict was applied to the Japanese, whose advanced state of mental, moral, and material civilization was said to make them the natural leaders of the Orient.[22] Japan was already the dominant power in the Korean peninsula, and within two months of the conclusion of the Edinburgh conference, on August 22, 1910, would annex Korea as a formal colony. The evangelization of Japan was thus an urgent imperative, not simply for the sake of its own inhabitants, but also because this ascendant Asian colonial power, in its growing rationalism and materialism, posed a potential threat to the allegedly "childlike faith" of Korean Protestants.[23] Koreans were thereby characterized as a childlike race whose ready acceptance of the Christian gospel was a cause for celebration, but also potential anxiety that they might prove equally ready to accept a rationalistic creed from their dominant neighbor.

As for the races which were branded as not merely childlike but "decaying" (Africans were clearly in mind here), they too needed the gospel urgently, but for precisely the opposite reason to that which impelled evangelism in China or Japan. Their traditional belief systems, labeled by the report as animism or fetishism, were, it was confidently predicted, destined to succumb "within a generation" to the first higher monotheistic religion with which they came into contact. In the light of the threatening advance of Islam into equatorial Africa, the only question, therefore, was whether "the Dark Continent shall become Mohammedan or Christian."[24] African religion had no future: "Paganism is doomed."[25]

In introducing its section on Africa the report made in passing the telling comment that "India and China were the two great mission fields of the world" and proceeded, as if in justification of this statement, to

21. World Missionary Conference, 1910, *Report of Commission I*, 85.
22. Ibid., 50–51.
23. Ibid., 66.
24. Ibid., 207, 365, 364.
25. Ibid., 21.

note the sparse nature of Africa's population, which was computed to be less than fifteen persons per square mile in comparison to China's ratio of over 260 to the square mile.[26] Mott expressed confidence that "under more settled and propitious conditions in the future" (an indication of the measure of trust that he placed in the beneficial impact of the colonial regimes, especially British), the meager population of Africa would increase "enormously."[27] Nevertheless, he was pessimistic about the survival of African "primitivism" which he saw as constituting peculiarly fertile soil for conversion: "There are but a few primitive races or peoples left in the world, and the opportunity afforded the Christian Church to reach them under most favourable conditions can last but a brief season."[28]

Africa thus had insistent claims of its own to make on the allocation of Western missionary resources, and even the occasional missionary voice from Asia was prepared to recognize this. D. E. Hoste, the British director of the China Inland Mission, urged in his questionnaire reply that "the situation in Africa constitutes perhaps the most urgent call upon the Christian Church at the present time." The record of existing well-organized work in Africa, Hoste believed, indicated that "it would, probably, be comparatively easy to win the rest."[29] The Commission I report concluded that the continent offered the prospect and indeed the necessity of an imminent battle with Islam for the soul of traditional religionists, and even of "rapid and widespread triumphs of the Gospel."[30]

Mott, however, appeared to believe that the strategic significance of Africa for the global fortunes of Christianity was limited. This may have been because he was ambivalent about the likely future trajectory of Islam. Although the Commission I report warned Edinburgh delegates of the aggressive nature of Muslim expansion in Africa, the Malayan peninsula, and Sumatra, and of the resurgence of Indian Islam particularly among low-caste groups, it paradoxically also informed them that globally Islam was "making no marked intellectual or spiritual progress." The religion, they were assured, was disintegrating philosophically into

26. Ibid., 204.
27. Ibid., 242.
28. Ibid., 23.
29. Hoste, answer to question XII (2), MRL 12, World Missionary Conference, 1910.
30. World Missionary Conference, 1910, *Report of Commission I*, 207-8.

competing sects and parties, lacking in "creative energy," and struggling to retain the allegiance of Muslims attracted to "modern learning."[31] Here Mott reflected the optimistic views expressed by the leading American advocate of missions to the Muslim world, Samuel Zwemer, who had written in 1907 that Islam was "doomed to fade away in time before the advance of humanity, civilization and enlightenment."[32] If Islam had no long-term future, the significance of the short-term religious contest in Africa, however urgent and fiercely fought it might be, was relativized.

One wonders how Mott or Zwemer would have reacted to the statistics published in 2009 in the *Atlas of Global Christianity*, which estimate that over the century since 1910, the average annual rate of growth of Islam worldwide has been 1.97 percent, compared with 1.33 percent for Christianity—so much for the prophecy of imminent disintegration.[33] They might have been rather less surprised, but considerably more gratified, to learn that in Africa, on the other hand, the rate of Christian growth over the century (3.82 percent) has surpassed the rate of Muslim growth (2.38 percent) with an ease that confounds the more pessimistic predictions made in 1910 that Africa stood on the brink of becoming a Muslim continent.[34] What Mott, along with almost all the delegates at Edinburgh in 1910, would have struggled to comprehend, is that traditional African understandings of the spirit world were not so comprehensively "doomed" in the face of encroaching modern enlightenment as they anticipated, but rather have been incorporated and substantially re-crafted within a Christian framework.

It is not easy for our generation—that has come to make an almost automatic mental association between Africa and the missionary—to appreciate that only a century ago the continent of Africa was still of distinctly secondary importance to India, the jewel in the imperial crown, in the minds of many British missionary thinkers, and of even more marginal significance to most American Protestant missionary strategists, whose attentions, like those of their compatriots who har-

31. Ibid., 13, 19, 207, 362.

32. Zwemer, *Islam*, 225; cited in Smith, "Christian missionary views of Islam," 362. I owe this reference to my former student, Ethan R. Sanders of the University of Cambridge.

33. Johnson and Ross, *Atlas of Global Christianity*, 7.

34. Ibid., 11, 110. Although questions may justifiably be asked about the basis of the figures of religious adherence used in the *Atlas of Global Christianity*, they are undoubtedly useful as indications of trends.

bored imperialist aspirations, were firmly fixed on the Pacific rim. The *Statistical Atlas of Christian Missions* prepared by Commission I at great expense[35] as a companion to the report revealed that there were more North American foreign missionaries working in Japan (769) than in the whole of the African continent (734). In east, southeast, and south Asia as a whole there were approximately 4,933 North American missionaries in 1910—nearly seven times as many as in Africa. In Britain, the disproportion between Asia and Africa was less marked, though still significant: the *Atlas* suggested that about 4,459 British missionaries were working in east, south-east, and south Asia, as compared with 2,261 in Africa.[36]

After the First World War, these ratios would begin to reverse, as the political conditions for missionary work in parts of Asia (notably China) deteriorated in the face of ascendant nationalist movements, while, conversely, missionary opportunities in Africa steadily expanded under the umbrella of colonial protection and educational subsidies. The number of Protestant missionary personnel serving in Asia decreased from 16,663 in 1925 to 14,318 in 1938, whereas those serving in Africa increased over the same period from 6,289 to 8,447.[37] After the Second World War, the transposition of Western missionary priorities became more marked, as the doors closed to Western missions, first in China and then in much of the Indian sub-continent. The corresponding re-orientation to tropical Africa was most marked in the case of American conservative evangelical or fundamentalist missions, though Catholic missions also contributed to the geographical shift. By 2010, according to the *Atlas of Global Christianity*, the number of North American missionaries (including Roman Catholics) working in Africa had reached 53,100, nearly ten times as many as those working in Asia (5,700), and

---

35. Stanley, *World Missionary Conference*, 47. Commission I had a budget of $9,900, excluding the cost of preparation of the maps for the *Atlas*, which was borne by the Student Volunteer Movement: World Missionary Conference, 1910, *Statistical Atlas of Christian Missions*, 7; see also minutes of Commission I, 9–10 September 1908, p. 7, MRL 12, World Missionary Conference, 1910.

36. World Missionary Conference, *Statistical Atlas of Christian Missions*, 65–74. The figures for Africa exclude Madagascar and Mauritius. The figures for North American and British missionaries working in Asia are necessarily estimates since the *Atlas* made no differentiation between British and North American members of the China Inland Mission (p. 67). I have estimated that 20 percent of the CIM force was drawn from North America, following figures in Austin, "Blessed adversity," 52 n. 13.

37. Parker, *Interpretative Statistical Survey*, 243.

even eclipsing the substantial American missionary presence in Latin America (40,200). In terms of North American missionary numbers, the *Atlas* suggests that Asia now ranks below even Oceania (the recipient of 6,900 missionaries). Whilst missionaries from Europe working in Africa also outnumber those working in Asia (21,600 compared with 13,000), it is interesting to note that European missions are now numerically a more significant presence in Asia than American ones.[38]

What is more pertinent still is the sobering observation that the striking geographical re-concentration of Western missionary forces over the last century has followed, rather than initiated, trends in the growth of world Christianity. Whether by political necessity or strategic choice, or a combination of the two, Western missions over the last century have refocused their attention on the continent where Christianity has taken independent root most easily, and have largely abandoned the goal that was uppermost in the allocation of missionary resources in 1910—the endeavor to capture the political and religious elites of Asia for Christ before they succumbed to the rival attractions of Western materialist ideologies.

For European Protestants from the era of Ziegenbalg onwards, the river of Christian mission had flowed primarily from west to east. This was because the first Protestant nations to establish themselves as imperial powers—Denmark, the Netherlands, and Britain—turned their attention increasingly to Asia and away from their initial preoccupation with the Caribbean or the Americas. British and European Protestant missionary priorities increasingly followed suit, all the more so after the achievement of slave emancipation in the British empire in 1833–34, which was followed with almost indecent haste by the withdrawal of most British missionary societies from the Caribbean.[39] American Protestants made this oriental preoccupation their own, though with a distinctive geographical emphasis on both the eastern and western rims of Asia rather than on the Indian sub-continent that absorbed so much British missionary energy. They also, of course, devoted substantial missionary resources to their southern continental neighbor, Latin America. The decision to exclude from the Edinburgh conference agenda all missions aimed at historic Catholic, Orthodox, or Oriental Christian populations, taken in April 1909 in deference to Anglo-Catholic scruples, was

---

38. Johnson and Ross, *Atlas of Global Christianity*, 262–63.
39. Stanley, "Twentieth-century world Christianity," 72.

thus a bitter pill for American evangelicals to swallow.[40] The forcible severance in 1910 of Latin America from the other fields of Protestant missionary activity had the effect of reinforcing still more strongly the unspoken equations in the minds of most European Protestants between "Christian" and "Western," "non-Christian" and "Eastern." Only gradually in the course of the twentieth century, as the balance of mission resources shifted from Asia to Africa, and as Latin American missions elbowed their way back onto the ecumenical Protestant agenda after the 1916 Panama Congress on Christian Work in Latin America,[41] did the old orientalist juxtapositions of religious geography begin to fade, to be supplanted by a new vertical ideological juxtaposition between Christian north and non-Christian south. This in its turn gradually inverted itself from the 1970s onwards into a third and diametrically opposite antithesis, which has now become a truism of religious studies discourse, namely that between the post-Christian north and the new Christian south.

INDIGENOUS AGENCY AND APPROPRIATION

The third premise discernible in David Cairns's address and John Mott's report is the tacit assumption that Christians from the non-Western world had only a subsidiary, if important, part to play in shaping the future of world Christianity. There were indeed speakers at Edinburgh who articulated a bold, if loosely defined, vision of what the face of future world Christianity would look like. It would not be a monochrome replication of Western styles but a truly catholic and universal family that incorporated, for example, distinctively Chinese, or Japanese, or Indian expressions of Christian truth and worship. Most notable in this respect was the Anglo-Catholic Bishop of Birmingham, Charles Gore, chairman of Commission III on Christian education, whose report insisted that the final eschatological vision held out by the New Testament in Revelation 21 was of "all nations" bringing the gifts of their distinctive racial characteristics into the inclusive community of the city of God.[42]

40. See Stanley, *World Missionary Conference*, 49–72.

41. Hogg, *Ecumenical Foundations*, 173–74.

42. For fuller expositions of Gore's statements see Stanley, *World Missionary Conference*, 193–98, and also Stanley, "From the 'poor heathen,'" 3–10.

But the efforts made at Edinburgh to articulate a theology of legitimate plurality within the catholicity of the global household of God were patchy and also founded on dubious notions of racial essentialism. They were rarely, if at all, extended to those races deemed to be "primitive," and they featured only minimally in Mott's activist program of winning the world through a program of evangelization led by Western missionary agencies. Both Cairns and Mott conceived of global evangelization as a movement that was ultimately dependent on the standards of Christian spirituality and evangelistic zeal set within Europe and North America. Indeed, the implicit but extraordinarily bold claim of Cairns's address in 1911 was that it was the wee nation of Scotland, with its particular inheritance of Reformed theology, democratic education, and missionary enthusiasm, whom God was calling to play a pivotal role in the divine strategy for the salvation of Asia's countless millions.

To be fair, the Commission I report did pay due homage to the necessary role of Asian and African Christians in the task of evangelization, and called in particular for more effective training of catechists, evangelists, and Bible women—figures who would be of central importance in the growth of popular Asian and African Christianity over the next hundred years.[43] However, the very next paragraph of the report went on to assert that "a crucial factor in the evangelisation of the non-Christian world is the state of the Church in Christian lands": the missionary movement would only become "irresistible and triumphant" if there was a higher level of spiritual consecration among members of what the report termed the "Home Church."[44] The opening chapter of the report had also revealed its presuppositions by drawing a comparison between the expansion of African Islam, which was essentially the work of indigenous agents, and Christianity, which "until a force of native workers can be prepared, must be spread by Europeans who differ greatly from the natives."[45] Although the comparison was not without foundation, even as early as 1910 this statement represented a serious undervaluation of the place that indigenous Christians already occupied in the process of evangelization in fields such as Uganda or Yorubaland. The largest British mission agency—the Church Missionary Society—

---

43. World Missionary Conference, 1910, *Report of Commission I*, 368–69; see also 241.

44. Ibid., 369.

45. Ibid., 20–21.

had in 1906 nearly ten times as many accredited "native" agents (8,850) as it had European missionaries (975).⁴⁶

Even observers of global religious trends in 1910–11 as perceptive as Mott or Cairns undoubtedly were made no essential distinction between the future of the Western missionary movement and the future of world Christianity: for the latter, they assumed, would be fundamentally dependent on, and coextensive with, the former. One hundred years later, it is patently obvious to us that these two global religious processes have proved to be, though not wholly unrelated, clearly separable and often markedly divergent. We are well aware that the players who scarcely made it onto the cast list at the World Missionary Conference in 1910 have proved to be among the key actors in the subsequent transformation of Christianity into a religion that is rooted increasingly in the cultural soil of the southern hemisphere. African American missionaries, Pentecostals, prophets, prophetesses, and African Initiated Churches feature hardly at all in the Edinburgh reports. There were at least six and perhaps eight or even more African–American delegates present at Edinburgh, and they even convened a separate caucus meeting for "all coloured delegates" during the conference which was advertised in the *Conference Daily Paper*, although we do not know who turned up to the meeting.⁴⁷ The Commission reports, however, give relatively little attention to the role of African American missions in the evangelization of West Africa. Pentecostals, of course, were becoming increasingly visible on the Christian stage by 1910, but since their rapidly growing presence as individuals scattered in different locations in Asia, Africa, and Latin America was not yet formalized into separate Pentecostal missionary agencies, they did not qualify for representation at Edinburgh. As for the first African Initiated Churches, the only mention they receive in Mott's report was of a sweepingly dismissive kind: the Ethiopian churches of South Africa are described as a "mischief" spreading through the country "a superficial and largely emotional form of Christianity unable to resist the disintegrating and corrupting influences of surrounding heathenism."⁴⁸

---

46. Cited in Williams, *The Ideal of the Self-Governing Church*, 262.

47. World Missionary Conference, 1910, *Conference Daily Paper* 5, 86; see Stanley, *World Missionary Conference*, 99–100.

48. World Missionary Conference, 1910, *Report of Commission I*, 229.

Nevertheless, the report did include a section specifically devoted to "organized evangelistic work on the part of the native churches." It took due note of such non-Western missionary initiatives as the west African missions of Jamaican Presbyterians and Anglicans; V. S. Azariah's National Missionary Society of India and Indian Missionary Society of Tirunelveli; the Telegu Baptist Natal Mission, whose first overseas missionary to the indentured sugarcane workers, John Rangiah, was a delegate at Edinburgh; and the earliest ventures by Korean Protestants to spread the gospel among the Korean diaspora in locations such as Jeju (Quelpart) Island, Siberia, Manchuria, and even Hawaii and California. Missions from what would now be termed "the global south" were thus already in evidence by 1910, and were warmly welcomed by Mott, even if he could not refrain from adding as a concluding comment that "In most of the cases referred to above, it should be noted that the counsel and guidance of the European missionaries have been fraternally asked and fraternally given."[49] Contrary to what is often alleged, Edinburgh 1910 did not confine its definition of overseas missions to Western endeavors, but it did assume that Western leadership of the whole enterprise was both appropriate and destined to remain intact for the foreseeable future.

CONCLUSION

David Cairns and John Mott were men of intelligence, insight, and exceptional breadth of vision, and in varying measure these qualities were shared by other leaders and delegates of the World Missionary Conference. In their perception that the leading nations of Asia were in an unusually "plastic" condition, peculiarly amenable at this pivotal point in their history to being molded by powerful ideologies from various quarters, they were not far wrong. At the same time, their field of vision had a number of blind spots. In the long term, Christianity would suffer more than it gained from the attempts of missions to yoke its message to Western scientific values and progress. They underestimated the capacity of the ancient faiths of Asia to retain their hold even on "modern," urban and educated people. They also seriously misjudged the capacity of Islam to survive and even flourish within a modern environment.

49. Ibid., 336–38.

They had very little sense of how far the future of world Christianity was to be shaped by African and other indigenous peoples whom they regarded as "decaying," "primitive," and devoid of the requisite cultural resources to articulate their own distinctive incarnations of the Christian gospel. Nevertheless, I have a suspicion that if the proceedings of the various centennial mission conferences held in 2010, in Edinburgh, Tokyo, Cape Town, and Boston, were to be subjected in one hundred years' time to critical dissection by scholars in the light of the course that world Christianity has actually taken in the twenty-first century, the diagnoses and policy prescriptions advanced in these conferences of our own generation will prove to be no less flawed, partial in perception, and ideologically conditioned than those of our predecessors a century ago. Ultimately our responses to the pronouncements made in 1910 will depend on our own theological and philosophical commitments. For all of their Western cultural biases, the delegates at Edinburgh 1910 shared a common conviction that the Christian gospel was good news for all human beings without exception, and was not, therefore, to be confined within the frontiers of European or American Christendom. This theological absolutism, so uncongenial to many palates today, was in fact the foundation for the construction of Christianity as a multi-cultural world religion.

WORKS CITED

Austin, Alvyn. "Blessed adversity: Henry W. Frost and the China Inland Mission." In *Earthen Vessels: American Evangelicals and Foreign Missions, 1880–1980*, edited by Joel Carpenter and Wilbert R. Shenk, 47–70. Grand Rapids: Eerdmans, 1990.

Cairns, David S. *The Vocation of Scotland in View of her Religious Heritage*. London: Student Christian Movement, 1911.

Cochrane, Thomas. "Church Union." *Chinese Recorder and Missionary Journal* 34.4 (April 1903) 179–82.

Commission I, 9–10 September 1908, p. 7, MRL 12, World Missionary Conference, 1910, series 1, box 7, folder 5, the Burke Library archives at Union Theological Seminary, New York City.

Garrett, Shirley S. *Social Reformers in Urban China: The Chinese Y.M.C.A., 1895–1926*. Cambridge: Harvard University Press, 1970.

Harper, Susan B. *In the Shadow of the Mahatma: Bishop V. S. Azariah and the Travails of Christianity in British India*. Grand Rapids: Eerdmans, 2000.

Hogg, W. Richey. *Ecumenical Foundations: A History of the International Missionary Council and its Nineteenth-Century Background*. New York: Harper & Brothers, 1952.

Hopkins, C. H. *John R. Mott 1865–1955: A Biography*. Grand Rapids: Eerdmans, 1979.
Hoste, D. E. answer to question XII (2), MRL 12, World Missionary Conference, 1910, series 1, box 5, folder 7, the Burke Library archives at Union Theological Seminary, New York.
Johnson, Todd M., and Kenneth R. Ross, eds. *Atlas of Global Christianity*. Edinburgh: Edinburgh University Press, 2009.
Kyounghan, Bae. "Chiang Kai-shek and Christianity: Religious Life Reflected from His Diary." *Journal of Modern Chinese History* 3.1 (June 2009) 1–10.
Middlebrook, J. B. *Memoir of H. R. Williamson: In Journeyings Oft*. London: Baptist Missionary Society, 1969.
Parker, Joseph I. *Interpretative Statistical Survey of the World Mission of the Christian Church*. New York: International Missionary Council, 1938.
Records: China Centenary Missionary Conference Held at Shanghai, April 25 to May 8, 1907. Shanghai: Centenary Conference Committee, 1907.
Salters, Audrey. *Bound with Love: Letters Home from China 1935–1945*. St. Andrews: Agequod, 2007.
Smith, Jane I. "Christian Missionary Views of Islam in the Nineteenth and Twentieth Centuries." *Islam and Christian-Muslim Relations* 9.3 (1998) 362.
Stanley, Brian. "From the 'poor heathen' to 'the glory and honour of all nations': Vocabularies of Race and Custom in Protestant Missions, 1844–1928." *International Bulletin of Missionary Research* 34.1 (2010) 3–10.
———. *The History of the Baptist Missionary Society 1792–1992*. Edinburgh: T. & T. Clark, 1992.
———. "Twentieth-Century World Christianity: A Perspective from the History of Missions." In *Christianity Reborn: The Global Expansion of Evangelicalism in the Twentieth Century*, edited by Donald M. Lewis, 52–83. Grand Rapids: Eerdmans, 2004.
———. *The World Missionary Conference: Edinburgh 1910*. Grand Rapids: Eerdmans, 2009.
Tartakov, Gary. "B. R. Ambedkar and the Navayana Diksha." In *Religious Conversion in India: Modes, Motivations and Meanings*, edited by Rowena Robinson and Satthianadan Clarke, 192–215. New Delhi: Oxford University Press, 2003.
Taylor, Jay. *Generalissimo: Chiang Kai-shek and the Struggle for Modern China*. Cambridge: Belknap Press of Harvard University Press, 2009.
Webster, J. C. B. *A History of the Dalit Christians in India*. San Francisco: Mellen Research University Press, 1992.
Williams, C. Peter. *The Ideal of the Self-Governing Church: A Study in Victorian Missionary Strategy*. Leiden: Brill, 1990.
World Missionary Conference, 1910. *Report of Commission I: Carrying the Gospel to All the Non-Christian World*. Edinburgh: Oliphant, Anderson & Ferrier, 1910.
———. *Statistical Atlas of Christian Missions*. Edinburgh: World Missionary Conference, 1910.
Zwemer, Samuel M. *Islam: A Challenge to Faith*. New York: Student Volunteer Movement for Foreign Missions, 1907.

PART II

Mission in the Twenty-first Century

5

Journey to the Center of Gravity

Christian Mission One Century after Edinburgh 1910

Athanasios N. Papathanasiou

"MISSIONS EXIST TO MAKE missions unnecessary." As we learn from Brian Stanley's monumental work, *The World Missionary Conference, Edinburgh 1910*, this statement was the conclusion reached with considerable enthusiasm by one of the participants at that conference.[1] For its time (that period was particularly paternalistic in spirit) this was a ground-breaking remark, insofar as it recognized that the new churches of the Third World needed to stand on their own feet as full churches, not just appendages of Western mother-churches.

This is a comment that I should like us to keep in mind, along with another matter also connected with the 1910 conference. That is a matter that is rather peripheral to the conference itself, but also has to do with the way local churches are understood. The Russian Orthodox clergyman and missionary to Japan Nicolas Kasatkin was invited to the Edinburgh conference, but did not take part.[2] Obviously, we shall never know what his particular contribution might have been if he had actually participated. I suppose, however, that it would have been very interesting had he presented his experience from the Russian-Japanese war that had been waged just five years before the conference. As soon as war

---

1. Stanley, *World Missionary Conference*, 111.
2. Ionita, "Cooperation and the Promotion of Unity," 263.

broke out, Nicolas (unlike the other Russians who were in Japan) did not return to his biological homeland. He stayed in Japan, feeling that his homeland was now his Japanese church community.[3] The inculturation process that he pursued in the Japanese context concerned his very being. His place, therefore, was no longer the place he had started from, but the place he had moved to.

I do not mention the case of Nicolas in order to be triumphalistic about Orthodox mission as a whole. After all, there are cases where Orthodox mission has been carried out not with the openness characteristic of Nicolas, but in a spirit of cultural colonialism.[4] The reason I have singled out both these points (the participant's remark and Nicolas's case) is that, each in its own way, they touch on a question of the utmost importance: the journey of faith towards otherness, towards the varied landscapes of the world and of history. And, of course, both bring to the fore the titanic battle over the *criteria* for this journey.

I consider the "criteria" a matter of decisive significance. They are what make each journey to be something different; in other words, to become either the journey of Ulysses (Odysseus) or the journey of Abraham. These two figures—Ulysses and Abraham—represent two radically different types of journey. No doubt, people consider the warrior Ulysses the traveler *par excellence*. And yet, the center of gravity for his travels, the center of gravity for his discovery of new places, and the center of gravity for his contact with otherness was the return to the point he had started from; the return to his homeland. That is the reason, after all, why his beloved Penelope waits for him back there—at home. Ulysses is an expression of human greatness, the human being who acts in history; but at the same time, he also expresses an impasse. He is a prisoner of naturalism. He cannot dream of a future radically different from what natural evolution can bring. The world in which Ulysses moves remains eternally what it was from the beginning. And that is why his epic, *The Odyssey*, culminates in the triumph of return, the triumph of land property, and the triumph of tribal gods.

With Abraham, the opposite happens. In his journey, there is no prospect of return. Abraham abandons his home forever. That is why he travels *with* his wife, Sarah. Abraham opens himself up to what is

---

3. See Cary, *A History of Christianity in Japan*, 417–18.

4. See, for example, Papathanasiou, "Missionary Experience and Academic Quest," 301–12.

different, what has not yet existed. He opens himself up to the future. In Abraham's case, the encounter with otherness is not merely one episode, it is the very core of the journey. Abraham moves into the realm of otherness, and in addition he himself becomes something other than what he was initially. He becomes a stranger, and accepts a god who appears to him at a very particular moment, the moment when Abraham is showing solidarity with strangers in need. Abraham is orientated towards surprise, and for that reason his story does not end with the story of his family. It continues as the history of the world and of the nations, of whom Abraham becomes the father.

As is well-known, Emmanuel Levinas and Miroslav Volf have underlined Abraham's journey as a metaphor of moving into the realm of the Other—as a model for true opening-up where the subject ceases to exist as an enclosed entity and is actualized only in relationship with the Other.[5] For Christians, this sort of journey is based on the fact that the biblical God moves into the realm of the radically Other. In taking flesh, God himself "changes" forever. He "became what He had not been hitherto,"[6] as an Orthodox hymn for the feast of Christmas says boldly and characteristically. Biblical syntax never ceases to amaze us. The moment God defines himself as "he who is and who was," the reader expects to hear that God is also "he who will be." Yet the biblical text says, "he who is and was *and who is coming*" (Rev 1:4, italics added)!

Here a special issue emerges. "Moving into the realm of the Other" out of love is often thought of as the direct opposite of mission. In other words, love is often thought of as a naturalistic attitude, in the sense that a person simply encounters the other and accepts the world as it is now. And yet in the Christian perspective, mission and encounter with the Other are not mutually contradictory, but are held together in a dialectical manner. "Moving into the realm of the Other" surpasses naturalism. It is the introduction of a vision into the natural order of the world; it is a witness to a different way of looking at the world. The natural order on its own contains harmony, but it also contains conflict, the dominance of the strongest. It contains life, but it *equally* contains death as well. Of course, as human societies grow wiser, they progress to toleration of the Other. But toleration is not the same as love! It can simply mean autonomous and enclosed individual entities existing in parallel. "Coming

---

5. Levinas, "The Trace of the Other," 177–79. Volf, *Exclusion and Embrace*, 42.
6. Christmas Matins, *Kathisma*.

into the realm of the Other" in the way of the sacrificial love shown to us by Christ is a different matter. In reality, for the world, sacrificial love is something absurd. In the natural order of the world, humans tend to see the stranger as a danger and the guest as something threatening, something that "interrupts" the self of the host, as Derrida would say.[7] Characteristic is the fact that already in the fourth century, when John Chrysostom was preparing to talk to the Christians of his time about solidarity with refugees, he began with the following warning: "I am going to tell you something annoying and onerous. I know you will be angry, but I will say it anyway. Yet I will not say it in order to harm you, but in order to correct you."[8]

If love is accepted as the essence of life, then it cannot be merely a sentiment; that is, it cannot be something that will be extinguished as soon as the bearer of it is extinguished. If we really recognize love as the essence of life, then we subscribe to the belief that the world is called upon to change; it is called to be delivered from any kind of death. Love itself, in short, is a testimony to the kingdom that is to come. Whether by word or by deed or by silence, love brings into history the way of life of a God who, as the Trinity, exists through the impulse of each person towards the others; an impulse that overflows so much that it creates others out of nothing in order to be in communion with them.

This impulse to journey towards open horizons is expressed in the very structure of the church community. As is well-known, the Eucharist is experienced as an *image* of the eschatological kingdom. Whenever the Eucharistic assembly takes place, the Spirit works anew and the future irrupts into history and it becomes clear what the kingdom we await will be like: existence will be transformed into co-existence, death will be done away with, and divisions between people will be removed. The fact that this vision concerns the whole universe, not just the Christian community, has been stressed by the Orthodox since mid-1970s with the famous phrase "liturgy after the Liturgy."[9] The phrase means that the vision of the Divine Liturgy needs to be witnessed to and spread into all the world. This emphasis is very valuable, yet I think that we must also notice something else. The journey towards the world is not simply the

---

7. Derrida, *Of Hospitality*, 125.

8. Chrysostom, "On Charity," 296.

9. Bria, *The Liturgy after the Liturgy*, 19–35. See also Vassiliadis, *Orthodox Perspectives*, 49–66.

result of the Eucharist; it is also the precondition for it. In other words, we do not need only a "liturgy after the Liturgy" but also a "liturgy before the Liturgy." The "liturgy before the Liturgy" is the sacrament of love. If solidarity, the journey towards the Other, and inviting the Other into the kingdom are not conditions and constitutive elements of the Liturgy, then the Liturgy risks lapsing into sheer ritualism, meaning a conviction that the performance of rites and cults without further conditions automatically produces salvific results.[10]

The very understanding of the Eucharist as an image of the kingdom that is to come reveals what sort of mission the church's mission is. God is ceaselessly working for the salvation of his creation in ways that we know, but also in ways that we do not know.[11] Thus, the church as the first fruits, a foretaste and anticipation of the future reality, is by nature the herald and minister of the kingdom. In other words, the church is first and foremost a missionary—a co-worker in God's mission, a witness to his promises and a servant of his love for his world. I repeat, however, that this does not imply naturalism. Even when Christians simply coexist with people of other faiths (or no faith) without inviting them to church membership, it is the vision of the kingdom (not some sort of neutrality) that inspires them. Mission, in consequence, is itself the reason for the church's existence and its mode of existence.

The participant's statement at Edinburgh 1910—"Missions exist to make missions unnecessary"—needs, then, a clarification. The establishment of a church community is not the culmination of a missionary journey. On the contrary, that is when the journey begins.

As a journey to the future, the Abrahamic journey is fascinating. Here, however, we need to clarify the meaning of the future. Being stuck in the past can become idolatry, but so can a leap into the void—the future can also become a fetish. The Abrahamic journey, then, is not based on the flow of time, but on a promise given by a living person. That is why the criterion for this journey is not the future *per se*. The criterion

---

10. On this issue see Papathanasiou, "The Church as Mission," 6–41.

11. Salvation as God's work even beyond the canonical boundaries of the church has been an issue well-attested in church tradition since early years. See Yannoulatos, "Facing People of Other Faiths," 131–52. See also the report of the fourth WCC-sponsored World Conference on Mission and Evangelism in San Antonio, Texas, in 1989. Wilson, ed. "Reports of the Sections: Section I," 31–32. Yannoulatos presided over the San Antonio conference, being the first Orthodox moderator of the Commission for Mission and Evangelism (1984–91).

is the One who gave the promise, and his promise does not concern only what natural time will bring. It has to do with the kingdom, with something truly new—with *novum*, to use Jürgen Moltmann's words.[12] It is that which cannot be produced by the world itself, but is given (introduced into history) by God. In the Abrahamic journey, then, there is a lurking temptation that the traveler will succumb to the fascination of the new landscapes that he encounters, that he will be captivated by them, and—to a greater or lesser extent—forget about the promise.

Conciliar Christianity has come a long way since 1910. It has freed itself from narrow-minded ideas such as the concept of Christendom and imperialistic mission, it has been enriched by the contribution of new theologies from the Third World, and so forth. Brian Stanley very characteristically remarks of the aftermath of Edinburgh: "The Christian faith was indeed to be transformed over the next century, but not in the way or through the mechanisms that they imagined. The most effective instrument of that transformation would not be western mission agencies or institutions of any kind, but rather a great and sometimes unorthodox miscellany of indigenous pastors, prophets, catechists, and evangelists, men and women who had little or no access to the metropolitan mission headquarters and the wealth of dollars and pounds which kept the missionary society machinery turning."[13]

In this superb flight, opening up to the future existed side-by-side with the temptations of the future. For instance, recall that from the paternalistic model of adaptation—which is indifferent to particular human contexts—we have progressed (since the 1970s) to contextualization, which quite rightly emphasizes the importance of contexts. But recall also that certain theological trends have made an absolute of every particular context at the expense of ecumenicity. On the other hand, recall how missiology has distanced itself from the narrow-minded belief that the church is the sole place of salvation, but also how certain people have proposed ignoring the church altogether.[14] The course of this century has really been a titanic battle over the criteria for the journey.

---

12. Moltmann, *The Coming of God*, 7.

13. Stanley, *World Missionary Conference*, 17.

14. See, for example, the case of J. C. Hoekendijk in the 1960s as well as the criticism against his famous plea "to desacralize the Church." Hoedemaker, "The Legacy of J. C. Hoekendijk," 166–70.

Nikos Nissiotis, an Orthodox theologian and pioneer of the ecumenical movement, made an appropriate point in 1973 regarding the gospel of Christ. In a way it was, I think, prophetic; Nissiotis spoke of the

> ongoing debate about a theology of evangelism which raises the question of what constitutes the essence of the Gospel itself. It seems to me that often we no longer work with a clear understanding of what the Gospel is. Our discussion no longer centres around the way, i.e., the methods and the means, or the "how" of proclaiming the Gospel in a pluralistic, polyformic, and rapidly changing world, but it raises the question of the "what," the content of evangelism for the world. The problem involved is that of a radically new interpretation of the Christian message to a world of revolution which is seeking perfect manhood as a God-given task in Christ. This is precisely where the study of evangelism becomes so difficult and, at the same time, exciting and decisive for the life and mission of the Churches.[15]

It seems that Nissiotis had in mind the currents in theology that, at that time, were welcoming secularization and confining mission to the purchase of worldly *shalom*. In my view, solidarity and the preferential option for the oppressed are integral parts of the good news. In the case that they are removed, what is in fact removed from Christianity is the primacy of love and the promise of ultimate victory over death. Beyond that, Nissiotis was right in discerning the development of theological tendencies that questioned not particular themes, but the very identity of Christianity itself. This questioning would become strikingly obvious in the decades immediately following, up to our own times; that is why I described Nissiotis' comment as prophetic. The same year that Nissiotis' comment was published, John Hick called for a "Copernican revolution in theology" and gave decisive impetus to the so-called "pluralistic theology," which precisely called into question basic tenets of Christianity.[16]

The hard core of pluralistic theology (which is not, of course, a unified and monolithic movement) is the radical relativizing of Christology and trinitarian theology, which pluralism considers not as universal truths but simply as contingent interpretations of a *Deus absconditus*—a hidden God. Some pluralistic currents accept Christ and his incarnation, but only as local actions of God without any

---

15. Nissiotis, "An Orthodox View," 184.
16. Hick, *God and the Universe of Faiths*, 120–32.

validity outside the context of the Mediterranean and Western worlds. Thus, the finality of Christ and the finality of the Trinity are radically negated. It is typical, speaking in a broad sense, that among major pluralist theologians virtually only Raimundo Panikkar has built his theology on trinitarian doctrine,[17] and perhaps only Aloysius Pieris maintains some kind of uniqueness of Christ.[18]

Pluralistic theology is, to a great extent, a well-intentioned attempt to respond to some particular problematic theologies. Such problems include an ungenerous "Christomonism" that undermines the Spirit and understands the church as an institution that holds the grace of God captive within itself; a fundamentalist theology that does not recognize the action of God outside the canonical bounds of the church; a theology that is stuck in one culture and refuses to be incarnate in every culture and accept every culture's own means of expression. Yet, I doubt whether it manages to address those problems adequately.

Pluralistic theology is regarded as an extreme liberal position. It is nevertheless my humble opinion that such theologies are the opposite—deeply conservative currents—in the sense that they affirm what they want to deny. Christomonism makes Christ a prisoner of an institution. Certain pluralistic theologies attack Christomonism, and yet they perpetuate it, affirming that Christ really is confined to one context, so they embark to a new universal theology without him. Within the purview of both (Christomonism as well as pluralistic theology), there is no such thing as a cosmic Christ, an eschatological Christ, a Spirit-conditioned Christ, one who works mystically throughout the universe, both within the church and outside it. Something similar has happened in the field of pneumatology. It is very important that we affirm the freedom of the Holy Spirit and his activity everywhere. Often, however, what develops is a pneumatomonism, which is a reaction against Christomonism and yet perpetuates its problems: it stresses the *autonomous* action of the Spirit, and in this way tends to break up the triunity of God.

To the extent that pluralistic theologies want to remain Christian, they inevitably get involved in contradictions. They accept one common destiny for all human beings: love and the kingdom (a position that I

---

17. Panikkar, "The Jordan, the Tiber, and the Ganges," 109–10. Cf. comment by Heim, *Salvations*, 171. See also, Williams, "Trinity and Pluralism."

18. Pieris, "A Liberation Christology of Religious Pluralism". For Pieris, the uniqueness lies in the belief in God crucified in Christ who is one body with the oppressed.

personally agree with). But the concept of *one* common destiny for all human beings is a decisively biblical and Christian idea! What would be a truly pluralistic position is pure polytheism: the self-sufficiency of each particular context and, in consequence, the absence of any belief about *one* end point for all people. Real pluralism should accept that for some faiths death will ultimately be abolished, whereas for other faiths death remains an eternal reality. If pluralism is based on the self-sufficiency of every context, then a pure pluralism should be equally accepting of liberation and slavery, if both are characteristics of one context or another! If, however, pluralistic theology accepts that all this variety ultimately ends in *one* reality, then it is not real pluralism, but simply henotheism. In any event, I believe that if we pass by the universality of Christ and the Trinity, then we do not take a step forward. We have to do with a return. We may hold Abraham's baggage, but eventually we take it to Ithaca. We understand Christ as a tribal deity, much as the gods were conceived of in the world that Abraham left behind.

Already today, we find a very interesting critique of the stated centennial turbulent journey. As is well-known, *missio Dei*—the idea that mission is first and foremost God's and that the church serves God's own mission—was a liberating formulation that came out of the Willingen conference in 1952. Recently, in the volume edited by Daryl Balia and Kirsteen Kim for the anniversary of the 1910 Edinburgh conference, various specialists have aptly talked about "rediscovery and reinterpretation of the ancient trinitarian concept of the *missio Dei*."[19] Much could be said here. Allow me, however, to give just a couple of examples: the case of Maximus the Confessor, who in the seventh century made fruitful use of biblical thought and formulated a theology exceptionally open to the universal work of God, as well as the case of Nicholas Cabasilas, an Orthodox theologian of the fourteenth century who focused on sacramental life.

Unlike other church figures such as Origen and Augustine, Maximus did not make a contrast between natural revelation and historical revelation. He considered that God reveals himself equally through the cosmos he created and through the word he addressed to humankind.[20] Maximus regards Christ as the giver of both the natural

---

19. Gonda et al., "Mission and Unity," 201.

20. Maximus the Confessor, "Ambigua" and "Questions to Thalassius, 9." See Balthasar, *Cosmic Liturgy*, 291–92.

law (to which those who do not belong to the church are subject) and the written law (that of the Bible). Therefore, Maximus sees Christ as the judge and recapitulation of all. Maximus does regard the church as the body of Christ, bound up with Christ forever, but he does not encase Christ in the church. For this reason he does not need to develop an autonomous hypostatic action of the Spirit in order to talk about God's grace outside the church. In quite a striking way, Maximus describes the church as an *image* and not merely as an institution: an image of God, an image of the world, an image of man, and so on. What does this mean? It means that the church manifests the common future of the whole world, serves *missio Dei* and ministers the journey of the entire cosmos towards that future, towards the kingdom.

Similarly, Nicholas Cabasilas explains the significance of baptism, but in parallel he also talks about people who have been mystically baptized by Christ himself and have in an unseen way become members of his church. Particularly significant is an aside showing that Christ is not confined and stresses the interpenetration of divine and human action: "If there are some members who appear to be helping the Head, how much more fitting if it is that the Head Himself should add that which is lacking for the members."[21] In other words, Cabasilas reverses Paul's comment that the church is the complement of Christ (Eph 1:23). Here, it is Christ himself who complements the church by his action outside its canonical boundaries. Christians, I would say, bear witness to Christ, but at the same time they encounter him in the person of the Other. Additionally, they are ready to acknowledge God's freedom to act everywhere and acknowledge God as the Lord of the surprise. Witness and dialogue together is the natural state for Christian believers.

What we need is a synthesis of Christology and pneumatology so that we do not fall every so often into forms of one-sidedness by emphasizing one element at the expense of the rest. Many prominent Orthodox theologians, such as Metropolitan of Pergamon John Zizioulas and Fr. Emmanuel Clapsis, have underscored the need for such a synthesis.[22] Allow me, however, to single out a recent statement from Jacques

---

21. Cabasilas and De Catanzaro, *The Life in Christ*, 88–89, 92–93. See also Khodr, "Christianity in a Pluralistic World," 118–28.

22. Zizioulas, *Being as Communion*, 110–14, 126–42. Clapsis, *Orthodoxy in Conversation*, 57–67. See also Breck, "The Lord is the Spirit," 57–67.

Matthey, former director of the World Council of Churches program on "Mission, Unity, Evangelism and Spirituality":

> We must move towards a pneumatological qualification of Christological approaches and a Christological qualification of pneumatological emphases. In this sense, it is to be positively acknowledged that the title of the Edinburgh celebration has finally acquired a Christological colour: "Witnessing to Christ Today" . . . Without a Christological concentration point, pneumatology may well move towards totally disincarnated spiritualities, fluid divine energies and a Gnostic understanding of the divine, like those in what is referred to as New Age. The question is whether these characteristics of the Spirit can automatically be interpreted as the moving force in humanity and creation in general . . . Unlike several contemporary authors, I am not convinced this is the best way, in particular because the New Testament does contain texts pointing to a universal and immanent presence of the triune God. The texts with the most universal soteriological horizon are, however, Christological ones.[23]

In other words, I am in deep consonance with Mark Heim in claiming that, "as Christians, in failing to explicitly use our particularistic grounds, we undermine true pluralism."[24] In my view, we should not talk about "hypostatic independence" of the Spirit, but about the seeming paradox of "relational independence." I mean that the Spirit is free to act wherever it pleases, but it always leads mystically to the Trinity and its kingdom. The conclusion of the book of Revelation is especially characteristic: not only the church, but also the Spirit anticipates the eschatological Christ. "The Spirit and the Bride say, Come! . . . Amen. Come, Lord Jesus!" (Rev 22:17–20). And it is the same Spirit that made Christ's incarnation possible (Matt 1:18; Luke 4:18)! It is obvious that a crucial issue emerges here: the interpretation of tradition. If one understands tradition in an essentialist way—as something static and unchanging—then one is tied to the past; one betrays the process of the incarnation and serves the cause of cultural imperialism. If, however, we understand tradition not as static forms but as the *criteria* for the journey, then we shall discover a very valuable dynamic—the impulse

---

23. Matthey, "Serving God's Mission," 32–33.

24. Heim, *Salvations*, 229. "The decisive and universal significance of Christ is for Christians *both* the necessary ground for particularistic witness *and* the basis for recognizing in other religious traditions their own particularistic integrity." Italics original.

towards the kingdom, the impulse that enables us to be open to surprise and to be creative. What, then, are the *constants* of mission through the ages? What elements go to make up the stable identity of the good news as the world changes and as Christians every so often re-examine their attitude? I think that the constants are not simply the questions that Christianity constantly needs to answer, as Bevans and Schroeder say in their classic monograph.[25] The constants are the *criteria* according to which the church *responds* to the questions of every age—and indeed to new questions that arise today that perhaps did not exist yesterday.

It is well-known that since 1991, when David Bosch published his magnum opus *Transforming Mission: Paradigm Shifts in Theology of Mission* (taking account the work of Hans Küng, which had appeared seven years earlier), it has become normal to search for new paradigm shifts—ever newer paradigm shifts—so as to renew our missiological perspectives. These intentions are obviously good, yet I think that sometimes this creates a problem. The notion of "paradigm" is often misused, and the result is to reinforce a superficial approach. I mean to say that people overlook the fact that according to Thomas Kuhn, who established the term in the sciences, a basic characteristic of a paradigm shift is incommensurability, that is, incompatibility between the previous paradigm and the one that follows it.[26] Bosch himself was aware of this when he warned, quite rightly, that in the realm of theology paradigms have to be understood in a different way. They often overlap, and elements that seem to belong to an old paradigm come back with full force.[27] When this is not understood, the label "paradigm shift" is applied to every new idea that in reality is nothing more than a shift in the center of gravity—an over-emphasis of one element—very often at the expense of the others. Cases of a true paradigm shift do indeed exist (for example, pluralistic theology really is a paradigm shift), but we need to be more sparing with use of the term. For example, the work of Matteo Ricci in China in the sixteenth century, the rekindling of interest in the

---

25. Bevans and Schroeder, *Constants in Context*, 34. "Six *constants* in Christianity, six questions that Christianity constantly needs to answer, six questions that shape the way the church will preach, serve and witness to God's reign" (questions that have to do with Jesus Christ, the church, eschatology, salvation, the human, and culture).

26. Kuhn, *Structure of Scientific Revolutions*, 148.

27. Bosch, *Transforming Mission*, 183–89.

church during the early 2000s,[28] or the occasional rejection of violence are really important directions and significant models but they are not (as some have claimed at various times) paradigm shifts![29] Historical consciousness is indeed valuable, and helps us understand that the gospel has always been expressed through various cultural media in every age. In fact, there is no other way of voicing the gospel. Parallel to this, a basic element in Christianity is the *continuity* of its message. Love and victory over death are elements that endure through time, not contingent data belonging only to certain contexts or paradigms. To give an example: reconciliation, as a new paradigm, cannot be regarded as invalidating the paradigm of liberation or the notion of conversion! We need synthetic work that can bring the various elements together around the center of gravity; a work with the daring sobriety, for example, of the "Antioch Agenda," which aptly speaks of reconciliation, accompanied by forgiveness, grounded in justice.[30]

On one occasion, the disciples had gone out into open water on a lake in order to meet Christ on the other side (Matt 14:22–33). But they met him in the realm of surprise: in the middle of the lake during a storm. They met as soon as Peter did the opposite of Jonah. He did not lock himself in the hold of the ship, but for the sake of the encounter with Christ, opened up to the uncertain. Christ joined his disciples as he who comes—as the master of surprise! Today, then, Christians are called to go out into the open waters of the seas of globalization, ready to bear witness in unforeseen circumstances. Allow me, please, to close my paper by singling out, in a broad outline, three areas of Christian mission that have particular importance today.

First area: from "mission to six continents," we must continue to the "mission to seven continents" or to the "mission to the seventh

28. Matthey, "Editorial," 6.

29. Some indicative instances: Bosch himself claimed to have set a postmodern paradigm (Bosch, *Transforming Mission*, 349–51), which Kim denies; see Kim, *Holy Spirit in the World*, 174. Others have understood *missio Dei* as a paradigm shift (Gonda et al., "Mission and Unity," 201), while Jeff Reed takes church-based mission as a new paradigm (see Reed, "Church-Based Missions"). For Alan Kreider, a real paradigm shift has been the formation of the Constantinian empire; see Kreider, "Beyond Bosch," 59–68. William R. Burrows proposed that the modern Catholic attitude should be considered as a special paradigm; see Burrows, "A Seventh Paradigm?," 121–38. Finally, Simon Shui-Man Kwan questions the understanding of contextualization as an absolute paradigm shift; see Kwan, "From Indigenization to Contextualization," 236–50.

30. Petersen, "Mission in the Context," 270–74.

continent." The seventh continent is the new universe that is being created by science—particularly physics and biology. With the new findings of science, it seems that the first literal globalization is being created: a reality truly common to all people based on objective data, not simply on the extension of a culture. In this unified world new challenges are emerging, such as the way the brain works, the dimensions of human freedom, the mechanism of decision-making, and so forth. As the philosopher Cornelius Castoriadis made clear, we have to discern between science and the meaning of life, since there is no science of the meaning. The meaning is not given (while natural phenomena are); it is always created by humans on the basis of their freedom.[31] The answers that have been given and will continue to be given to the new challenges are culturally conditioned, but they also change the traditional cultures and shape new cultural forms. The church, then, has the special mission of articulating a witness amidst the new realities, without identifying the gospel with antiquated world-images or images of man. Peter Phan has aptly spoken of a triple dialogue as the Christians' *modus operandi*: dialogue with the poor (liberation), dialogue with cultures (inculturation), and dialogue with the religions (interreligious dialogue).[32] I personally would go on speaking rather of a quadruple dialogue, adding one more dimension: dialogue with modern atheism, which makes new appeals to science.

Second area: the place for Christian witness is in the public sphere. It does not belong to either state authority or the private sphere. The historian Glen Bowersock has shown that the martyrologies of Christians in late antiquity mark an unprecedented innovation initiated by the church. The Christian martyrologies do not simply recount feats, as do other martyrologies (pagan ones, for instance), but consist of the proceedings of the martyr's trial—his or her public dialogue with the authorities and with society.[33] Here, Bowersock concurs with Jürgen Habermas, who stresses that the place for religion is in the public sphere, and underlines the necessity for all parties to find a common language of communication instead of inward-looking jargons.[34] Would it be an

---

31. Castoriadis, *Crossroads in the Labyrinth*, 33–38.
32. Phan, "World Missionary Conference," 105–8.
33. Bowersock, *Martyrdom and Rome*, 41–56.
34. Habermas, "Religion in the Public Sphere," 1–25.

exaggeration to compare this with the obligation to incarnate the gospel in each concrete context?

Third area: Abraham's journey expresses a requirement of vital importance—the requirement for religious freedom. We are talking about the possibility for a human being to "go out from his land and his kindred" (cf. Gen 12:1), to choose his or her own direction and not necessarily to remain tied to the context in which he or she happens to have been born.[35] It is the possibility for a person to be converted and to repent.

The journey goes on, always into unforeseen landscapes. A map is not needed in advance, but a compass is needed. A compass that indicates the center of gravity.

WORKS CITED

Balthasar, Hans Urs von. *Cosmic Liturgy: The Universe According to Maximus the Confessor*. San Francisco: Ignatius, 2003.

Bevans, Stephen B., and Roger P. Schroeder. *Constants in Context: A Theology of Mission for Today*. Maryknoll, NY: Orbis, 2004.

Bosch, David J. *Transforming Mission: Paradigm Shifts in Theology of Mission*. Maryknoll, NY: Orbis, 1992.

Bowersock, G. W. *Martyrdom and Rome*. Cambridge: Cambridge University Press, 2002.

Breck, John. "The Lord is the Spirit." In *Come Holy Spirit, Renew the Whole Creation: An Orthodox Approach for the Seventh Assembly of the WCC, Canberra, Australia, 6–21 February 1991*, edited by Gennadios Limouris, 57–67. Brookline, MA: Holy Cross Orthodox Press, 1990.

Bria, Ion. *The Liturgy after the Liturgy: Mission and Witness from an Orthodox Perspective*. Geneva: World Council of Churches, 1996.

Burrows, William R. "A Seventh Paradigm? Catholics and Radical Inculturation." In *Mission in Bold Humility: David Bosch's Work Considered*, edited by Willem Saayman et al., 121–38. Maryknoll, NY: Orbis, 1996.

Cabasilas, Nicholas. *The Life in Christ*, translated by Carmino J. De Catanzaro. Yonkers, NY: St. Vladimir's Seminary Press, 1974.

Cary, Otis. *A History of Christianity in Japan: Roman Catholic and Greek Orthodox Missions*. St. Clair Shores, MI: Scholarly, 1970.

Castoriadis, Cornelius. *Crossroads in the Labyrinth*. Cambridge, MA: MIT, 1984.

Chrysostom, John. "On Charity." In *Patrologia Graeca #51*. Paris: Migne, 1862.

Clapsis, Emmanuel. *Orthodoxy in Conversation: Orthodox Christian Engagements*. Brookline, MA: Holy Cross Orthodox Press, 2000.

Derrida, Jacques. *Of Hospitality*. Palo Alto, CA: Stanford University Press, 2000.

---

35. Papathanasiou, "An Orphan or a Bride?"

Gonda, László, et al. "Mission and Unity—Ecclesiology and Mission." In *Edinburgh 2010: Witnessing to Christ Today*, edited by Daryl Balia and Kirsteen Kim, 199–221. Oxford: Regnum, 2010.
Habermas, Jürgen. "Religion in the Public Sphere." *European Journal of Philosophy* 14.1 (2006) 1–25.
Heim, S. Mark. *Salvations: Truth and Difference in Religion*. Maryknoll, NY: Orbis, 1995.
Hick, John. *God and the Universe of Faiths: Essays in the Philosophy of Religions*. Oxford: Oneworld, 1973.
Hoedemaker, Bert. "The Legacy of J. C. Hoekendijk." *International Bulletin of Missionary Research* 19 (1995) 166–70.
Ionita, Viorel. "Cooperation and the Promotion of Unity: An Orthodox Perspective." In *Edinburgh 2010: Mission Then and Now*, edited by David A. Kerr et al., 263–75. Oxford: Regnum, 2009.
Khodr, Georges. "Christianity in a Pluralistic World: The Economy of the Holy Spirit." *The Ecumenical Review* 23 (1971) 118–28.
Kim, Kirsteen. *The Holy Spirit in the World: A Global Conversation*. Maryknoll, NY: Orbis, 2007.
Kreider, Alan. "Beyond Bosch: The Early Church and the Christendom Shift." *International Bulletin of Missionary Research* 29.2 (2005) 59–68.
Kuhn, Thomas S. *The Structure of Scientific Revolutions*. Chicago: The University of Chicago Press, 1996.
Kwan, Simon Shui-Man. "From Indigenization to Contexualization: a Change in Discursive Practice Rather Than a Shift in Paradigm." *Studies in World Christianity* 11.2 (2005) 236–50.
Levinas, Emmanuel. "The Trace of the Other." In *Continental Philosophy: An Anthology*, edited by William McNeill et al., 177–79. Oxford: Wiley-Blackwell, 1998.
Matthey, Jacques. "Editorial." *International Review of Mission* 372 (2005) 6.
———. "Serving God's Mission together in Christ's Way: Reflections on the Way to Edinburgh 2010." *International Review of Mission* 99 (2010) 32–33.
Maximus the Confessor. "Ambigua." In *Patrologia Graeca* #91, 1128C-D. Paris: 1862.
———. "Questions to Thalassius, 9." In *Patrologia Graeca* #90, 308A-C. Paris: Migne, 1862.
Moltmann, Jürgen. *The Coming of God: Christian Eschatology*. London: SCM, 1996.
Nissiotis, N. A. "An Orthodox View of Modern Trends in Evangelism." In *The Ecumenical World of Orthodox Civilization: Russia and Orthodoxy, Volume II, Essays in Honor of Georges Florovsky*, edited by Andrew Blane, 184. Paris: Mouton, 1973.
Panikkar, Raimundo. "The Jordan, the Tiber, and the Ganges: Three Kairological Moments of Christic Self-Consciousness." In *The Myth of Christian Uniqueness*, edited by John Hick and Paul Knitter, 89–116. Maryknoll, NY: Orbis, 1987.
Papathanasiou, Athanasios. "An Orphan or a Bride? The Human Self, Collective Identities and Conversion." In *Thinking Modernity: Towards a Reconfiguration of the Relationship between Orthodox Theology and Modern Culture*, edited by Asaad E. Kattan and Fadi A. Georgi, 133–63. Balamand and Munster: St. John of Damascus Institute of Theology, University of Balamand, Lebanon; and Westphalian Wilhelm's University, Centre of Religious Studies, 2010.
———. "Missionary Experience and Academic Quest: The Research Situation in Greece." In *European Traditions in the Study of Religion in Africa*, edited by Afe Adogame et al., 301–12. Wiesbaden: Harrassowitz, 2004.

———. "The Church as Mission: Fr Alexander Schmemann's Liturgical Theology Revisited." *Proche-Orient Chrétien* 60 (2010) 6–41.

Petersen, Rodney. "Mission in the Context of Racism, Restorative Justice and Reconciliation." In *Antioch Agenda: Essays on the Restorative Church in Honor of Orlando E. Costas,* edited Daniel Jeyaraj et al., 270–74. New Delhi: Indian Society for the Promotion of Christian Knowledge, 2007.

Phan, Peter C. "The World Missionary Conference, Edinburgh 1910: Challenges for Church and Theology in the Twenty-First Century." *International Bulletin of Missionary Research* 34 (2010) 105–8.

Pieris, Aloysius. "A Liberation Christology of Religious Pluralism." In *Lieve Troch Felicitation Volume.* Sao Bernardo do Campo, Brazil: Nhanduti, 2009.

Reed, Jeff. "Church-Based Missions: Creating a New Paradigm." No pages. Online: http://www.bild.org/download/paradigmPapers/2_Church%20Based%20Missions.pdf.

Stanley, Brian. *The World Missionary Conference, Edinburgh 1910.* Grand Rapids: Eerdmans, 2009.

Vassiliadis, Petros. *Orthodox Perspectives on the Unity and Mission of the Church.* Geneva: World Council of Churches, 1998.

Volf, Miroslav. *Exclusion and Embrace: A Theological Exploration of Identity, Otherness, and Reconciliation.* Nashville: Abingdon, 1996.

Williams, Rowan. "Trinity and Pluralism." In *Christian Uniqueness Reconsidered: The Myth of a Pluralistic Theology of Religions,* edited by Gavin D'Costa, 3–15. Maryknoll, NY: Orbis, 1990.

Wilson, Frederick R. ed. "Reports of the Sections: Section I: Turning to the Living God." In *The San Antonio Report: Your Will be Done—Mission in Christ's Way,* 25–36. Geneva: World Council of Churches, 1990.

Yannoulatos, Anastasios. "Facing People of Other Faiths, from an Orthodox Point of View." *The Greek Orthodox Theological Review* 38 (1993) 131–52.

Zizioulas, John D. *Being as Communion: Studies in Personhood and the Church.* Yonkers, NY: St. Vladimir's Seminary Press, 1985.

6

Mission and Interreligious Dialogue

Edinburgh, Vatican II, and Beyond

Peter C. Phan

SEPARATED FROM EACH OTHER by six decades, both the World Missionary Conference (Edinburgh, June 13–24, 1910) and Vatican II (1962–65) are arguably the most defining events of their respective communities, the Protestant churches and Roman Catholicism. Compared with Vatican II, Edinburgh of course is smaller in scope—1,200 delegates vs. over 2,500 churchmen, the council adorned with all the pomp and circumstance that would be the envy of Hollywood special effects artists, and that only the Catholic Church has the wherewithal to produce. Edinburgh also lasted much shorter than Vatican II—ten days versus forty weeks spread out in four years. Yet, the World Missionary Conference (WMC) can be said to have foreshadowed Vatican II in many respects, in doctrines as well as in church reforms. Among these, no doubt mission and interreligious dialogue figured prominently at both church events.[1]

That Christian mission lies at the heart of the WMC is clear from its official name and from its subtitle, "To Consider Missionary Problems

---

1. In this essay the term "mission" in the singular is used to connote both the fact that the church is essentially sent by the triune God to continue the *missio Dei* in the world and the various activities, especially evangelization, by which it carries out its mission (often referred to as "missions" in the plural).

in Relation to the Non-Christian World." Of its eight commissions, the first and most important—whose chairman was none other than the charismatic conference leader John R. Mott himself (1865–1955)—was entitled "Carrying the Gospel to All the Non-Christian World." The conference was both the climax and the catalyst of the modern Protestant missionary. It was, in the words of the eminent historian of missions Andrew Walls, "a landmark in the history of missions; the starting point of the modern theology of mission; the high point of the modern Western missionary movement."[2] In contrast, mission cannot be said to be at the center of Vatican II's agenda, and it is treated only in a decree and not in a constitution, the most authoritative teaching genre.[3] Nevertheless, a persuasive case can be made that mission is the overriding *ad extra* concern of the council's *ad intra* task of defining its identity and instituting church reforms. In other words, Vatican II's *raison d'être* as conceived and convoked by Pope John XXIII is the renewing and revitalizing of the church's mission.

In contrast to mission, interreligious dialogue occupies only a peripheral position at both Edinburgh and Vatican II. It is the theme of the WMC's Commission Four, entitled "The Missionary Message in Relation to Non-Christian Religions," which produced a 280-page report. Vatican II issued an analogous document, entitled "Declaration on the Relation of the Church to Non-Christian Religions," but it is only a declaration, the lowest of the council's three teaching genres, and a very short one at that, with only 2,000 words.[4] Its main theme is the theological status of non-Christian religions vis-à-vis Christianity, and it is much less mission-oriented than Edinburgh's Commission Four's Report.

The focus of my paper is neither mission nor interreligious dialogue *per se* in both the WMC and Vatican II. Rather it is the *interrelationship* between these two activities of the church as they were understood by the two historic assemblies, as well as the theological tensions and

---

2. Walls, *Cross-Cultural Process*, 53.

3. Vatican II's sixteen documents are divided into three categories, in descending order of authority: constitution (which is subdivided into "dogmatic" and "pastoral"), decree, and declaration. The decree on the mission activity of the church (*De Activitate Missionali Ecclesiae*), which was promulgated by Pope Paul VI on December 7, 1965, is commonly referred to by its first two Latin words *Ad Gentes* (*AG*). The English translation of the council's documents is taken from Flannery, *Vatican II*.

4. The declaration was promulgated on October 28, 1965 and is known by its first two Latin words *Nostra Aetate* (*NA*).

problems this intricate and uneasy conjunction poses to our churches today. Both Edinburgh and Vatican II assume that mission in the sense of evangelism can go hand-in-hand with a positive relationship with non-Christian religions—part of what we call interreligious dialogue today. They were not, however, fully alert to the severe theological and pastoral tensions and problems inherent in their taken-for-granted inclusion of interreligious dialogue within mission, once interreligious dialogue is understood in its full scope, purpose, procedure, and dynamics.

The essay first seeks briefly to delineate how Edinburgh and Vatican II viewed mission and the place of interreligious dialogue within it. It argues that though interreligious dialogue played second fiddle to mission in the agendas of both Edinburgh and Vatican II, by contrast, in their aftermaths it has emerged as one of the most urgent and controversial aspects of Christian mission and missiology. Secondly, the essay highlights the fact that subsequent disputes, in both the Catholic and Protestant churches, at times quite acrimonious, about the nature, purpose, and practice of interreligious dialogue in relation to mission stem from the unresolved tensions and ambiguities, both theological and pastoral, inherent in Edinburgh and Vatican II and their aftermaths. Thirdly, drawing on the insights of the Federation of Asian Bishops' Conferences (FABC) and Asian theologians, the essay concludes with suggestions on how to move beyond the current impasse between mission and interreligious dialogue.

MISSION AND INTERRELIGIOUS DIALOGUE AT EDINBURGH AND VATICAN II

As a preliminary observation, it may be objected that linking the WMC with Vatican II (and the Roman Catholic Church in general) seems to be an arbitrary and unjustified effort, especially in view of the fact that participation of Roman Catholics was excluded from the Edinburgh conference. There is, however, a little-noted historical incident that makes this linkage instructive.[5] It began with the friendship between the American Episcopal layman Silas McBee (1853–1924), vice-chairman of the WMC's Commission Eight ("Cooperation and the Promotion

---

5. For an account of this historical incident, see Delaney, "From Cremona to Edinburgh," 418–31.

of Unity"), and the Italian bishop of Cremona, Geremia Bonomelli (1831–1914). As editor of the *Churchman*, McBee had published in 1906 an article entitled, "An Italian Bishop on Church and State," which was originally Bonomelli's pastoral letter in which the prelate argued for separation of church and state, a position quite controversial at his time and dubbed "Americanism" by its opponents. In April 1910 McBee visited the bishop of Cremona and asked if he would send a message to the WMC, to which the bishop enthusiastically agreed. Shortly after, McBee, fearing that Bonomelli would meet with his strong disapproval from his Roman superiors, had a change of heart and withdrew his request. Bonomelli, however, brushed off McBee's qualm and wrote an unusually lengthy letter, translated into English by Countess Sabina Parravicino Revel, in which he heartily applauded the conference for its work on behalf of ecumenical unity. McBee published Bonomelli's letter in *Report of Commission VIII on Cooperation and the Promotion of Unity* and read it at the last session of the conference to an electrified audience.

There is another historical incident that invites linking the WMC with Vatican II. It was the same Bonomelli who had suggested in 1908 to a visiting young priest named Giuseppe Roncalli that the church needed an ecumenical council to deal with the many challenges facing it, a suggestion that the future Pope John XXIII took to heart and carried out some fifty years later. There are, as will be shown below, more substantive reasons to join the Edinburgh conference and Vatican II together, but it is comforting to know that there were already some historical threads sewing the two church events together.

Among the many substantive links between the WMC and Vatican II, no doubt mission stands out as the most obvious and the strongest. The Edinburgh conference was originally entitled "The Third Ecumenical Missionary Conference," succeeding those at London in 1888 and New York in 1900. The conference's title conveys its participants' triumphant conviction that by the beginnings of the twentieth century, Protestant mission had reached the whole inhabited world—the *ekoumene*—and that its main task was to devise the most effective ways and means to bring this enterprise to a successful conclusion by literally carrying the gospel to the remaining non-Christian world.

Thus, Christian mission is the heart of the Edinburgh conference and the focus of its flagship commission, chronologically first and theologically foundational, which is appropriately entitled "Carrying the

Gospel to All the Non-Christian World." The other seven commissions simply investigate the various ways that the missionary mandate can effectively be fulfilled. The adjective "non-Christian" that qualifies "world" refers mainly to Africa, Asia and the Pacific Islands, to the exclusion of Europe, North America, and South America, which were judged already Christianized. The Commission One Report presents a survey of the non-Christian world from the perspective of mission. It exudes the optimism born of the conviction that, given the then-available means such as communications, railway transport, treaties, and trade, the possibility of converting the whole world lay within reach, famously epitomized in John Mott's adoption of the watchword of the Student Volunteer Movement for Foreign Missions: "The evangelization of the world in this generation." Along with incandescent optimism and unbounded enthusiasm, there was a burning sense of urgency that mission was reaching its providential *kairos*, to be missed by the church at its own peril. The report noted that there was "a rising spiritual tide," particularly in the non-Christian world, and the opportunity must be seized, now or never.

Edinburgh 1910 has been rightly hailed as an event of momentous significance, a keystone, a beacon, and a point of reference in the history of Protestant mission. This is especially so because of its establishment of the Continuation Committee and through it, the International Missionary Council (IMC) in 1921. The IMC in turn spawned conferences in Jerusalem (1928), Tambaram, India (1938), Whitby, Canada (1947), Willingen, Germany (1952), and Achomota, Ghana (1958) until it merged with the World Council of Churches in 1961. It would be redundant to expound here in detail the theology of mission that undergirds the WMC. A plethora of studies, both laudatory and critical, have been published on the theme, especially on the occasion of the worldwide centenary celebrations of the conference, chiefly in Edinburgh (June 2–6, 2010) and, of course, during these days in Boston.[6] There is no gainsaying the fact that the Edinburgh conference marked the coming-of-age of the Protestant missionary movement and laid the foundations for contemporary Protestant missiology. The Edinburgh conference affirmed most emphatically, as Vatican II would do half a century later,

---

6. For a comprehensive history of the conference, see Stanley, *World Missionary Conference*. For studies in connection with the project Edinburgh 2010, see Kerr and Ross, *Edinburgh 2010*; Balia and Kim, *Edinburgh 2010*; and Ross, *Edinburgh 2010*. For the Edinburgh 2010 project, see www.edinburgh2010.org.

that the church is missionary by nature, that mission devolves on each and every Christian, and that the gospel can take root and produce good fruits in any place, society, and culture.

To understand the context of the WMC's position on the relationship between mission and interreligious dialogue, it would be useful to mention briefly the main criticisms that have been leveled against the Edinburgh conference.[7] First, Edinburgh was limited by a territorial or Christendom conception of mission as expansion of Western Christianity into non-Christian lands. Second, it labored under the assumptions of Western imperialism and colonialism, especially in its view of Africa. Third, its theology of mission was vitiated by overwhelmingly militaristic and triumphalistic metaphors. Fourth, its attitude towards the so-called "younger churches" was tinged with a sense of moral superiority and racism. Fifth, its decision to exclude from discussion doctrinal and ecclesiastical issues papered over profound differences that were bound to emerge later. Finally, its optimism about the possibility of evangelizing the non-Christian world proved to be unfounded. No doubt all of these deficiencies in the WMC's theology of mission, as will be argued below, influenced the way it understood the function of interreligious dialogue.

As mentioned above, the WMC dealt at length with the issue of mission and non-Christian religions in Commission Four, entitled "The Missionary Message in Relation to the Non-Christian Religions." It is important to note that the theme of the commission was not what is referred to today as interreligious or interfaith dialogue, but how to present "Christianity to the minds of non-Christian peoples." In other words, its perspective on non-Christian religions is thoroughly missiological. The commission had twenty members, with David S. Cairns (1862–1946) as chair and Robert Speer (1867–1947) as vice-chair, the former a leading Scottish theologian, the latter an American distinguished mission administrator. Eleven questions were sent to missionaries and there were 187 responses. On the basis of these submissions the committee wrote a 280-page report divided into chapters dealing with "animistic religions" of the Bantu peoples of Africa, the tribal religions of India and the Pacific, the religions of China (Confucianism, Buddhism, and

---

7. See the succinct list of criticisms in Ross, *Edinburgh 2010*, 30–34.

Daoism), the religions of Japan (the same three Chinese religions, plus Shintoism), Hinduism, and the Baha'i faith.⁸

Again, there is no need to analyze in detail here the Commission Four Report.⁹ Suffice it to highlight some of its key affirmations concerning mission and interreligious dialogue. First, it is to be noted that of the eleven questions only three deal specifically with the nature and characters of non-Christian religions. Question two asks respondents to distinguish between the "traditional and formal" doctrines of these religions and "forms of religious observances," a very insightful observation on the frequent gap between official church teachings and popular practices. Question six asks respondents to identify "points of contact" with Christianity so that non-Christian religions can be regarded as "preparation" for it. This question, more than any other, reveals the Edinburgh conference's undergirding theology of religions. Question eight focuses on the belief in immortality and the existence of God, presumably examples of the sought-for points of contact.

Second, pervading the responses is a strong recommendation for all Christians to treat other religions with great sympathy, respect, and even reverence, and to be in solidarity with their adherents as fellow-pilgrims of faith. This attitude must however be coupled with a readiness both to bear witness to specifically Christian truths and practices and to learn from those of other religions. Interreligious dialogue is thus understood as an authentically *mutual* witness.

Third, with respect to a theology of religions, the Commission Four report is undergirded by what is subsequently known as "fulfillment theology." As Kenneth Cracknell's careful analysis of the theology of religions of the Edinburgh conference has shown,¹⁰ this fulfillment theology did not originate with the Edinburgh conference but had deep roots in nineteenth-century theologians and missionaries, notably Frederick Denison Maurice (1805–72), Thomas Ebenezer Slater (1840–1912), and John Nicol Farquhar (1861–1929). Grounded in the philosophy of evolution, the biblical affirmation that Jesus did not come "to abolish but to fulfill" (Matt 5:17), and the patristic *Logos* and *logoi spermatikoi* Christology, fulfillment theology, in Cracknell's summary,

---

8. See *Report of Commission IV*.

9. A comprehensive study of Commission Four against its historical and theological contexts is available in Cracknell, *Justice, Courtesy and Love*.

10. See ibid., 181–260.

proposes a fivefold view of non-Christian religions: (1) they act as tutors (*paidagogos*) to Christ; (2) they are *praeparatio evangelica*, as it were, stepping stones to Christianity; (3) they are fulfilled, and even superseded, by Christianity; (4) they are like "dawn" transfigured by the "perfect day" of Christianity, just as Christ's light has shone upon the "shadow" of Judaism (Heb 10:1); and (5) they are "gathered up" or "summed up" (Eph 1:10) until all things reach "the measure of the full stature in Christ (*eis metron ēlikias tou plērōmatos tou Christou*, Eph 4:13).

Interestingly, some fifty years later, Vatican II promulgated almost identical teachings on mission and interreligious dialogue often with the same expressions, though of course there is no reference in the council to the Edinburgh conference. As mentioned above, Vatican II's main statement on mission is the decree *Ad Gentes*, and its statement on the relationship of the church to non-Christian religions is the declaration *Nostra Aetate*. These two documents cannot, however, be rightly understood except in the context of the council's overall ecclesiology. It has been rightly said that Vatican II's central theme was the church, *ad intra* and *ad extra*. The church's face turned toward the outside, hence mission and interreligious dialogue (among other tasks) flows from the church's internal self-understanding. Indeed, Vatican II is the first council in the Roman Catholic Church to make a conscious effort at self-reflection to understand its very nature and mission. The church's *ad intra* face is presented in the Dogmatic Constitution on the church known by its first two Latin words *Lumen Gentium* (LG), while its *ad extra* face is presented in the *Pastoral Constitution on the Church in the Modern World* known as *Gaudium et Spes* (GS).[11]

There is currently a debate on how to interpret the legacy of Vatican II; that is, whether it constitutes a smooth and gradual development from the church's past ("the hermeneutics of continuity"), or a rupture ("the hermeneutics of discontinuity"), the former predictably favored by conservatives and the latter by liberals. With regard to ecclesiology, especially in issues of mission and interreligious dialogue, Vatican II did mark a decisive break with the past. This is symbolized by the council's out-of-hand rejection of the draft *De ecclesia* (On the Church) that had been prepared by the Theological Commission headed by the archconservative cardinal Alfredo Ottaviani, prefect of the Supreme

---

11. *Lumen Gentium* was promulgated on November 21, 1964 and *Gaudium et Spes* on December 7, 1965.

Congregation of the Holy Office (now the Congregation for the Doctrine of the Faith). It was famously criticized by Bishop Joseph De Smedt of Bruges, Belgium as vitiated by the triad of "triumphalism," "clericalism," and "juridicism." Another draft, written no longer under Ottaviani's dominance and subsequently modified by the council, rejects the then-prevalent neo-scholastic, juridical approach to ecclesiology and uses a plurality of images to describe the church. The American ecclesiologist Richard McBrien highlights the six themes and images that the council employs to describe the church, namely, church as mystery or sacrament, people of God, servant, communion, an ecumenical community, and an eschatological community.[12]

To these six themes I would add two more, with reference to our topic at hand, that is, the church as a missionary movement and a religious community among other religious communities. It is here that there are deep resonances between the WMC and Vatican II, with the latter echoing, sometimes verbatim, albeit unintentionally, the former. The council's Decree on the Church's Missionary Activity (*Ad Gentes*) is composed of six chapters, the first providing the "doctrinal principles" and the rest dealing with various practical aspects of mission.[13] By and large they correspond to the eight commissions of the Edinburgh conference, though of course reflecting the specific concerns and culture as well as socio-political conditions of the Catholic Church in the 1960s. Again, there is no need to give a summary of the document here; suffice it to highlight the affirmations that echo those of the WMC. First, like Edinburgh, Vatican II affirms that "the church on earth is by its very nature missionary since, according to the plan of the Father, it has its origin in the mission of the Son and the holy Spirit" (*AG*, no.1). Hence, mission constitutes the church into being and is not simply one of its many activities. The church exists for the sole purpose of mission and not the other way round; that is, mission is not for the sake of the church, its numerical expansion, or even its spiritual well-being.[14]

---

12. See McBrien, *The Church*, 162–81. The American church historian John Malley insightfully suggests that in addition to specific teachings Vatican II is different because of its "style," one that privileges "dialogue," "collaboration," and "collegiality." See Malley, *What Happened at Vatican II*. Another incisive study of Vatican II is Pieris, *Give Vatican II A Chance*.

13. For a commentary on *Ad Gentes*, see Vorgrimmler, *Commentary on the Documents of Vatican II*. Vol. IV. 87–181.

14. Pope Paul VI expresses the intrinsic link between mission and church in

Second, Vatican II emphasizes more explicitly than Edinburgh that the mission of the church is essentially a prolongation of the mission of God (*missio Dei*), or more precisely, of the Trinity. Mission is placed in the context of the Father sending the Son, the Son's own mission, and the Spirit's being sent by the Father through the Son: "Missionary activity is nothing else, and nothing less, than the manifestation of God's plan, its epiphany and realization in the world and in history; that by which God, through mission, clearly brings to its conclusion the history of salvation" (*AG*, no. 9).

Third, not unlike Edinburgh but without its beamy optimism, Vatican II perceives an urgent call to mission, noting the different circumstances that had been produced in the intervening half-century. "In the present state of things which gives rise to a new situation for humanity, the church . . . is even more urgently called upon to save and renew every creature" (*AG*, no. 1).

Finally, like Edinburgh, Vatican II recognized "elements of truth and grace which are found among peoples, and which are, as it were, a secret presence of God." And, like Edinburgh, it stressed that these elements of truth and grace derive from Christ and must be restored to him, so that "whatever goodness is found in people's minds and hearts, or in the particular customs and cultures of peoples, far from being lost, is purified, raised to a higher level and reaches its perfection" (*AG*, no. 9).

This last statement brings us to Vatican II's view of non-Christian religions. It is an almost verbatim citation of an earlier text in *Lumen Gentium*, paragraph 17. In paragraphs 15 and 16 of *Lumen Gentium*, the council presents a series of concentric circles signifying decreasing degrees of relationship to the unique church of Christ. At the innermost circle are Catholics who are said to be "fully incorporated" into the church. The church of Christ is said to "subsist"—that is, continue to exist fully, albeit not exclusively—in the Catholic Church (*LG*, no. 8). The next two circles are occupied by catechumens and non-Catholic

---

his 1975 apostolic exhortation *On Evangelization in the Modern World* (*Evangelii Nuntiandi*): "Evangelizing is in fact the grace and vocation proper to the Church, her deepest identity. She exists in order to evangelize, that is to say in order to preach and to teach, to be the channel of the gist of grace, to reconcile sinners with God, and to perpetuate Christ's sacrifice in the Mass, which is the memorial of his death and glorious Resurrection" (no. 4). The statement on mission from the Catholic Bishops of the United States (November 12, 1986) puts it succinctly: "To say 'church' is to say 'mission.'" (no. 16).

Christians. Finally, in the remaining five circles stand first Jews, then believers in the creator (especially Muslims), then those who "in shadows and images seek the unknown God"; then "those who, through no fault of their own, do not know the Gospel of Christ or his church, but who nevertheless seek God with a sincere heart, and, moved by grace, try in their actions to do his will as they know it through the dictates of their conscience." Lastly, "those, without any fault of theirs, have not yet arrived at an explicit knowledge of God, and who, not without grace, strive to lead a good life." All of these five groups of non-Christians are said to be able to be saved, always by God's grace given in Christ and mediated by the church.

It is important to note that Vatican II only affirms the possibility of salvation of non-Christians as *individuals*. In this, it must be pointed out, Vatican II goes further than Edinburgh. But it does not make any statement, positive or negative, on whether non-Christian *religions* themselves as institutions function as ways of salvation for their adherents. It simply says that "whatever of good or truth is found amongst them [that is, non-Christians, not their religions *per se*] is considered by the church to be a preparation for the Gospel" (*LG*, no. 16).

These ideas are picked up again in the "Declaration on the Relation of the Church to Non-Christian Religions" (*Nostra Aetate*).[15] The new focus here is with non-Christian *religions* as such, and not just non-Christian individuals. In ways reminiscent of the report of the WMC's Commission One, the council first speaks of peoples who possess "a certain awareness of a hidden power" and even "a recognition of a supreme being" (the "animist religions" of Commission One), next Hinduism, then Buddhism, and finally religions which offer "a program of life covering doctrine, moral precepts and sacred rites" (Commission One's religions of China and Japan). Of these, the council states:

> The Catholic Church rejects nothing of what is true and holy in these religions. It has a high regard for the manner of life and conduct, the precepts and doctrines which, although differing in many ways from its own teaching, nevertheless often reflect a ray of that truth which enlightens all men and women ... The Church, therefore, urges its sons and daughters to enter with prudence and charity into discussion and collaboration with mem-

---

15. For a commentary on *Nostra Aetate*, see Vorgrimmler, *Commentary on the Documents of Vatican II*. Vol. III, 1–154.

bers of other religions. Let Christians, while witnessing to their own faith and way of life, acknowledge, preserve and encourage the spiritual and moral truths found among non-Christians, together with their social life and culture (*NA*, no. 2).

The council goes on to speak about Islam and Judaism, acknowledging their many historical and doctrinal commonalities with Christianity. Regarding Islam, the council urges both Christians and Muslims to forget their histories of mutual hatred and violence and to work toward mutual understanding and to collaborate together to promote justice and peace. With regard to Judaism, the council recognizes the "common spiritual heritage" binding Jews and Christians together. Most importantly, the council affirms the continuing validity of God's covenant with the Jews, rejects the charge of deicide, and condemns all forms of discrimination.

Clearly, then, on mission and the relations between the church and non-Christian religions, there are between Edinburgh and Vatican II more than occasional and superficial similarities. Despite their deep confessional differences, their theologies of mission and interreligious dialogue are almost identical, at times even word-for-word. They are basically predicated upon the concept of "fulfillment." Both Silas McBee and Geremia Bonomelli would have heartily rejoiced in such ecumenical convergences.

The Catholic Church did not come to this position without deep soul-searching and intellectual conversion. It did not—and indeed could not—appeal to the WMC had it known its teachings; the mere fact that *Protestants* held them would render them theologically suspect. However, anyone passably familiar with the pre-Vatican II attitude of the Catholic Church toward non-Christians and non-Christian religions, epitomized in the axiom *extra ecclesiam nulla salus* [outside the church there is no salvation], can readily recognize the "discontinuity," a disingenuous euphemism for the 180-degree turn, between "before" and "after" Vatican II. Suffice it to contrast declarations of *Lumen Gentium*, *Ad Gentes*, and *Nostra Aetate* with the declaration of the Council of Florence (1438–45): "Those who not living within the Catholic Church, not only pagans, but also Jews and heretics and schismatics, cannot become participants in eternal life, but will depart 'into everlasting fire which was prepared for the devil and his angels' (Matt 25:41), unless before the end they are joined to the Church."[16]

16. Denzinger, *Sources of Catholic Dogma*, 715.

No amount of hermeneutical prestidigitation can bridge the abyss that separates Florence and Vatican II. The participants at the WMC, who would fall under the Council of Florence's "heretics," never framed the difference between Christianity and other religions in such stark terms as salvation or perdition. Still, both Edinburgh and Vatican II, while recognizing the "elements of truth and grace" in non-Christian religions, never failed to affirm most emphatically, and in the same breath, that mission is absolutely necessary, that Christ is the universal and unique savior, that the goal of mission is to bring non-Christians to Christ and to plant the church through baptism, and that Christianity (or the Catholic Church) brings all other religions to their fulfillment. How then is interreligious dialogue understood in relation to mission?

MISSION AND INTERRELIGIOUS DIALOGUE: BETWEEN SCYLLA AND CHARYBDIS

It is important to note that neither Edinburgh nor Vatican II was engaged in interreligious dialogue in the proper sense of the term. Participants in these assemblies discoursed among themselves *about* other religions and their relations to Christianity, not *with* their adherents. Though both gatherings supplied rich information about various non-Christian religions—and here Edinburgh had a distinct advantage over Vatican II as its reports came not only from theologians and scholars of religion, but also veteran and experienced missionaries in the field—their overriding perspective was thoroughly and explicitly missiological. Their main interest was to search for "points of contact" or the *logoi spermatikoi*. Non-Christian religions are seen as stepping-stones towards Christianity or *praeparatio evangelica*. Furthermore, their vantage point was their conviction about the spiritual and moral superiority of Christianity. To put it bluntly, in spite of their genuine openness to and sincere admiration for other religions, the ultimate and not-so-covert goal of both Edinburgh and Vatican II in knowing other religions better was to be more effective in converting their adherents to Christ and/or Christianity. It was for this purpose that both Edinburgh and Vatican II strongly recommended what we would regard today as "interreligious dialogue." Vatican II urged Catholics to "enter with prudence and charity into discussion and collaboration with members of other religions"

(*AG*, no. 2). Though neither Edinburgh nor Vatican II used the expression "interreligious dialogue" to refer to this "discussion and collaboration with members of other religions," clearly it is what they intended, at least in its inchoate forms, and it is no less clear that they understood it to be at the service of mission understood as evangelism.

Perhaps this intrinsic connection between mission and interreligious dialogue, or more precisely, the subordination of the latter to the former, is most sharply articulated by Pope John Paul II in his 1990 encyclical *On the Permanent Validity of the Church's Missionary Mandate Redemptoris Missio* (*RM*) "Interreligious dialogue is a part of the Church's evangelizing mission. Understood as a method and means of mutual knowledge and enrichment, dialogue is not in opposition to the mission *ad gentes*; indeed, it has special links with that mission and is one of its expressions . . . In the light of the economy of salvation, the Church sees no conflict between proclaiming Christ and engaging in interreligious dialogue. Indeed, she feels the need to link the two in the context of her mission *ad gentes*" (*RM*, no. 55).

Here, I suggest, lie the *skandalon* and the *crux* of the matter: if the goal of the mission *ad gentes*, that is, mission to those who do not know Christ, is as commonly assumed, persuading them humbly and graciously to accept Christ and baptism and join the church, and if interreligious dialogue is "a part of the Church's evangelizing mission" and "has special links with that mission and is one of its expressions," as John Paul II states, then what is the ultimate purpose of interreligious dialogue? Precisely what is the nature of these "special links," and in what ways is interreligious dialogue an "expression" of mission? It is very interesting to note that in the same paragraph that John Paul II asserts that interreligious dialogue is "a part of the Church's evangelizing mission," the pope goes on to say that the two activities "must maintain both their intimate connection and their distinctiveness; therefore they should not be confused, manipulated or regarded as identical, as though they were interchangeable" (*RM*, no. 55).

John Paul's statement can be interpreted in two opposite ways. On the one hand, it may be taken to mean that mission in the sense of evangelization and conversion cannot be substituted with interreligious dialogue, as some Asian theologians have been accused of doing. On the other hand, it may be taken to mean that because evangelization and interreligious dialogue are not interchangeable, the latter must be distinguished from the former. If so, must not interreligious dialogue have its own purpose, method, procedure, and dynamics so that it does not become mission-for-conversion in camouflage?

It is, I submit, this ambiguous relation and tension between mission and interreligious dialogue inherent in Edinburgh and Vatican II that spawned the at times fierce theological debates in the wake of the two assemblies, especially after the Second World War. In the post-Edinburgh era, on the Protestant side, the WMC's positive attitude toward non-Christian religions and its fulfillment theology exercised powerful influence on the International Missionary Council (IMC) conference in Jerusalem (1928) in its response to the challenge of secularism, and also on the influential book *Rethinking Missions* (1932). But it was not long before fulfillment theology was severely challenged by the Dutch missionary to Indonesia and missiologist Hendrik Kraemer, in his book *The Christian Message in a Non-Christian World* (1938), written specifically for the next IMC conference at Tambaram, India, which emphasized discontinuity rather than continuity between Christianity and other religions.[17] The same line of attack was later mounted by Karl Barth with his theology of religions that views all religions—including Christianity as a religion—as idolatrous human works in opposition to Christianity as the locus of divine self-revelation. Finally, the merging of the IMC with the World Council of Churches (WCC) at New Delhi in 1961 and the subsequent founding of the WCC's sub-unit on Dialogue with People of Living Faiths and Ideologies (especially under the directorship of Stanley J. Samartha between 1968 and 1971) sparked fears among conservative Protestants that an ecumenical agenda and interreligious dialogue (and socio-political activism) were replacing mission as the church's fundamental task. As a result, the Lausanne Committee for World Evangelization (LCWE) was founded in 1971 as a counter-movement (with Billy Graham as one of its leaders) with the stated aim to reclaim the Edinburgh conference's priority of "world evangelization." Subsequently, the LCWE held conferences in Lausanne (1974), Pattaya, Thailand (1980), Manila, Philippines (1989), Pattaya again (2004), and Cape Town (2010). The issue of mission vs. interreligious dialogue returned with a vengeance in recent decades with the

---

17. Kraemer, *The Christian Message*.

emergence of Evangelical charismatics as the fastest-growing and most mission-minded Christian group.[18]

In the post-Vatican II era on the Catholic side, the debate on mission and interreligious dialogue as well as the role of non-Christian religions has been no less intense. On the theological scene, the most influential figure was the German Jesuit Karl Rahner (1904–84). On the basis of God's universal will to save in Christ (1 Tim 2:4) and of God's real and gracious self-gift to every human being (which he calls the "supernatural existential"), Rahner argues that all persons who live a good life are "anonymous Christians." As for non-Christian religions, in Rahner's view, they remain valid so long as the preaching of the gospel has not reached their adherents in a real way. Rahner's thesis of "anonymous Christians" and "anonymous Christianity" was fiercely attacked by both liberals and conservatives. The former, notably the Swiss theologian Hans Küng, rejected it for trying to surreptitiously baptize non-Christian religions and not respecting their "otherness"; the latter, led by Hans Urs von Balthasar, another Swiss theologian and an admirer of Karl Barth, for jeopardizing the role of Christ as the unique and universal Savior and the missionary task of the church. Meanwhile, a theology of religions typology, organized by distinguishing the three paradigms of exclusivism, inclusivism, and pluralism, and with both Catholic and Protestant proponents and opponents in each camp, was much in vogue, with conservatives espousing the first paradigm, moderates the second, and liberals the third.[19]

On the part of papal teaching, two landmark documents have been issued since Vatican II. Reference has already been made to Pope Paul VI's 1975 apostolic exhortation *Evangelii Nuntiandi*. Reflecting the concerns of liberation theology, the pope grounds Christian mission in Jesus' preaching, serving, and witnessing the kingdom of God and emphasizes the integral and total development of the human person in all its dimensions as the goal of mission. Some fifteen years later John Paul II issued his encyclical *Redemptoris Missio*. One of its many purposes is "to clear up doubts and ambiguities regarding missionary activity

18. For an informative discussion of interreligious dialogue from an Evangelical perspective, see Yong, *Discerning the Spirit(s)*; Yong, *Beyond the Impasse*.

19. For a rich discussion of Roman Catholic theology of religions, see the works of Jacques Dupuis, especially *Christian Theology of Religious Pluralism* and *Christianity and the Religions*. One of the best introduction to contemporary theologies of religions is Knitter, *Introducing Theologies of Religion*.

ad gentes" (no. 2) that were alleged to be widespread, especially among Asian theologians. John Paul II reasserts the necessity and urgency of the evangelization of non-Christians (*ad gentes*), which, in his view, were running the risk of being replaced by interreligious dialogue and social activism. The pope vigorously affirms that Jesus is the universal and unique Savior and that the church is the universal sacrament—sign and instrument—of salvation. Other religions may be regarded as "participated forms of mediation of different kinds and degrees," but "they acquire meaning and value *only* from Christ's own mediation, and they cannot be understood as parallel or complementary to his" (no. 5).

Other Roman authorities also weighed in on the discussion regarding mission and interreligious dialogue. A year after *Redemptoris Missio*, the Pontifical Council for Inter-Religious Dialogue and the Congregation for the Evangelization of Peoples issued a joint document entitled *Dialogue and Proclamation* (*DP*). Explaining the relationship between these two activities, the document says that they are "interrelated yet not interchangeable":

> Interreligious dialogue and proclamation, though not on the same level, are both authentic elements of the Church's evangelizing mission. Both are legitimate and necessary. They are intimately related, but not interchangeable: true interreligious dialogue on the part of the Christian supposes the desire to make Jesus Christ better known, recognized and loved; proclaiming Jesus Christ is to be carried out in the Gospel spirit of dialogue. The two activities remain distinct but, as experience shows, one and the same local Church, one and the same person, can be diversely engaged in both (no. 77).

With regard to the role of non-Christian religions in salvation, the document makes a new and critically important statement. As Jacques Dupuis notes in his commentary, the fifth draft says that "concretely, and in normal circumstances, it will be in the sincere practice of what is good in their own traditions that the members of other religions who are saved respond positively to God's will and receive salvation in his Son, even while they remain unable to identify their Savior and to name him." This text was judged to concede too much autonomy to non-Christian religions to the detriment of Jesus and the church. It was suggested to delete it and simply repeat the phrase found in *Lumen Gentium*, no. 16: "by following the dictates of their conscience." However, the suggestion was also rejected as too conservative and the final text combines both phrases to read: "in the sincere practice of what is good in their own religious traditions and by following the dictates of their conscience" (*DP*, no. 29). Dupuis notes that according to *DP*, "the members of other religions, then, are not saved by Christ in spite of, or beside, their own tradition, but in the sincere practice of it, and, in some mysterious way, through it."[20]

Another document of the Roman magisterium, published in 2000 by the Congregation for the Doctrine of the Faith (CDF), then under the leadership of Josef Ratzinger, now Pope Benedict XVI, is entitled *On the Unicity and Salvific Universality of Jesus Christ and the Church*, known in Latin as *Dominus Iesus*. The document stunned not only non-Catholic Christian communities with its affirmation that Christian communities that have not preserved a valid episcopate, and the genuine and integral substance of the Eucharist are not "Churches in the proper sense" (no. 17), but also non-Christians with its statement that "*objectively speaking they are in a gravely deficient situation in comparison with those who, in the Church, have the fullness of the means of salvation*" (no. 22).

Whether or not *Dominus Iesus* simply restates, albeit in uncomfortably stark and uncompromising terms, what the Catholic Church has always believed, or has betrayed the deep insights of Vatican II, clearly it touched a raw theological nerve. This was made obvious by the visceral reactions of anger and sadness both on the part of Christians and non-Christians who disagree with it, or of relief and gratitude on the part of those who feel that finally the Vatican has found the courage to teach the truths of the Catholic faith that have been thrown in doubt by those seeking dialogue with other religions rather than mission. Both sides can, of course, appeal to Vatican II for support and vindication, apparently with equal plausibility, and the reason for this is that there are inherent ambiguities and tensions in the council's position on mission and interreligious dialogue. These tensions and ambiguities had not been dispelled during the aftermath of the council, nor have they been resolved and settled by *Dominus Iesus*.[21]

That Ratzinger and the CDF felt that the current theology of religions and interreligious dialogue was getting out of hand and needed to be reined in was demonstrated by the fact that writings judged

---

20. Burrows, *Redemption and Dialogue*, 152.
21. For a nuanced evaluation of *Dominus Iesus*, see Pope and Hefling, *Sic et Non*.

dangerous were officially condemned and punitive measures applied to their authors (e.g., Jacques Dupuis, Roger Haight, Jon Sobrino, and a host of minor theologians). Far from settling theological disputes, however, *Dominus Iesus* and the CDF's disciplinary actions serve as a clarion call to revisit the relationship between mission and interreligious dialogue that both Edinburgh and Vatican II assumed to be obvious. Are these two activities the Scylla and the Charybdis between whom the church is caught? Or are they identical twins, or first cousins, or best friends, or total strangers? Or are they alienated family members that need to be reintroduced to each other so that their relationship may be based on a new foundation?

"MISSION, PLEASE MEET INTERRELIGIOUS DIALOGUE"

It is an undeniable historical fact that both mission understood narrowly as proclamation of what God has done in Christ for the whole humanity and a corresponding invitation to all to accept God's self-gift (evangelism/evangelization) and, on the other hand, interreligious dialogue have been practiced by Christian churches—the latter especially since the second half of the twentieth century. This does not mean that there has been unanimity regarding their theological validity. For some Christians, such as the traditionalist Catholic followers of Archbishop Marcel-François Lefebvre (1905–91)[22] and the majority of Evangelicals,[23] the main, if not only, task of the church is professed to be the exclusive depository of divine revelation: evangelization; that is, preaching the gospel to save the lost. Hence, interreligious dialogue is to be rejected

---

22. One of the many reasons why Lefebvre and his followers (e.g., the members of Saint Pius X Society) rejected Vatican II is its positive teachings on non-Christian religions, especially Judaism, and its promotion of interreligious dialogue, as contained in its dogmatic constitution *Lumen Gentium* (no. 16) and its declaration *Nostra Aetate*. After his schism Lefebvre claimed that he wanted to protect the Catholic Church from the council's perfidies, among them the approval of interreligious dialogue, and from Pope John Paul II's activities in favor of interfaith understanding, in particular his prayer for peace with leaders of other religions at Assisi in October 1986.

23. Not all Evangelicals are opposed to interreligious dialogue of course. See the works of, e.g., Clark Pinnock, Charles E. Van Engen, Harold Netland, David Hesselgrave, Carl Braaten, Mark Heim, Andrew Kirk, Ajith Fernando, Veli-Matti Kärkkäinen, Amos Yong, Timothy Tennent, and many others.

since it erroneously implies that the church does not already possess the fullness of truth and therefore still needs to learn from other religions.

On the opposite side of the theological spectrum are those who hold that mission directed toward converting non-Christians (mission *ad gentes*) is no longer appropriate in our age of religious pluralism where all religions are to be considered simply as alternative and equally valid ways that lead to God and salvation. For them, only interreligious dialogue, where people of different faiths share their religious experiences and doctrines as equals, is theologically justified.

Between these two extremes a majority of Christians maintain that evangelization must be the church's primary mission, but also acknowledge that dialogue with people of different faiths is useful and even necessary. They would subordinate interreligious dialogue to mission and regard it as a part of the church's task of converting non-Christians. Lately some, for example, Pope Benedict XVI, believe that such dialogue must not be extended to matters of faith (interreligious or interfaith dialogue) since interfaith dialogue would require a bracketing of faith, but must be restricted to cultures (intercultural dialogue).

Finally, a number of theologians maintain that both evangelization and interreligious dialogue are constitutive and irreplaceable, yet distinct elements of the church's mission. However, they hold that the intimate conjunction of these two activities is only possible if they are radically re-envisioned in both their nature and method.

It can safely be presumed that for the Catholic Church and mainline Protestant churches the first two views—broadly characterized as exclusivism and pluralism—are not theologically acceptable, though the former is still prevalent among the more conservative groups and the latter among the more liberal ones. With regard to the third view, in its two versions—broadly characterized as inclusivism—it is clear, from the various documents of the Edinburgh conference, Vatican II, and the post-Vatican II era, that there is a fear that interreligious dialogue might replace mission *ad gentes*. Whether such fear is well-grounded or not need not concern us here; what is to be noted is that it has led to the subordination of interreligious dialogue to mission as "part" or "expression" of it. Of course, as we have seen above, there is no lack of statements in the Roman Catholic magisterium affirming the necessity of interreligious dialogue and even its distinction from and non-interchangeability with mission. Nevertheless, it is undeniable that while there is the fear that interreligious dialogue may replace mission, there is no similar fear or even a faint perception of the danger that by subsuming interreligious dialogue into mission (understood in the narrow sense of evangelism), interreligious dialogue might be robbed of its distinctive nature, purpose, procedure, and dynamics. In other words, there is an asymmetrical relation between mission and interreligious dialogue, with the latter suffering from a subordinate position and a likely loss of authenticity and integrity.

This refusal to grant an equal status to interreligious dialogue, I suggest, is rooted in the theology of fulfillment of religions, according to which non-Christian religions are at best *praeparatio evangelica* and destined to be superseded by Christianity, notwithstanding possible "elements of truth and grace" present in them. At the roots of this theology lie a Christology with an exclusive claim about Jesus as the only and universal savior and about the church as the unique sign and instrument of salvation. In support of such theology of fulfillment, certain biblical passages such as Mark 16:16, John 14:6, Acts 4:12, and 1 Tim 2:4–6 are without fail cited as irrefutable proofs. I am not suggesting that these exclusive-sounding texts be ignored, explained away, or denied. Rather I propose that they be interpreted in light of the overall biblical and patristic attitude, both negative and positive, toward non-Christian believers and non-Christian religions; their past imperialistic and colonialist interpretations, and the history of their (mis)uses for violence and marginalization. Above all, they should be interpreted in the new context of interreligious dialogue that is not, of course, their original context, but one in which their meaning and import will necessarily be modified and deepened.

Before expounding the differences between interreligious dialogue and mission, it would be useful to ponder briefly on the purpose, forms, and dynamics of interreligious dialogue as elaborated by *Dialogue and Proclamation*. The document helpfully distinguishes four forms of dialogue: (1) the *dialogue of life*, where people of different faiths "strive to live in an open and neighborly spirit, sharing their joys and sorrows, their human problems and preoccupations"; (2) the *dialogue of action*, in which Christians and non-Christians work together "for the integral development and liberation of people"; (3) the dialogue of *theological exchange*, in which scholars seek "to deepen their understanding of their respective religious heritages, and to appreciate each other's spiritual values"; and (4) the dialogue of *religious experience*, "where persons, rooted in their own religious traditions, share their spiritual riches, for instance with regard to prayer and contemplation, faith and ways of searching for God or the Absolute" (no. 42).

As daily experiences, especially in Asia, have undeniably shown, these four forms of interreligious dialogue can be, and in fact have been, carried out quite successfully without presupposing a fulfillment theology of religions, or the proclamation of Jesus as the unique or universal savior, or the affirmation of the church as the only ark of salvation. This is obvious for the first two forms of dialogue. While common life and collaboration for justice, peace, and the well-being of creation may be inspired and sustained by the conviction that Jesus, or Krishna, or the Buddha, or the Qur'an is the only true word of God, they do not presuppose this faith confession as a starting point, or foundation, or indispensable conditions for their successful execution or goal. On the contrary, as conflict-resolution experts have persuasively argued, a successful overcoming of violence and conflicts must *not* be made to depend on religious convictions, especially in situations where religions have been manipulated to incite and justify violence.

The third form of dialogue, theological exchange, only demands that religious and theological convictions of each religion must be honestly, clearly, and accurately expounded. Its purpose may be to overcome misunderstandings and to enrich one's understanding and living of one's own faith. Its goal is not and cannot be to convert others to one's own faith and religion, and as far as Christians are concerned, to make non-Christians into disciples of Jesus and members of the church through baptism (interreligious dialogue for conversion). Nor is the goal of this form of interreligious dialogue to show that non-Christian religions are simply the same as Christianity, only in imperfect or anonymous form (the "anonymous Christian" theory); or that they secretly and unconsciously tend toward Christianity and will eventually be fulfilled by it (the *praeparatio evangelica* or fulfillment theology); or that non-Christians can be saved only on condition of their "invincible ignorance" of Christ and the church. If these were the intended goals of interreligious dialogue, honesty requires that Christians state them openly at the outset. But then it is right that non-Christians should refuse the Christians' invitation to interreligious dialogue, just as Christians should reject interreligious dialogue if it is initiated by non-Christians with similar aims. Hence, none of the above goals should be ascribed to the third form of interreligious dialogue. Rather, its only goal is and must be simply and wholly for each participant to understand more deeply his or her own religious tradition and to obtain a better appreciation of the truths and values of other religions, and as a result, each participant will be able to live his or her faith more perfectly.

Only the fourth form of dialogue, that of sharing religious experience, seems to be explicitly founded on one's faith convictions, or as *DP* says, is "rooted in their own religious traditions." But even here nothing is said about the duty or even the intention to "proclaim" these faith convictions to convince others of their truth. Of course, one shares one's faith to others because one is convinced of its truth and value, and perhaps one feels compelled to do so, or as the apostle Paul puts it, "the love of Christ impels us" (2 Cor 5:14). However, sharing is by no means the same as preaching and proclaiming and persuading. This is true especially in the sharing of "prayer and contemplation," which must in its highest moment culminate in wordless and silent adoration. To use an analogy: if as a Vietnamese, I am convinced that Vietnamese foods are tasty and healthy, it is natural that I want to share them with others. However, this act of hospitality and sharing in no way demands that I make other peoples into Vietnamese, or that only Vietnamese foods should be eaten by everybody, or that Vietnamese foods should be considered the only true and good foods, or that other ethnic foods should be regarded as pale imitations of Vietnamese foods. The only thing that is required by hospitality is that I offer the most authentic Vietnamese foods possible, *and* also that I be willing to eat whatever foods others wish to share with me.

Let it be noted that the analogy of food-sharing and hospitality for interreligious dialogue is by no means trivial and inappropriate. Indeed, for Asians, there is no interreligious dialogue unless it is accompanied by eating and hospitality for people of different faiths. In fact, the most effective interreligious dialogue occurs not in academic halls or even in churches but at dining tables where food and drink are shared with everyone.

As to the dynamics of interreligious dialogue, it is important to note that in none of these four forms of dialogue there is a requirement that the participants must lay aside or bracket their religious convictions. On the contrary, as mentioned above, each participant must present the beliefs and practices of his or her religious tradition clearly, accurately, and fully. Thus, interreligious dialogue by no means implies or leads to relativism. It does not espouse the view that all religions are "equal" or "alternative" ways to God. In fact, all participants in interreligious dialogue, Christians and otherwise, are deeply and passionately convinced of the truth of their religious traditions and defend them with vigor and rigor. Each participant may believe that his or her religious way is the best, even the only, way to achieve the goals intended by his or her religion, if such belief is an essential part of its creed. Otherwise the participants in interreligious dialogue would not be what they are in terms of religion. But they are also aware that their understanding and practice of their faith always remains partial and distorted and are in constant need of correction and enrichment from other religious traditions. Thus, the real challenge in interreligious dialogue is not to retain one's religious convictions but to remain firmly rooted in one's religious tradition *and* at the same time be open to learn from as well as be challenged by other, often different, and at times contradictory traditions. *Dialogue and Proclamation* puts it well: "Christians may have to challenge them [other religious traditions] in a peaceful spirit with regard to the content of their belief. But Christians, too, must allow themselves to be questioned. Notwithstanding the fullness of God's revelation in Jesus Christ, the way Christians sometimes understand their religion and practice it may be in need of purification" (no. 32).

With regard to religious conversion, participants in interreligious dialogue, Christians and otherwise, of course would be very pleased if others decide to "convert" and accept their religious tradition. But this applies *both* ways, that is, non-Christians may become Christian and vice versa. This is a possibility, some would say a risk, which each participant—especially Christians—must be aware of. As a result of interreligious dialogue, Christians may feel called by God to "convert" to other religion(s), or, as often the case, to be "interreligious."[24] It is quite acceptable that the participants wish and even pray for the conversion of the others. But conversion is not and must be made into the goal of interreligious dialogue itself; otherwise interreligious dialogue is corrupted into evangelism- or mission-in-camouflage.

If interreligious dialogue is understood and practiced in this way, it is no threat to mission, nor, conversely, is mission understood as

24. On this issue, see Knitter, *Without Buddha*.

evangelism a threat to it. They are simply two distinct activities, with their own goals, methods, and dynamics. One is not a "part" or "expression" of the other, much less reducible to or replaced by the other. At both the WMC and Vatican II, mission was elevated to the role of the master that interreligious dialogue must serve. In the aftermaths of both church assemblies, a whole battery of theologies of religions, Christologies, and ecclesiologies was elaborated to consolidate the subordination of interreligious dialogue to mission. Now reintroduced to each other on the basis of a different kind of relationship, mission and interreligious dialogue can recognize themselves as non-identical twins, or as good friends, or as reconciled family members, or as equal partners. In this new relationship, mission itself does not remain unaffected. In this new context, the so-called Great Commission, the Christological and ecclesiological presuppositions of mission, and the modes of mission must be reconfigured. Only in this way will the intuitions and intentions of both the WMC and Vatican II that took place in the twentieth century be fully implemented in the twenty-first century.

WORKS CITED

Balia, Daryl, and Kirsteen Kim, eds. *Edinburgh 2010: Witnessing to Christ Today*. Oxford: Regnum, 2000.

Burrows, William. *Redemption and Dialogue: Reading* Redemptoris Missio *and* Dialogue and Proclamation. Maryknoll, NY: Orbis, 1993.

Cracknell, Kenneth. *Justice, Courtesy and Love: Theologians and Missionaries Encountering World Religions, 1846–1914*. London: Epworth, 1995.

Delaney, Joan. "From Cremona to Edinburgh: Bishop Bonomelli and the World Missionary Conference of 1910." *The Ecumenical Review* 52.3 (2000) 418–31.

Dupuis, Jacques. *Christianity and the Religions: From Confrontation to Dialogue*. New York: Orbis, 2002.

―――. *Toward a Christian Theology of Religious Pluralism*. Maryknoll, NY: Orbis, 1977.

Denzinger, Heinrich. *The Sources of Catholic Dogma*. Translated by Roy J. Defarrari. Fitzwilliam, NH: Loreto, 1955.

Flannery, Austin. *Vatican II: Constitutions Decrees Declarations. A Completely Revised Translation in Inclusive Language*. North Port, NY: Costello, 1996.

Kerr, David A., and Kenneth R. Ross, eds. *Edinburgh 2010: Mission Then and Now*. Oxford: Regnum, 2009.

Knitter, Paul F. *Introducing Theologies of Religion*. Maryknoll, NY: Orbis, 2002.

―――. *Without Buddha I Could not be a Christian*. Oxford: Oneworld, 2009.

Kraemer, Hendrik. *The Christian Message in a Non-Christian World*. Grand Rapids: Kregel, 1938.

McBrien, Richard. *The Church: The Evolution of Catholicism*. New York: HarperOne, 2008.
Malley, John. *What Happened at Vatican II*. Cambridge: Harvard University Press, 2008.
Pieris, Aloysius. *Give Vatican II a Chance: Yes to Incessant Renewal No to Reform of the Reforms*. Gonawala-Kelaniya, Sri Lanka: Tulana Research Centre, 2010.
Pope Paul VI. *On Evangelization in the Modern World (Evangelii Nunciandi)*. Boston: Pauline, 1976.
Pope, Stephen, and Charles C. Hefling, eds. *Sic et Non: Encountering Dominus Iesus*. Maryknoll, NY: Orbis, 2002.
Report of Commission IV: The Missionary Message in Relation to Non-Christian Religion. Edinburgh: Oliphant, Anderson & Ferrier, 1910.
Ross, Kenneth. *Edinburgh 2010: Springboard for Mission*. Pasadena, CA: William Carey International University Press, 2009.
Stanley, Brian. *The World Missionary Conference, Edinburgh 1910*. Grand Rapids: Eedrmans, 2009.
Vorgrimmler, Herbert. *Commentary on the Documents of Vatican II*. Vol. III. New York: Herder and Herder, 1969.
———. *Commentary on the Documents of Vatican II*. Vol. IV. New York: Herder and Herder, 1969.
Walls, Andrew F. *The Cross-Cultural Process in Christian History: Studies in the Transmission and Appropriation of Faith*. Maryknoll, NY: Orbis, 2002.
Yong, Amos. *Beyond the Impasse: Toward a Pneumatological Theology of Religions* Grand Rapids: Baker, 2003.
———. *Discerning the Spirit(s): A Pentecostal-Charismatic Contribution to Christian Theology of Religions*. Sheffield: Sheffield Academic, 2000.

7

Wooden Boxes and Latticed Windows

Christian Confession and Post-colonizing Mission

Ruth Padilla DeBorst

WHAT COMES TO YOUR mind when I say "South Africa 2010"? If you are like most of the world, surely you will think of the 2010 FIFA World Cup. Photos of the Cape Town stadium on Green Point Common, with breathtaking views of Table Mountain and the entire bay are now etched in the memories of millions of fans. In contrast, not many know of an unassuming, old church building a mere two miles away. On the outside wall, a small plaque beckons to passersby:

> *All who pass by: Remember with shame the many thousands of people who lived for generations in District Six and other parts of this city, and were forced by law to leave their homes because of the color of their skins. Father, forgive us . . .*

When you step inside the small District Six Museum, you take in the graphic horror of an entire populated neighborhood bulldozed to the ground. A yellowed sign calls visitors to again remember:

> Remember Dimbaza, remember Botshabelo/Onverwacht . . . remember District Six, remember the racism which took away our homes and our livelihood and which sought to steal away our humanity. Remember also our will to live, to hold fast to that which marks us as human beings: our generosity, our love of justice, and our care for each other . . . In remembering we do not

> want to recreate district six but to work with its memory: of hurts inflicted and received, of loss, achievements and of shames. We wish to remember so that we can all, together and by ourselves, rebuild a city which belongs to all of us, in which all of us can live, not as races but as people.

The more wrenching tragedy of apartheid is that the flagrant abuse of power was undergirded and justified by religious, theological, "Christian" scaffolding. Consequently, the complex and painful way forward in South Africa continues to demand the rule of just law but also the incarnation of a reconciliation politics on the part of the Christian church. The witnessing church in South Africa and in the rest of the world today must confess publicly, deconstruct, and reform its use of power according to the model of the incarnate Christ in order to make God's reconciling work visible today. A mission that is truly to bring good news to the world in the twenty-first century cannot shy away from the complex double task of extricating mission from power and intermingling it, instead, with reconciliation.

Like the network of roads laid out by the Roman Empire throughout its domain, current globalization and technology provide a global reach of messages and messengers of all sorts and from many places. Today we are going to consider several unsettling actions called for if Christians are to make known the good news of God's good purposes for the entire creation across borders, and not merely serve as agents of cultural or economic colonization. We begin with a story of reordering of power in the early church. We then fly over centuries of world history, and we finally land in proposals for Christian mission in the twenty-first century. I venture to propose public confession—which entails remembering, releasing and reconciling—as a necessary means for replacing power and his sons, pride and prejudice, with incarnation and her daughters, humility and embrace.

THE FIRST CHRISTIAN REFORMATION: RE-ORDERING OF POWER IN THE EARLY CHURCH

Along the network of Roman roads—built with the heavy taxes levied upon the people under imperial domination—moved people, products, and ideas. Also along those roads marched the armies sent to secure borders and impose peace. The biblical book of Acts records the name of a centurion posted in the regal city of Caesarea. Cornelius, a devout and generous man who prayed to God regularly, had called to God and sought out the apostle Peter. Remember, Cornelius served in the powerful imperial army that had executed Jesus and continued crushing Israel militarily and strangling it economically. To make matters worse, although he was said to fear God, Cornelius had never taken the steps required to become a Jewish proselyte. He and his household adhered to traditions, habits, diets, and values abhorrent to religious Jews. In spite of all these barriers, however, the Holy Spirit guides Peter and enables him to transcend pride and prejudice. Much to the initial consternation of the "central" church in Jerusalem, Peter not only responds to the summons of this Roman centurion, but also daringly and humbly enters into the intimacy of this man's world. He spends days partaking of the same food under the same roof with someone who represents everything the Jewish people fear, hate, and reject. He obediently shares "the good news of peace through Jesus Christ,"[1] and in so doing, *he* receives the good news of God's reconciling love for all people afresh. Peter is no longer free to conceive of himself and his inner circle of fellow-Jewish Christ followers as the only brokers of God's action in the world; he is forced to step out of his neatly constructed borders and categories and embrace his "unlikely" brother: "I now realize how true it is that God does not show favoritism but accepts men [and women] from every nation who fear him and do what is right."[2] No longer can he hold a leash on God, constricting the Spirit to gift only people akin to him in religious tradition, ethnic background, or social or political status. He cannot but confess publicly to his critical fellow-disciples: Who was I, that I could hinder God? God gave *them*—the gentiles, those we excluded—the same gift as he gave *us*.[3] You can imagine a typical Jewish response to Peter's revelation: The same? Can anyone have the same value, giftedness, even closeness to God as we do? We are God's chosen people. We are insiders; others are outsiders! And if they want to share in power and belonging, they must eat what we eat and reject what we reject; they must become like us!

---

1. Acts 10:36, NIV.
2. Acts 10:34–35, NIV (with author's addition).
3. Acts 11:17, NIV.

The passage points to an issue that threatened to tear the early church apart. From here on out, the biblical narrative and historical records depict the ongoing struggle of a church attempting to come to grips with the gospel—with the implications of the radically equalizing and all-embracing good news that transcended the boundaries and categories so easily preset by the dominant group of Jewish disciples. Stories of controversy, condemnation, conflict, and church councils blend in with those of celebration, confession, acceptance, and hospitality throughout the book of Acts and the epistles. It is well worth noting that the title "Christian" was first attributed to the followers of Jesus not in Jerusalem (the initial center of power) but on the margins among new believers in the multi-cultured and oft looked-down-upon gentile city of Antioch.[4] God was clearly fulfilling God's good purposes through those Christian communities, calling people to reconciliation in Jesus Christ, to full life in the Spirit, and to relevant witness in the broader community. This witness took on concrete, economic form: in spite of the prejudice held against them by their fellow believers in Jerusalem, the Christians in Antioch reached out with a generous offering when the Jerusalem church hit on hard times![5] Theirs is a public confession of faith that alters the ruling power structure and refashions relationships according to the paradigm of King Jesus, who rules by giving himself away. And over time, by engaging in the practice of God's border-crossing mission, the church in Jerusalem did come to the humble recognition that God was active outside the confines of their ethnic and linguistic structures; they realized that they had as much to receive from other Christian communities as they had to give, in creating mission partnerships with Christ followers, both women and men, from other areas of the empire.

CHRISTIAN MISSION AND COLONIZING POWER THROUGHOUT HISTORY

Similar dynamics have played out in Christian mission throughout history. Love of money and self-sacrifice, fear and forgiveness, and power and reconciliation are entangled threads that resist unraveling. Kreider characterizes the church of the first several centuries as a "peace church,"

---

4. Acts 11:26.
5. Acts 11:27–30.

a church that understood its very existence as an expression of God's peace-building in the world.[6] Witness of the gospel was written along with persecution, prison, and death for many followers of Jesus who dared confess his lordship in direct confrontation of imperial decree. However, with the "Constantinian reversal" of AD 313, (once the power and interests of the empire and those of the church intertwined), it became increasingly difficult for the church to sort out its allegiances. It appears undeniable that, in Lois Barrett's words, "Whenever the church has a vested interest in the status quo—politically, economically, socially—it can easily be captivated by the powers, the institutions, the spirits and the authorities of the world. And whenever the church becomes captivated by the powers, it loses the ability to identify and name evil."[7] The uncritical blend of power and mission rests on the proud assumption that the centers of power and their emisaries own the pure gospel, the inspired theology, the appropriate ecclesiology, and the right ethical answers to the questions of Christian life in the world. Blinded by this assumption, the church runs the risk of carrying the "good news" of the power of the day and serving as agents of cultural colonization, be it the Rome of the first Christendom, the cross-and-sword-brandishing conquistadores, the "enlightened and reformed" nation-states, the "civilizing" British empire, the recent crusaders against the "axis of evil," or the current Western marketing schemes for converting the "unreached."

Throughout the history of world Christianity, people on the receiving end of Western mission often experienced it as yet another form of colonialism or foreign imposition.[8] They sometimes reacted strongly, even violently,[9] with nationalist assertions of indigenization and independence from missionary input and Western control,[10] including calls for a moratorium on missions.[11] Some of these voices ring loud and clear:

6. Kreider, *Missio Dei*, 3.
7. Guder, *Missional Church*, 113.
8. Bosch, *Transforming Mission*, 302–13.
9. Examples are the 1851 edict against Christians in Vietnam (Koschorke, *History of Christianity*, 75), the 1900 Boxer Rebellion in China, during which Chinese Christians and Western missionaries were martyred (Bevans and Shroeder, *Constants in Context*, 216); and the 1904 rebellion in Namibia (Ibid.).
10. Regarding Asia, see Koschorke, *History of Christianity*, 90–92, 101–6; Africa, 216–20; Latin America, 390–418.
11. John Gatu at the CWME meeting in Bangkok in 1973 (Bevans and Shroeder, *Constants in Context*, 262).

"I am suspicious of 'African experts' who, without being invited, come from outside our black experience and propose theological as well as sociological programs ... It must be a black man who best knows how to live as a black man today." Manas Buthelezi, bishop of the Central Diocese of the United Evangelical Lutheran Church of South Africa, 1973.[12]

"We Christians can and must fight against tyranny ... The revolution is not only permissible but obligatory for those Christians who see it as the only effective and far-reaching way to make the love of all people a reality." Camilo Torres, Colombia, 1965.[13]

"We in the younger churches have to learn the discipline of freedom to accept and to refuse, to place resources at the service of mission rather than to have mission patterned by resources ... If, in order to do that, we must say to you, our friends, 'Stay home,' we will do so because before God we have this grave responsibility of our integrity." José Miguez Bonino, addressing a group in the USA, 1974.[14]

The patchy history of Christian mission forces the question: Is there any hope today, in the midst of the pulls and tugs of current globalizing and counter-globalizing forces, of differing theological outlooks and internecine tensions, that Christians in mission can make known the good news of God's good purposes for the entire creation across borders, and not merely serve as agents of cultural or economic colonization?

PUBLIC CONFESSION IS AT THE HEART OF NON-COLONIZING MISSION

We live in days of what Walsh and Keesmaat denominate "a homogenized global consumerist consciousness."[15] Mass media, business, travel, and concerted trade agreements work together to erase local tastes, life-styles, and values, converting the globe into one big McWorld (in Tom Sine's words).[16] Everything is susceptible of being bought, sold, bartered, and marketed—including people. Even the gospel in some circles

12. Koschorke, *History of Christianity*, 259.
13. Ibid., 392.
14. Anderson, *Moratorium*.
15. Walsh and Keesmaat, *Colossians Remixed*, 29.
16. Sine, *Mustard Seed vs. McWorld*.

is being wrapped in the trappings of economic success and reduced to a seal of approval of the idols of our syncretistic and pagan consumer society. These idols, building on Chris Wright's daring denunciation at the recent Lausanne III congress, are: (1) the power and pride that breed self-seeking thirst for status and position, name and fame; (2) the popularity and success that lead us into manipulation, dishonest statistics, and untruthful success stories; (3) the wealth and greed that blind us and make us accomplices in social injustice and the abuse of creation.[17]

The world church today—as in the days of Peter and the early church, the days of St. Francis, Huss, Luther, Calvin, and Wesley, the days of massacres of native peoples, of slave trade, and of apartheid—is in dire need of reformation. The greatest stumbling block to God's work in God's world, Wright warned the 4,500 Christians gathered in Cape Town, is the unfaithfulness of the church. "We need to hear the prophetic word: 'Repent and believe!'" "Before we go out to the world," Wright exhorted, "we need to come back to the Lord. Before we take the gospel to the world, we must confess our lack of faithfulness to God. Before we seek the lost, we must fall on our knees before the Lord."[18] Similarly, the British mission leader Max Warren writes, "The validity of our claim to have a gospel for the world depends in part upon the integrity with which we are prepared to face our failures."[19] Confession truly is at the heart of all reformation. But, what kind of confession?

I grew up in Argentina, worked for years in Ecuador and El Salvador, and currently live in Costa Rica. Catholic cathedrals stand out in the skyline of all Latin American cities, a daily reminder of the power of a church that imposed Christianity at the point of a sword. The gilded altars and images bespeak of centuries of oppression of our native peoples. But I want to call your attention to another piece present in all Catholic churches. If instead of walking down the center aisle, you stop at the back of the church or edge your way along the sides, you will see them. They are wooden boxes with small, latticed windows behind which the priest can hide. You know what I am referring to: the confessional. Devout Catholics kneel at these boxes at least weekly, and there spill out the list of accumulated sins before they partake of communion.

17. Wright's address can be heard at http://ispss.istreamplanet.com/director/CapeTown2010/Plen2_Sat_Seg1_Wright_WEB2974987157.mp4.

18. Chris Wright, "Integrity: Confronting Idols."

19. Warren, *I Believe*, 75.

Now, do not get me wrong. There is nothing wrong with confession. I am actually insisting that it is a non-negotiable for the people of God! So, what's the problem? Well, the danger lies in that confession in this tradition has been sacramentalized into a private, one-on-one ritual, isolated from community and sectioned off from everyday life and relationships. The ritual can be performed, and once the doorframe of the church is crossed, life can continue as usual.

Let's not, however, be too quick to bash Catholic Christians. Stop for a moment and think. What space do we assign confession in Evangelical, Pentecostal, or Protestant churches? Granted, among some of us, there is a practice of "giving testimony." But the sharing tends to focus on the marvels of the Spirit's work, the triumphant overcoming of temptation and sin in people's lives. And truly, in more traditional liturgies there always is a moment assigned to confession and absolution of sin. However, it too is often sacramentalized into a private, one-on-one ritual, isolated from community and sectioned off from everyday life and relationships. The ritual can be performed, and life can continue as usual.

I dare say this individual mea culpa confession is *not* the type that brings transformation. It is gutless; in it rests no transformative power. Out of it, no new sending is issued; no post-colonial mission is possible. In contrast, listen to the prophet Isaiah: "Woe to me!" he cried, as he was confronted with the scary holiness of God's presence that shed light on the social scene of his time. "I am ruined! For I am a man of unclean lips, and I live among a people of unclean lips, and my eyes have seen the King, the Lord Almighty!"[20] His was a public confession and one that, as the biblical text shows, laid bare the injustices perpetrated by the people of Israel, the oppression so endemic even to its religious system, the abandonment of God's project to bless *all* people through them. And it is only once he has made this public confession that Isaiah is ready to be sent. Sent to what? Sent to call on his people, time and time again, to own up to their condition, their utter disregard for God's nature and good purposes, to confess God's sovereign and life-giving rule, and to live justly in light of it by the power of God's Spirit.

What is being called for here is public confession. In *Honest Patriots* Donald Shriver denounces the crippling effects of the "sacramentalization of confession" and the "privatization of forgiveness" that keep evils

---

20. Isa 6:5.

hidden from the public eye and individuals and institutions unaccountable for them. Evils, crimes perpetrated, and social wounds must be *publicly* remembered, named, faced, confessed, and mourned. Space must be created for all voices and stories to be heard, and for collective repentance and forgiveness to take place. Symbols, sites, and art in everyday spaces can contribute to intergenerational cooperation. Plaques like the one on the public wall of the District Six Museum, memorials like those of the Holocaust and Vietnam, museums like the one of the Inquisition in Mexico City, and the one in memory of the thousands of "disappeared" in Buenos Aires—all these help people remember. They are constant reminders of horrors that should never be repeated. "Never again!" they cry out to all who pass by. Remembrance, not avoidance, is the way towards release and reconciliation.

What might communities of Jesus' followers need today to remember in order to release and be reconciled? What issues beg for public confession today?

Perhaps Christians around the world—but especially those in centers and positions of power—need to confess that we have made God too small and ourselves, our institutions and denominations, agencies and buildings, programs and egos, even our nations, our race, our ethnicity, our sexuality, far too big. We have made God in our own image rather than recognizing God's image in our fellow human beings. When we reduce God's awesome holiness to chummy buddyness, the life of our neighbors also loses importance.

Father, forgive us, for we know not what we do! Or, we know all too well, but find it too costly to change!

Perhaps Christians of European descent need to confess that much of their privilege, opportunity, success, and prosperity is built on the backs of people native to other lands; individuals whose very lives, land, and future were taken—and continue to be taken—hostage for their own advancement, with no redistribution for generations. Additionally, these Christians infinitely add disgrace upon disgrace when this abuse is done while affirming that "in God we trust."

Father, forgive us, for we know not what we do! Or, we know all too well, but find it too costly to change!

Perhaps the rest of us need to confess that the dark oppression of anger and even revenge is never too far from our hearts. We often nurse and build our identity around our festering wounds, unready to be healed. In so doing, we stifle the work of God's Spirit in and through us.

Father, forgive us, for we know not what we do! Or, we know all too well, but find it too costly to change!

Perhaps some of us need to confess that, blinded by Enlightenment articulations, pride, and prejudice, we easily assume the categories we have constructed and the issues we fight over are actually of global concern. Perhaps some of us need to confess the belief that the entire world church should line up on our "right" side of the debate: dispensational or non-dispensational, egalitarian or complementarian, left or right, and so on. Believing the West has figured it all out, theology has been written that truth—cast as propositional and absolute—is absolutely clear and objective in every context, and the rest of the world can simply translate and apply it. In doing so, we often deprive ourselves and our communities of fresh insights and the renewal stemming from unlikely places around the globe.

Father, forgive us, for we know not what we do! Or, we know all too well, but find it too costly to change!

Perhaps Christians at the centers of world power and prosperity need to confess that it is simple to pay lip service to the now famous "shift of the center of gravity of Christianity," but actually more difficult to truly acknowledge, respect, include and open up space to people from the majority world. This means inclusion in decision-making, setting of priorities, and defining what integral witness of the good news looks like in the world today (aside from the dichotomies that have governed many Western debates and church practices—religious vs. secular, spiritual vs. material, personal vs. social, and lay vs. ordained). Perhaps the writer of a recent *Economist* article reviewing Lausanne III is insightful in assessing, "If the ecumenists of the WCC and certain evangelicals are getting on better, it's probably because Christianity's centre of gravity is moving south—to Africa and other poor places, where the ideological rows of the northern hemisphere often ring hollow, and churches dare not neglect either the spiritual or the material."[21]

Father, forgive us, for we know not what we do! Or, we know all too well, but find it too costly to change!

Perhaps all who claim to follow Jesus need to confess that Jesus' way of humble incarnation—of giving himself away in favor of others in both life and in death, of forgiveness and embrace—goes against all our natural instincts and learned strategies of self-protection and self-aggrandizement. We would much rather mold our values and lifestyles according to those of the prevailing culture. Perhaps we, as Peter, stand in need of conversion before we can fully further God's kingdom and God's justice.

Father, forgive us, for we know not what we do! Or, we know all too well, but find it too costly to change!

Perhaps, with Roland Allen, we need to confess our lack of faith in the work of God's Spirit when we engage in mission. "*Want of faith has made us fear and distrust native independence.* We have imagined ourselves to be, and have acted so as to become, indispensable." "We have desired to help them . . . And we have done much . . . We have done everything for them except acknowledge any equality. We have done everything for them but very little with them. We have done everything for them except give place to them. We have treated them as 'dear children,' but not as 'brethren.'"[22] Perhaps we need to recognize, that even if others do not do things our way, "There is no stage in which it is necessary that they should be slaves of a foreign system."[23]

Father, forgive us, for we know not what we do! Or, we know all too well, but find it too costly to change!

Perhaps when we think of South Africa, we should join in the recent Statement of Lament for Evangelicals and the Legacy of Apartheid, and confess the silence and complicity of much of the world church. While we need to reject the theological heresy that undergirded apartheid and

---

21. *The Economist*, "Heaven and earth."
22. Allen, *Missionary Methods*, 143.
23. Ibid., 146.

lament the socioeconomic suffering that is apartheid's ongoing legacy, we also need to "open our eyes to see the pain and wounds of the current realities and injustices which the church fails to protest and engage in our own contexts today. We are called to deeds of repentance and to resist injustices."[24]

Father, forgive us, for we know not what we do! Or, we know all too well, but find it too costly to change!

Perhaps the list goes on, and includes men and women, insiders and outsides, academics and practitioners, and people from North, South, East, and West. Dividing walls and stereotypes are erected with ease. Exclusionary attitudes and practices abound. Only confession born out of a humble awareness of God's incomprehensible, self-giving love can begin to crack those barriers.

A FINAL CALL TO UNCOMPROMISING CONFESSION

He was in serious trouble. I actually feared for his life. No, he was not into drugs, trafficking, or other shady deals. He had no criminal record and his name was not on a "wanted" list—but his very life was in jeopardy. Why? This megachurch pastor in the city of San Salvador dared to confess publicly—in newspapers, sermons, and speeches—the evils of his society and the connivance of religious power in the ruling injustice. He was unwilling to serve as a court prophet for a government that was unconcerned about the plight of the poor. He would not—as other religious leaders did—offer a stamp of approval to policies that perpetuated injustice at home and abroad. He would not sit at the banquet table of the powerful nor barter the vote of his congregation of over 100,000. This uncompromising confession gained him insistent calls from the Presidential Palace: "Who does he think he is?" stormed the president, outraged that the pastor would not shake his hand in official photo opportunities. Public confession unmasks power and renders the idols of our day powerless.

---

24. "Statement of Lament for Evangelicals and the Legacy of Apartheid" was drafted and circulated during Lausanne III at Cape Town by the Lausanne Special Interest Group on Reconciliation.

Mario Vega is not the first person to provoke anger and persecution by living out of his faith, even in direct confrontation with ruling powers. He stands in a long line of women and men who, through the ages, have refused to circumscribe confession of God's kingdom and God's justice to the realm of things personal, private, religious, intra-church, and spiritual. He communes with the likes of the very Son of God, Jesus of Nazareth; of Stephen, James, and Chloe in the early church; of Thecla, Perpetua, and Felicity of later days; of Casas and Claver a few centuries ago; and of King, Rosa Parks, Ida Clark, and Romero in recent years. For Mario, as for them, witness of the incarnate, crucified, risen, and ruling Christ cannot be anything but public, social, and yes, political. Theirs is a stance that challenges the powers-that-be, not with the weapons and categories of hegemony, imposition, and violence, but with the power of the Spirit who indwells in them and enables them to stand outside the ruling framework and critique it, and to make their lives available for its re-creation. These sisters and brothers exemplify a stance that I believe is non-negotiable for the people of God who seek to live a post-colonial and post-colonizing paradigm of church and mission. May we, as they, shed our pretenses of power and actively avail ourselves to remember and release. May we make visible, here and now, the reconciliation God has effected in Christ of women and men with God, with one another, and with the rest of creation. May we engage in bold, humble, public confession so that God's good purposes are fulfilled on earth as they are in heaven.

WORKS CITED

Allen, Roland. *Missionary Methods: St Paul's or Ours?* Grand Rapids: Eerdmans, 1962.

Anderson, Gerald H. "A Moratorium on Missionaries?" *Christian Century* 91.2 (January 16, 1974) 43–45.

Bevans, Stephen, and Roger Schroeder. *Constants in Context: A Theology of Mission for Today.* Maryknoll, NY: Orbis, 2004.

Bosch, David Jacobus. *Transforming Mission: Paradigm Shifts in Theology of Mission.* Maryknoll, NY: Orbis, 1991.

Guder, Darrel. *Missional Church: A Vision for the Sending of the Church in North America.* Grand Rapids: Eerdmans, 1998.

Koschorke, Klaus, Frieder Ludwig, and Mariano Delgado, eds. *A History of Christianity in Asia, Africa, and Latin America, 1450–1990: A Documentary Sourcebook.* Grand Rapids: Eerdmans, 2007.

Kreider, Alan. *Missio Dei. Exploring God's Work in the World. Peace Church, Mission Church: Friends or Foes?* Elkhart, IN: Mennonite Mission Network, 2004.

Lausanne Special Interest Group on Reconciliation. "Statement of Lament for Evangelicals and the Legacy of Apartheid." No Pages. Online: http://reconcilers.wordpress.com/2010/10/22/apartheid-legacy-lament/.

Sine, Tom. *Mustard Seed vs. McWorld: Reinventing Life and Faith for the Future.* Grand Rapids: Baker, 1999.

The Economist. "Heaven and Earth: An Intra-Christian Gap Has Closed a Little." No pages. Online: http://www.economist.com/node/17361406.

Walsh, Brian, and Sylvia Keesmaat. *Colossians Remixed: Subverting the Empire.* Downers Grove, IL: InterVarsity, 2004.

Warren, Max Alexander Cunningham. *I Believe in the Great Commission.* London: Hodder and Stoughton, 1976.

Wright, Chris. "Integrity: Confronting Idols." Plenary Address at Lausanne III, Cape Town, South Africa. October 23, 2010. Video. Online: http://conversation.lausanne.org/en/conversations/detail/10978.

8

Finding the Seventh Story

Brian D. McLaren

WE LIVE BY STORIES. Just as the sixty billion or so human cells that constitute your body are united by the story of you, the seven billion bodies alive today are united in the story of humanity. And within that human story, we create uncountable sub-stories that unite and identify us—first, the mega-stories of civilizations, and within civilizations, the big stories of religions, nations, ethnic groups, and states.

And within those stories, we live, move, and have our being in smaller stories of denominations, sects, parties, and communities, within which we also find ourselves in the cozier stories of families, circles of friends, companies, and other associations.

Some years ago I became curious about those stories—why some of them seem to make us smarter and kinder, why some of them seem to make us stupider and meaner, why some bias us towards peace and others towards hate and violence. I started trying to classify stories according to their dominant plot-line, and over several years of study, conversation, and reflection, I came up with six stories of violence. They have proven themselves (to me, anyway) both discrete and comprehensive.

The first of these violent narratives is, I believe, at the heart of the whole conversation about post-colonialism. It is the story that drives nations to become empires and create colonies: the story of domination.

1. Domination

The story of domination is a familiar one: we used to be oppressed and marginalized by others. But we were too wise, brave, and proud to let ourselves be dominated (or we were chosen by God for better things, or both). So we began the long struggle for ascendancy. Now we are on top, and we will only be safe if we retain our position of hegemony.

Of course, those who have come under our dominion aren't as happy about our ascendancy. They have a different story to tell.

2. Revolution

In this story, we used to be free and proud, but "they" brutally and deceitfully rose to power. Now, they have the upper hand, and we must retain the memory of all their injustice so as to motivate us to throw off, at the right time, their oppression and regain our lost freedom and pride.

Of course, if such a revolution happens, we then inhabit the story of domination. What happens, though, when we are firmly in control, but things still are amiss? Then we need the third story.

3. Purification

All would be well, according to this story, if it weren't for some insidious minority groups who are among us, but not really of us. They are the source of our greatest problems. They are like a cancer within our body politic, robbing us of health and threatening our future. Left unchecked, they will destroy us, so we will only be safe when we have purged their destructive influence from among us.

The domination (or imperial) narrative, the revolution (or revenge) narrative, and the purification (or scapegoating) narrative account for a surprisingly high percentage of violent human behavior. But three other stories also contribute to human violence.

4. Isolation

Our group may decide we don't want to be part of the previous three narratives. Perhaps we have been scapegoated by the purification narrative, or have tried revolution and failed, or are a former empire who has been dethroned from domination. We may choose instead to isolate—either geographically by becoming refugees who seek another homeland, or socially by maintaining customs of clothing, diet, speech, and so on that will mark us as different from others and keep us separate from them. Our goal? Simply to survive without participating in the presiding systems of domination, revolution, and purification, because we know we're only safe if we're separate and distinct.

This isolation narrative often coexists with two sister narratives of self-preservation.

5. Accumulation

In this story, you're only safe if you've got a lot of land, money, or weapons to protect you from the insanity and unpredictability of others around you. You'll dip into the system to compete as necessary, but your goal is not to be in the center of the action: your goal is to squirrel away resources to create an island of prosperity and security on the margins. There you can ride out the storms of conflict created by other less enlightened people.

But what if you've tried the isolation and accumulation narratives and have either failed or been prohibited from living by them? You have one remaining option:

6. Victimization

In this story, we tell the truth about our misfortune and mistreatment at the hands of others. By keeping these painful memories alive, we keep at bay the accusation of inferiority by which others might mock us: it's not our fault that we're like this—it's their fault. By telling and retelling these stories, we keep alive the hope that our powerful tormentors may acknowledge their injustice and desist from it, opening up a better day for us. We present ourselves as innocent victims, which can help us gain certain advantages by sympathy and guilt that we couldn't gain otherwise. And perhaps we await a leader who will rouse us to redress these injustices by leading us in a revolution narrative.

As I began to trace the shapes of these six narratives and see them played out in our contemporary world, I also began to see them in the Bible, especially in the Gospels.[1]

The Romans, for starters, embody the domination narrative. The Sadducees and Herodians have decided to hitch their wagons to that imperial narrative as well, thinking, "If you can't beat the colonizers, why not join them?" The tax collectors have similarly figured out a way to

---

1. My thought process in this regard unfolds in *The Secret Message of Jesus, Everything Must Change*, and *A New Kind of Christianity*. My first attempt at articulating the gospel as story can be found in *The Story We Find Ourselves In*.

profit from the colonial system, securing personal good at the expense of the common good.

At the other extreme, the Zealots live by the revolution narrative, always keeping a dagger hidden under their cloak, waiting for the chance to slit the throat of a Roman soldier peeing on a wall. Who knows whether the next small act of terrorism might be the spark to light a wildfire of revolution?

The Pharisees are the champions of the purification narrative, scapegoating prostitutes, drunks, and all those who are flagging in rigor to keep the law.

Although they are peripheral in the gospel narratives, the Essenes and related groups clearly represent the isolation narrative.

The accumulation narrative runs through the wealthy Judeans in the south who buy up small farms in Galilee to the north and create huge agri-business vineyards that employ (or exploit) the former landowners as tenant farmers. These accumulators then deploy an army of stewards to extract their tribute.

That leaves the Galileans, the landless day-laborers, the scapegoated prostitutes, the excluded lepers, the despised Samaritans, and all the others who are sick and paralyzed and thus unable to thrive. They find their place in the victimization narrative.

Against this backdrop of stories and counter-stories, Jesus' masterstrategy of communication suddenly appears incandescent: he tells stories—parables about the players in these various narratives. And in parable after parable, he cracks open these six dominant stories to make room for another story to emerge, one he calls "the kingdom of God."

This story is a reversal of all previous stories. The kingdom of God rejects the domination narrative and leads through service, sacrifice, and love. It rejects violent revolution and revenge and calls instead for forgiveness and reconciliation. It rejects purification, and instead invites the outcasts to the table for inclusion rather than scapegoating. It subverts the normal standards of purity (what goes in through the mouth, for example), and focuses instead on purity of heart (which is evidenced by the words that come out of the mouth). It counters isolation with incarnation, penetration, and solidarity, drawing near to touch lepers, eat with sinners, mix with the masses in Galilee, and even confront injustice in the centers of power. The kingdom of God, by assessing *giving* superior to receiving, judges accumulation inferior to self-giving. And the kingdom of God empowers victims, assuring them that their little bit of faith can move big mountains of injustice, inviting them to become the salt of the earth and the light of the world—protagonists in their own story of liberation.

To put it differently, rather than the us-over-them narrative of domination, or the us-instead-of-them narrative of revolution, or the us-purified-of-them narrative of purification, or the us-apart-from-them narrative of isolation, or the us-protected-from-them narrative of accumulation, or the us-under-them narrative of victimization, Jesus' good news of the reign of God celebrates a some-of-us-on-behalf-of-all-of-us narrative, a healing story of us-for-the-common-good.

In light of this radical message of the kingdom of God, it is heartbreakingly tragic that our ancestors in our Christian religion soon domesticated Jesus' message and accommodated it to the narratives it originally sought to heal and replace.

Our religious forefathers—for many reasons that resist easy explanation—reduced Jesus' rich, three-dimensional reign-of-God story of creation, liberation, and reconciliation to a flat linear narrative of condemnation (of all), election (of a few), and damnation (of the remainder). The subversive Jewish storyline of a God who sides with slaves, not Pharaohs, was all but lost to us, and in its place we constructed—largely within the confines of Greek philosophy and Roman imperial politics—a storyline in which the few, the chosen, the elect—in short, the Christians—were destined for heaven in the afterlife *and for domination in this life.*

The Christian religion thus became the chaplaincy for the domination narrative in the waning Roman Empire. In the fifteen or so centuries since Rome's fall, the dream of domination has resurrected again and again—for example, in the Holy Roman Empire, in the Crusades, in the Spanish conquistadores, in the British Empire, in the system of apartheid, and currently in American exceptionalism.

Where Christian domination was not an option, Christianized versions of the other narratives have also framed the lives of millions, so that Christian revolution, Christian purification, Christian isolation, Christian accumulation, and Christian victimization narratives abound.

But when these narratives prove themselves violent and show themselves to be part of the problem rather than the solution, the witness of Jesus in the Gospels still shines against the darkness, and we again seek the power of a seventh story, a story that leads to peace rather than violence—the good news, the healing story of the reigning of God.

The postcolonial conversation provides us such a moment. Christian domination has proven itself little if at all better than other domination narratives. Millions of people have abandoned Christianity as they abandoned its favorite narrative. Whether through Christians (like Dr. Martin Luther King, Jr.) or non-Christians (like Mohandas Gandhi), we have seen that violence can't cure violence. The wide, smooth highways that lead to mutually assured destruction have lost their appeal for many of us, and we seek a less-traveled path once again—an alternative story that was judged unrealistic by some, but now seems the only path of hope.

Some words attributed to Austrian philosopher, social critic, and ex-priest Ivan Illich (1926–2002) speak powerfully to our post-colonial moment: "Neither [violent] revolution nor [political] reformation can ultimately change a society, rather you must tell a new powerful tale, one so persuasive that it sweeps away the old myths and becomes the preferred story, one so inclusive that it gathers all the bits of our past and our present into a coherent whole, one that even shines some light into the future so that we can take the next step . . . If you want to change a society, then you have to tell an alternative story."

It is my hope and prayer that more and more of us will discover or rediscover the alternative story of the kingdom of God proclaimed by Jesus in life and deed as well as in parable and teaching. Hopefully, many Christians who are raised to revere Jesus as Lord will lead the way in this rediscovery. But perhaps many others will participate and lead as well—Muslims who revere Jesus as a prophet, Jews who understand him as an itinerant rabbi in the tradition of the prophets, Hindus and Buddhists who have long believed that human beings can embody and teach enlightenment, and perhaps even agnostics and atheists who have grown tired of the six narratives of violence and will welcome a hopeful alternative story from wherever it arises.

Christians who resist this possibility—that Jesus' gospel, rather than the Christian religion, is the hope of the world, and that Jesus and his gospel were gifts to the world and not just to one religion within it—perhaps need to reflect on our history and be chastened and humbled by our repeated habits of domination, revolution, purification, isolation, accumulation, and victimization. Perhaps that chastening and humility are another legacy waiting to be claimed from the tragic history of colonialism.

If the modern missionary movement was the unwitting accomplice of Spanish Catholic colonialism and British Protestant colonialism—two species in the genus of Euro-domination, it is not at all surprising that the term "missionary" itself has been tainted. Nor is it surprising that many have developed an aversion to all things missionary, as complicit in domination and violence. It would be sad, however, if this needed reassessment led to a foreclosure upon the possibility of a new era of post-colonial—and we could even say, anti-colonial—mission.

Such a new era of mission would not be framed by the flat linear narratives of colonial Christianity. Rather, it would spring from the rich, alternative, multidimensional narrative space known as Jesus' good news of the reigning of God, and from its native soil—the Jewish narratives of creation (in Genesis), liberation (in Exodus), and new creation or reconciliation (in Isaiah and the prophets).

Such a post-colonial missional movement would not be a restorationist attempt to repristinate mission, seeking to repudiate Christian history and return to an idealized "New Testament" gospel. Rather, it would seek at every moment to be both instructed and humbled by our history, never forgetting that we can't be protected from losing our way simply by using words like "Jesus," "kingdom," "God," and "gospel," or by extracting quotations from the New Testament, oblivious to the narrative purposes for which they have been extracted. Instructed by our past, and especially by its failures, this movement would never forget how "the neighbor" can be so easily dehumanized into "the other," and how, according to Jesus, if one wishes to encounter God, one must do so through the loving encounter with the stranger, the other, the outcast, the outsider, and the enemy.

For all the failures of the modern missionary movement, we can celebrate that it thrust some of "us" into the territory of "them," usually without weapons and usually with concrete demonstrations of love. In spite of collusion and complicity with alien, anti-gospel narratives, those us-them encounters then in many cases began to sow the seeds for the subversion of the alien narratives, making room for authentic gospel seeds to take root. We, who look back on the tragic failures of our ancestors, thus have the opportunity to seek to heal rather than repeat those failures. And that, no doubt, is an essential part of our post-colonial mission.

What will happen when the descendents of the colonizers and the descendents of the colonized together seek to live out the seventh story? These sage words adapted from Catholic missionary and missiologist Vincent Donovan provide the beginnings of an answer: "Do not leave others where they are, and do not try to bring them where you are, as beautiful as that place might seem to you. Rather, go with them to a place neither you nor they have ever been before."[2] That is the adventure of the seventh story, a journey upon a less-traveled way that leads to life, shalom, salaam, peace.

WORKS CITED

Donovan, Vincent J. *Christianity Rediscovered: An Epistle from the Masai*. 25th Anniversary Edition. London: Orbis, 1978.

McLaren, Brian D. *A New Kind of Christianity: Ten Questions that are Transforming the Faith*. New York: HarperOne, 2010.

———. *Everything Must Change: Jesus, Global Crises, and a Revolution of Hope*. Nashville: Thomas Nelson, 2007.

———. *The Secret Message of Jesus: Uncovering the Truth that Could Change Everything*. Nashville: Thomas Nelson, 2006.

———. *The Story We Find Ourselves In: Further Adventures of a New Kind of Christian*. San Francisco: Jossey-Bass, 2003.

---

2. Donovan, *Christianity Rediscovered*, xii–xiii.

Theological Education and Mission in Euro-American Institutions of Higher Learning

A Non-Western Reflection

Daniel Jeyaraj

A NUMBER OF DETAILED WORKS and essays have been published on the development of theological education in Euro-American institutions from 1910 until our current time. I would like to highlight only two representative works. Professor Olav G. Myklebust's writings provide a historical analysis of the relationship between theological education and missiology in Euro-American institutions from 1910 to 1989.[1] Secondly, Dr. Dietrich Werner and his team dealt with the sixth theme of Edinburgh 2010, namely Theological Education and Formation. His expertise in organizing team works has produced an insightful book that contains not only historical surveys of various types of theological education, but also gives useful case studies.[2]

---

1. Myklebust, *The Study of Missions*. These two volumes examine the development of mission studies in Euro-American theological institutions until 1950. For further development see Myklebust, "Missiology in Contemporary Theological Education," 87–107.

2. Werner, et. al., *Handbook of Theological Education*.

Without narrating or critiquing what others have written on theological education and mission in Euro-American institutions of higher learning, I wish to briefly address three themes: (1) manifestations and perceptions of Euro-American Christianity; (2) necessity of biblical literacy among students of theology; and (3) teacher-practitioners as living role models. I will review certain Euro-American causes that hinder the witness of my fellow Christian sisters and brothers in theological institutions and churches. I will place before you two suggestions that might help us to reverse the situation.

MANIFESTATIONS AND PERCEPTIONS OF EURO-AMERICAN CHRISTIANITY

The modern West European Protestant missionary heritage is now 304 years old. In 1706 it began with the first Lutheran missionary Bartholomäus Ziegenbalg (1682–1719) and the work of the Royal Danish-Halle Mission among the Tamil people in the Danish colony of Tranquebar, South India.[3] Yesterday Professor Dana Robert explained the origins of the Protestant missionary movement among Americans in and around Boston; it started with the establishment of the American Board of Commissioners for Foreign Missions in 1810. Thus, for 300 years Protestant missionaries have been going from their Euro-American countries and serving among non-western peoples. From there the number of Christians constantly grew—not so rapidly, but steadily and gradually. However, the number of Christians belonging to the institutional forms of Christianity in Euro-American contexts was decreasing.

CONCEPT AND REALITY OF CONVERSION

I wish to share with you some of my observations that I have gathered in Western Europe and in the United States. Our sisters and brothers in Western Europe and the United States have been good at financially supporting missionary work among non-western people. However, they are preoccupied with a Christendom mentality, mission as crossing geographical distances, and the violent experiences of their ancestors under

---

3. Jeyaraj, *Bartholomäus Ziegenbalg*.

Frankish, British, French, German, and Scandinavian rulers. These preoccupations prevent them from purposely engaging with the experiences, difficulties, and successes of non-western Christians. Their ancestors did not have the opportunity to freely choose their religious adherence, therefore some of them imposed their version of Christianity on the native peoples of the Americas or Africa. In doing so, they did not endorse the concept of personal religious conversion. Thus, Western Christians deprive themselves from cross-cultural learning. Additionally, they understand conversion in terms of imposition of political violence through military expeditions, colonialism, imperialism, social dislocation, economic depravity, cultural destruction, pacification of minds to make them unable to agitate, and proselytism in a sense of superficial change of religious identity for material benefits (such as education, medical help, relief during catastrophes, and employment).

The New Testament, however, teaches a different meaning of conversion. It is associated with the Greek concept of *metanoia* ("change of mind" resulting in new ways of thinking and living). Most Christians have often understood it as repentance (that is, remorse over past sins). The New Testament understanding of conversion implies that each human culture contains some elements that affirm and sustain life and some elements that deny and destroy life. Therefore Christians do not and cannot completely renounce their ancestral heritages, languages, traditions, cultural settings, and social habits. Instead they focus them towards the Lord Jesus Christ. They keep what is compatible with the teachings of Jesus Christ, renounce any cultural element that is demonic and injurious to human flourishing, and recast other elements that fit their new lifestyle. Culture as an organic entity implies change through additions, deletions, and modifications.

Any society that denies the possibility of conversion can become dictatorial and ultimately cause more damage than good. Conversion as new thinking and behaving has political, economic, and social consequences; while it is liberation for those who have been oppressed, it is bad news for the oppressors. Literature written by oppressors obviously blames the conversion of their subordinates. But the life stories of those who of their own freewill choose to become Christians tell a different story. They speak of liberation from oppression, regaining previously denied dignity and self-worth. Now they have a new approach to life, fellow human beings, creation, and their ancestral cultures. Religious communities that do not allow this freshness of life through conversion will experience a period of stagnation after which they will deteriorate gradually.

IGNORANCE OF INTERCULTURAL THEOLOGY

Euro-American theological educators compete with one another in publishing theological essays and monographs, flooding the market with their contributions. Most of them invariably operate within their own socio-cultural milieu because they are monolinguals. They use theological categories that are indebted to Greco-Roman ways of philosophical and legal thinking and living. They quote authors who agree with and differ from them; thus, in many ways, they recycle popular ideas. If they knew more than one language—especially a non-Euro-American language—they would be able to interact better with other literature. The possibility of cross-fertilization of ideas is more likely for educators who can learn from theological writings in languages such as Chinese, Hindi, Swahili, and Yoruba. While the Hispanic theologians in the United States can partially operate in Spanish, their thinking categories are indebted not to Mayan, Aztec, or other native cultures of Latin America, but to Greek and Latin. Theological literature in German, French, and English—mostly developed in academies and without any significant reference to real-life situations in parishes or societies—does not seem to provide a viable answer to halt the obvious decline of Christians in Euro-American contexts.

Euro-American theologians have written how the gospel should be preached to others and practiced by others. The large research libraries and archives in Euro-American theological institutions and mission agencies preserve countless documents on mission. Theological knowledge is available on the Internet, via mass media, and is even accessible with iPhones. Yet, young couples with children, students attending colleges, seminaries, and universities, and youth are often not in the churches. The grand church buildings with great history (and often with sizable endowments) do not attract these people. A sense of impasse, stagnation, and even resignation is prevalent.

If only theological educators incorporated mission literature into their curriculum and invited their students to creatively exegete them, all would benefit. These writings tell how certain translations and interpretations of the Bible have affected the lives of countless people in other parts of the world. They also illustrate how non-Christians faced and overcame difficult socio-cultural and economic-political issues. We need the help of each other to become aware of our failures, limitations, and opportunities in order to benefit from mutual and interdependent theological learning.

Jesus Christ was, after all, a West Asian. His socio-cultural milieu was Aramaic, Hebraic, and Greco-Roman. His parables are derived from nature, agriculture, and business. Euro-American industrialized societies seem to be far removed from the society that Jesus Christ and his apostles lived and worked in. Currently, societies that are similar to the ones in the New Testament abound in Sub-Saharan Africa, India, and other Asian countries. They live by agriculture and cattle breeding. They have not yet fallen prey to Euro-American types of extreme individualism. People in rural areas know and interact with each other. Their cosmologies include not only deities, angels, and saints, but also demons, malicious spirits, and departed ancestors. Practices such as animal sacrifices, witchcraft, and respect for elderly persons abound. Euro-American theologians who learn insights from non-western peoples can create new syntheses that can help theological students. Writings of missionaries also provide excellent insights into the worlds of non-western peoples.

INABILITY TO COPE WITH MILITANT SECULARISM

Euro-American secularism is secular and absolutist. The postmodern suspicion of metanarratives, carefulness to be politically correct, and obvious affirmation of multiculturalism are meant to belittle Christianity. It is really interesting that secularists who decry conversion to Jesus Christ silently affirm or indirectly welcome the conversion of their fellow citizens to Islam, Buddhism, Hinduism, and even to Paganism. They do not realize that any religion that is associated with politics, monetary wealth, immovable properties, and control of production and distribution of goods can become violent, absolutistic, and exclusive. Neither Islam, Buddhism, or Hinduism has been immune to this problem.

Additionally, the prolonged controversies over creationism and evolution, ordination of women for sacramental office, the legitimacy of homosexual people in church offices, and ethical scandals concerning certain clergy have polarized Christian denominations. Long existing interdenominational rivalries, competitions, and survival strategies have prevented church leaders from collaborating. These and other reasons have created a situation where people avoid belonging to an institutionalized church. Some have even proposed a model of "believing without belonging."[4] In this environment, many churches continue to lose members. Their theological models that were developed in the West and taught to students from Edinburgh 1910 to Boston 2010 have not been able to halt the decline. This situation should not be allowed to deteriorate into resignation, inactivity, and disappearance; such has occurred in many British cities where church buildings are being turned into Hindu temples, mosques, houses, movie theaters, furniture depots, shopping centers, and even into strip clubs. An important key to recovering and reclaiming Christianity among militant secularists lies in theological education that specializes in what it professes; namely, preparation of biblically well-informed pastors who are engaged in mission work.

NECESSITY OF BIBLICAL LITERACY AMONG STUDENTS OF THEOLOGY

In Euro-American countries the Bible is the most sought-after, but least read, book. It is available in all Euro-American languages and in many different versions. Those who have access to the Internet or an iPod can study the Bible in these different languages and versions. Bible societies and various mission agencies (such as Scripture Union) focus their attention on spreading biblical literacy among their contemporaries; yet biblical illiteracy abounds among people, even among those who are in the habit of attending Sunday worship services. It is not difficult to discover the reason(s) for growing biblical illiteracy.

The basis for Christian theological education is the Bible and its allied subjects: history of Christianity, systematic theology, practical theology (including missiology), and the study of religions (including new religious movements). Sound biblical knowledge provides interpretive

---

4. Davie, *Religion in Britain*.

insights to understand the meaning and implications of a particular biblical text. This simple truth is the hardest for Christian friends in theological institutions. Nowadays it is not uncommon among theological educators and students that while they know the books of the Bible in order, they do not know the key data and teachings of each book. Many of them do not have the habit of reading and meditating on the Bible. Their busy schedules and commitment to simply cover the subject or to complete assignments within the allotted time, for example, occupy their minds and hearts.

Without detailed knowledge of the Bible, both theological educators and students cannot understand what Christian mission should or could mean in their situation. They might use the word "mission" because nowadays it is used by everyone from military generals to sales persons. For Christians, this Latin word (derived from *missio*, "to send") can embody different ideas and meanings that have nothing to do with biblical meanings and values in general, and with Jesus Christ and his cross in particular. Like social workers, they can engage either in preventive or curative activities among the homeless, the unemployed, and battered women and men. These activists often refer to Francis of Assisi's famous statement that one should preach the gospel of Jesus Christ by living it, and only use words if necessary. Seen from this perspective, Christian philanthropy does not really differ from the good works done by other social activists. This dominant worldview does not require a person to get acquainted with the Bible and its teaching, or the church and Christian traditions, but only with the goodwill of human beings. I am amazed by the goodwill activities of average people in the United States. Their concern for the welfare of people in other parts of the world is truly praiseworthy.

Having mentioned the unparalleled philanthropic work done by social activists in the Western Hemisphere, I must point out the pervasive biblical illiteracy among Euro-American Christians. This illiteracy is disturbing and it invariably leads Christians to forget their distinctiveness and thus lose their Christian identity. A significant number of Christian pastors in Euro-American churches do not take the Bible seriously. They do not improve their knowledge of the Bible. Their indifference to the Bible and its total teaching does not help them to educate their congregants in biblical knowledge. Thus, even the small number of people who regularly attend Sunday worship services do not have the necessary linguistic and cognitive tools to articulate their Christian faith in an intelligent manner. As a result, they are not in a position to describe the "reasons for the hope" that they have (1 Pet 3:15).

I am fully aware that there are Christian pastors who take the Bible seriously and teach it regularly—they are in the minority. I laud them for their faithfulness and courage to adhere to the Bible in an age that seeks to wean them away from it. However, many Christian pastors and their congregations seem to have fallen prey to this temptation. Let me mention two contrasting examples. In August 2010, I visited a Baptist church in a suburb of Chennai. On the weekends, young students gathered in this church to read the books of Kings and Chronicles. They told me that the youth from all Baptist churches in Chennai and its vicinity would participate in a public quiz program; this team had won first prize for the past three years, and this year they also wanted to win it. On a Sunday I was asked to preach in this church. Even before I finished referring to a verse in the Bible, two or three persons stood up to read it aloud. They had read the Bible so many times that they knew the arrangement of the books and their chapters. The biblical literacy of this congregation astonished me. Their efforts to commit the biblical verses to memory and to recite them in times of joy and sorrow are truly great. They are not theological students, but they relate to day-to-day occurrences from biblical perspectives. Their pastor studied in a theological school that emphasized the importance of studying the biblical texts.

A week later I sat in an Anglican Church in Great Britain; all members of this church are well-educated people who work in various high-level companies. Some of them conduct Bible studies, and some of them participate in an Alpha Course. But the priest has great difficulty in educating the congregants in biblical knowledge. Before every message he spends a lot of time explaining the background information of the text at hand. Even then, the people do not know or understand what is going on around them. They must be asked to turn to a specific page number in their pew Bibles; if they are left to turn to a specific book or an epistle, they do not know where to find it. Their biblical illiteracy astonished me.

Another example from a Christian congregation in the United States can illuminate the consequences of biblical illiteracy further. Recently, I participated in a worship service on a Sunday. Two members of the congregation came forward and read the prescribed biblical passages. First they announced the page number of the assigned readings in the pew Bibles; even then most people did not care to take the Bible in their hands and follow the readings. After the readers returned to their seats, the preacher came forward. His speech had very little to do with the biblical passages; he spoke about politics and the recent rallies in Washington D.C. (conducted by leading comedians). This pastor somehow did not realize that people came to the church not to listen to a political speech—they could get the same or even better information from newspapers, television, or the Internet. He missed an opportunity to educate those people theologically and to equip them to respond to the needs of everyday life in a responsible manner. People who do not find necessary spiritual food for their life do not come to church.

Additionally, I have noticed how preachers use selective readings of certain biblical texts that seem to affirm their preconceived ideas. Passages such as the Exodus narratives and the Nazareth Manifesto are used endlessly to highlight the need for socio-economic justice and practical service to the needy. The Exodus story is powerful, indeed. It transformed the life of my mother when she first heard it in an evangelistic meeting in 1972 in Dindigul, a small town in Tamil Nadu, south India. She was a daily waged worker; the assurance that God listened to the cry of his people in misery, came down to deliver them from oppression, personally led them during the day as a pillar of cloud and during the night as a pillar of light, and enabled them to settle down in a good place led to the conversion of my mother. Her changed attitude impacted her life positively. She no longer worshipped the Seven Virgin Spirits that she venerated earlier, and her piety became intense. Her change in life orientation strengthened many people whom she knew. Her personal liberation had social implications. She could not cause any systemic change in the village, but became a symbol of strength to many people—including myself—in many ways. She helped me get out of poverty and enabled me to enlarge the horizon of my knowledge and experience.

Liberation in Euro-American contexts has a different meaning. Much has been written about liberation from systemic evils engrained in the dynamics of politics, the economy, and broader society. Even after about fifty years of vigorous rhetoric about liberation and consciousness-building activities, the gap between the rich and the poor paradoxically increases. The people to whom liberation was preached are still in poverty and oppression. Even the few people who courageously spoke against the brutality of oppression were eliminated (e.g., Archbishop Oscar Romero [1917–80]). Euro-American people could do little or nothing to stop unequal trade treaties or arms races of their governments. Gradually, Christian pastors have changed the focus of their social activities. Sermons on God's love for human beings abound, especially for the homeless and the unemployed. Representatives of countless Christian congregations (for example, in Greater Boston) regularly distribute free meals to the poor and the unemployed. Their participation in the Common Cathedral is impressive. Yet, at best they treat only the outward symptoms of a sick society that has forgotten its Christian values and heritages. Many families are broken. Abuse of the social benefits provided by the state and other private organizations continues. Public trust has noticeably decreased. Insurance companies benefit from every kind of social sickness that torments people. Social stress is mounting. As a result, even some knowledgeable preachers who loudly proclaim love and service for others are unable to live in a relationship of love and service within their own household. They are either divorced or live as single parents. Their personal lives are a mess. People who listen to them do not take them seriously. The sermons on liberation do not address the causes of social problems in individuals, families, societies, and countries. They have a "massage effect" on their listeners, making them temporarily feel good. As individuals they are not motivated to mend their relationships through forgiveness, love, and covenanted commitments. As collective citizens, they are not encouraged to speak against the systemic injustices that their policy-makers decide and execute in terms of education, unequal trade agreements, taxes, weapon use and sale, and ecological violence. Consequently, people are unable to cope with uncertainties and ambiguities in life. Christian theologians have tried to address these problems through "contextual" and other theologies. The practical effect of these theologies, however, seems to be extremely limited.

It is not the first time in history that society faces monumental challenges. It is also not the first time that Christians have tried to address them from a biblical perspective. A survey of the history of world Christianity provides us many examples of Christian leaders who took biblical teachings seriously and ventured to transform their society. In 1675-76, Philip Jacob Spener (1635–1705),[5] father of German

---

5. Wallmann, *Der Pietismus*; Albrecht-Birkner, *Hoffnung besserer Zeiten*.

Pietism, published his famous *Pia Desideria*.[6] He did not stop deploring the pathetic situation of German society or his Lutheran church. He proposed six practical means to remedy the situation. He encouraged theological educators to move the Bible from its peripheral position to the center of theological education and use it extensively to shape the attitudes and character of their students. When they dealt with differences of opinion and interpretations of biblical passages, they were to be gentle with each other. It was the duty and privilege of theological educators to demonstrate to their students that Christianity does not consist of mere knowledge, but in practicing it in a tangible manner. For this purpose he initiated several *ecclesiolæ in ecclesia* ("little churches within the church"). The members of these small groups within the Lutheran churches, also known as the *Konventikel*, attended the regular morning worship services on Sundays; in the evenings they gathered together as small groups to study the Bible, to deepen their fellowship, to pray for and to support the mission of the church. They were led by the *Prediger* ("preachers") who were expected to be living examples of what they preached. The relationship between these small groups and the state Lutheran churches had many facets, from strained negotiations to cordial cooperation. In any case, the *Landeskirchliche Gemeinschaften* ("fellowships of the state church"), as they are called nowadays, serve the seedbed for local and overseas mission activities that are inseparably associated with their teacher-practitioners (based on the theological conviction of the priesthood of all baptized Christians).

TEACHER-PRACTITIONERS AS LIVING ROLE MODELS

The fifth practical means that Philip Jacob Spener proposed for church renewal is concerned with training theological students in universities. It contains three parts: first, he proposed that university professors support and accompany theological students in their efforts to understand theology and practical works. Second, he advised theological students to form small groups to discuss biblical texts and piety. Third, he encouraged professors to introduce theological discussions with their students

---

6. Spener, *Pia Desideria*. For a modern print, see *Pia Desideria: Umkehr in die Zukunft* (Giessen: Brunnen, 1995). For an English edition, see *Pia Desideria* (Philadelphia: Fortress, 1964).

on matters of interest in which they take a personal stance. Over time, several theological faculties in German universities established *Konvikt*, hostels for theological students under the care of a professor of theology. Spener recommended that professors of theology develop their teaching materials—including books—to, on the one hand, glorify God, and on the other edify people in Christian faith and service. He reminded them that the "kingdom of God is not in words, but in power" (1 Cor 4:20). Spener viewed professors of theology as both mentors and parents. The teaching and lifestyle of teachers would have a positive impact on the ministerial formation of their students. In this context it is understandable that some of Spener's friends founded the first Protestant mission enterprise, the Royal Danish-Halle Mission (1705–1845), also known as the Tranquebar Mission. These friends included theologians and pastors such as Franz Julius Lütkens (1650–1712), Laurentius Gensichen (1674–1742), Johann Lysisus (1675–1716), and Joachim Lange (1670–1744). Lütkens and Lange were involved in selecting Ziegenbalg as the first Lutheran missionary. Ziegenbalg himself knew Spener and had received a study scholarship from him. Thus, active Bible-based Pietism among theological educators and students produced the first missionary movement. This model would be repeated in the history of Protestant missionary movements.

When I began my theological studies, I was privileged to learn under Albert Davis, who was both an educator and missionary at heart (working with an Indian mission agency). Later, I was appointed as a lecturer on the history of Christianity and had the joy of teaching a few Indian missionaries who were many years my senior. They had many years of pioneer experience in establishing Christian congregations in various parts of India. Their mission agency sent them to seminary so they could gain additional insight into what was going on in the rest of the world. I wanted to check the theoretical principles of my teaching against their practical wisdom. Therefore I went to their homes in the evenings and asked them what they thought about the relevance of my class lectures for actual missionary work in Indian villages, towns, and cities. I would revise my lecture notes accordingly and present them to the class for discussion and verification. Thus, from the beginning I had the opportunity to combine theological education and mission.

When I began to teach in Euro-American theological institutions of higher education, I experienced a separation between academic studies of theology, popularly categorized under *Wissenschaft* (the intellectual pursuit as a "science"), and student's practical engagement informed by theology. After they complete their formal academic studies in a university, they would begin their practical training. By this time they would have little or nothing to do with their theological educators. Instead, their ecclesial officers begin teaching them the art of managing church properties, investing endowments, balancing incomes and expenditures, managing business meetings, and familiarizing themselves with the most recent government regulations regarding interpersonal relationships. A pastor's duty resembles the duty of a chief executive officer of a business institution. Thus, their theological education is separated from their actual pastoral work.

I have noticed that most theological educators in seminaries and divinity schools do not have sufficient pastoral or mission experience. Some of them do not attend any church services, nor do they even belong to a church. Yet they teach theology and mission; their intellectual pursuit deals with theoretical concepts and evaluations often measured against the criteria established by anti-Christian, Euro-American scholars. Therefore, their teaching on the Bible and mission remains highly theoretical. Even their examinations of church- and mission-related case studies are not balanced with practical insights. They believe that their conscious distance from the church and its mission makes them impartial teachers. Their views, observations, and critiques of church and its mission should not be taken lightly because they can detect in them certain elements that can easily escape the attention of a practicing insider. But they cannot be role models for students in theology and mission because mission is not limited only to theories alone, but it is extended into practice.

It is a fact that most theological educators are monolinguals. They can speak and write in American or British English. They might know Hebrew, Greek, Latin, or Spanish. But their academic discussion partners are predominantly Euro-American. They seldom incorporate into their syllabi materials produced by non-western theological scholars and practitioners. In this way they deprive themselves and their students an opportunity to learn from insights and experiences of world Christianity. As a result, they are unable to address the concerns raised by non-Euro-American peoples in their midst. It would be great if at least some theological educators would deal with theological literature in Arabic, Chinese, Hindi, or Swahili, however meager or non-academic they might seem to be. In this manner they would soon realize that Euro-American theological education should not be kept parochial, and their questions—often posed by their civil society—are not the normative concerns of the entire world. They would also see how theological educators and students in other parts of the world solve problems and bear witness to Jesus Christ in their everyday lives in the midst of poverty and religious pluralism. The focus on world Christianity-oriented learning would help theological educators and students in Euro-American theological institutions to recognize the true fact that the church is much bigger than they actually think. They are privileged to belong to the church as the worldwide body of Christ that is alive, active, and increasing. Euro-American congregations can be rejuvenated by a new confidence in the power of the global church.

Bible-centered Christian theological education is imperative for meaningful interreligious living and sharing. Almost all Muslims value the Qur'an greatly. They will hesitate to speak with Christians who do not take the Bible seriously or mishandle it even in the name of academic freedom. Most Hindus and people of other religions derive inspiration from their sacred scriptures and from interpretations of their spiritual masters. In this context it becomes essential for theological educators to not only know the Bible and its teachings, but to live by it. Once I met a Muslim taxi driver in Malaysia. When he came to know that I was a Christian, he began to recite several Qur'anic verses that talk about Mother Mary and Jesus Christ. His memory power was so sharp that he could easily quote large sections of the Qur'an. The existence of non-Christians in our societies requires us to know our sacred text—as well as the texts of other religious traditions—so that we can guard ourselves not only against their misuse, but also against their abuse. It is not true that Christians alone misused and abused the Bible to conquer other peoples, subjugate women, and silence people in the name of God. Christians, however, should be ready to acknowledge these failures and repent. It is also true for people of other faiths, whether they are Jews, Muslims, Buddhists, or Hindus. They are aware how their politicians, military commanders, economists, and fundamentalists have misused and abused their sacred texts. Therefore, it is important for all Christian theological educators to be familiar with the sacred scriptures and histories, of other faiths and ideologies. Their careful examination will help us to transcend unguarded emotionalism and unfounded romanticism regarding peoples of non-Christian faiths and ideologies. In addition, they will help lead us to evaluate the missing links between the ideals in their scriptural teachings and interpretations on the one hand and their actual practices on the other. Only then will Christian theological educators and students be able to meaningfully relate to people of non-Christian faiths and ideologies living in multicultural societies. In this context it is worth remembering the sober words of Friedrich Max Müller (1823–1900), stating that a person who knows only one religion does not know any religion at all.[7]

In our efforts to engage with people of other world religions, it is right to ask what has kept these religions alive, active, and growing. As far as Hinduism is concerned one can easily find the answer in their *gurukula*s ("the house of a guru"), *ashram*s (a place where a guru leads his disciples in theology and service), temples, and homes. In a *gurukula* the priests-to-be live with their teacher, learn from his oral teachings, watch him perform liturgies and sacrifices, and imitate his lifestyle. In an *ashram* the disciples live under the guidance of a spiritual master and engage in social work. Spirituality and practical service are inseparably interwoven. Temples are places not only of spiritual worship, but also of festivals, social gatherings, public engagements, and learning. Life in the temple does not know the difference between intellectual theology and practical life; they are seamlessly interconnected. Each Hindu house has a separate place where they keep the images of their deities and offer them worship. These four institutions together have preserved the lifeline of Hinduism for over 5,000 years. Similarly, Christian theological educators and students can learn to combine their teaching and religious practices in their theological institutions, churches, and homes. After all, biblical literacy that begins in Christian homes and continues in Sunday schools should be carried on and intensified in theological institutions of higher learning. The changing student scenario in American theological institutions, however, poses a great challenge. Most of the students in mainline seminaries and theological schools are commuters; they just come to classes and return to their homes far away. Some of them complete their courses online without ever seeing their teachers. In this case, it is important for theological educators and students to organize a mandatory period to meet each other in person.

7. Müller, *Introduction to the Science of Religion*, 11f.

I have met several students who have benefited greatly from theological educators who know the Bible in its entirety, critique it in an informed manner, and bring out practical implications. The practical relevance of the Bible is not always clearly definable. Among the options that are available, theological educators and students can choose the best alternative and approach it from a theological perspective. People as living beings react and respond to practical issues in certain ways; sometimes their reactions are unpredictable. Therefore theological educators and students should be prepared for surprises, setbacks, and disappointments. Instant success is not guaranteed, yet their informed theological orientation counts. They will learn from their achievements and failures, and press on further. By contrast, if theological educators make fun of the Bible, based on their perception and interpretation of higher biblical criticism, their students are troubled and confused. When these students become pastors or leaders of Christian congregations, they are unable to guide people spiritually and theologically.

Theological educators must point out the textual variations of the biblical texts not only in Hebrew, Aramaic, and Greek manuscripts, but also in various vernacular translations.[8] These difficulties should not be glossed over. The knowledge and acknowledgement of these difficulties shows that we are dealing with an ancient text that has been handed down to us through countless generations of scholars and others. The insights that we gain collectively will remain partial by making use of the best scholarship and tools that are currently at our disposal. Often, things that we do not know do not trouble us as much as those things that we know well and understand. As biblical scholars continue to unravel textual difficulties and suggest various interpretations, we can allow ourselves to be guided by the teachings of the texts that we know for sure and understand well. In this regard, we can perhaps refer to Professor Andrew Walls' teaching on the "the indigenizing principle" and "the pilgrim principle" of a church.[9] He writes of the indigenizing principle as the day-to-day activities of a local congregation in its time and space. The pilgrim principle, on the other hand, encourages the local congregation to become what God wants them to become. Similarly, biblical scholars continue to bring out new insights from the textual

---

8. For a collection of these difficulties and suggested solutions see Archer, *New International Encyclopedia*.

9. Walls, "The Gospel as Prisoner and Liberator of Culture," 7f.

composition, transmission, and preservation of the Bible, and thus expand the horizon of our biblical knowledge (the pilgrim principle). In doing so, we can safely operate with the text of the Bible that we know, understand, and interpret in its entirety (the indigenizing principle).

Theological educators who have taken the biblical texts seriously have often played an important role in the mission of the church. I would like to draw our attention to August Hermann Francke (1663-1727), who was a trusted friend and admirer of Philip Jacob Spener. In 1693 he instructed his congregation in Glaucha, a suburb of the city of Halle (Saale) in Saxony, Germany to properly deal with the Bible as God's word and to appropriate it for their life as individuals, families, and as a congregation.[10] Francke was a Hebraist before he became a professor of theology (1698) at the newly founded Frederick University (1694).[11] He began to focus on biblical theology and practical theology (without neglecting systematic theology, polemics, and Aristotelian philosophy). He encouraged the preachers, educators, and teachers whom he had been training to earnestly look for practical ways of using and living the theological principles that they were learning.[12] He developed the concept of *tätige Nächstenliebe* (love for neighbor in action). His love for the biblical texts in their original languages led him to require his students to read through the Hebrew Bible at least once a year and the New Testament in Greek at least thrice a year. In 1720, his co-worker and successor Johann Heinrich Michaelis (1668-1738) published a critical, annotated text of the Hebrew Bible that was the fruit of a team work of Pietist theological educators in Halle (Saale).[13] Thus, his teachings laid a foundation not only for pietistic theological education and mission, but also for various kinds of philanthropy, first in Halle (Saale), and then in different parts of the world (including Tranquebar and Chennai, India; Philadelphia,

---

10. Peschke, *August Hermann Francke*, 74-91.

11. In 1817 this university and the Leucorea University (founded in 1502 by Elector Friedrich the Wise), where the reformers Martin Luther (1483-1546) and Philip Melanchthon (1497-1560) worked, joined together and became known as the United Friedrich University. On 10 November, 1933 it got its present name: Martin Luther University Halle-Wittenberg. For further history, see www.international.uni-halle.de/university/history/ (accessed November 9, 2010). I am proud to be an alumnus of this university.

12. Wallmann, *Der Pietismus*, 73.

13. Wallmann, "Scriptural Understanding and Interpretation," 906-25. See also Rengstorf, "Johann Heinrich Michaelis und seine Biblia Hebraica von 1720," 15-64.

USA; and St. Petersburg, Russia). Some of his students and followers like the abovementioned Ziegenbalg, Johann Ernest Gründler (1677–1720), Benjamin Schultze (1689–1760) and several others became missionaries and translators of the Bible into Tamil (1728), Telugu (1740s), and other languages. Count Nicholas von Zinzendorf (1700–1760), one of his famous students, would play an important role in the establishment of the Moravian church and its mission activities in different parts of the world. Zinzendorf's followers would have direct impact on the English Methodists (like John Wesley) and Baptists (like William Carey).[14] These and other role models manifest the inseparable link between Bible-centered theological education and Christian mission.

CONCLUSION

Christian theological education has to do with being and becoming. Christians exist in their congregations, yet they are constantly becoming into those whom God wants them to be. The exhibition entitled *Vatican Splendors: A Journey through Faith and Art*, currently held in the Senator John Heinz History Center in Pittsburgh, illustrates the relationship between Christian being and becoming. It presents the apostle Peter as the bishop who takes care of the sacramental and administrative needs of the local people within the institutionalized form of a church. Simultaneously, it portrays the apostle Paul as the missionary who focuses his attention on inviting people outside who do not yet belong to the church. This exhibition states that both Peter and Paul together are the inseparable twin pillars of the church that is indigenized and is constrained to go out. This bishop-missionary principle is a good example for Christian theological educators and students.

The apostle Paul became a model for his disciples, such as Timothy and Titus. He urged his readers to imitate him (1 Cor 4:16) in his mission. He reminded his Christian readers to function as living epistles who are being read by all people (2 Cor 3:2). Likewise, the writer of the letter to the Hebrews (13:7) advises his readers to remember their leaders, who spoke the word of God to them. He urged them to consider the outcome of their way of life and to imitate his faith. I believe that biblical

---

14. For additional information on the impact of the Tranquebar Mission see Jeyaraj, "Mission Reports from South India, 21–42.

literacy and teacher-practitioners as living role models can inspire the missionary activity of every church.

Let me conclude this lecture by referring to a teaching of the Tamil poet Tiruvalluvar on *kalvi* ("education").[15] He describes the quality and purpose of education as follows: *karkka kacadara-k karpavai karrapin nirka atarku-t taha* (Tirukkural, 391). This short poem can be interpreted as follows: "By clarifying all doubts we should learn flawlessly that which we intend to learn. After we have learnt it, we should live accordingly." Thus, this poem reiterates the fact that our lives must manifest the good things that we have learned. Theological education is meant to produce meaningful and fruitful lives.

WORKS CITED

Albrecht-Birkner, Veronika. *Hoffnung besserer Zeiten: Philipp Jacob Spener und die Geschichte des Pietismus*. Halle/Saale: Franckeschen Stiftungen, 2005.

Archer, Gleason L. *New International Encyclopedia of Bible Difficulties Based on the NIV and the NASB*. Grand Rapids: Zondervan, 1982.

Blackburn, Stuart. "The Legend of Valluvar and Tamil Literary History." *Modern Asian Studies* 34.2 (2000) 449–82.

Cutler, Norman. "Interpreting Tirukkural: The Role of Commentary in the Creation of a Text." *Journal of American Oriental Society* 112.4 (1992) 549.

Davie, Grace. *Religion in Britain since 1945: Believing without Belonging*. Oxford: Blackwell, 1994.

Jeyaraj, Daniel. *Bartholomäus Ziegenbalg: The Father of Modern Protestant Mission: An Indian Assessment*. New Delhi: Indian Society for Promoting Christian Knowledge and Gurukul Lutheran Theological College, 2006.

———. "Mission Reports from South India and Their Impact on the Western Mind: The Tranquebar Mission of the Eighteenth Century." In *Converting Colonialism: Visions and Realities in Mission History, 1706–1914*, edited by Dana Lee Robert, 21–42. Grand Rapids: Eerdmans, 2008.

Müller, Max Friedrich. *Introduction to the Science of Religion: Four Lectures Delivered at the Royal Institution, Two Essays on False Analogies and the Philosophy of Mythology*. London: Longmans, 1873.

Myklebust, Olav Guttorm. "Missiology in Contemporary Theological Education." *Mission Studies* 7.12 (1989) 87–107.

———. *The Study of Missions in Theological Education: An Historical Inquiry into the Place of World Evangelisation in Western Protestant Ministerial Training*. 2 vols. Oslo: Forlaget Land og Kirke, 1955, 1957.

---

15. Modern scholarship assumes that Tiruvalluvar lived in the fifth or sixth century A.D. For further details see Cutler, "Interpreting Tirukkural," 549. For his identity, see Blackburn, "The Legend of Valluvar," 449–82.

Peschke, Erhard. *August Hermann Francke: Werke in Auswahl*. Berlin: Evangelische, 1969.
Rengstorf, K. H. "Johann Heinrich Michaelis und seine Biblia Hebraica von 1720." In *Zentren der Aufklärung: I: Halle: Aufklärung und Pietismus*, edited by Norbert Hinske, 15-64. Heidelberg: Schneider, 1989.
Spener, Philipp Jacob. *Pia Desideria: Oder Herzliches Verlangen nach Gottgefälliger Besserung der wahren Evangelsichen Kirchen/sampt einigen dahin einfältigen abzweckenden Christlichen Vorschlägen*. Frankfurt am Main: Zunner, 1676.
———. *Pia Desideria*. Philadelphia: Fortress, 1964.
———. *Pia Desideria: Umkehr in die Zukunft*. Giessen: Brunnen, 1995.
Wallmann, Johannes. *Der Pietismus*. Göttingen: Vandenhoeck & Ruprecht, 2005.
———. "Scriptural Understanding and Interpretation in Pietism." In *Hebrew Bible/Old Testament: The History of Its Interpretation: II: From the Renaissance to the Enlightenment*, edited by Magne Sæbø, 902-95. Göttingen: Vandenhoeck & Ruprecht, 2008.
Walls, Andrew F. "The Gospel as Prisoner and Liberator of Culture." In *The Missionary Movement in Christian History: Studies in the Transmission of Faith*, 3-15. Maryknoll, NY: Orbis, 1996.
Werner, Dietrich, David Esterline, Namsoon Kang, and Joshva Raja, eds. *The Handbook of Theological Education in World Christianity: Theological Perspectives, Ecumenical Trends, Regional Surveys*. Oxford: Regnum, 2010.

PART III

Student Perspectives

10

The Student Paper Workshops of 2010Boston

Travis L. Myers

THE REALITIES NOTED BY the 2010Boston theme, the "changing contours of world mission and Christianity," were most clearly and broadly on display through the student paper presentation component of the conference. The workshop sessions on Friday and Saturday (coordinated by Br. Larry Whitney, chaplain for community life at Boston University) were the venue provided for collaborative reflection upon the eight transversal themes, with professors from the Boston Theological Institute (BTI) serving as moderators for each workshop.[1] A variety of interests and concerns were reflected in the thirty-six papers presented, such as: the many ambiguities, complex dynamics, and local implications of globalization; ecological crises and Christian responsibilities toward creation; the contested meaning and value of short-term mission (or "Christian service") trips; the liberation and restorative care of women and children in sex slavery; and the appropriate theological impetuses and practical modes for interreligious dialogue, evangelism, and disciple-making activities (including catechesis, sacramental theologies, and education for mission). More context-specific studies included topics like emergent/missional liturgical forms among Anglicans in "post-Christian" England; post-conflict reconciliation initiatives in Colombia; and student movements for Christian mission in China.

---

1. See Appendix I for the complete conference schedule, including the list of student presenters and BTI faculty moderators.

Students presented work from different academic disciplines (including history, biblical studies, theology, philosophy, sociology, and demography), with most of the studies being interdisciplinary to some degree. Several students also exhibited the creative and ecumenical incorporation or synthesis of resources from theological traditions other than their own. In addition to BTI schools, students who either presented papers or participated in responsive dialogue during the workshops came from a variety of academic institutions, such as Yale Divinity School (New Haven, CT), Pittsburgh Theological Seminary, Palmer Theological Seminary (Philadelphia, PA), Westminster Theological Seminary (Philadelphia, PA), Asbury Theological Seminary (Wilmore, KY), Fuller Theological Seminary (Pasadena, CA), Luther Theological Seminary (St. Paul, MN), Trinity Evangelical Divinity School (Deerfield, IL), and Wake Forest University (Winston-Salem, NC). International students from these schools originated from nations such as Germany, Japan, Korea, China, Taiwan, Indonesia, and India. Therefore, as evidenced by the regions of the world and theological traditions represented, the issues in and for pastoral ministry raised, and the global concerns addressed, the students and their papers—more than any other component of the conference—represented the current shape of world Christianity and Christian mission.

This, of course, was a fitting reality and an aspect of the conference intended by its planners. In the first plenary address, Dana Robert demonstrated the critical, catalytic place of students in movements of Christian mission from the earliest cusp of the modern era. "Young people try to change the world," she stated. "When the disciplines of piety and study converge in the social milieu of student life[2] then movements to change the world result."[3] She recounted as examples the Society of Jesus, John Wesley's Oxford Holiness Club (later becoming Methodism), and the "Haystack" prayer meetings of Williams College and Andover Theological Seminary (eventuating in the American Board of Commissioners for Foreign Missions).

---

2. That is, a group of individuals experiencing together the idealistic and energetic pursuit of God's purpose for their lives, constant intellectual stimulation in gaining new knowledge about the world, and the encounter of other cultures and peoples by meeting international students.

3. See Robert's chapter in this volume.

Robert even asserted that the 1910 Edinburgh conference would have been impossible "without the rich history of student mission movements behind it . . ."[4] Brian Stanley has argued elsewhere the indebtedness of Edinburgh 1910, both in its very occurrence and in its style and ethos, to the interdenominational and transatlantic student mission movements originating in the late nineteenth century.[5] Stanley also notes that several students present at Edinburgh 1910 as ushers or stewards later became well-known theologians and church leaders.[6] The fact that many of the students who presented papers at 2010Boston had been involved already in pastoral ministry, the theological education of others, and/or leadership in cross-cultural mission was evident in the content of their presentations. This previous engagement with the global church also contributed to the robust way in which the student component represented the global church at the conference. In this volume, Gina Bellofatto points out that 2010Boston was the only one of the four widely publicized centennial celebrations[7] (with Tokyo, Cape Town, and Edinburgh) to make student contributions a core part of the planning and actual event process.[8] Perhaps a future archbishop or theological school president was among us as a student in November 2010!

The following five papers were chosen to represent the student paper workshop component of 2010Boston. Some of the BTI faculty members who moderated workshops recommended the "best" presentations from their sessions, and the editorial team added to this initial list of candidates a few others from our own survey of the papers. There were a number of exceptional papers that qualified for consideration but are not included here. We finally selected these five particular papers for their originality, creativity, scholarship, and readability, as well as the various specific "contours" of world mission and Christianity reflected by their respective topics. In addition, this set of student authors does provide a somewhat representative (though by nature limited) sample of

---

4. See Robert's chapter in this volume.

5. Stanley, *World Missionary Conference*, 6–9, 88–90. See also Kerr and Ross, *Edinburgh 2010*, 5–6 on John R. Mott's influence on Edinburgh 1910.

6. Stanley, *World Missionary Conference*, 6–7; Cf. Bevans, "From Edinburgh to Edinburgh," 3.

7. For example, Winter, "Global Cross-Cultural Mission Collaboration"; and "Spotlight: The Future(s) of Missions."

8. See Bellofatto's chapter in this volume.

the institutional, ecclesial/denominational, disciplinary, vocational, geographic, and ethnic diversity of the three dozen students who presented papers at 2010Boston.

"FROM AMONG HER OWN CHILDREN": AFRICAN AMERICANS AND THE EVANGELIZATION OF AFRICA IN THE NINETEENTH CENTURY

Mary Cloutier is a PhD candidate (Intercultural Studies) at Trinity Evangelical Divinity School and a former missionary (1999–2001) with the Christian and Missionary Alliance in Burkina Faso and Gabon. Her contribution to 2010Boston, a retrieval of the lives and ministries of three nineteenth-century female African-American missionaries to Africa, is an exemplary case of the "new historiography."[9] Cloutier recovers the missionary agency of three women marginalized in both life and memory, considered alter and subordinate by their white American missionary co-laborers and neglected by traditional histories of mission. Cloutier constructs the brief biographies from a close examination of mission reports, magazine articles, biographies of male associates, unpublished personal correspondence, and interviews with descendants. She brings to the fore the fact that these African-American women were considered "ethnic others" by both their missionary colleagues and the Africans of their respective host cultures. The biographies are set against the backdrop of an introductory survey of various arguments made in the nineteenth century for the viability and advantages of African-American missionaries to Africa. Cloutier notes a decline in the number of African-American overseas missionaries in the early to mid-twentieth century and proposes theories to explain it (all involving black responses to racism in the United States). Her frequent employment of the original voices of her subjects may prove disturbing, though illuminating, to readers in "post-racial" Western settings.

---

9. See the editor's introduction and contributor essays in Shenk, *Enlarging the Story*.

DISCIPLES IN MISSION: EVANGELIZATION, LIBERATION, AND A "THEOLOGY OF NEIGHBOR"

Marcus Mescher is pursuing a PhD in Theology and Education at Boston College's School of Theology and Ministry. His concentration on Christian discipleship draws from several years of ministry to high school and college students, especially through service programs and international immersion trips. While an undergraduate student at Marquette University, he spent four years working as a youth minister in the Archdiocese of Milwaukee. In his paper, Mescher primarily follows the theological project of Gustavo Gutiérrez while interacting with other contemporary commentators and theologians to present a "potent" reading of Jesus's parable of the good Samaritan (Luke 10:25–37) that takes seriously the biblical text and remains in interlocution with the Thomistic tradition. A crucial turn in the argument is the observation that the parable shifts the meaning of "neighbor" from object to subject; the neighbor is not "a receptacle" of mercy but rather "one who proactively reaches out with compassion." Mescher works from an interpretation of the parable to construct a "theology of neighbor" that entails generous solidarity, reciprocal friendship, and community-building commitments with persons on the socio-economic margins of society toward whom Christians are called to intentionally move. The paper suggestively calls into question the possible prejudices, presumptions, and "limit-questions" that relatively wealthy Christians might bring to their mission endeavors in a globalized world (and even to their relationship with God).

DO-IT-YOURSELF MISSIONS: THE RISE OF INDEPENDENT FAITH-BASED ORGANIZATIONS AND THE CHANGING CONTOURS OF MISSIONS

Eva Pascal taught at McGilvary School of Divinity in Chiang Mai, Thailand (2006–10) before beginning a PhD in Religious Studies at Boston University. In her paper, Pascal sets forth socio-cultural, religious, and political developments as well as theological factors during the past two and half centuries that have given rise to the contemporary proliferation of independent faith-based organizations (FBOs) engaged cross-culturally in relief and development work. She demonstrates the continuity of this more recent phenomenon with the historical trajectory of evangelical Protestant voluntarism in world mission, the emergence of the paradigm of "development" in international relations after World War II, and the increase of non-governmental organizations (NGO's) in general since the end of the Cold War. Pascal then presents brief case studies of four FBOs in Thailand from which she draws five common characteristics that are basic to such entrepreneurial, action-oriented, and layperson-driven "do-it-yourself" Christian missions. In her case studies and conclusions, Pascal reveals the multifaceted way in which FBOs promote in local contexts a "tangible salvation," facilitated by and exemplifying aspects of globalization.

METHODIST BORDER FRIENDSHIP COMMISSION: A CASE STUDY

Lisa Beth White is an ordained UMC minister and a candidate for the PhD in Practical Theology at Boston University's School of Theology. Her paper is an extended case study of a single faith-based organization working on the U.S.-Mexico border in the Lower Rio Grande Valley region, the Methodist Border Friendship Commission (MBFC). White's introductory account of the geographic, ecological, demographic, economic, and political situation of this particular border region vividly portrays the complexity of this context in which many persons live and minister. She notes the fluidity and high frequency of two-way traffic across the border and the interdependent relationship between communities on both sides of it. The MBFC is a collaborative effort of the United Methodist Church and the Iglesia Metodista de México whose leaders and volunteers must navigate the "maze" ramified by an international economy and multiple governmental jurisdictions in order to coordinate an array of projects (which White succinctly surveys) that address both the occasional as well as ongoing needs of the region's many poor families. White concludes by posing a set of theological questions she believes should be considered by short-term mission teams from the United States that visit the region.

A PRELIMINARY STUDY OF SYMBIOTIC MISSION THROUGH FLORAL BEAUTY

At the time of the 2010Boston conference, Megumi Yoshida was a visiting fellow at Yale Divinity School and a scholar in residence at the Overseas Ministries Study Center in New Haven, CT. She is a doctoral student at the Doshisha University School of Theology in Kyoto, Japan, and a master practitioner of *ikebana*, a traditional Japanese form of artistic floral arrangement. In her paper, Yoshida incorporates biblical exegesis (of Jer 1:11–12 and Luke 12:13–38), history, cultural studies, and contextual theology to explain how *ikebana* can be employed to communicate the trust-inspiring faithfulness and love of God in sustaining creation and fulfilling his promises. She calls for "symbiotic mission" in which Christians think and behave in awareness of their vital relationship to an ecological order in crisis that is continually dependent upon God's active preservation of it.[10] At the heart of Yoshida's paper is the story of Joseph Neesima (1843–90), the son of a Samurai who risked his life to stow away for the United States and became a corresponding member of the American Board of Foreign Commissioners for Foreign Missions after graduating from Amherst College and Andover Theological Seminary. The first ordained Japanese Protestant, Neesima established Doshisha University in 1875 after returning home from Boston. During a severe winter near the end of his life, he composed the poem "Winter plum blossoms in my garden" to express his hope in God's steadfast care of him, which he recognized in the emergence of those flowers.

The "contours of world mission and Christianity" that are identified and exposited in these five papers are critical issues that will engage missiological reflection for years to come. May the insights and proposals these students offer, as well as the passion, rigor, and imagination with which they offer them, serve as catalysts to meaningful global engagement by the body of Christ in the twenty-first century.

WORKS CITED

Bevans, Stephen. "From Edinburgh to Edinburgh: Toward a Missiology for a World Church." In *Mission After Christendom: Emergent Themes in Contemporary Mission*,

---

10. The current volume was still in production when the devastating earthquakes and tsunami of March 2011 struck Japan.

edited by Ogbu Kalu, Peter Vethanayagamony, and Edmund Kee-Fook Chia, 1–11. Louisville, KY: Westminster John Knox, 2010.

Kerr, David A., and Kenneth R. Ross, eds. *Edinburgh 2010: Mission Then and Now*. Pasadena, CA: William Carey International University Press, 2009.

Shenk, Wilbert R. *Enlarging the Story: Perspectives on Writing World Christian History*. Maryknoll, NY: Orbis, 2002.

"Spotlight: The Future(s) of Missions." *Christianity Today*, August 2010. Accessed June 24, 2011. http://www.christianitytoday.com/ct/special/pdf/0812spotlightmissions.pdf.

Stanley, Brian. *The World Missionary Conference, Edinburgh 1910*. Grand Rapids: Eerdmans, 2009.

Winter, Ralph. "Global Cross-Cultural Mission Collaboration: Edinburgh 1910." *Mission Frontiers* (January-February 2009) 9–11.

11

"From Among Her Own Children"

African-Americans and the Evangelization of Africa in the Nineteenth Century

Mary Cloutier

"MISSIONARIES ... MUST BE RAISED UP FOR AFRICA FROM AMONG HER OWN CHILDREN"

IN HIS ADDRESS DELIVERED at Christ Church in Hartford, Connecticut, on the occasion of the founding of the African Mission School Society in August of 1828, Rev. J. M. Wainwright expressed the desire (shared by many) to see Americans of African descent carrying the gospel to the land of their ancestors. At that time, he noted that there was but one "colored missionary" in Africa (the Rev. Lott Carey). Wainwright felt that it was

> the design of Providence that that land should be evangelized chiefly by its own sons, and that *American* churches should prepare and send these missionaries: "We rejoice ... in the establishment of the African seminary in Hartford, as furnishing a pledge that these claims and wants are not to be neglected. And we hope the day is near which shall see not one but many schools in the United States devoted to the training up of young persons

of color for usefulness among their brethren, both in this and in their native land."[1]

God did, indeed, enable a great many Americans "of color" to spread the gospel in Africa. It is interesting to note the historic events that both precipitated and hindered this missionary effort, as well as the rationales and concerns offered by American Christians of that time period. The purpose of this paper is to consider these rationales and concerns, which were largely based on the ethnic heritage of African-Americans, and to juxtapose them with the stories of three such missionary women of African ancestry, who became "ethnic others" in the circle of their missionary co-laborers, as well as their African host culture.

RATIONALE FOR SENDING BLACK MISSIONARIES TO AFRICA

Health

Though opinions and statistics varied on the subject, there was widespread belief in the nineteenth century that American negroes, by virtue of their African ancestry, were more likely than whites to survive the West African climate and diseases. One report from the year 1854 gave a long list of white missionaries who had died or had returned to the United States in broken health. The writer then added, "Now during all this time, but four of the colored preachers have died, though their numbers have been to the whites *as ten to one*."[2] More than four decades later, M. E. Strieby polled the secretaries of nearly all the mission boards, asking whether "colored missionaries" in Africa endured the climate better, and whether they had freer access to the natives than white men. While answers varied, he reported that, "as a rule, the testimony was decidedly in favor of the colored missionaries."[3]

Freedom, Liberty, Empowerment

Lamin Sanneh writes extensively on the subject of antislavery and antistructure efforts, pointing out that nineteenth-century American blacks not only sought freedom, but also endeavored to "preach the gospel of

---

1. Wainright, "Discourse on the Occasion of Forming the African Mission," 540.
2. Newcomb, *Cyclopedia of Missions*, 101. Italics original.
3. Strieby, "The Destiny of the African Race," 371.

human freedom and political reform." Sanneh further asserts that the modern missionary movement "began largely as the initiative of freed slaves and ex-captives and carried the message of abolition as the timely expression of the message of Christianity."[4]

Wilmore Gayraud, Professor of Afro-American Religious Studies at New York Theological Seminary, has marveled, "What is most incredible is that these impoverished and uneducated Black preachers, many with a price still on their heads, had the audacity to think that they could do for Blacks overseas what they could scarcely do for themselves at home."[5] Gayraud adds that these early black missionaries to Africa were undaunted by white prejudice; their concerns were not only for evangelism, but also racial pride and self-respect.[6]

Divine Providence

After reporting the 1844 death of pioneer missionary Benjamin Griswold, *The Presbyterian* remarked, "Perhaps the indication of Providence is that the church should direct special attention to the raising up a band of colored missionaries to occupy these vacated fields."[7] A similar statement appeared in *The Baptist Missionary Magazine* in March of 1851, after the deaths of several missionaries: "Yet God has a people there, and if the white man cannot live to evangelize them, he can and will raise up other agencies. Educated colored men, in all probability, must and will be the only instrumentality employed in the conversion of Africa."[8]

In the first half of the nineteenth century, this idea of "divine providence" was often based on the alarming death tolls of whites, compared to the lower death rates of black missionaries. However, subsequent writers on the subject saw other indications of divine providence in sending African-American missionaries.

In 1890, the secretary of the American Missionary Association, Michael E. Strieby, also spoke of God's divine purpose in preparing black Americans to be gospel-bearers to the land of their fathers, by virtue of their common heritage. Comparing black Americans to the Hebrews,

---

4. Sanneh, *Abolitionists Abroad*, 62.

5. Gayraud, "Black Americans in Mission," 99.

6. These early efforts to evangelize Africa led to the founding of the American Baptist Convention in 1840.

7. *The African Repository* XXI, 29.

8. Quoted in Christy, *Pulpit Politics: Ecclesiastical Legislation on Slavery*, 135.

he asserted that they were "brought into contact with the most enlightened nation of the old world and disciplined by their hard bondage, and thus prepared for the important part they were to take in the work of the world's redemption . . ."[9] He added that the enslavement of blacks was "America's guilt" and that their Christian education was "America's duty"—when this duty is fully performed, "these ex-slaves will be fitted for their great work in Africa, their religion will prompt them to it, the climate will be congenial, the ties of kindred, color and of fatherland will draw them there."[10]

Later, in 1902, African-American William A. Hunton (the first black person to serve as an International Secretary for the YMCA) also spoke of God's providential preparation of the American negro for mission work in Africa, but in terms of education and economic progress. Hunton outlined three "indications" of this providence: (1) young, educated negro men and women were already heading to Africa, not as missionaries, but as "pioneers in commercial and industrial life and work";[11] (2) African-born students were coming to America for education and training; young black Americans were "talking with them and learning of their spirit";[12] and (3) missionaries and Africans were saying (to American blacks), "You have been living in America; you have been enjoying the light and freedom of this country; you have been receiving the blessings of education and training; you have heard, best of all, the gospel of Jesus Christ. Why don't you come over and help us?"[13]

Lamin Sanneh contributes an intriguing perspective from his twenty-first century vantage point: that nineteenth-century African-American missionaries, "the same slaves or their descendants, whose capture and sale had supported and justified chiefly power, arrived back as bearers of the Gospel, their extorted status as slaves the most powerful incentive for their mission whose central premise was that no human being deserved to be made slave because no human being was such before God." Those whom God had liberated from bondage became mes-

---

9. Strieby, "The Destiny of the African Race," 374.
10. Ibid., 372.
11. Hunton, "Providential Preparation," 295.
12. Ibid.
13. Ibid., 296.

sengers of freedom to the very ones that had sold them into slavery. It was a message of forgiveness and reconciliation.[14]

While nineteenth-century Christians spoke of God's divine providence in preparing African-Americans for the evangelization of Africa, there arose necessary discussions on proper training and recruitment, their willingness to go as missionaries to Africa, and sensitivity to the African's perception (and reception) of these missionaries. One must also take into account during this period in history the tremendous socio-political impact of the Atlantic slave trade, the emancipation of slaves in America, the colonization of American blacks in West Africa, and the European colonial system.

CONCERNS

Proper Preparation and Training

Secretary Strieby, in his 1890 report, attributed some of the failures of black missionaries to "immaturity of knowledge and character," though he felt that these difficulties would be removed "by more thorough education and riper experience."[15] A similar report from 1876 also cited problems, including immorality, immaturity, dissension, and lack of training. The author quickly pointed out the disparate backgrounds between white and black missionaries: "The Anglo-Saxon race has behind it 17 centuries of culture; the Negro race in America, 17 years. This should make a difference as to the races."[16] The question was not whether the black American had the *capacity* for missionary work, but whether he or she had been and would be given the opportunity for training, education, and placement on the field. During the latter half of the nineteenth century, countless denominations and missions organizations were networking to establish training schools to prepare black American missionaries for overseas service. Various women's missionary societies supported these schools, including their graduates who went on to missionary service, with a special emphasis on women missionaries. Churches and Sunday schools also participated in identifying and supporting those called to missions.

14. Sanneh, *Abolitionists Abroad*, 64.
15. Strieby, "The destiny of the African race," 374.
16. *The American Missionary*, 33.

Africa's "Acceptance" of Black Missionaries

This was another area where opinions of seasoned missionaries differed widely, though most indicated that a black missionary would be just as capable as a white missionary in evangelizing and serving in Africa. At the 1902 Student Volunteer Movement conference on missions, a young female African-American missionary candidate, Altha Brown, directed a question to missionary Isabella Nassau, asking whether a "thoroughly qualified American negro would be more acceptable and more efficient in an African mission than a white man." Nassau replied that, while native pastors are most effective in evangelizing and governing the church, she felt that educated "colored brethren" would be received as a white man is received.[17] Nassau had, in fact, spent most of her first twenty years of missionary service working side-by-side with African-American women.[18] Another missionary, answering the same question, stated that their mission already had several West Indian negro missionaries serving in Africa, and hoped to receive more. He explained that a white missionary makes an impression that a black missionary would not make at first, but that as Africans "they look upon him as one of themselves and do not care for him offhand; but if that man is full of love for Jesus Christ, and if he is not puffed up with his own conceit, he will make his way finally better than any white man going out there could do ... It is a the question of what kind of a man is sent, not a question of whether the man's face is colored or white."[19]

Availability and Willingness of Qualified Black Americans to Serve in Africa

In 1847, missionary John Leighton Wilson gave a survey of the mission in Africa, and noted the need for "the colored race" to help in Christianizing Africa, but not without the proper training, preparation,

---

17. Nassau was well into her seventies at this time, and still serving on the mission field.

18. Charity Sneed, who emigrated with her family to Liberia as a child, served with Miss Nassau from the late 1860s to the mid-1870s. Mary Lucy Harding, a missionary teacher, served with Miss Nassau in Gabon, 1882–89. This is evident in numerous missionary magazines and Robert Hamill Nassau's *My Ogowe*. *Woman's Work for Woman*, in general, mentioned Misses Nassau, Sneed, and Harding in their joint missionary work.

19. Hunton, "Providential Preparation," 298. It is not evident whether the author's comment is based on past incidents, or whether it is his personal opinion.

and character. However, he was concerned that there were few in number who were both qualified and *willing* to engage in missionary work, stating, "The churches of the West Indies have been recently looked into with a good deal of interest; and it has been hoped that a supply of just such men and women as are needed, in almost any quantity, might be here obtained. But if this hope is realized immediately, or shall be for some time to come, it will be the most wonderful achievement of modern missions."[20]

In 1861, African-American Rev. Alex Crummell, in a published letter to Charles B. Dunbar, M.D., listed several theories why the American black man had "difficulties" in doing good work in Africa. He was quick to point out that these were more subjective than objective, and they pertained only to American black Christians, not Christians of the West Indians, nor to the "infant church of Sierra Leone [which] is already, in sixty years from its birth mother of missions."[21] Crummell felt that the black American (Christian) religion lacked missionary zeal, and that it was "not diffusive, but rather introversive. It does not flow out, but rather inward."[22] Crummell also borrowed a theory of phrenologists of his day: that the black race has a quality of stolid inhabitativeness, adding his opinion that "as a people we cling with an almost deadly fixity to locality . . . we lack speculation . . . we look where we stand, but few beyond."[23] Additionally, Crummell felt that American blacks were hindered by "a reluctance on the part of even some good and zealous Christians to engage in the propagation of the gospel in Africa on the ground 'that its ultimate tendency must be to subserve the objectionable scheme of African colonization.'"[24]

There are plenty of examples of missionaries who served in sharp contrast to Crummell's opinion. Amanda Smith, a woman born in slavery in 1837, was converted as a young adult, gifted by the Holy Spirit to preach, and was sent to do so in the US, Great Britain, India, and West

---

20. Wilson, "Mr. Wilson's Survey of the Mission," 254.
21. Crummell, *Relations and Duties*, 48.
22. Ibid., 48–9.
23. Crummell noted that this was the opinion of Horace Greeley and Gerrit Smith, and disputed by Douglass and Watkins, *The Relations and Duties of Free Colored Men in America to Africa*, 49.
24. Ibid., 51.

Africa.[25] While only ordained men were considered "clergy," there were a number of such nineteenth-century missionary women who "itinerated" throughout towns and regions, preaching the gospel, and discipling believers of both genders and of diverse cultures. One can imagine that remarkable African-American women preachers and teachers in Africa (such as Smith) had an impact on the local women, and reinforced the status and worth of women in the church body. Far too often in mission history, the ecclesiastical "structure" has marginalized women, and the mission-established churches in Africa have largely overlooked the indigenous societal and religious norms that recognized spiritual leadership qualities in women.[26]

Happily, Crummell's criticisms were also refuted by the next generation of young black American Christians, many of whom were earning college degrees and expressing zeal to serve overseas.[27] Rev. George Moore made the comment that Fisk University was the first school for negroes in the South to send missionaries to Africa. He noted in an address at the Student Volunteer Convention of 1902, that Altha Brown was going overseas that year, and that there was "a number of others who are anxious to go, if the boards will offer them work. We hope that they will encourage us by giving them the opportunity to carry the gospel back to the fatherland."[28]

In the mid-twentieth century, however, there was a decided shift towards the "introversion" and "inhabitativeness" described by Crummell. According to Marilyn Lewis,[29] the participation of American black churches in worldwide evangelism dropped precipitously, beginning in the 1930s. The term "missionary" was redefined as "a woman who did good works and taught the Bible in small women-led groups";[30] this "missionary work" was neither evangelistic nor cross-cultural, and

25. Smith, *An Autobiography*, 17, 30.

26. Adeney, "Do Missions Raise or Lower the Status of Women?" 211–21.

27. Among them were prominent medical missionaries such as William Sheppard, M.D., Louise Fleming, M.D., and Emma Delaney.

28. Student Volunteer Movement, 298.

29. Marilyn Lewis (1951–2000) was both a historian and promoter of Christian mission, as well as "guest editor" of the special African-American edition of *Mission Frontiers* magazine (April 2000). The issue also reports her untimely death of a heart attack on February 20, 2000, and can be found at http://www.missionfrontiers.org/pdf/2000/02/tribute.htm.

30. Lewis, "Overcoming Obstacles."

did not seek to fulfill the Great Commission of Matthew 28:18–20. Marilyn Lewis attributed this to a "protective mechanism" towards missions, and suggested that it may be "in part a response to racism and discrimination."[31]

WHAT OF TODAY?

Given the vast numbers of godly, committed, and accomplished African-American missionaries who served in Africa in the nineteenth and early twentieth centuries, there is a lamentable lack of recognition given to them in mission history resources. This may be a contributing factor to the low percentage of African American Christians participating in long-term overseas ministry today. One of the reasons for this lack of mission history detail is the tendency of historians to focus on certain missionary "heroes"—usually men, and almost invariably Europeans or white Americans. Recent scholarship has added details of the work of nonwhite missionaries, of women, and of local believers who have had a significant impact on the work of worldwide missions.[32]

The following biographies are not available in mission history texts, but have been pieced together from snippets of missionary reports, personal diaries, and private correspondence with descendants of the missionaries. All three are women "of color" whom God used to write his redemptive story in equatorial Africa. Two, if not all three, of the women were born in slavery; one was illiterate, while the other received a basic education; the third, born circa 1860, benefited from the post-Emancipation era's educational opportunities provided through church and missionary organizations. In each case they responded to God's call, were enabled by influential people, and faithfully served in places where they were the "ethnic other"—both in their respective missionary circles, and in their host communities. Their ethnicity was simultaneously a qualifier for their presence on the mission, and a potential detriment to their legitimacy within the mission structure. In most cases, the resolve and faithfulness necessitated by their social situation equipped them to fill missionary roles that may have otherwise been closed to them, for want of formal degrees or church licensing.

31. Ibid.
32. Tucker, "The Role of Bible Women," in Robert, *Gospel Bearers, Gender Barriers*.

MRS. LAVINIA SNEED AND CHARITY SNEED

A brief notation on a ship's passenger list tells a great deal about the early history of the Sneed family of Danville, Kentucky. James Sneed, 34, his wife Lavinia, 26, and their eleven-year-old daughter, Charity, were newly-freed slaves, bound for the Afro-American colony in Liberia in 1854. The registry indicated that Mrs. Sneed and Charity were "emancipated by Chas. Henderson," while Mr. Sneed was "purchased and set free to go with his wife."[33] Little is known about their time in Liberia, other than the fact that Mr. Sneed died in 1861, and was an elder in the Presbyterian Church.[34]

The Presbyterian Corisco Mission reports began listing Charity Sneed as part of the mission as early as 1860.[35] Still a teenager, Charity was an assistant to Phoebe Ogden, who taught the young girls of the mission school. When Rev. Thomas Spencer Ogden suddenly died, Charity accompanied his widow and baby son back to the United States, and then returned to the Corisco Mission, where she was next associated with Isabella Nassau.[36] Charity very likely attained only a basic education in Liberia, and was not considered a full "missionary" at Corisco. Yet, she was involved in Nassau's itinerating ministries to the interior villages, evangelizing and giving "religious instruction."[37] The two women opened the Bolondo Mission station in 1870. Early on, Charity's name did not appear on the missionary list, but as she took on added roles and responsibilities, she was acknowledged as an "assistant." Women's Mission Society reports show that Charity Sneed was supported for many years by one particular group from West Virginia.[38]

Seven years after Charity's arrival in Corisco, her mother also joined the mission family, assuming the role of housekeeper and baby nurse for

33. "List of Emigrants of the Ship Sophia Walker"; *The African Repository and Colonial Journal*, 217.

34. Personal papers of Peter Menkel, entry dated February 20, 1883. Peter had visited friends of the Sneed family in Monrovia on his way back to Gabon from the US, and informed them of his wife's death.

35. Corisco is a small island just off the coast of what is now Gabon and Equatorial Guinea.

36. Nassau, *Crowned in Palmland*, 98.

37. Isabella Nassau's letter is referenced in the report on The Bolenda School in *The Presbyterian Monthly Record*, Feb 1871, 50.

38. As per Isabella Nassau in her July 1879 letter, quoted in *Woman's Work for Woman*, December 1879, 407.

the Nassau family. A year later, Mrs. Sneed's expertise was needed for the "confinement" period of another missionary wife, Mrs. Harriet Menaul. Two weeks after giving birth, the young mother died. Mary Nassau expressed in a letter home what "a great comfort" Mrs. Sneed had been to the Menauls.[39] Six months later, Mary Nassau died, and Mrs. Sneed once again comforted and cared for a grieving family.

Mrs. Sneed was likely illiterate, but was exceptionally qualified for the many familial needs of the mission, especially related to childbirth, childcare, and basic nursing. She was often a comforting presence when missionary colleagues were gravely ill and dying.[40] While this is not found in the annual mission reports, it is a common theme in private missionary papers that mention Mrs. Sneed.

In 1872, the Sneeds left for an extended stay in Monrovia. During their absence, two Corisco missionary wives left suddenly for the US. The mission met the crucial need for female missionaries by placing Charity and her mother at that site, where Charity resumed the women's work.[41]

In 1874, Charity Sneed married fellow missionary, German-American Peter Menkel, who served as the mission boat captain. There seemed to be no negative reaction to this interracial marriage, and Charity carried on her mission role, as before, including taking "entire charge" of the Bolondo Girls' School for many months, while Miss Nassau was ill.[42] However, her name moved further up the missionary list, as "Mrs. Menkel."[43]

Peter Menkel's diary contains personal details of their life, but does not mention any issue of race until 1882, when Peter (on a health furlough) took their five-year-old daughter to the US so that she could receive a formal education. Menkel was shocked and heartbroken when his family expressed embarrassment of his mulatto child, unwilling to provide for her housing and care; local schools also rejected her because

---

39. Nassau, *Crowned in Palmland*, 28.

40. Reading, *Ogowe Band*, 188.

41. Letter from Rev. Albert Bushnell, dated July 11, 1872. *Presbyterian Monthly Record October 1872*, 312.

42. Nassau, *Woman's Work for Woman*, 407.

43. The name of her mother, Mrs. Lavinia Sneed, never appeared on the missionary list, and only rarely in the text of the mission reports in the twenty-four years she served among the missionaries. Hers was a labor of love.

of her ethnicity. After a visit of eight months, Menkel prepared to return to Gaboon with the child. While still in the US, he received word of the sudden death of his wife, Charity, at the Gabon mission. In a brief mention in the Annual Report for the year 1882, the mission said this about Charity Sneed Menkel: "She was held in much esteem as a faithful and excellent missionary..."[44]

Fellow missionary Laura Kreis Campbell, whose private diary and letters have been preserved by her descendants, described Charity's death and also wrote at great length about the character and personality of Mrs. Sneed: "She was born in America, both she and her husband were slaves, but with different masters. Mrs. Sneed's master set her free before the war, and also bought her husband's freedom. So we rightly judge that she was appreciated by her master. They immediately came to this country [sic]. She spent most of her time after her arrival here in caring for missionaries and still continues in this service. We are very glad to have Mrs. Sneed in Gaboon; she is such a good nurse."[45] Campbell's diary reveals that Mrs. Sneed traveled fairly often from mission to mission, to nurse various sick missionaries and to help missionary wives during their confinement and first months of motherhood. Campbell was delighted when Mrs. Sneed visited her home: "She's such good company!"[46] Yet, there is a subtle line of demarcation between Mrs. Sneed and the other American missionaries, as Mrs. Campbell noted that Mrs. Sneed "has always done a great deal for our missionaries, so much so that she seems like one of us."[47]

Mrs. Sneed remained at the mission nine years beyond the death of her daughter, Charity. In 1891, she warmly welcomed her son-in-law, Peter, and his new bride. Her three living grandchildren (one had died in Gabon), by that time, had been sent to the US, and were placed in three different schools for "colored children." Mrs. Sneed approached Dr. Nassau, who was preparing for a furlough in the US, and expressed to him the desire "to lay her old bones down in America." Nassau—remembering her kindness and friendship over the years, as well as her

---

44. *Forty-Sixth Annual Report of the Board May 1883*, 39.

45. Laura Kreis Campbell, private letter to family, from Gabon, West Africa, December 21, 1881. In using the phrase "this country," Campbell referred to the *continent* of Africa, as the Sneeds first lived in Liberia.

46. Diary of Laura Kreis Campbell, May 1882.

47. Laura Kreis Campbell, letter dated December 21, 1881, from Gabon, Africa.

importance in his family as the children's nurse—booked her first-class passage on the same ship, and also secured her placement in a "home for colored people" in Philadelphia. One might rush to judgment at Mrs. Sneed's placement in a "home for colored people," but further research reveals that this establishment was founded by an accomplished and wealthy African-American man, Stephen Smith,[48] and was designated "for the relief of that worthy class of colored persons who have endeavored through life to maintain themselves, but who, from various causes, are finally dependent on the charity of others."[49]

Mrs. Sneed's early years as a slave, and her intimate knowledge of suffering and loss, equipped her for her unique role as comforter and caregiver of the missionaries and their children. None of her colleagues would have questioned her preparation and qualifications for these vital ministry roles.

MARY LUCY HARDING

Mary Lucy Harding entered the mission field of Gabon in 1882, having just graduated with high honors from Ann Arbor University.[50] There is no information available about her life prior to her university years. Various missionary magazines of the 1880s followed her progress as the first "colored" missionary to (equatorial) Africa, appointed by the Presbyterian Mission, sent out under The Women's Board of the Northwest, and fully supported by Letitia Grace Chandler of Detroit, Michigan.[51]

Harding sailed to Africa with her seasoned missionary colleague, Isabella Nassau. Because the two women expected to be appointed to the northern mission of Batanga (Cameroon), Harding spent the voyage studying the Benga language; she was able to read it fluently by

---

48. Stephen Smith (1795–1873) was a former slave who purchased his freedom. He then built a business empire in Columbia, PA, and became one of the wealthiest African-Americans in America. His lumber business helped to transport fugitive slaves to Canada. Smith donated $250,000 to establish the Stephen Smith Home for Aged and Infirm Colored Persons. See http://www.preservationalliance.com/programs/aai/index.php/inventory/detail/372.

49. Gibbs, *Shadow and Light*, 10.

50. *The Gospel in All Lands*, 168.

51. *The Church At Home and Abroad*, 331. Chandler was the widow of Zachariah Chandler, former mayor of Detroit. The couple was active in the anti-slavery movement and in the Underground Railroad.

the time they landed.[52] The mission, however, appointed them to the far southern mission station, in what is now Lambarene, in the interior of Gabon. This was yet "pioneer" mission work, and the women knew they were serving among largely unreached people, speaking a wide variety of languages, and who were frequently at war with one another over territory and trading rights. Missionary reports during her seven years of service describe Harding's many travels by canoe to various interior villages. Readers could not help but notice that much of this work was done among the Fang people, who were said to be fierce warriors and cannibals. Harding, at various times, taught and supervised the mission schools, preached the gospel, discipled new believers, studied several local languages, and printed materials in these languages on her own press.

Perhaps the most remarkable aspect of Harding's ministry is the lack of recognition given to it by her male missionary colleagues; while she is mentioned in several books written by Robert Hamill Nassau, he only wrote of her presence at given events or places, and her acts of hospitality. Nassau described her in this succinct way: "Miss Harding, a highly-educated lady, was of negro extraction; but, of so slight an admixture that she was regarded as [a] 'European.'"[53] This lack of recognition of her fruitful ministry was less likely due to her ethnicity than to her marital status and place in the recognized church structure. In the nineteenth century, the female missionary (married or single) was more often recognized for her dedication to (and exemplary conduct in) the home and family, and for hospitality; all were esteemed characteristics of the godly woman, whose role was to "complement but not compete with what missionary males were doing."[54]

While private missionary papers indicate that Harding was a welcome part of the missionary circle, she seemed to have had interpersonal conflicts with her co-worker, Isabella Nassau;[55] Nassau's book, *My Ogowe*, also alludes to conflict with a male colleague, Rev. Adolphus Good, "relative to some difficulties [between them] as to station control."[56] After seven years of service, Harding was removed from the field. She

52. Nassau, *Woman's Work for Woman*, 182.
53. Nassau, *My Ogowe*, 420.
54. Robert, "The Christian Home," 148.
55. Nassau, *My Ogowe*, 472.
56. Ibid., 571.

immediately began serving with the Presbyterian Freedmen's Bureau, teaching in schools for "colored children." Traces of her life disappear at the turn of the century. There are no known extant photos of Harding, only long-forgotten published reports of her mission work in Gabon and Arkansas tell fragments of her story.

The stories of these three women represent a wider perspective on the history of Christian missions than is not yet well-known: a story that involves African-American men and women. While nineteenth-century rationales and concerns might now seem outdated and irrelevant, there remains a concern that present-day missions organizations and strategies are overlooking the potential unique contributions of African-American churches and missionaries. Through careful research and a retelling of God's mission history by persons from diverse nations and ethnicities, the Church will be able to correct past attitudes of apathy and suspicion, both of which have produced the exclusion of others. In viewing mission history through this broader lens, individuals will be able to foster a new interest and passion in reaching the nations together for Christ. Churches and mission organizations might discover their need to repent and seek reconciliation for past prejudices and injustices against those who were qualified and willing but not invited to serve as missionaries due to their ethnicity, gender, or marital status.

WORKS CITED

Adeney, Miriam. "Do Missions Raise or Lower the Status of Women? Conflicting Reports from Africa." In *Gospel Bearers, Gender Barriers: Missionary Women in the Twentieth Century,* edited by Dana L. Robert, 211–21. Maryknoll, NY: Orbis, 2002.
American Missionary Association. *Annual Report of the American Missionary Association, Volumes 30–39.* New York: American Missionary Association, 1876.
Bushnell, Albert. Letter from the Gaboon Mission, dated July 11, 1872. *The Presbyterian Monthly Record.* XXIII.10 (October 1872) 312.
Christy, David. *Pulpit Politics: or, Ecclesiastical Legislation on Slavery, in its Disturbing Influences on the American Union.* Cincinnati: Faran & McLean, 1862.
Crummell, Alex. *The Relations and Duties of Free Colored Men in America to Africa—A Letter to Charles B. Dunbar, M.D., Esq., of New York City by the Rev. Alex Crummell, B.A.* Hartford, CT: Lockwood, 1861.
Forty-Sixth Annual Report of the Board of Foreign Missions of the Presbyterian Church. Volume 46 (May 1883) 38–43.
Gayraud, Wilmore S. "Black Americans in Mission: Setting the Record Straight." *International Bulletin of Mission Research* 9.3 (July 1986) 98–102.
Gibbs, Mifflin Wistar. *Shadow and Light: An Autobiography.* USA: Arno, 1968.

Hunton, William. A. "The Providential Preparation of the American Negro for Mission Work in Africa." In *World-Wide Evangelization, the Urgent Business of the Church*, edited by Student Volunteer Movement for Foreign Missions, 294–98. New York: Student Volunteer Movement for Foreign Missions, 1902.

Lewis, Marilyn. "Overcoming Obstacles: The Broad Sweep of the African American and Mission." *Mission Frontiers* (April 2000). No pages. Online: http://www.missionfrontiers.org/pdf/2000/02/200002.htm.

Nassau, Robert Hamill. *Crowned in Palmland: A Story of African Mission Life*. Philadelphia: Lippincott, 1874.

———. *My Ogowe: Being a Narrative in Daily Incidents During Sixteen Years in Equatorial West Africa*. New York: Neale, 1914.

Nassau, Isabella. "News from the Field." *Woman's Work for Woman* IX.12 (December 1879) 407.

———. *Woman's Work for Woman* XIII.6 (June 1883) 181–83.

Newcomb, Rev. Harvey. *Cyclopedia of Missions; Containing a Comprehensive View of Missionary Operations throughout the World; with Geographical Descriptions and Accounts of the Social, Moral, and Religious Condition of the People*. New York: Scribner, 1854.

Reading, Joseph Hankinson. *The Ogowe Band: A Narrative of African Travel*. Philadelphia: Reading, 1890.

Robert, Dana L., ed. *Gospel Bearers, Gender Barriers: Missionary Women in the Twentieth Century*. Maryknoll, NY: Orbis, 2002.

———. "The 'Christian Home' as a Cornerstone of Anglo-American Missionary Thought and Practice." In *Converting Colonialism*, edited by Dana L. Robert, 134–65. Grand Rapids: Eerdmans, 2008.

Sanneh, Lamin. *Abolitionists Abroad: American Blacks and the Making of Modern West Africa*. Cambridge: Harvard University Press, 1999.

Smith, Amanda. *An Autobiography: The Story of the Lord's Dealings with Mrs. Amanda Smith, the Colored Evangelist; Containing an Account of Her Life Work of Faith and Her Travels in America, England, Ireland, Scotland, India and Africa, as an Independent Missionary*. Chicago: Meyer and Brother, 1893.

Strieby, Michael E. "The Destiny of the African Race." *The American Missionary* XLIV.12 (December 1890) 371–75.

Student Volunteer Movement for Foreign Missions. *World-Wide Evangelization: The Urgent Business of the Church. (Addresses Delivered before the Fourth International Convention of the Student Volunteer Movement for Foreign Missions, Toronto, Canada, February 26–March 2, 1902)*. New York: Student Volunteer Movement for Foreign Missions, 1902.

The African Repository and Colonial Journal XXI.1 (January 1845) 29.

The African Repository and Colonial Journal XXX.7 (1854) 214–19.

The American Missionary XXXIV.11 (November 1880).

The Church at Home and Abroad. Vol. 3. Philadelphia: Presbyterian Board of Publication and Sabbath School Work, 1888.

The Gospel in All Lands. Vol. 6 (July–December 1882).

The Presbyterian Monthly Record XXII.2 (February 1871).

Tucker, Ruth A. "The Role of Bible Women in World Evangelism." *Missiology: An International Review* XIII.2 (April 1985) 133–46.

Wainwright, J. M., D. D. "Discourse on the Occasion of Forming the African Mission School Society, Delivered in Christ Church, in Hartford, Connecticut, on Sunday evening, Aug. 10, 1828." *The Christian Spectator* II.X (October 1828) 539–40.

Wilson, John Leighton. "Mr. Wilson's Survey of the Mission." *The Missionary Herald* XLIII.8 (August 1847) 253–61.

12

Disciples in Mission

Evangelization, Liberation, and a "Theology of Neighbor"

Marcus C. Mescher

INTRODUCTION: DISCIPLES IN MISSION FOR LIBERATION

THE PARABLE OF THE good Samaritan (Luke 10:25–37) may be the most well known of Jesus' parables. It has long served to inspire people of many faiths, along with those of no particular religious affiliation, to serve others in need. In fact, sociologist Robert Wuthnow reports that in one study of individuals involved in community service, half of those who did not identify as religious and two-thirds of churchgoers cited the parable of the good Samaritan as part of their motivation to serve.[1] For some, the widespread knowledge and acceptance of this parable's moral lesson may be interpreted as a promising sign of the potential to translate Gospel themes into a wider, pluralistic cultural context and globalized reality.

But this parable calls for much more than benign benevolence or humanitarian aid. In fact, through this parable (as with the pericope of the last judgment in Matt 25:31–46), Christ calls disciples to conversion to the "other" and even identifies himself with the "other" in need. These passages are often cited by moral theologians as paradigmatic texts for uniting love of God to love of neighbor, but what relevance do they bear

---

1. Wuthnow, *Acts of Compassion*, 161.

for mission and evangelization? Thirty-five years after Pope Paul VI's apostolic exhortation *Evangelii Nuntiandi*, we are reminded that the link between Christ, the church, and evangelization cannot avoid the work of liberation.[2] Gustavo Gutiérrez cites the parable of the good Samaritan to suggest that a "theology of the neighbor" provides the basis for a spirituality of liberation and the heart of Christian discipleship.[3]

Given the widespread familiarity of this parable and its unique significance for inter-personal right-relationship, the parable of the good Samaritan offers special value to disciples in mission, for evangelization, and liberation. In the pages that follow, we will highlight some of the most potent themes in this parable: namely, what it means to recognize the "other" as neighbor and to *be* neighbor to the "other." We will also explore how this "theology of neighbor" provides meaningful insight for discipleship in mission marked by solidarity through friendship. And finally, we will consider how all of this calls disciples to the margins of our church and world.

---

2. "The Church," Paul VI writes, "has the duty to proclaim the liberation of millions of human beings, many of whom are her own children, the duty of assisting the birth of this liberation, of giving witness to it, of ensuring that it is complete. This is not foreign to evangelization." He continues, "Between evangelization and human advancement—development and liberation—there are in fact profound links. These include links of an anthropological order, because the man who is to be evangelized is not an abstract being but is subject to social and economic questions. They also include links in the theological order, since one cannot dissociate the plan of creation from the plan of Redemption. The latter plan touches the very concrete situations of injustice to be combated and of justice to be restored. They include links of the eminently evangelical order, which is that of charity: how in fact can one proclaim the new commandment without promoting in justice and in peace the true, authentic advancement of [humanity]? . . . it is impossible to accept 'that in evangelization one could or should ignore the importance of the problems so much discussed today, concerning justice, liberation, development and peace in the world. This would be to forget the lesson which comes to us from the Gospel concerning love of our neighbor who is suffering and in need'" (§§30–31).

3. "Our attitude towards [the other, especially the poor and oppressed], or rather our commitment to them, will indicate whether or not we are directing our existence in conformity with the will of the Father. This is what Christ reveals to us by identifying himself with the poor in the text of Matthew [25:31–46]. A theology of the neighbor, which has yet to be worked out, would have to be structured on this basis" (Gutiérrez, *A Theology of Liberation*, 116).

WHO IS MY NEIGHBOR?

In the Hebrew Bible, Israel receives both covenant and law as the way to *shalom*. *Shalom* is often translated into English as "peace," but it is better understood as "balance," "wholeness," and fullness of life in "right-relationship." This is a process of right-ordering relations in three ways: between the self and God, between oneself and others, and one's own inner sense of *shalom* (in that order of priority). The *Shema* is the clearest articulation of one's primary duty to "love the Lord, your God, with all your heart, and with all your soul, and with all your strength" (Deut 6:5), but this is complemented by repeated emphasis on a horizontal responsibility to "love your neighbor as yourself" (Lev 19:18). By law and covenant, the nation of Israel was a people set apart,[4] but this did not mean the law only applied to how Jews were to treat fellow Jews. In fact, the command to "love your neighbor" is repeated only twice in the Hebrew Bible, whereas the command to "love the stranger" is reiterated no fewer than thirty-six times.[5]

Jesus captures the spirit of this dual mission *par excellence* in the parable of the good Samaritan. In this scene, a lawyer asks Jesus what he must do to inherit eternal life. Jesus asks him what is written in the law (Luke 10:25–26). The lawyer replies by reciting the *Shema* and adds the duty to love one's neighbor as oneself, which Jesus confirms as an apt interpretation of the law.[6] The lawyer, perhaps a bit embarrassed that he has answered his own question when he was aiming to "test" Jesus (v. 25), then asks "Who is my neighbor?" (v. 29). The lawyer's query is a self-interested, ethnocentric limit-question, seeking to learn the minimum that must be done in order to follow the law (and inherit eternal life). This limit implies an exclusion of others, or non-neighbors, to whom the lawyer is less accountable or not obligated at all.

---

4. They were aware of this as they traveled without a place to call home; Yahweh reminds the Israelites, "the land is mine; for you are strangers and guests with me" (Lev 25:23).

5. Sacks, *To Heal a Fractured World*, 103.

6. This passage resembles similar exchanges in Mark (12:28–34) and Matthew (22:34–40), though in Mark and Matthew, "love of neighbor" is considered secondary to "love of God." The fact that Luke connects these vertical and horizontal commands indicates that love of God is incomplete without love of neighbor. Interestingly, in John's Gospel, there is no commandment to love God, only to "love one another as I have loved you" (John 13:34).

To answer this theoretical limit-question, Jesus responds with a concrete example of unexpected, excessive care. But it would be a mistake to focus on the actions themselves and reduce the Samaritan to a benign humanitarian. The weight of this parable comes from the fact that the lawyer—and Jesus' audience—would have been scandalized to learn that the moral hero of the story was a Samaritan.[7] The Samaritan's compassionate actions break the boundaries of mutual animosity that separated Jew from Samaritan, which Jesus uses to undermine the justifications of his contemporaries to deny care or restrict one's duty to another in need. The example of the Samaritan illustrates that neighbor-love is anything but a calculation of who does and does not deserve compassion or mercy. Moreover, as Augustine points out, the concept of "neighbor" is not to be confined based on geographical proximity, ethnic similarity, or reciprocal relationship; the parable teaches us that "all people must be recognized as neighbors."[8]

By this standard, the answer to Jesus' question, "Which of these three, in your opinion, was neighbor to the robbers' victim?" (v. 36) is obvious. The Samaritan is the one who showed mercy, the one whose example we are to follow to "Go and do likewise" (v. 37). But such an easy answer belies the significance of the question. By asking who was neighbor *to* the victim, Jesus shifts the meaning of neighbor from *object* to *subject*. The neighbor is not just an object to me, a receptacle for my mercy; rather, the neighbor is the one who proactively reaches out with

---

7. If the parable were only a reinforcement of the duty to love one's neighbor, it would have been sufficient for a lay Israelite to tend to the victim (presumably a fellow Jew) on the side of the road. If the parable was designed to reiterate Jesus' call to love one's enemy (cf. Luke 6:27–35), it would be fitting for the victim to have been a Samaritan and have a lay Israelite tend to his enemy's needs. For a Jewish audience, the moral hero of this parable is "one of the most odious characters possible," such that "Any self-respecting, pious Jew in a ditch would rather be left for dead than be helped by such a person" (Keesmaat, "Strange Neighbors and Risky Care," 280, 282). The following illustrates this well: "An American cultural equivalent would be a Plains Indian in 1875 walking into Dodge City with a scalped cowboy on his horse, checking into a room over the local saloon, and staying the night to take care of him" (Bailey, *Through Peasant Eyes*, 52).

8. Augustine, *De Doctrina Christiana*, Book I, Chapter 30, §§31–32. In English, the word "neighbor" is usually considered as a geographical term (one who lives nearby, in my neighborhood). But Augustine uses the word *proximum* (person close to me) not *vicinum* (determined by vicinity, geography) to emphasize that recognizing others as neighbor and being neighborly to others is about drawing close *to* others—not vicinity by happenstance.

compassion. In other words, the lawyer's question is irrelevant because loving one's neighbor is necessary but insufficient; disciples must also *be* loving neighbors to others.[9]

For all these reasons, the parable of the good Samaritan is a valuable paradigm text for our purposes. It addresses the relationship between the triad of right-relationship because the Samaritan's exemplary display of compassion is predicated by a devout love of God.[10] In terms of horizontal right-relationship and responsibility, it is important to note that Jesus is asked a hypothetical limit-question and provides a most practical answer and guide for discipleship, reinforced by Luke's use of "do" as bookend markers in verses 28 and 37.[11] Furthermore, the example of the good Samaritan demonstrates that love is about *possibility* rather than bare minimum requirements. This is not to suggest that

---

9. Robert Funk comments on the passage, saying: "When we understand the parable we shall no longer be concerned with the question." He expands on this, saying, the "parable of the Good Samaritan is a language trap which the lawyer could not comprehend. He asked a straightforward question; he got an enigmatic answer. Jesus in effect is saying: If you knew what love means, you would not have asked the question. I asked you how you read, and you answered with the right words; now I ask you whether you understand—and your answer is your life" (Funk, "How Do You Read?" 57, 61).

10. Bonaventure explains how the Samaritan is the most theocentric figure, since to "love your neighbor as yourself" means to love "*from the source* you love yourself, namely, from love that is affective and effective," to love "*whom* you love yourself, that is, in God," to love "*on whose account* you love yourself, scilicet, on account of God," to love "*to what end* you love yourself, that is, for grace in the present life and glory in the future," to love "*how* you love yourself, that is, above material things and your own body and inferior to God" (In Karris, *Works of St. Bonaventure*, 976–77). Moreover, it is worth noting that the word for "compassion," which commentators concur is the fulcrum on which the story turns, is *esplangchnisthē*, which is related to the word for "innards," conveying a deep, visceral reaction (rather than a cerebral rationalization *against* helping the one in need). Gustavo Gutiérrez translates this as "his heart was melting" (*A Theology of Liberation*, 114). Interestingly, in Luke's Gospel, this word only appears in two other passages: with reference to Jesus, when he raises the widow's son (7:13) and with reference to the father in the parable of the prodigal son (15:20), who personifies God's unfailing mercy and providence. Although this fact is not meant to allegorize the passage as solely Christological, it is also interesting to note that when the Samaritan promises the innkeeper he will return, the word *epanerchesthai* is used, a word that only appears one other time in the New Testament, in reference to Christ's return at the end of time (Luke 19:15) (Hendrickx, *The Parables of Jesus*, 89). Taken together, the Samaritan is a Christ-like figure, a suitable example for our own *imitatio Christi*.

11. "Of all Jesus' parables, this might be said to be the most practical. It deals with the most practical of all problems in the most practical way" (Barclay, *And Jesus Said*, 82).

Jesus reduces the complexity of what compassion and love entail, but rather that prejudice, social boundaries, or concerns about recognition, reciprocity, or reward should not impede or restrict love from being fundamentally action-oriented and always inclusive.[12] For these reasons, we can agree that "there is no other parable in the Jesus tradition which carries a comparable punch."[13]

But what relevance does the parable hold for disciples in mission? First and foremost, the Samaritan's compassionate care is demonstrative of the kind of conversion and commitment to the "other" that is at the heart of Jesus' teaching and healing ministry. Additionally, it demonstrates how human solidarity trumps any distinction between "us" and "them," "in" and "out," or "worthy" and "unworthy." For disciples in mission, this serves as a reminder that missionary work is not unilateral; evangelization isn't about epistemic privilege so much as it is about an openness to the "other;" to become aware of how the "seeds of the gospel" have already taken root.

HUMAN SOLIDARITY AND LIBERATION

As we have seen, in the pericope of the parable of the good Samaritan, Jesus is asked a limit-question and turns it on its head, providing an answer that seeks the highest possibility from the human person and draws *every* person toward universal solidarity through an ethic of proactive, compassionate neighborliness. In *Jesus Before Christianity*, Albert Nolan uses this parable as evidence that Jesus' primary concerns were about the liberation of all people in compassionate action rooted in faith.[14] Nolan

---

12. Eduard Lohse emphasizes this point vigorously: "[t]he conquering power of love is limited by no boundary; it is made dependent neither on the consideration of whether the act is in behalf of people who are worthy of love nor on specifying the circle of potential recipients of helpful deeds. By naming even enemies as those to whom one should act in loving care, every hesitating deliberation is excluded as to whether the 'neighbor' must first meet some qualification, as is usually supposed. The command of love knows no condition and no presupposition; it is valid for every place and every time" (*Theological Ethics of the New Testament*, 56–57).

13. Funk, *Parables and Presence*, 65.

14. Nolan states that Jesus was motivated by compassion, not by a need to prove his divinity or moral authority. He explains, Jesus' "only desire was to liberate people from their suffering and their fatalistic resignation to suffering" and continues, "What [Jesus] wanted to do most of all was to awaken the same compassion and the same faith in the

argues the point of Jesus' teaching and healing ministry is to challenge disciples to transcend group solidarity in favor of a more inclusive and ultimately universal human solidarity.[15] This means seeing every other person as our neighbor and being a neighbor to every other person.

And like the parable of the good Samaritan, in Nolan's view, compassion is the key to Christian neighbor-love. He contends that the "root cause" of oppression and domination of some persons under others is a lack of compassion, and that compassion alone is what can teach a person what solidarity with others means.[16] Jesus' own compassionate care for the sick, sinful, and suffering, along with his inclusive table fellowship, is predicated by a counter-cultural focus on exceptionless human dignity rather than status or prestige. His relationships with people who were poor, outcast, and despised would have meant that these individuals "would have interpreted his gesture of friendship as God's approval of them."[17] Truly, these gestures of friendship are crucial for the way they bestow dignity upon people who are often deprived this kind of recognition and respect. But in moving beyond our positions of privilege and power, we are confronted by the urgent need for liberation, for resistance against dehumanizing forces, and collaborative commitment against the systems and structures that undermine human solidarity and right-relationship.[18]

Just as to recognize others as neighbor and to be neighborly to others requires an ongoing give-and-take, so friendship is a fitting example of mutuality in right-relationship. Thus, friendship is not mere leverage for human liberation; it is about fostering intimate relationships to cultivate deeper and wider solidarity. This process begins with "reception" (of the Holy Spirit, and in hospitality toward the other person[s]), is marked by dialogue, and is carried forward in sharing of all kinds (from

---

people around him. This alone would enable the power of God to become operative and effective in their midst" (Nolan, *Jesus Before Christianity*, 43–44; see also 82, 117).

15. Nolan, *Hope in an Age of Despair*, 108.
16. Nolan, *Jesus Before Christianity*, 116, 82.
17. Ibid., 48.
18. Here Joerg Rieger's *Christ and Empire: From Paul to Postcolonial Times* is a valuable resource for addressing problems of power. Rieger reminds us that "The need for liberation only becomes clear from the underside. It is the repressed neighbor who helps us to see the reality." Rieger also notes that freedom is more than emancipation from oppression; it is "also the grace of a true encounter with Jesus Christ at the margins that is inseparable from our true freedom" (320).

emotional to material possessions, for example), which Nolan stresses is an essential demand of Jesus' message and a signal of the Spirit at work in bringing about the reign of God.[19] Second, sharing also bears significant implications for the power dynamics at play because friendship is about empowerment through self-gift, something entirely oppositional to the systems and structures of power that dominate, oppress, and dehumanize individuals. In a small-scale sense, these relationships are liberatory for all involved.

For both Nolan and Gutiérrez, the most fundamental aspect of friendship is to overcome the "tyranny of selfishness" that makes what is most convenient, comfortable, and conducive to self-interest trump any other concern.[20] Friendship requires the temperance of the *id*. Gustavo Gutiérrez suggests that this is at the heart of the meaning of the parable of the good Samaritan.[21] Gutiérrez uses the Samaritan as an example of a much-needed "conversion to the neighbor," which is essentially the most basic step toward a theology of liberation.[22] Gutiérrez adds that this conversion is an ongoing, even permanent process that begins with "watchfulness" and sensitivity to others, engenders a loyalty to individuals usually cast out in isolation, and perhaps most importantly, seeks to conquer fear ("more than unbelief, the enemy of faith") and its "offspring, despair and indifference."[23] Neighborliness and friendship aim to conquer fear—fear that might muzzle evangelization, mollify work for liberation, and manipulate mission to make it superficial and safe. This is no marginal concern; Jon Sobrino contends that the "greatest

---

19. Nolan states quite unequivocally, "Nothing in the Gospel has been so consistently and unashamedly watered down as Jesus' teaching about money and sharing" (*Hope in an Age of Despair*, 104; see also 127).

20. Ibid., 146. This point is reinforced by Gustavo Gutiérrez, who states rather strongly, "we can stand straight, according to the Gospel, only when our center of gravity is outside ourselves" (*A Theology of Liberation*, 118).

21. Gutiérrez writes, "The neighbor was the Samaritan who *approached* the wounded man and *made him his neighbor*. The neighbor, as has been said, is not the one whom I find on my path, but rather the one in whose path I place myself, the one whom I approach and actively seek" (*A Theology of Liberation*, 113).

22. Gutiérrez explains, "A spirituality of liberation will center on a *conversion* to the neighbor, the oppressed person, the exploited social class, the despised ethnic group, the dominated country. Our conversion to the Lord implies this conversion to the neighbor" (*A Theology of Liberation*, 118).

23. Nickoloff, "Church of the Poor," 535.

hurdle facing evangelization is the lack of conviction that good news is possible."[24] Indeed, friendship and the formation of good neighborhoods can serve as valuable sources of hope and faith in the possibilities of love as we strive to cooperate with the Holy Spirit at work in the world.

FRIENDSHIP AT THE MARGINS

In their recent book, *Friendship at the Margins*, Christopher Heuertz and Christine Pohl explain how faithfulness to God takes shape in cultivating friendships in the margins of our church and world. Heuertz and Pohl outline several key requirements and benefits of friendship: they contend that friendship begins with sacrificial love; from there, friendship is marked by mutual respect and humility, accountability, integrity, long-term commitment, fidelity, and stability. They also contend that friendship is predicated by gratitude and sustained by generous sharing. What is more, friendship proves revelatory of truth, accounts for power dynamics, and is conscious of possessions (especially if they are found lacking or in excess). Friendship also helps constitute one's identity and value; being offered friendship (and as Pohl adds, hospitality), means that the other is worthy of this gift of time and talent. As Henri Nouwen attests, "we will never believe we have anything to give unless there is someone who is able to receive. Indeed, we discover our gifts in the eyes of the receiver."[25]

Indeed, it is this mutual exchange that provides the greatest benefit, on both a personal and collective level. On the most basic level, these interpersonal relationships work against categories of "otherness," challenge assumptions about "other" people (the poor, the ignorant, the unsaved), and engages each participant in a process of not only conversion (the word that Nolan and Gutiérrez use), but unfolding transformation. Friendship puts us on a path or journey of ongoing formation: my identity is in flux as relationships develop and change. Friendships reveal who I am, someone who is more than the sum of what I have or do; friendship is about who we become together, in relationship with one another and in a web of other relationships, as well.

24. Sobrino, *Christ the Liberator*, 215.
25. Quoted by Heuertz and Pohl in *Friendship at the Margins*, 80.

The parable of the good Samaritan is often used to showcase the need for awareness of others, empathic concern, and compassionate, merciful care for those in need. This has long been a useful model for service, but one that focuses too much on the outcome of interactions, rather than the process of forming relationships. Mission work, like service, can put too much stress on specific results (x number of people served dinner or y number of converts); it can tempt disciples to log more hours or ramp up their effort to produce even greater results. Not only can this distorted view of mission and ministry exaggerate the importance of specific outcomes, but it can also lead to an inflated perception on one's own importance.

But friendship isn't outcome-based. And because friendship is at least bilateral and often multi-lateral (we have more than one friend at a time and friendships with one person can lead us to get involved in our friend's friends' lives, as well), friendship teaches individuals to humbly accept one's finitude and to put faithfulness ahead of every other goal, whether success, efficiency, or effectiveness.

Despite the fluid nature of friendships, the concept of being-on-the-way (*homo viator*) is critiqued by Heuertz and Pohl. The problem with journey-imagery or reference to being a "pilgrim people" suggests that it is possible to get up and leave when the going gets tough. Heuertz and Pohl respond by claiming that friendship is about putting down roots in order to make people feel safe, needed, and that they belong.[26] To return to the example of the good Samaritan, it is the difference between being a good neighbor in a single episodic act and building a good neighborhood through commitment to lasting relationships. As Pohl notes, overemphasis on "large-scale, structural change and to individual, personal change" has "eclipsed the importance of friendship and hospitality with poor people and strangers," a central way to foster and sustain communities based on understanding and acceptance.[27] Commitment to a specific people or place does not mean that friendships become closed upon themselves; Heuertz and Pohl insist that disciples must always consider who we are excluding from sharing in these reciprocal benefits and blessings.

This is not to suggest that intimate relations on the margins are free from complication or frustration; Heuertz and Pohl are forthright about

26. Ibid., 79.
27. Pohl, *Making Room*, 84.

how such relationships are fraught with difficulty. Chief among this list is the fact that these friendships lead us into complex, ambiguous situations that require integrity, humility, and prayerful, moral discernment. Relationships with marginalized persons inevitably lead into difficult territory. These are opportunities to more fully depend on God and turn outwards in reliance upon a prayerful, truthful, and loving community.[28] When dealing with people who are disadvantaged or disenfranchised, it may be tempting to expect success stories and clear categories between good and evil, saint and sinner. Friendship disabuses disciples of any such illusion.

FRIENDSHIP IN A NEW LIGHT

At this point, we have come to see friendship in a new light, even in comparison with the Aristotelian[29] and Thomistic[30] traditions. Friendship is a significant aspect of moral life, not only for the ways we benefit from these relationships, but through the discipline and authenticity they require. We have learned from Nolan and Gutiérrez that friendships have important implications for human solidarity and liberation. These relationships require openness, conversion, and commitment to the other, especially the one in grave need. Heuertz and Pohl add shape and substance to this relationship by describing the mutual benefits and blessings of friendship specifically located at the margins of society. Friendships as such involve self-awareness and self-criticism as we confront basic assumptions about others, carefully examine our own self-deception, and grow more sensitive to self-indulgent and excessive lifestyle choices that reinforce oppressive forces of power and prestige.

Friendship at the margins requires that we seek out opportunities to take us *to* the margins, wherever they may be in our personal relationships,

---

28. Heuertz and Pohl, *Friendship at the Margins*, 98–99.

29. For Aristotle, friendship exists only between equals and is ranked, in increasing value by utility, pleasure, and virtue. Friendship has three marks: goods in common, to will the good of the friend (loving the self as another self—not for own benefit) and mutuality (*Nicomachean Ethics*, 1155a–57b).

30. For Thomas Aquinas, the most noble human love is friendship; charity is friendship between the human person and God (*ST* II–II.23.1). The effect of this love is union (*ST* II–II.28.1); friendship with others is to be sought for God's sake (*ST* II–II.25.1; 27.7).

neighborhoods, churches, and larger communities. Disciples recognize how Jesus modeled this through inclusive table fellowship and his teaching and healing ministry, as he consistently reached out to and connected with the despised and downtrodden. Of course, this rapport is not unique to Jesus. As Rabbi Jonathan Sacks explains, the call of faith in Judaism is to be a healing presence, to enact covenantal love (*hesed*). Love, which typically also means loyalty in the Hebrew Bible, is worked out in "covenantal relationships" on an interpersonal level, day in and day out: "love moralized into small gestures of help and understanding, support and friendship: the poetry of everyday life written in the language of simple deeds . . . *Hesed* is the gift of love that begets love."[31] Therefore, the path to *shalom* (peace, right-relationship) involves *tikkun olam*, that is, mending or perfecting the world through *darkhei shalom*, the ways of peace.[32] In other words, the Judeo-Christian mission is community, not just a cause; mission is embraced and spread outwards in incrementally more inclusive relationships, not simply through unilateral acts of proselytization or charity. Liberation is not to be understood as only political or economic, but in a holistic sense: personal, social, and spiritual, as well.

The parable of the good Samaritan is significant for this work of liberating evangelization because it reminds us to recognize every person as a neighbor and to be neighborly towards every other. It is to begin to realize human solidarity in terms of ever-inclusive friendship. It is to recognize the church's communion and mission calls disciples beyond the walls of our churches and pages of our membership lists to seek and cultivate more relationships, to form good neighborhoods and communities of faith where people are welcomed, supported, and held accountable to one another. Thus, *shalom*, solidarity, neighborliness, and friendship are inextricably linked—and most urgently needed at the margins of our church and world.

WORKS CITED

Aquinas, Thomas. *Summa Theologica*. Translated by Fathers of the English Dominican Province. Vol. 1–5. Notre Dame, IN: Ave Maria, 1981.
Aristotle. *Nicomachean Ethics*. Translated by Joe Sachs. Newburyport, MA: Focus, 2002.

31. Sacks, *To Heal a Fractured World*, 46.
32. Ibid., 72, 98.

Augustine. *De Doctrina Christiana*. Edited and Translated by R. P. H. Green. Oxford: Clarendon, 1995.
Bailey, Kenneth E. *Through Peasant Eyes: More Lucan Parables, their Culture and Style*. Grand Rapids: Eerdmans, 1980.
Barclay, William. *And Jesus Said: A Handbook on the Parables of Jesus*. Philadelphia: Westminster, 1970.
Funk, Robert W. "'How Do You Read?' A Sermon on Luke 10:25–37" *Interpretation* 18 (1964) 56–61.
———. *Parables and Presence: Forms of the New Testament Tradition*. Philadelphia: Fortress, 1982.
Gutiérrez, Gustavo. *A Theology of Liberation: History, Politics, and Salvation*. Translated by Sister Caridad Inda and John Eagleson. Maryknoll, NY: Orbis, 1988.
Hendrickx, Herman. *The Parables of Jesus*. New York: Harper & Row, 1986.
Heuertz, Christopher L., and Christine D. Pohl. *Friendship at the Margins: Discovering Mutuality in Service and Mission*. Downers Grove, IL: InterVarsity, 2010.
Karris, Robert J. *Works of St. Bonaventure: St. Bonaventure's Commentary on the Gospel of Luke*. Chapters 9–16. Saint Bonaventure, NY: Franciscan Institute, 2003.
Keesmaat, Sylvia C. "Strange Neighbors and Risky Care." In *The Challenge of Jesus' Parables*, edited by Richard N. Longenecker, 263–85. Grand Rapids: Eerdmans, 2000.
Lohse, Eduard. *Theological Ethics of the New Testament*. Translated by M. Eugene Boring. Minneapolis: Fortress, 1991.
Nickoloff, James B. "Church of the Poor: The Ecclesiology of Gustavo Gutiérrez." *Theological Studies* 54 (1993) 512–35.
Nolan, Albert. *Hope in an Age of Despair*. Maryknoll, NY: Orbis, 2009.
———. *Jesus Before Christianity*. Maryknoll, NY: Orbis s, 2001.
Paul VI. *Evangelii Nuntiandi*. Vatican: 8 December 1975.
Pohl, Christine D. *Making Room: Recovering Hospitality as a Christian Tradition*. Grand Rapids: Eerdmans, 1999.
Rieger, Joerg. *Christ & Empire: From Paul to Postcolonial Times*. Minneapolis, MN: Fortress, 2007.
Sacks, Jonathan. *To Heal a Fractured World: The Ethics of Responsibility*. New York: Schocken, 2005.
Sobrino, Jon. *Christ the Liberator: A View from the Victims*. Translated by Paul Burns. Maryknoll, NY: Orbis, 2001.
Wuthnow, Robert. *Acts of Compassion: Caring for Others and Helping Ourselves*. Princeton: Princeton University Press, 1991.

Do-It-Yourself Missions

The Rise of Independent Faith-Based Organizations and the Changing Contours of Missions

Eva Pascal

CONTEMPORARY CHRISTIAN MISSIONS AND outreach have proved creative and resilient. Many Christians in "developed" countries find themselves in a philanthropic milieu driving them toward altruism and outreach to those in "less fortunate" lands. Christians have answered the call for outreach in cross-cultural missions through the formation of new and the strengthening of established faith-based, non-governmental organizations. In addition to church-based and para-church faith-based organizations (FBOs), the past few decades have witnessed a proliferation of independent Christian missions and faith-based organizations. Independent faith-based organizations bring some unique characteristics to the world of mission as autonomous, creative forces for sharing the gospel amidst tangible problems. This paper explores the rise of faith-based organizations in the context of religion and development work, looking particularly at faith-based organizations engaged in cross-cultural missions. The paper will also look at case studies of independent faith-based organizations' missions in Thailand. In these case studies we see an important addition to the foreign mission scene with organizations that are independent, self-initiated, creative, "do-it-yourself" approaches to mission and ministry. Since the mid-twentieth century, burgeoning Christian faith-based organizations, particularly independent organizations, have represented the changing contours of missions. This paper focuses on this contour as an important evolution in Christian mission and outreach.

TRACING THE ROOTS OF INDEPENDENT FAITH-BASED NGOS IN EARLY MODERN MISSIONS

As Andrew Kirk has aptly said, in the last two centuries of missionary expansion, the church has been involved in almost every kind of development project conceivable. Propagating the gospel has gone hand in hand with using scientific discoveries and technologies to improve the material lives of people.[1] The term "faith-based organization" has a broad meaning that runs across religious traditions. G. Clarke defines the term as any organization that derives inspiration and guidance for its activities from the teachings and principles of faith. He also outlines different types of activities that this might cover: (1) an organization that governs the faithful; (2) a charitable or development organization running projects and providing services for marginalized people; (3) a socio-political organization that mobilizes the faithful politically; (4) a missionary organization that promotes the faith, and; (5) an illegal or terrorist organization engaged in an arms struggle in the name of religion.[2] These are ideal categories, with significant overlap; our interest here is Christian faith-based organizations engaged in cross-cultural missions that promote the faith through charity, development, and community building.

Some of the "historic" faith-based organizations were created by churches or denominations; others have the support of multiple churches and tend to be para-church agencies, not directly linked to formal church structures. Some are recognized by churches, and some see themselves as an extension of churches (such as World Vision). Independent FBOs can be differentiated from "historic" FBOs in that they have a much looser affiliation to church structures, they tend to have variegated funding, are often driven by non-professionals, and are commonly initiated from the ground up.

The rise of independent Christian faith-based organizations can be traced to various evangelical movements in the early modern waves of

---

1. Kirk, *What Is Mission?*, 109.
2. Clarke, "Faith-based Organizations and International Development."

foreign missions. In the late eighteenth century, transatlantic evangelicalism thrived due to various revivals and awakenings that continued well into the nineteenth century. Among the common threads within this new movement was an emphasis on conversion—the need for Christians to be born again, to come to Christ or to have a renewed spiritual experience. Activism, such as evangelism and mission-based relief efforts, was also strongly encouraged. Such revivals increased interest in and formation of voluntary societies, and some of these societies set to work abroad.[3] A second wave of evangelical movements also led to increased interest in voluntary societies, resulting in the mushrooming of interest in overseas missions. Among these is William Carey's Baptist Missionary Society (1792), representative of "modern mission" based on church-building that often included at least a school and a health clinic.[4] These societies spawned greater possibility for autonomy from parent churches, leading to more autonomous missions.[5]

By 1910, the Edinburgh World Missionary Conference (EWMC) was very optimistic and strident about evangelizing the non-Christian world. There was a great sense of confidence in this ambitious task because for the first time in history—with the vast power of the West and an increase in globalization through modern modes of transportation and communication—Christians could finally safely reach all parts of the world to evangelize non-Christians.[6] At the heart of the EWMC's idea of mission was the concept of expanding the kingdom of God. The nexus of gospel, conversion, and salvation was at the center of the 1910 understanding of mission. The building of the kingdom also involved other mission activities of the church, many of them associated with the mission station. This might be called the "action-model of mission" activity. School (education), medical clinics (health care), and printing technology (literature, literacy) all contributed to the betterment of non-Christians, and went hand in hand with expanding God's kingdom. Proclamation and action were both components of cooperative mission goals.[7] The autonomy from churches in home countries with the focus

3. Bebbington, *Evangelicalism in Modern Britain*, 2ff.
4. See Stanley, *The History of the Baptist Missionary Society*.
5. Brian Stanley posits that this may have created more autonomy from churches for overseas missions than was possible in the Catholic Church. See *The Bible and the Flag*.
6. Stanley, *The World Missionary Conference*.
7. The building of churches and public preaching and proclamation was primarily

of self-sufficient mission stations was prototypical of contemporary independent FBOs in foreign countries.

Other historical developments in missions contributed to the fostering of independence in foreign missions. Under the influence of Holiness revivals, people like James Hudson Taylor founded a new generation of "faith missions" in the form of the China Inland Society (later OMF International). Certain innovations resulted from these faith missions. They were careful not to clash with established churches, choosing rather to focus on conversion and church planting while leaving maintenance and church-building to indigenous Christians. Those involved in these missions were identified by spiritual *calling* rather than *qualifications* (ordination or special training). Missionaries were expected to identify with indigenous people and their concerns in their own environments. With the emphasis placed on spiritual calling, single women and wives could now be treated as peers.[8] A new generation of faith missions grew rapidly, particularly in the United States.[9] As David Bosch has pointed out, "The relationship between the evangelistic and the societal dimensions of the Christian mission constitutes one of the thorniest areas in the theology and practice of mission."[10] Although faith missions placed an emphasis on proclamation, more room for relief and development initiatives was carved by the allowance of laypersons who had a vision and a calling to participate in missions. The dual emphasis on spiritual calling and contextual knowledge of the field would help lay the groundwork for future independent FBO ventures.

---

the responsibility of ordained or trained missionaries, which at the time were almost exclusively men. Women and lay members were tasked with more social action roles, such as education, medical care, and other functions generally described as "philanthropic or reformatory work." By 1910, women made up the majority of missionary personnel (55 percent for Protestants; 65 percent for Catholics). Robert, "Missionaries Sent and Received Worldwide," 258–59.

8. See Fielder, *The Story of Faith Missions*. See also, Svelmoe, *A New Vision for Missions*, 61–63, 83, 123–29, 131–34, 153–64.

9. Kim and Kim, *Christianity as a World Religion*, 40–42.

10. Bosch, *Transforming Mission*, 401.

THE RISE OF INDEPENDENT MISSIONS AND FBOS

At the beginning of the twentieth century, the majority of foreign missions and missionaries were organized and financed by either denominational bodies or ecumenical missions boards. This structure began to change, especially in the US, in the decades just before World War II. The new structure allowed missionaries to receive funding outside of denominational bodies and ecumenical structures, which severed financial ties to their home churches. In these independent mission structures, the missionaries themselves became more financially independent, and churches and mission boards were not always in a position to approve or deny missionary candidates.

The end of World War II and the start of the Cold War prompted the emergence of international organizations such as the United Nations (UN) and the World Bank (WB), in addition to the rise of the United States as a hegemonic political and economic power. With these changes emerged the idea of development through non-governmental organizations (NGOs), a term applied to any structure outside government that would foster development in third world countries. The establishment of new non-governmental organizations that embraced developmental goals was encouraged, and thus these various transnational bodies became new sources of funding for non-governmental organizations that are religious or faith-initiated (FBOs).

An account of the rise and proliferation of faith-based NGOs must be construed by piecing together important data from several different sources. As Denoulin and Bano have said, no inventory exists for NGOs in general or FBOs in particular, but the proportion of FBOs among similar organizations and their overall impact is significant.[11] As Ian Linden reminds us, it is important to remember that it is difficult to assess whether an NGO is in fact faith-based because so many begin as explicitly religious and then gradually become more secular in tone.[12] However, there is a worldwide increase in the number of NGOs in general, among them FBOs. The US alone has about two million NGOs.

---

11. Séverine and Bano, *Religion in Development*, 83. The UN has proposed a handbook for developing data on non-profit organization by country, but a comprehensive study has yet to be completed. *Handbook on Non-Profit Institutions in the System of National Accounts*, New York: UN, 2003.

12. Linden, "The Language of Development." For example, Oxfam and Amnesty International started out as faith-based.

India has about one million grassroots groups, while more than 100,000 NGOs sprang up in Eastern Europe between 1989 and 1995.[13]

In the last ten to fifteen years in particular there has been an increase in the global granting structures that provide large pools of funding for existing FBOs, while prompting the creation of independent FBOs that meet funding criteria. These include multi-lateral and philanthropic funding sources such as the Global Fund, the Gates Foundation, USAID, and PEPFAR. Billions of dollars are given to different charities and small non-governmental organizations that fit the specifications of such grants.[14] As of July 2007, the Global Fund gave out 7.7 billion dollars for HIV/AIDS prevention projects alone; likewise, since 2003, PEPFAR has given 30 billion dollars for similar projects.[15] In 2007, the Bush administration required one-third of its 3 billion dollar international AIDS prevention budget to be put towards programs that promoted abstinence until marriage. We can deduce that a large portion of that money went to FBOs, which are known for promoting similar views on pre-marital sex. New independent FBOs have thus emerged as a response to the availability of funding. Although Christians are only a small percentage of the population in India, the Catholic Church today is the second largest provider of health care, after the government.[16] In 2000, the World Bank estimated 50 percent of health and education delivered to people in Sub-Saharan Africa was done by faith-based or religious organizations.[17]

Additionally, individual donor contributions to faith-based organizations have also greatly increased,[18] leading to the strengthening of the funding base for new and existing FBOs. As Robert Wuthnow has

13. Office of the United Nations High Commissioner for Refugees, *The State of the World's Refugees*. Smillie and Minear, *The Charity of Nations*, show the importance of NGOs for foreign aid by pointing out the curious fact that some individual NGOs have country specific programs with larger budgets than the governmental ministries to which they relate. See also "The Non-Governmental Order."

14. Specific funds are allocated for malaria and various other health needs that create niches for development organization. See Berkley Center for Religion, Peace and World Affairs Malaria: Scoping New Partnerships.

15. Berkley Center for Religion, Peace and World Affairs. Faith Communities Engage the HIV/AIDS Crisis, 44–45, 52.

16. United Nations General Assembly Session on HIV/AIDS, "India Progress Report."

17. Marshall and Keough, *Global Balance*, xii.

18. Ibid., 25–26.

pointed out, many of the major historic faith-based organizations increased their annual budgets over the last two decades of the twentieth century. The top 25 FBOs had a combined expenditure of 2.3 billion dollars and were present all over the world.[19]

Another indicator of the growth of FBOs is that institutions like the WB and UN have come to embrace FBOs as too numerous and critical to the success of efforts on the ground to exclude from development initiatives. The importance of FBOs to development has only in the last few years come to be seen as an important part of the development conversation (as seen in a growing field of literature devoted to the subject).[20] This shift to engage FBOs started with the initiative of former World Bank president James Wolfensohn working with Archbishop of Canterbury, George Carey. Together, they created the World Faith Development Dialogue (WFDD) in 1998. This brought together the World Council of Churches and helped establish the Development Dialogue on Values and Ethics (DDVE). The United Nations has also recently hosted meetings with religious leaders and FBOs.[21] This new perspective sees religion as inseparable from development, as evidenced by the input of religious leaders and organizations that helped create a consensus for the Millennium Development Goals.[22]

More specifically, it is well known to those on the ground that independent faith-based organizations are proliferating. However, although they are "far more numerous," they are "less well-known or understood."[23] Independent FBOs are more difficult to trace because they tend not to register in their host country, since a majority of their funding comes from the founding missionaries' home countries or from multi-lateral organizations. Definite numbers are also hard to come by because of the instability of many organizations; non-profit organizations and projects of all kinds start up but sometimes often dissolve

---

19. Wuthnow, *Boundless Faith*, 132–3. These figures are based on IRS 990 forms and auditors' reports for 2003. As an example, World Vision's expenditure since 1981 increased by 326 percent.

20. See, for example Haynes, *Religion and Development*; Séverine and Bano, *Religion in Development*; and van Ufford and Schoffeleers, *Religion & Development*.

21. Marshall, United Nations Population Fund.

22. Katherine Marshall has documented the conversation of the WB and FBOs. Marshall and Keough, *Millennium Challenges for Development and Faith Institutions*. See Marshall and van Saanen, *Development and Faith*.

23. Berkley Center Report, "Faith Communities Engage the HIV/AIDS Crisis," 15.

or morph into other organizations. An example of this is the Chiang Mai-based FBO, The Garden of Hope. Began as a rehabilitation center for former sex workers, it was forced to rethink its approach and settle on a new mission focus (to be detailed below). Another example, The Human Development Center (an FBO based out of Bangkok) started out modestly by providing kindergarten education for a handful of slum children, but now offers many services including a health clinic and vocational training.

Robert Wuthnow has posited that US missionary activities across the globe have been strengthened by a combination of voluntary associations, a philanthropic ethos, and the thickening of international networks producing an increase in funding to faith-based organizations.[24] The trend of independent missions, which began in the pre-WWII years, was thus further enhanced by missions adapting hybrid NGO structures.[25] In this environment, independent missions also find new visions (as expressed by the language of development), new sources of funding, and further independence from established missionary structures. The ensuing FBOs embraced concrete programs meant to tackle specific needs within a vision of "human flourishing" that often fit well with those expressed in the UN development goals. The UN Millennium Development Declaration adapted in 2000 consists of the following goals: ending hunger and poverty, universal education, gender equality, child health, maternal health, combating HIV/AIDS, environmental sustainability, and global partnership. Many FBOs work within these spheres and have an important voice in human development advocacy.

CASE STUDIES IN THAILAND: INDEPENDENT MISSIONS "ON THE GROUND"

The growth of Christian populations in Asian regions dominated by other world religions (for example Hinduism in India and Nepal, Islam in Malaysia and Indonesia, Buddhism in Thailand and Cambodia) has been slow but steady. The relatively small number of Christians in Asia may obscure the fact that within these minority settings there are dynamic centers of independent Christian missions and FBOs.

24. Wuthnow, *Boundless Faith*, 139.
25. Ibid., 118–39.

Do-It-Yourself Missions 201

Thailand is a good place to look at independent mission organizations because of the trending number and diversity of faith-based organizations. There have been some attempts to create a database of the more historic FBOs.[26] The region of Northern Thailand in particular has become a strategic regional point as well for missions due to its proximity to Southwestern China and various countries across Southeast Asia. The majority of people in many Southeast Asian countries identify themselves as (Theravada) Buddhists.[27] In this tradition, Buddhism is linked closely with national identity. FBOs bring an action-centered model of mission that might be more effective for the region. They are able to forge long-term relationships, building the trust of locals through a "dialogue of action" where Christian FBOs can engage locals by working for mutual causes.[28]

An action-model of missions is also, in some cases, the only way for a Christian organization to carry out international missions. Political constraints on missions in, for example, China, Laos, and Vietnam—not to mention complications and repression by the military dictatorship in Myanmar (Burma)—render a proclamation-model of evangelization (focusing primarily on conversion and baptismal incorporation into congregations) impractical, if not impossible, for cross-cultural missions. Furthermore, Thailand offers an open door policy and sufficient infrastructure to serve as a base from which independent organizations and missionaries can work with and within countries that prohibit missions. Northern Thailand, besides being the region with the highest concentration of Christians in the country, has the advantage of proximity to Southwestern China, Laos, and Burma.

---

26. See the Directory of Development Organizations: Guide to International Organizations. Thailand has a large number of FBOs. The following representative organizations are selected from a much longer list: Adventist Development and Relief Agency (ADRA), Caritas International Thailand, Catholic Office for Emergency Relief and Refugees (COERR), Eaglesrest, Help for Pastors, Friends of the Samaritans, Lydia House for migrant workers, Jesuit Refugee Service (JRS) Thailand, Rejoice Urban Development Project, Catholic Mission in Human Development Centre, Spirit in Education Movement (SEM), The New Light Foundation, The Rahab Beauty Shop, The Love Line Family Centre, National Catholic Commission on Migration (NCC).

27. Johnson and Ross, *Atlas of Global Christianity*. For example, the percentages of Buddhists in the following Southeast Asian countries are: Thailand, 86.8 percent; Cambodia, 84.9 percent; Myanmar, 73.6 percent; and Laos, 52.9 percent.

28. Fitzgerald and Borelli, *Interfaith Dialogue*. They note four kinds of dialogue: dialogue of life, of action, of theological exchange, and of religious experience.

In the last few decades Northern Thailand and the surrounding regions have experienced unique social, economic, and political challenges. It is home to a sizeable population of marginalized people, such as ethnic minorities without citizenship rights and economic, political, and religious refugees fleeing from the repressive military regime in neighboring Myanmar. The concentration of these marginalized people creates acute needs in the areas of health care, education, poverty reduction, and human rights (including human trafficking for the purposes of exploitation, such as child prostitution). FBOs minister to locals by directly responding to their medical, educational, material, and spiritual needs. In this way, FBOs share the gospel through the action of showing Christian love. Salvation is not understood solely as religious conversion, but also as salvation from material poverty, oppression, ignorance, disease, and suffering. Some FBOs also simultaneously use a proclamation-model, but their primary mode of operation is action-centered. The need for development combined with the advantage of existing infrastructure in Southeast Asia, along with increased funding to development organizations, have led to more activity in the region by various religious groups.[29]

CASE STUDIES OF INDEPENDENT FAITH-BASED ORGANIZATIONS IN THAILAND

Estimates by various local ministry personnel suggest there are over 400 non-governmental organizations in Chiang Mai alone. The examples put forth in this paper come from my experience of living and teaching in Thailand for four years. For the purposes of this paper I would like to look at four independent FBOs, three in the Chiang Mai area and one in Bangkok. I have identified these four organizations because they are diverse in nature, but they share some basic commonalities in their independent structures.

The Garden of Hope (GOH)

The Garden of Hope, located in Chiang Mai, is "a community that protects vulnerable and at-risk children and women from abuse and exploitation in Southeast Asia and equips and enables them to develop

29. Berkley Center Reports 2010, Faith-Inspired Organizations.

maturity and responsibility, bearing fruit for the glory of God."[30] In doing so, it hopes to "transform the lives of the sexually exploited for God's glory." The work of the Garden of Hope revolves around three programs: children's drop-in center, women's resources, and a teen rescue operation. At the drop-in center, children in the red-light district are provided physical, emotional, spiritual, and educational support through a variety of activities. The Garden of Hope also reaches out to women and teens working in the red-light district that are involved in, at-risk of, and coming out of prostitution. This FBO is dedicated to showing the children, youth, and women who find themselves in situations of sexual exploitation "the way, the truth, and the life of Christ through outreach, fellowship, comfort, counseling, vocational training and evangelism." The Garden of Hope is served by a group of national staff and international volunteers, the majority of whom are laypersons.

Free Burma Rangers (FBR)

The Free Burma Rangers is an organization whose vision and mission are "to free the oppressed and to stand for human dignity, justice and reconciliation in Burma" and "to bring help, hope and love to people of all faiths and ethnicities in the war zones of Burma, to shine a light on the actions of the dictators' army, to stand with the oppressed, and to support leaders and organizations committed to liberty, justice and service."[31] To carry out these objectives, trained teams of four or five persons are sent into Myanmar to conduct relief, advocacy, leadership development, and unity missions among internally displaced persons. These missions provide emergency medical, educational, spiritual, material and general assistance to people who suffer under the oppression of the Myanmar government. The evangelistic mission of these FBR teams is evident in the fact that educational supplies they provide include Bibles and hymnals.

Agape Home (Nikki's Place)

Agape Home, started in 1996 in Chiang Mai, is a faith-based organization that provides "love and care to abandoned or orphaned babies and

---

30. For more information, see GOH's website: http://www.thegardenofhope.org/index.html.

31. For more information, see FBR's website: http://www.freeburmarangers.org/.

children with, or at risk of, HIV/AIDS."[32] It offers multiple programs primarily aimed at young children whose parents are either suffering from HIV/AIDS or have died from the disease. If the mothers are still alive but are too ill to self-support and take care of their children, they and their young children are placed in a Mother-Baby Unit (MBU, essentially a group home), where shelter, food, and basic care are provided. If an HIV positive mother is sufficiently healthy but unable to work, she and her children (with or without HIV) can qualify for "Project Lek," where Agape Home provides a monthly stipend to allow the family to remain together in their own home. The organization's largest project is a residential facility that accommodates dozens of abandoned or orphaned children with, or at risk of, HIV/AIDS. Many children are referred to Agape Home by hospitals, social agencies, other NGOs or churches. While not explicitly stated on the group's website, it is likely from the frequent references to God and God's love that being a "believer" is one of the most basic requirements for both local and international volunteers.

The Human Development Center (HDC)

The Human Development Center was founded by an American Catholic priest in a Bangkok slum in 1973, illustrating that self-starting FBOs are not an exclusively Protestant activity or interest.[33] Serving as a parish priest and living among his parishioners in the slaughterhouse area, Father Joseph Maier soon realized that their needs were more than spiritual. Noting that many children were not going to school, his first project was to build a kindergarten to provide the slum children with a basic education. From this humble beginning, the HDC grew into an umbrella organization with thirty-one schools all over the slums of Bangkok—thirty kindergartens and one primary—with nearly 4,000 students taught by 110 teachers.

Over the years, HDC operations expanded to include: a medical clinic providing general as well as pre- and post-natal care seven days a week; an All-Slum Savings and Loan program lending money for slum dwellers to rebuild their homes after frequent fires; vocational

---

32. See, http://www.nikkisplace.org/.

33. For an article about this organization, see the Normita Thongtham, "A Catholic Mission," *Bangkok Post*, June 2, 1998. http://www.bangkokpost.com/outlookwecare/020698_Outlook01.html

training and employment programs for poor mothers; a graphic design department producing novelty items like T-shirts and placemats, whose profits are used to finance other HDC programs; a Community Health Development Centre providing care for HIV/AIDS victims and serving as a hospice for the terminally ill; and a Mercy Centre providing shelter, food, caring personal interaction, and education if the children wish to go back to school. HDC employs full-time social workers, available to provide family counseling and teach the community about AIDS and drugs. To deter drug abuse among the youth, sports programs are organized; the HDC soccer, basketball, and volleyball teams compete on a regular basis. HDC also has a prison program, providing assistance to young offenders and illegal immigrants in detention centers around Bangkok.

BASIC CHARACTERISTICS OF "INDEPENDENT" FAITH-BASED ORGANIZATIONS

All cross-cultural FBOs share a common adherence to Christian values, either explicitly on the level of their mission statement or more implicitly in their motivation. Their governing members also uphold those values and bring them to an action-centered sharing of the love of Christ. The *modus operandi* of FBOs is to share the gospel through an action-model of problem solving. From the four case studies described above, several common characteristics can be identified among independent FBOs.[34]

Loose affiliation with church structures. Some newer FBOs are more independent because they are not attached to church or para-church organizations; historic FBOs are often funded by, and thus accountable to, church administration. Of the four case studies, HDC operates alongside local churches. However, even HDC's relationship to the church is lateral, as it has a high degree of freedom to operate various programs and internally allocate money for its programs. The three other cases have the support of many churches of the founders' countries of origin, along with local church support. Thus they are even more loosely affiliated with less church oversight. FBOs that are not under the umbrella

---

34. Ferris, "Faith-Based and Secular Humanitarian Organizations," 311–25. Ferris points out that an important distinction of "independent" FBOs from historic FBOs is loose ties to church structures.

of church bodies, or in a lateral but accountable relationship to church bodies, operate with a high degree of self-governing autonomy.

Diversity of funding sources. Historic FBOs that operate under a large church organization or ecumenical body receive funding through the affiliate umbrella group, and in addition may tap into multi-lateral national and international grant funds. Independent FBOs are not directly affiliated with and thus not financially dependent on a church, denomination, or para-church organization. The access of independent FBOs to funding may be varied, with funding coming from multiple churches, individual donors, and/or secular sources. As funding sources might be varied, securing funding can be difficult before the organization is established or self-supporting. Some independent FBOs, like Garden of Hope and Agape Home, initially found it easier to secure funding by either being initiated or supported by founders and patrons. FBOs may take advantage of secular funding sources, especially funding available for health and HIV/AIDS prevention, which allow even more independence from church structures. Organizations like the FBR tend to secure funding primarily from individuals and by appealing to churches abroad.

Because of the instability of funding for many independent FBOs, securing long-term funds and, ideally, becoming self-sustaining can become a major preoccupation. This might be one of the reasons for the short life cycles of small-scale independent FBOs. Funding might also be a source of competition between many types of non-governmental organizations. Yet, secured funding from a lucrative funding source or wealthy or steady stream of donors (or the founders themselves being independently wealthy) can allow much more room for innovation in problem solving programs. The importance and need of funding for FBOs is driven home in all four examples of FBOs discussed earlier. Their publicity material and websites promote an appeal for donations from private individuals.

Non-professionals and lay people. Professional training as a missionary or a formal education in theology or ecclesial ordination is not a prerequisite or priority for independent FBOs. This is evident by the use of "international volunteers" in all the examples previously mentioned. As indicated earlier, much of the burden of work in non-church building mission, even in 1910, was assigned to the non-ordained, women, and laity. These tasks were in areas such as education and health care, but necessary for evangelizing efforts.

The lack of importance of ministerial credentials for work in faith-based organizations does not imply, however, that leaders are any "less" Christian. Credibility depends on their spiritual "calling" and good relationship with churches. Of the case studies, only the HDC was started by an ordained individual. In this case, he also ventured into areas outside of his field of expertise. The other examples began with people working outside of their primary vocational training.

The leaders of the four organizations documented above did not start as experts in the niche of their particular FBO. However, some founding members became interested in their particular mission because of general knowledge regarding both the specific areas and the particular people that the organization targets. Some of the founders of the FBOs have experience in the military, for example, but no medical training. One founding member of the Garden of Hope has a Harvard law degree and worked for international organizations related to law and human trafficking. Although it is obviously advantageous to have professionals in the area of interest, it is not a necessity for starting an organization. Often training and expertise develop as the organization grows, expands, and partners with professionals and other more technically skilled organizations.

Self identification as Christian mission and ministry Although leaders of independent FBOs are often non-professionals, they often self-identify as Christian missionaries, engaged in cross-cultural missions. Christian networks are important to all four organizations examined; for FBRs and Agape Home, fund raising efforts are aimed at Christians, tugging at the "Christian" heart and financial generosity. As Christian organizations, all FBOs share in common the objective of showing the saving work of God in alleviating suffering and providing a more fulfilled life in the present.

Self-initiated missions and ministry. As independent FBOs are not created directly out of the decision-making bodies of churches, many are initiated from the level of voluntary individuals or small groups. Independent FBOs are difficult to document because they do not operate under direct affiliation with church, denominational, or ecumenical bodies, they tend to be initiated by individuals and small groups that are non-professional, and often self-identify as missionary without registering as such with host governments. As funding often comes from a variety of sources, there might be volatility, but also a heightened degree of creativity, in beginning a mission.

THE MILIEU "DO-IT-YOURSELF" MISSIONS: PROBLEMS AND POTENTIALS

With the rise of independent FBOs it seems that anyone with a concrete vision for helping others abroad, and with sufficient financial resources, can engage in missions. If the Christian message of a salvation starting here on Earth is heeded, serving people in their current needs becomes imperative. As Gary Gardner has put it: "Religious people in wealthy countries are in an enviable position; they often have enough wealth and, increasingly, the creative institutions, to move their societies closer to the ideals to which they are committed."[35] We find ourselves immersed in a milieu of "do-it-yourself" altruism that is both fashionable and encouraged. This is evident in both secular and faith-based circles, as the distinctions begin to blur when it comes to encouraging individual potential to help others in need.[36] Nicholas Kristof calls this an "unnamed revolution" happening as we speak, a "do-it-yourself" approach to philanthropy and foreign aid in which many women are involved.[37] Kristof identifies this trend of "do-it-yourself" foreign aid particularly in idealistic young adults; altruism is contagious, he says. He asks, "Are these young idealists unsophisticated about what it takes to change the world? Yes, often. At first, they don't always appreciate the importance of listening to local people and bringing them into the management of projects, and they usually overestimate the odds of success. They also sometimes think it will be romantic to tackle social problems, a view that may fade when they've caught malaria."[38]

Kristof suggests that it is fair to object that some of these do-it-yourself organizations, without distinguishing between secular or

35. Gardner, *Inspiring Progress*.

36. Indeed, Gilbert Rist has put forth the argument that altruism and development in the West functions as a religion and arises out of a western linear view of history and progress. See *The History of Development*.

37. Kristof, "D.I.Y. Foreign Aid Revolution." Here, Kristof looks at the proliferation of individual effort to solve problems and create positive change.

38. Ibid.

faith-based ones, only accomplish miniscule results. Many challenges are deeply rooted, such as the child sex and HIV/AIDS prevention that require structural, cultural, and governmental changes in order to make long-term impact. But it is equally true that self-start organizations make a difference: if you happen to be an HIV positive child or an orphan, you may have a longer and more fulfilling life upon coming into contact with an FBO. One of the potential strengths of independent FBOs is the fact that they can cultivate networks of Christians wanting to engage in altruism, thus tapping into resources from local and foreign churches and Christian individuals. Even some secular NGOs are cognizant of the fact that FBOs have a wide reach into local communities and church networks, particularly concerning health resources and issues. A team from Management Sciences for Health, a secular NGO in Cambridge, MA, reiterated the importance of working with FBOs for health programs, especially in Africa where religious life is very important to many local people.[39] Management Sciences for Health has partnered with Christian Connections for International Health, an organizational network of 165 Christian health organizations and 300 individuals across the globe, many of them independent FBOs. An interview with members suggests that FBOs have much potential, but sometimes they do not cultivate and leverage Christian networks to secure a variety of funding sources.[40]

39. Meeting with the Management Sciences for Health leadership team for a course Mission Enacted, December 6, 2010, Cambridge, MA. See www.msh.org for more information. They highlighted the importance of FBOs and also the challenges and potentials in the following ways (Handout entitled, "MSH and Faith-Based Organization: Strengthening Partnership and Collaboration for Health"): (1) FBOs play an important role in international health; they are major providers of health care in many countries through mission hospitals, clinics, and community programs; (2) Increasingly, FBOs are partnering with each other in order to take on major health initiatives—e.g., the Interreligious Council in Uganda; (3) FBOs have existing and extensive networks and influence at the community level to achieve improved health outcomes, e.g., home-based care for HIV/AIDS and directly-observed treatment for tuberculosis, especially in remote and underserved areas; (4) Missionaries are often leaders in providing high-quality health services and effective strategies; (5) FBOs can have considerable influence on health policies and advocacy, as seen in Africa, where governments have been pushed to provide treatment for AIDS and in Afghanistan and Senegal, where *mullahs* actively support contraceptive use; (6) Despite these positive features, FBOs also have unrealized potential and a desire to strengthen their capacity and effectiveness. Understanding FBOs and how to better work with them at the country level is important for MSH's work, just as it is important that we understand other dimensions of social structure and cultural values in the communities we serve.
40. Conversation with Douglas Huber from Christian Connections for International

CONCLUSION

The recent surge in viable multi-lateral funding for development projects and donations to charities, coupled with the historic development of independent mission structures, have contributed to a current proliferation of independent, self-started, "do it yourself" missions in the form of faith-based organizations. In the case studies above from Thailand, I have attempted to show examples of "independent" FBOs. What these independent FBOs focus on in mission is a tangible salvation and an attempt to remedy human, social, economic, medical, and developmental needs that are not being met fully by the established churches, other international organizations, or by the various governments. Thus, these FBOs identify felt needs and fill the gaps with their own dedication and acquired expertise. They accomplish their goals using concrete acts designed to solve specific problems. As independent FBOs, there is much potential for creativity and innovation, but also many challenges for growth. At the same time, the challenge for independent FBOs is to take responsibility for their organizations in local contexts while not imposing themselves on others. They must work more closely with local communities. They also must communicate and cooperate with donor and local churches, other NGOs, and local power brokers to maximize influence toward structural and governmental change. In doing so, long-term transformation is made possible. The growth in independent FBOs represents an evolution in the changing contours of missions facing human spiritual and developmental needs in the twenty-first century.

WORKS CITED

Bebbington, David W. *Evangelicalism in Modern Britain: A History from the 1730s to 1980s*. London: Unwin Hyman, 1989.

Berkley Center for Religion, Peace and World Affairs, Georgetown University. Faith Communities Engage the HIV/AIDS Crisis: Lessons Learned and Paths Forward. Fall 2007.

———. Malaria: Scoping New Partnerships. January 9, 2009.

Berkley Center Reports 2010. Faith-Inspired Organizations and Global Development Policy: A Background Review: "Mapping" Social and Economic Development Work in Southeast Asia.

Health, for a course Mission Enacted, December 6, 2010, Cambridge, MA. See www.ccih.org for more information.

Bosch, David. *Transforming Mission: Paradigm Shifts in Theology of Mission.* Maryknoll, NY: Orbis, 1991.
Clarke, G. "Faith-based Organizations and International Development: An Overview." In *Development, Civil Society and Faith-Based Organizations,* edited by G. Clarke, M. Jennings and T. Shaw, 17–45. New York: Lang, 2007.
Directory of Development Organizations: Guide to International Organizations, Governments, Private Sector Development Agencies, Civil Society, Universities, Grantmakers, Banks, Microfinance Institutions and Development Consulting Firms, Edition 2008. Volume II/A, Asia and the Middle East: Thailand.
Ferris, Elizabeth. "Faith-Based and Secular Humanitarian Organizations." *International Review of the Red Cross* 87.858 (June 2005) 311–25.
Fielder, Klaus. *The Story of Faith Missions.* Oxford: Regnum, 1994.
Fitzgerald, Michael, and John Borelli. *Interfaith Dialogue: A Catholic View.* Maryknoll, NY: Orbis, 2006.
Gardner, Gary T. *Inspiring Progress: Religions' Contributions to Sustainable Development.* New York: Norton, 2006.
Haynes, Jeffrey. *Religion and Development: Conflict or Cooperation?* New York: Palgrave Macmillan, 2007.
Johnson, Todd M., and Kenneth R. Ross, eds. *Atlas of Global Christianity 1910–2010.* Edinburgh: Edinburgh University Press, 2009.
Kim, Sebastian, and Kirsteen Kim. *Christianity as a World Religion.* London: Continuum, 2008.
Kirk, Andrew J. *What is Mission? Theological Explorations.* Minneapolis, MN: Fortress, 2000.
Kristof, Nicholas. "D.I.Y. Foreign Aid Revolution." *New York Times Magazine.* No pages. Online: http://www.nytimes.com/2010/10/24/magazine/24volunteerism-t.html?ref=magazine.
Linden, Ian. "The Language of Development: What Are International Development Agencies." In *Development, Civil Society and Faith-Based Organizations,* edited by G. Clarke, M. Jennings and T. Shaw, 72–93. New York: Lang, 2007.
Marshall, Alex. United Nations Population Fund, Second United Nations Inter-agency Consultation on Engaging Faith-based Organizations for the MDGs, August 5, 2009.
Marshall, Katherine, and Marisa Bronwyn van Saanen. *Development and Faith: Where Heart Mind and Soul Work Together.* Washington, D.C.: World Bank, 2007.
Marshall, Katherine, and Lucy Keough. *Global Balance: Common Ground between the Worlds of Development and Faith.* Washington, D.C.: World Bank, 2005.
Marshall, Katherine, and Richard Marsh. *Millennium Challenges for Development and Faith Institutions.* Washington, D.C.: World Bank, 2004.
Office of the United Nations High Commissioner for Refugees. *The State of the World's Refugees.* Oxford: Oxford University Press, 2000.
Rist, Gilbert. *The History of Development: From Western Origins to Global Faith.* London: Zed, 2008.
Robert, Dana. "Missionaries Sent and Received Worldwide, 1910-2010." In *Atlas of Global Christianity 1910–2010,* edited by Todd M. Johnson & Kenneth R. Ross, 258–59. Edinburgh: Edinburgh University Press, 2009.
Séverine, Deneulin, and Masooda Bano. *Religion in Development: Rewriting the Secular Script.* London: Zed, 2009.

Smillie, Ian, and Larry Minear. *The Charity of Nations*. Bloomfield: Kumarian, 2004.

Stanley, Brian. *The Bible and the Flag: Protestant Missions and British Imperialism in the Nineteenth and Twentieth Centuries*. Leicester, UK: Apollos, 1990.

———. *The History of the Baptist Missionary Society 1792–1992*. Edinburgh: T. & T. Clark, 1992.

———. *The World Missionary Conference, Edinburgh 1910*. Grand Rapids: Eerdmans, 2009.

Svelmoe, William Lawrence. *A New Vision for Missions*. Tuscaloosa: The University of Alabama Press, 2008.

"The Non-governmental Order." *The Economist*. December 11, 1999.

Thongtham, Normita. "A Catholic Mission." *Bangkok Post*, June 2, 1998. No pages. Online: http://www.bangkokpost.com/outlookwecare/020698_Outlook01.html.

Ufford, Quarles van, and J. M. Schoffeleers, *Religion & Development: Towards an Integrated Approach*. Amsterdam: Free University Press, 1988.

United Nations General Assembly Session on HIV/AIDS. "India Progress Report on the Declaration of Commitment on HIV/AIDS." New Delhi: Ministry of Health and Family, 2005.

Wuthnow, Robert. *Boundless Faith: The Global Outreach of American Churches*. Berkeley: University of California Press, 2009.

14

Methodist Border Friendship Commission

A Case Study

Lisa Beth White

THE METHODIST BORDER FRIENDSHIP Commission is a faith-based organization working within the Lower Rio Grande Valley region, on both the U.S. and Mexican sides of the border. It is a joint organization of the United Methodist Church and the Iglesia Metodista de México. This case study will examine geographic, demographic, political, ecological, and theological issues that inform and shape the work of the Methodist Border Friendship Commission (MBFC).

GEOGRAPHY

The Lower Rio Grande Valley is located at the southernmost tip of Texas where the Rio Grande runs shallow. MBFC begins its work in Del Rio and Ciudad Acuña, located just south of the Amistad Reservoir, all the way down to Brownsville and Matamoros just a few miles from the Gulf of Mexico. There are two major dam projects on the border-forming Rio Grande, the Amistad Reservoir and Falcon Reservoir. These dams have contributed to the shrinking of the river farther south. Once a lush grasslands river area with wetlands near the coast, the border area is now marked more by dry brush land overgrazed by cattle. The area is rural, with small towns dotting the landscape. Agriculture and cattle ranching are the main industries.

Agriculture has played a major role in the border region throughout its history. Early "Anglo" settlers brought in new crops and irrigation methods (most notably, canals) that increased production. In addition to the canals, there is a smaller river called the Arroyo Colorado, which flows through Hidalgo, Cameron, and Willacy counties on the U.S. side. There are also bodies of water called *resacas* that flowed into the Rio Grande many years ago, but are now cut off from the river.

The border region is well known as a birder's paradise, as many species winter in the area and migrating birds rest in the region on their way north or south. The World Birding Center is actually located in Brownsville. The arroyo, *resacas*, and Rio Grande provide habitat for fish, waterfowl, amphibians, and reptiles. However, with recent changes in water quality, air quality, and the construction of the border wall, many species are now threatened. Agriculture on the Texas side of the border continues to be an important part of the economy, with cotton, citrus, sorghum grain, peppers, cabbage, and aloe as major crops.

DEMOGRAPHICS

The demographics of the border area are difficult to interpret, as statistics are gathered by both the U.S. and Mexican governments.[1] U.S. Census Bureau statistics for Cameron County, Texas—the southernmost county along the border—give a general picture of the demographics of the region on the U.S. side. The population of Cameron County was estimated to have grown at a rate of 15 percent during the period between 2000 and 2007. Nearly 35 percent of the population is under the age of eighteen, and only 55 percent of the adult population has graduated high school. 86 percent of the population is Hispanic and 13 percent is Caucasian, or "Anglo" (the term commonly used in Texas), with 79 percent speaking a language other than English at home. In 2007 the median income per household was $29,589 while the per capita income was only $10,960. Thirty-four percent of the population lives below the poverty line.[2]

---

1. For this case study, only U.S. statistics are considered.
2. U.S. Census Bureau, *State & Country QuickFacts*.

These statistics do not reveal the complex nature of life along the border. People must often travel back and forth across the border. Upper- and middle-class Mexican citizens travel to the U.S. for shopping and to stay in resort hotels on South Padre Island, Texas. Working-class Mexican citizens travel across the border for both work and shopping. Texans travel across the border for work, tourism, and dining. Many times families will have relatives on both sides of the border; this is illustrated in my own family by two of my brothers' marriages. They each married women who were born on one side of the border but raised on the other, and who still have family on both sides of the border.

The situation at the elementary school that my brothers and I attended as children illustrates the changing dynamics of power and language in the area. My sister-in-law, Eloisa Ackerman, is now principal of Dishman Elementary School in Combes, Texas, just outside Harlingen in Cameron County. When my brothers and I attended, the school kept Spanish-speaking students in segregated classrooms, where they were taught English until they could be mainstreamed into grade-level classes. Now every employee at the school is bilingual, and students are placed according to academic needs rather than language skills. As a Hispanic woman, Mrs. Ackerman represents a shift among the power holders from an Anglo-only group to that which is more representative of the demographics of the area.

Another demographic factor in the region that is not represented in the statistics is the seasonal influx of Winter Texans. While the actual number of Winter Texans is difficult to estimate, they provide several million dollars to boost the economy each year (estimates range from $225 million to $900 million). Winter Texans are typically from the upper mid-west, retired, many are military veterans, and many form long-lasting friendships by returning to the same RV park year after year. Winter Texans come for the mild winter weather, often volunteer in the area, and spend money at tourist attractions and festivals.

I want to summarize and restate an important aspect of life and ministry on the border: the movement of people across the border is not a one-way or permanent movement. Historically, people have moved to find temporary work, returning to their homes and families after a period of time. People often have family on both sides of the border, and the flow of persons back and forth across the border is common. Winter Texans go to Mexico for tourism, pharmaceutical needs, and inexpensive dentistry. Mexicans come north for shopping, tourism on South Padre Island, and for work.

Another dimension to the demographic picture is religion. Franciscan priests came to Texas in the 1600s as a part of Spanish colonization efforts, establishing many Catholic missions. Anglos brought other Christian denominations into the state during the late 1800s. Religious preference statistics are available for the state of Texas, but these are not representative of the border area. On both sides of the border the population is heavily Catholic. A popular pilgrimage destination is the Virgen de San Juan del Valle Shrine, in San Juan, Texas. Between 10,000 and 20,000 people visit the shrine weekly, attending mass, visiting the outdoor Stations of the Cross, and praying to the Virgin. Other denominations along the border are Southern Baptist, United Methodist, Presbyterian, and Pentecostal. On the Mexican side, there are autonomous versions of these denominations.

POLITICAL CONSIDERATIONS

The history of the border region is one marked by conflict and treaty. Originally inhabited by Native Americans, the area was colonized by Spain in the 1500s. In 1821 Mexico won independence from Spain and allowed Anglos to begin settling in Texas. The border region did not see many Anglo settlers until the 1850s and later. The border itself was in question after the war between Texas and Mexico that resulted in Texas' independence as a republic in 1836. Mexico did not recognize Texas' independence, and when a battle took place between U.S. and Mexican troops just north of the Rio Grande in 1846, the U.S. formally declared war on Mexico. The Treaty of Guadalupe Hidalgo established the border in 1848. In the years since, Mexicans have come north looking for safety (especially during the Mexican Revolution, 1910–29) and for work, with varying restrictions placed on them by the U.S. government.

The border region is governed by a number of entities, several of which impact the work of the Methodist Border Friendship Commission. In addition to the federal governments of the United States and Mexico, the area is divided by state and municipal units. The Texas state government contains several border counties: Val Verde, Kinney, Maverick, Webb, Zapata, Starr, Hidalgo, and Cameron. On the Mexican side, the states are Coahuila, Nuevo León, and Tamaulipas. The border crossings are maintained by the U.S. Border Patrol, with customs and immigration officers on each side of the border for their respective countries. Each municipality has its own local government and regulatory agencies, some of which impact the work of the MBFC.

A significant factor for the work of the MBFC is the existence of *colonias*. According to Texas Secretary of State Esperanza "Hope" Andrade, *colonias* are unincorporated subdivisions, usually in floodplains, with little to no infrastructure.[3] Land and substandard housing are cheap, and for residents whose per capita annual income ranges from $5,559 to $8,899, the *colonias* are an affordable option. Limited public funds at the county level are not enough to provide water and sewer services to all of the *colonias*. There are over 2,000 *colonias* in Texas with approximately 400,000 residents, mainly located along the border. *Colonias* often resemble the shantytowns seen in the global south: houses built with scrap wood, corrugated tin, and cardboard. Residents build temporary structures while continuing to work on their actual homes, digging septic tanks, and struggling to pay their contract for deed (land contract), a system of payment in which ownership of the land remains with the seller until the final payments are made. Disease rates are higher in *colonias* than in the rest of the state, with tuberculosis occurring at twice the state rate. Unemployment rates are staggering, from 20 to 60 percent, compared to the overall unemployment state rate of 7 percent.[4]

ECOLOGY AND ECONOMY

Ecology and economy are interconnected in the border region. The ecology of the area has changed since the devaluation of the peso and the implementation of the North American Free Trade Agreement. According to the Texas Environmental Almanac, the border region has experienced dramatic population growth.[5] The Mexican states tracked population growth in the border region from 1980 to 1990. In that time, the state of Tamaulipas experienced 36 percent growth while Nuevo León

---

3. Andrade, *Colonias FAQ's*.
4. Ibid.
5. Texas Center for Policy Studies, "NAFTA and the Texas/Mexico Border Environment."

experienced only 2 percent growth. This difference is directly related to the growth of *maquiladora* plants in Tamaulipas and the devaluation of the peso in 1982. On the Texas side, Cameron County experienced 24 percent growth, and Hidalgo County 35 percent growth during the same time period. The border cities have become clogged with people, straining the public works systems.

Maquiladora plants are foreign owned assembly plants located in Mexico that use imported materials for assembly and export to the U.S. Tariff changes implemented with NAFTA allowed the duty-free import of machinery, equipment, and raw materials to the plants. There are nearly 2,300 *maquiladora* plants along the U.S.-Mexico border.[6] According to the Texas Secretary of State, Texas' trade with Mexico has increased by 448 percent since the inception of NAFTA.[7]

The Rio Grande is the second-longest river in North America. Ramón Eduardo Ruiz argues that pesticides, carcinogens, industrial solvents, and raw sewage are dumped into the river. He notes that Nuevo Laredo, Reynosa, and Matamoros do not have waste treatment plants.[8] NAFTA opened the way for increased truck traffic by decreasing the restrictions of tariffs and quotas. This has worsened air quality in the region. New structures have had to be implemented in order to address environmental issues on this international border. The Mexican government does not have the resources to provide inspectors to keep up with the number of plants in the area, and enforcement of regulations proves difficult. In recent years, the border area has been struggling with drought conditions as well. Plants, animals, and people are all beginning to suffer the consequences of these conditions.

METHODIST BORDER FRIENDSHIP COMMISSION

The context in which the MBFC works is clearly one of poverty, a maze of international business and government concerns, and a confusing border situation. The Methodist Border Friendship Commission was started as a way to organize the work of the Methodist churches along the border. Leaders from the Southwest Texas Annual Conference and

---

6. Ruiz, *On the Rim of Mexico*, 61–63.
7. Andrade, *Border Commerce Coordinator Report*.
8. Ruiz, *On the Rim of Mexico*, 199.

from the Iglesia Metodista de México met to form the agency as an intentional effort to cooperate in mission outreach to the poor in the area.

Structure

The Methodist Border Friendship Commission is a joint project of the United Methodist Church and the Iglesia Metodista de México; specifically, the Southwest Texas Annual Conference and the Rio Grande Conference of the UMC, and the Eastern Conference of the Methodist Church of Mexico. The Rio Grande Conference has its roots in Methodist mission outreach to Mexicans in the early 1850s, and was formalized in the creation of the Rio Grande Mission Conference in 1882.[9] At that time, there were three conferences in Texas: one for English speakers, one for German speakers, and one for Spanish speakers. The Rio Grande Conference now covers Hispanic/Latino congregations across Texas and New Mexico, which overlap geographically with other annual conferences such as the Southwest Texas Annual Conference. Several districts are also part of the MBFC, the Distrito San Pablo and Distrito Fronterizo in Mexico, the Southern District of the Rio Grande Conference, and the McAllen District of the Southwest Texas Annual Conference.

The MBFC has two coordinators: Guillermo "Willie" Berman is the Mexican Methodist Border Mission Coordinator for the Eastern Conference of the Methodist Church of Mexico; Susan Hellums is the Border Area Mission Coordinator, working out of the First UMC of McAllen. Volunteers in Mission is the short-term mission-sending program of the United Methodist Church, under the umbrella of the General Board of Global Ministries (GBGM). Each annual conference in the UMC administers its own Volunteers in Mission program, and all projects are listed through the GBGM offices. What is unique about the MBFC is that it is a program with coordinators from two different Methodist churches on both sides of the border working together to create a program that addresses issues common to Mexico and Texas.

Funding

The MBFC is an Advance Special of the General Board of Global Ministries of the UMC. Formerly known as The Advance for Christ, Advance Specials were created following World War II (1948) in an

---

9. Vernon, *Methodist Excitement in Texas*, 196.

effort by the Methodist church to provide relief for immediate needs while at the same time proclaiming the gospel. At that time, secular development theory focused on infrastructure and economic aid. Current development theory has shifted to focus on human needs such as maternal health, childhood education, environmental concerns, and poverty reduction, as reflected in the United Nations' Millennium Development Goals.

Specific programs submit applications to become Advance Specials; the Methodist Border Friendship Commission is one of those programs. Individuals or groups within the UMC can designate which ministry is to receive their donation, with 100 percent of donated funds going to the designated agency or program; this is one method through which the MBFC receives funding. Other funding sources include direct donations by individuals and support from churches.

MBFC distributes funds to several local projects. The website includes reports for the budget years 2003–4 and 2004–5. In the more recent report, grants and in-kind gifts were listed, as well as numbers of volunteers and teams who worked as short-term missionaries with the MBFC. A total of $32,150 was given to programs, such as: $4,900 for a breakfast and lunch program at three churches in Mexico, feeding between fifty and seventy children per day; $300 to assist a Volunteers in Mission team from Mexico to travel to San Luis Potosi for a construction project; $5,000 for a Pastors' Children Scholarship fund, helping over forty Mexican children with school fees and supplies; and $4,000 for pastoral support in both districts of the Methodist Church of Mexico that are part of the MBFC's structure. In-kind gifts were received and distributed through the MBFC, such as computers, sewing machines, school supplies, bicycles, clothes, health care items, medical equipment, and hand tools.[10]

Short-term mission teams provide their own funding for projects. Volunteers in Mission teams pay for their own travel, housing, food, and contribute both funds and labor for construction projects. Medical and dental teams provide labor and supplies for their projects. Youth mission projects such as U.M. ARMY (United Methodist Action Reach-out Mission by Youth) also pay for their own travel, stay in churches that donate sleeping space, provide their own food, and pay for supplies used in building wheelchair ramps, painting projects, and porch or floor repairs.

10. Methodist Border Friendship Commission, "Construction Ministries."

Projects

Projects for the MBFC are divided into three categories: construction, non-construction, and "wish list" ministries in need of funding. Construction projects are further divided as to their location, whether on the Texas side or Mexico side of the border. On the Texas side, projects include disaster relief (following hurricanes, for example), home construction and repair in the *colonias*, counseling services, a food pantry, community health and wellness services, and a literacy center. Projects on the Mexico side of the border are similar to those in Texas and include repairs to churches and parsonages, kindergarten programs, breakfast and lunch programs, sewing classes, and after-school programs. Spanish language Bibles are purchased for distribution in Vacation Bible Schools. A backpack and school supplies project helps to provide resources for more than 1,250 students who cannot afford supplies or uniforms. The farm animal and agriculture program provides chicks and quail in three Mexican communities.

Clinica Betania, Eleazar Kindergarten, and Betania Elementary School are ministries of the Iglesia Metodista de México. These are also Advance Special projects of the UMC. The kindergarten and school were founded by the denomination and have been incorporated into the public school system of Mexico. Classroom expansion and scholarships are provided by the ministry. The clinic provides health care for low-income families. Scholarship programs support pastors' children with school fees, as the average monthly salary for Methodist pastors in Mexico is $240–$270. Secondary school fees are also part of the scholarship program to help keep students from dropping out to find work. Breakfast and lunch programs have been started by the Iglesia Metodista de México in communities where funds are not available for the federal feeding program.[11]

THEOLOGICAL ISSUES

There are several theological issues to which we now turn our attention. The first is that of boundary crossing, as the border region provides both literal and figurative boundaries that must be crossed. Both the

---

11. Methodist Border Friendship Commission, "Ministries offering opportunities for service (other than construction)."

North American Free Trade Agreement (NAFTA) and *maquiladora* plants send the message that Mexican labor and a good working relationship between Mexico and the U.S. are desired. Yet the border wall sends a clear, visual message that Mexicans are "the other" and are to be kept out of the United States. Crossing the border from one country to another can cause anxiety, even for those who cross legally and with proper documentation. The purpose statement of the Methodist Border Friendship Commission states that it exists "to promote friendship and fellowship, evangelism and mission, and to promote service to others as a clear response to the love of God, a love that knows no boundaries, no borders."[12] In the midst of the contradictory messages of commerce and international relations, the MBFC works toward a different vision of humanity. The churches are separate and yet they work in greater cooperation than do the governments of Mexico and the U.S. The City of Brownsville called for $1.2 billion in funds designated for wall construction to be diverted to health care, education, job training, housing, and infrastructure that would contribute to a reduction in diabetes and preventable diseases. This call went unheeded by the federal government. As an organization of Christian missionaries, the MBFC can work with and for the people of the region, in spite of the government's refusal to prioritize human rights and needs. In this way the MBFC crosses boundaries to work with and for the poor, following the example of Jesus and the early church.

The early church spread along routes of commerce and transportation. By building upon existing structures of commerce and transportation and by working in the face of dehumanizing forces such as NAFTA, *maquiladora* plants, migratory farm labor, and substandard housing, the MBFC works in a subversive way, using the structures of power to build friendship and fellowship instead of profit. What remains unclear to me is whether or not MBFC agents are aware of the subversive nature of their work. Has MBFC work gradually become a counter-narrative in response to the dominance of commerce and international relations, or did it intentionally set out to be this kind of agency from the beginning of its existence? To what degree has an actual subversive or counter-narrative theology been explicitly proposed or considered by the leadership of the MBFC? Can this aspect of their work be articulated as an

---

12. Methodist Border Friendship Commission, "Methodist Border Friendship Commission."

explicit rationale to the short-term mission teams who come to work on the border?

It appears that the MBFC is an organization that attempts to fill the "middle gap" that exists in the modern framework of development and government policies along the border. The structures that gave rise to border commerce, trade, and transportation are government structures, international trade agreements, and law enforcement agencies. In response to the pollution and poor housing conditions along the border, it is often secular development organizations or government agencies that work in the *colonias*. The MBFC is clearly a church organization, yet its primary focus is addressing a variety of needs of people along the border. Providing Bible studies and pastors' salaries are part of their work, woven into the fabric of meeting a multitude of physical needs such as housing, food, and health care. The split between secular and sacred is not so obvious in their work. The MBFC emerges from the relatively minor role that the Methodist church plays in the religious demographics of the largely Catholic region. Yet it manages to function in the middle ground, weaving together resources of the "secular" and "sacred" spheres to work with and for the poor. How much formal development theory has played a part in the strategy of the MBFC is a question that deserves more study.

Another set of theological questions this case study raises are related to short-term missioners, their understanding of the relationships formed during their work, and the implications of their experience for mission and lifestyle choices in their home contexts. Residents on the border cannot help but notice the issues surrounding them. U.S. citizens who live in Texas but work in the *maquiladora* plants are faced with daily border crossings and labor practices that cannot be overlooked. Inequities in pay and housing quality are obvious to these people and those who live near *colonias* or work with public services. A dilemma is posed when people come down to serve on the border and then return home: How engaged are they in the political and economic issues that affect the border? These issues are a part of their lives, as the products assembled in the *maquiladora* plants and the food grown in the Rio Grande Valley are shipped to their stores for consumption. The missioners support to some degree the U.S. government and economy that directly impacts the lives of the people they serve; and yet, do they examine these assumptions and commitments as part of their short-term mission experience?

As one crosses out of his or her own context, it might become easier to see injustice and prejudice. The recognition of similar situations of injustice, poverty, and prejudice when crossing back into one's home context should be an explicit goal for short-term mission. Anthony Gittins states that "in the postmodern world, every city is multicultural and every neighborhood is surrounded by invisible barriers separating prosperity from poverty. Anyone who wants to can encounter poor or needy people; anyone who chooses to can pass over and come back."[13] The challenge for pastors is to invite missionaries to come educate their congregations about cross-cultural ministry, then work with those missionaries to help the congregation discover the boundaries that need to be crossed right in their own backyards. The greatest need might not be thousands of miles away, but just a few blocks down the street. Likewise, the greatest injustice might not be in another country but in the city and neighborhood where the church is located. These can easily be ignored unless an intentional effort is made to continue and transfer the work of discernment learned via international boundary crossing.

Discerning the contours of the *missio Dei* is a complex task for short-term missioners. Questions that must be considered include: How and why did they select the MBFC as their project in the first place? How do they understand God's mission in their lives, in their church, and in their community? How do they understand God's mission at the border? These questions are especially relevant when one considers how many short term-missioners participate in the work of the MBFC. According to the report for June 2004–May 2005, there were over 2,000 short-term missionaries: thirty-seven medical teams with over 480 team members serving in Mexico; eighty-five construction teams with over 1,300 team members serving in Mexico; twenty-two Volunteers in Mission teams serving in Texas; twenty-two NOMADS teams with eighty-nine team members (Nomads On a Mission Active in Divine Service, people who travel in their own RVs to work sites); an U.M. ARMY work camp with over 100 youth; a Houston-area United Methodist Church team with over 200 youth; and twenty teams for site visits and tours.[14] Each person who comes to work on the border encounters the multi-faceted issue of

---

13. Gittins, *Ministry at the Margins*, 15.
14. Methodist Border Friendship Commission, "Construction Ministries."

poverty, including the danger of dependence, as well as what God is at work doing there.

Another theological issue requiring reflection is that of the balance between meeting basic needs and cultivating personal relationships. Should one or the other be prioritized? Some argue that without first meeting basic needs, forming relationships is impossible. Others say that it is in the meeting of basic needs that relationships are formed. Still others argue that genuine cross-cultural relationships are more significant than merely accomplishing tasks and should therefore occupy more of the time and attention of short term missioners. Willie Berman, MBFC coordinator for the Methodist Church of Mexico, states on the organization's webpage describing construction projects that "after the goodbyes are said and the team is gone, the family has a new house, but they're still the same family with the same root problems."[15] His declaration to those who come in service is that "it's not about the house"; rather, the "Methodist Church of Mexico feels the call to address the rest of the family's social, economic, and spiritual problems."[16] Building a long-term, multifaceted, and more beneficial relationship between the recipient and the Methodist church is the larger reason for the construction of a house.

The short-term mission team plays a role in the development of this relationship, but they are not the intended beneficiaries of the relationship. The Methodist Church of Mexico clearly sets the agenda and priorities for work teams, which means they are not powerless in this relationship, as can often be the case between givers and receivers. However, one wonders about the agenda of the work teams. Do they come to give of themselves and to be at the service of others, and therefore relinquish their power in the relationship? Or do they come with a focus on their own spiritual benefit? Many youth short-term mission trips are designed as programs for the spiritual development of the youth. This carries with it the danger of objectifying "the other" or "the poor." Jonathan Bonk argues that "it is hard to assume the role of a servant when one is rich and powerful, while those whom one ostensibly serves are mired in poverty and powerlessness."[17] One of Bonk's major arguments is that the wealth and privilege of Western missionaries and

15. Ibid.
16. Ibid.
17. Bonk, *Missions and Money*, 60.

mission agencies compromises their ability to establish relationships and communicate the gospel authentically.[18]

CONCLUSION

The Methodist Border Friendship Commission is a rare cross-border agency that works in a cooperative manner, often in conflict-ridden situations. There is a lot of good work done by the MBFC, by residents of the border region, and by short-term mission teams who come to work with the MBFC. Yet dynamics are involved that invite theological reflection and further study. It is my hope that agencies such as the MBFC will benefit from short-term mission teams that want to engage in deep theological reflection, the ongoing work of relationship building, and a new kind of discernment and living in their own localities in addition to their labors along the border. Cooperative models of ministry such as this one provide an excellent opportunity to stimulate questions regarding the *missio Dei*, poverty, power in relationships, and how we care for one another across borders.

WORKS CITED

Adeney, Miriam. "Shalom Tourist: Loving Your Neighbor While Using Her." *Missiology* 34.4 (2006) 463–76.

Andrade, Esperanza. *Border Commerce Coordinator Report: January 30, 2009*. No pages. Online: http://www.sos.state.tx.us/border/forms/2008-bcc-report.pdf.

———. *Colonias FAQ's (Frequently Asked Questions)*. No pages. Online: http://www.sos.state.tx.us/border/colonias/faqs.shtml.

Bonk, Jonathan J. *Missions and Money: Affluence as a Missionary Problem . . . Revisited*. Maryknoll: Orbis, 2006.

First United Methodist Church of McAllen. "Missions." No pages. Online: http://www.mcfirst.com/default.aspx?name=missions.

Gittins, Anthony J. *Ministry at the Margins*. Maryknoll: Orbis, 2004.

Methodist Border Friendship Commission. "Construction Ministries on the US Side of the Border." No pages. Online: http://www.mcfirst.com/default.aspx?name=MBFC_constructministry

———. "Methodist Border Friendship Commission." No pages. Online: http://www.methodistbfc.org/.

---

18. For further reading on the issue of short-term mission and power, see Adeney, "Shalom Tourist"; Priest and Priest, "They See Everything"; and Slimbach, "First, Do No Harm."

———. "Methodist Border Friendship Commission Ministries and Projects." No pages. Online: http://www.methodistbfc.org/default.aspx?name=MBFC_ministries.

———. "Methodist Border Friendship Commission Report." No pages. Online: http://www.mcfirst.com/docs/MBFC2005Report.pdf.

———. "Ministries Offering Opportunities for Service (Other Than Construction)." No pages. Online: http://www.mcfirst.com/default.aspx?name=MBFC_otherministry

Priest, Robert J., and Joseph P. Priest. "They See Everything, and Understand Nothing: Short-Term Mission and Service Learning." *Missiology* 36.1 (2008) 53–73.

Ruiz, Ramón Eduardo. *On the Rim of Mexico: Encounters of the Rich and Poor.* Boulder, CO: Westview, 1998.

Slimbach, Richard. "First, Do No Harm." *Evangelical Missions Quarterly* 36 (2000) 428–41.

Texas Center for Policy Studies. "FOCUS: NAFTA and the Texas/Mexico Border Environment." In *The Texas Environmental Almanac.* 1995. No pages. Online: http://www.texascenter.org/almanac/NAFTA-FOCUS.HTML.

"The Rio Grande Conference of the U.M.C." No pages. Online: http://www.riograndeconference.org/.

U.S. Census Bureau. *State & Country QuickFacts: Cameron County, Texas.* No pages. Online: http://quickfacts.census.gov/qfd/states/48/48061.html.

Vernon, Walter N., Robert W. Sledge, Robert C. Monk, and Norman W. Spellmann, eds. *The Methodist Excitement in Texas: A History.* Nashville, TN: The Texas United Methodist Historical Society, 1984.

15

A Preliminary Study of Symbiotic Mission through Floral Beauty

Megumi Yoshida

INTRODUCTION

IN RECENT YEARS, ABNORMAL weather has caused severe droughts and forest fires in some areas, but rainstorms and floods in other areas. The size of typhoons and hurricanes is increasing. Many people in the world have been struck by unusual natural calamities, causing many of them to become homeless and suffer from poverty. The El Niño and La Niña phenomena are well known; in Spanish, the former means "little boy" or even connotes "the Christ child," while the latter means "little girl."[1] The fact that some weather phenomena are named after Jesus Christ reminds us that Christianity and ecological issues are in some ways connected. Natural calamities caused by freakish weather patterns illustrate the urgency demanded in dealing theologically with ecological issues. We cannot avoid ecological issues in Christian mission, especially if we take into account "the whole gospel."[2]

In the 1970s, the World Council of Churches (WCC) became aware of the interconnections between justice, peace, and ecological

---

1. "Information on the names El Niño and La Niña."
2. Bonk, "The Gospel and Ethics," 47.

sustainability. At the WCC Vancouver Assembly in 1983, "justice, peace, and the integrity of creation" (JPIC) was addressed. Over the past twenty-five years since that meeting, this theme has been a concern of churches and their members to varying degrees. Non-Christians have also become increasingly aware of ecological issues. For example, in my home country of Japan we have to sort out our rubbish into a variety of categories for recycling: aluminum cans, steel cans, brown-colored bottles, clear bottles, other-colored bottles, batteries, electric light bulbs, ceramics, newspapers, home electrical appliances, and so on. In addition, we must wash all bottles and cans completely. In Japan, recycling is a part of our daily life, and the recycling system seems to be much more efficient than the one in the U.S. Although consumerism has not yet abated in the U.S.—even after the most current economic crisis—some individuals and businesses have taken small steps toward greater eco-responsibility for ensuring environmental sustainability, such as using reusable shopping bags and returning more cans and bottles.

At the Overseas Ministries Study Center (OMSC) in December 2009, a participant provided an interesting perspective on this topic in the weekly seminar, "Climate Change and Catastrophe: Paradigms of Response in Christian Mission." She said that secular people have already been long-involved in ecological issues and activities, but Christians—believing both in God and that the Earth is God's creation—do not know how to be involved in this issue. Theological thinking in mission has yet to seriously take up such emergent global issues instead of just following secular trends. Since missionaries and ministers are living on the "frontier" of the world's concerns, theological educators have to be involved in global emergent issues.[3] Without taking leadership in secular issues, both Christian persons and Christianity itself will lose an opportunity for influence in society.

In this presentation I would like to consider a new approach toward mission through floral beauty. Flowers and plants are all around us, sustaining and enhancing our lives. In seeing our relationship with flora in terms of a "cross-cultural matrix" for mission,[4] human sensitivities to the environment are finely honed. Doing so helps Christians to approach important issues ecologically in what I would like to call "symbiotic" mission. First, I will introduce the aesthetic power of flowers and

3. Yeow, *Minister as Theological Educator*.
4. Yoshida, "'Cross-Cultural Matrix' for Mission," 161–79.

plants through my experience in *ikebana* (traditional Japanese flower arrangement) at OMSC during my stay for the 2009–10 academic year. *Ikebana* was born in a Japanese context, but enables us to do theology in different contexts as well. Flowers and plants themselves are beautiful to behold even without any hermeneutical skill. Second, I will briefly exegete two biblical examples of how plants and flowers have inspired faith in the promises of God, recounting the way in which flowers encouraged the Christian faith of a particular Japanese missionary and educator. Third, I would like to consider a new role for floral beauty in moving the church toward a symbiotic mission of creation care and Christian witness. Through a mutually agreeable relationship between the environment and mission, ministry will be enriched, becoming holistic and more engaged with the Japanese worldview.

MY EXPERIENCE OF THE POWER OF FLORA IN *IKEBANA*: GOING BEYOND BOUNDARIES

In October 2009 I held a solo exhibition, "Beauty of Life through *Ikebana*," in the entrance way of Doane Hall at OMSC as part of the Twelfth Annual City-WideOpen Studios (CWOS) exhibition by ArtSPACE in New Haven, Connecticut. Through *ikebana* arrangements, I expressed the eternal word of God that sustains our transient daily lives, but of which we are hardly aware. *Ikebana* is a part of Japanese traditional culture that has developed in the local context of Japan, but is not familiar in the U.S. However, many people in the U.S. have warmly appreciated my *ikebana* images. The beauty of flowers and plants goes beyond any cultural boundary. Indeed, beauty has no boundary; who can deny the beauty of flowers when one looks at them? Anyone can appreciate beauty in live flowers and plants without any preliminary background knowledge. One staff member of OMSC told me that he often cannot understand the beauty of fine art, but could easily appreciate the beauty of flowers and my *ikebana* exhibit.

Spiritual Phase of Plants and Flowers

In ancient Japan people regarded the evergreen tree as a symbol of eternal life; the evergreen tree is where divine gods were believed to reside. It is still called *yorishiro*, meaning "the place where deities come to lodge."

This is preserved in cultural custom: for example, a pine tree is always painted on the back screen of Noh theatre, or is used as *kadomatsu* or *wakamatsu* at the New Year.[5] The evergreen tree and its branches are also offered in Shinto ceremonies.

The spiritual aspect of *ikebana* comes not only from Shintoism but also from Buddhism. The custom of placing flowers on an altar as a ritual offering (*kuge*) began when Buddhism was introduced to Japan by way of Korea around 538 A.D. In the Heian period (794–1185), flower arrangement spread widely in people's worship along with Pure Land Buddhism. Apart from altar offerings, the practice of enjoying flowers arranged beautifully in a vase also became popular among aristocrats. Gradually the enjoyment of arranging flowers likewise developed, and with the appearance of the bourgeoisie, the art of flower arrangement, *ikebana*, emerged. *Ikebana* has remained a cultural facet, widely inhabiting the Japanese environment and aesthetic.

Ikebana *is the Way of Rebirth: Re-creating Life in Beauty*

Ikebana means to enjoy nature in our daily lives. Etymologically, "*ikebana*" is derived from *ike-ru* ("to live," "to give life," "to arrange") plus *hana* ("flowers"). *Ikebana* is also sometimes called *kadou*, composed of *ka* ("flowers") plus *dou* ("Dao"). *Ikebana/kadou* is the Dao of giving life to flowers that is "caught" by viewers through the artist's arrangement of the flowers and plants.

In the process of floral arrangement, artists/arrangers enter Dao to meet Dao's great creativity and to receive vitality.[6] They cultivate themselves in the process of their giving life to flowers and plants in vases. In other words, through people conducting the Dao of flowers, they themselves derive and express life in their own contexts. Through the Dao, human beings and flowers are at the same time reciprocally permeated.[7]

Through arranging flowers and plants, people communicate with the heart of nature, and express not only the visible beauty, but also

---

5. *Kadomatsu* means a pair of arranged pine trees that decorates the main entrance of a house at the New Year in order to welcome the deities of the New Year. *Wakamatsu* is the young branches of a pine tree arrangement at the New Year that is placed in the home's *tokonoma* (alcove).

6. Chang, *Creativity and Taoism*, 70.

7. Ames and Rosemont, *The Analects of Confucius*, 46.

the invisible existence of it. In this sense, plants are cut, removed from their native milieu, and put in an artificial container so that they are re-created, filled with new beauty when placed in a new environment. *Ikebana* artists do not just imitate and re-create the shape that a plant has had in nature, but create a new world with branches, leaves, flowers, as well a human impression of the plants' beauty in order to express the real nature of both the visible and the invisible, now "seen" together by the eyes of the soul. In this creative process, the beauty of each branch, leaf, and flower begins to assert its own nature to the artist, attracting and inspiring the artist. At the same time, the artist's hands and soul respond to them. The artist and plants are not separate, but one. The human enters into communion with the plants. This esoteric experience is the reason why arranging flowers is called *kadou* ("the Dao of flower").

Ikebana is not "natural," but an artificial environment where each branch, leaf, and flower retains its short-lived nature. The artist changes the water of the container to keep them fresh. For instance, at an exhibition, the artists change the water every morning before opening time and every evening after closing time, and replace withered flowers with fresh ones. In this process, the artist lives together in this fragility, and realizes that his life cannot be separated from it, but is a part of humanity and nature, living together wholly in the universe.

Ikebana maintains the natural element, in spite of the artificial environment brought about in the containers. Plants begin to pass away as soon as they are cut, but by the artist's hands they are given even more beauty in their transient life in the container; then they move people's hearts more beautifully. It may be said that *ikebana* is a kind of rebirth of life.[8] Created floral beauty and the artist become one to *re-create* God's beauty in the vase. The ordered unity of the arranged flowers showcases the single moment of life as perceived by the viewer and created by the arranger. Action, creation, observation, and communion between God and all creatures come together.

Ikebana *as Perichoretic Experience*

Ikebana enables us to go beyond a subject/object dichotomy. It can be considered a perichoretic experience. To state it briefly in the words of Jürgen Moltmann, *perichoresis* is the concept that "all things are in God

---

8. Yoshida, "Looking at a Continuity in Cultural Heritage."

and God is in all things."⁹ Originally, *perichoresis* was a term used to explain relationships within the trinitarian Godhead. Its biblical basis is John 14:11 ("I am in the Father and the Father is in me") and John 14:20 ("I am in my Father, and you in me, and I in you"), meaning, God is in Jesus Christ, and Jesus Christ is in God; Jesus Christ is in us, and we are in Jesus Christ; God is in us, and we are in God. Moltmann expanded the concept to involve God and all creation, including humans, in his theological project for a "sustainable society."¹⁰ In my proposal, *perichoresis* can refer to the realities and relationships that floral beauty in *ikebana* images represent and communicate: a mutually dependent relationship between humans and nature as well as a shared dependence on God.

In that way, using the lessons of *ikebana* in mission and theological education for mission enables us to enhance our sense of symbiosis. In order to keep flowers and plants fresh in *ikebana*, we have to care for them. By cultivating Dao through *ikebana* like awareness and living, a sense of perichoretic type union between humans and nature can be attained. This is part of what it means to live together with nature in a symbiotic way. With a real sense of symbiotic existence, we can begin to address ecological issues from a Christian theological perspective.

GOD COMMUNES WITH HUMANS THROUGH FLOWERS AND PLANTS

In the Bible, God communes with humans through flowers and plants. For example, in Jeremiah 1:11–12, immediately after he was appointed a prophet, Jeremiah was looking at an almond branch when Yahweh queried him. These two verses narrate "the vision of the call."¹¹ "The word of the LORD came to me, saying, 'Jeremiah, what do you see?' And I said, 'I see a branch of an almond tree (*shaqed*).' Then the LORD said to me, 'You have seen well, for I am watching (*shoqed*) over my word to perform it'" (NRSV).

---

9. Moltmann, "Response to Megumi Yoshida," 117–18. In the same paper, Moltmann also briefly described pantheism and panentheism. Pantheism is the belief that all *is* God and God *is* all. Pan*en*theism is that all is *not* God and God is *not* all, but all is *in* God. For my assessment of Moltmann's explanation of perichoresis, see Yoshida, "The Icon Image of 'The Holy Trinity.'"

10. Moltmann, "Perichoresis," 113.

11. Lundbom, *Jeremiah 1–20*, 227.

It is difficult to notice the wordplay in English translations, but in the original Hebrew it is clear. In Jeremiah, the verb *shaqad* is used with the connotation of threat (Jer 5:6; 31:28; 44:27).[12] This wordplay, then, implies that the budding of the almond branch and the Lord's activity are interrelated and equally near, especially considering the divine "watching."[13] The image of a blooming almond (*shaqed*) points to the fact that Yahweh is watching over (*shoqed*) his words to soon perform them.

In late January or early February in Canaan, almond trees blossom before their leaves appear. Their flowers are white and tinted with pink. About ten weeks after the flowers appear the almond fruit begins to ripen.[14] The almond tree is the first blossoming tree of spring. The almond blossoms herald that spring is coming in the midst of the cold winter season in Canaan. Jeremiah could see God's calling on his life in the newly blooming almond branch of winter when all green plants were still withered.

Similarly, about one century ago in Japan, Joseph Hardy Neesima (Niijima Jo, in Japanese; 1843–90) saw a sign of God's message in plum blossoms breaking through a very cold winter and composed the poem *Teijou no ichi kanbai* ("A winter plum blossom in my garden"). Neesima was a Japanese Christian who worked for the American Board of Commissioners for Foreign Missions (ABCFM) and founded Doshisha University in Kyoto.[15] In February, plum trees (*ume* in Japanese) have beautiful blossoms with a sweet aroma. In Japan, plum blossoms herald spring's coming in the cold of late winter. It is especially cold in Kyoto where Neesima lived (and I also live). The poem in English reads:

> I see a branch of plum in my garden.
> It dares to bloom despite snow and wind.
> Without an attitude of contention or pretension
> With a spirit of harmony and laughter
> It signifies the coming of the hundred flowers of spring.[16]

---

12. King, *Jeremiah*, 153.
13. Craigie et al., *Jeremiah 1–25*, 16.
14. King, *Jeremiah*, 152.
15. Hardy, *Life and Letters*, 167.
16. Takenaka, *Consider the Flowers*, 52.

Neesima was born the first son of a samurai after four daughters in Edo (now Tokyo) on January 14, 1843.[17] Commodore Matthew Perry (1794–1858) first entered Uraga Harbor near Edo when Neesima was ten years old. Japan had closed its doors to foreign countries, allowing only Holland and China to trade on Dejima, a small artificial island in Nagasaki Bay. The arrival of Perry compelled the opening of Japan to the West with the Convention of Kanagawa in 1854. When Neesima was about sixteen he found an atlas titled *History of the United States* written by missionary Elijah Coleman Bridgman (1801–61) in Chinese, containing information about subjects like the American presidency, free schools, and hospitals. "I read it many times," he wrote to a friend in a letter, now famous, about why he wanted to flee Japan. "I was wondered [sic] so much as my brain would melted [sic] out from [sic] my head . . ."[18]

Neesima also later encountered an abridged Chinese Bible in the library of a friend. He was now captivated not only by a desire to learn about the U.S., but also about the Christian God's dealings with all humankind and the world.[19] In defiance of an overseas travel ban (and thus risking his life), Neesima boarded an American merchant ship by stealth and stowed away out of Japan in 1864.[20] In Shanghai, he boarded a ship, the *Wild Rover*, bound for Boston. Neesima gave his Samurai long sword as his travel fee to Captain Horace S. Taylor (1829–69), and sold his short sword for eight dollars to Captain Taylor in order to buy the New Testament in Chinese.[21] At that time, long and short swords were regarded as a samurai's life. Soon after arriving in Boston, Captain Taylor introduced him to Alpheus Hardy (1816–87), the owner of the *Wild Rover* and a Christian merchant who had given up an earlier aspiration to the ministry but was still interested in mission.[22] Hardy and his wife were deeply impressed by Neesima's profound interest in the U.S.

---

17. This date is according to the old Japanese lunar calendar. According to the solar calendar presently used, the date is February 12. See Ueno, *Doshisha Hyakunen Shi*, 12. For more on the history of Japanese Congregationalism, see Alika and Okawara, "Sho-Chiku-Bai."

18. Hardy, *Life and Letters*, 3–4.

19. Ibid., 7.

20. Ibid., 1–2, 9.

21. Ibid., 40. In 1920, Arthur Sherburne Hardy, a son of Alpheus Hardy, returned Neesima's swords to the president and trustees of Doshisha University. See Hardy, "Woodstock, Connecticut."

22. Kato, *Niijima Jo Sensei Ryakuden*, 35.

and in Christianity as they read the letter he had written out in English.[23] With the support of the Hardys, Neesima was baptized on December 30, 1866.[24] Captain Taylor had called him "Joe," and so Neesima began to use the name Joseph Hardy Neesima.

Hardy had enrolled Neesima in the Phillips Academy at Andover, Massachusetts in 1865, and arranged his board at the house of Miss Mary E. Hidden, who was a strict Puritan and influenced him. Neesima did well, and proceeded to Amherst College (a Congregational institution) from which he graduated in 1870. Neesima was the first Japanese person ever to earn a degree from a Western university, studying science and technology. He decided to become a minister, and so studied at Andover Theological Seminary (also a Congregational school), graduating in the summer of 1874. For ten months in 1872, he traveled as a translator together with Japan's Commissioner of Education in Europe to learn Western educational situations. He became the first Japanese person to be ordained a Protestant minister, joining the Congregational Church (now the United Church of the Christ, America). He was appointed a corresponding member of the Japan Mission of the American Board of Commissioners for Foreign Missions (ABCFM).[25]

In October of 1874, not long before he was to finally return to Japan, Neesima spoke at the sixty-fifth annual meeting of the ABCFM held at Grace Congregational United Church of Christ in Rutland, Vermont. Pleading for the establishment of a Christian school in Japan, he declared with a broken voice: "I cannot go back to Japan without money to found a Christian college, and I am going to stand here until I get it."[26] The

---

23. Hardy, *Life and Letters*, 3–45.

24. Ueno, *Doshisha Hyakunen Shi*, 42–43. Neesima wrote letters to Mrs. Hardy about his decision to become a Christian, dated October 27 and December 25, 1866. See Hardy, *Life and Letters*, 57–59.

25. Ueno, *Doshisha Hyakunen Shi*, 56, 687.

26. Davis, *A Sketch of the Life*, 33. In these words of Neesima one can hear echoes of Martin Luther's famous words, "Here I stand. I can do no other." In *The Missionary Herald*'s November report of the annual meeting of the board were two simple references to "Rev. Joseph Neesima," one noting his appointment to the Committee on the Japan Mission. ("The Committee.") The other appears in a section titled "Farewell Address" and notes Neesima was "a native of Japan, and about to return there (who was introduced by Hon. Alpheus Hardy, briefly stating some of the singular facts of his history)." ("Farewell Address.") However, the December 1874 issue of *The Missionary Herald* did report more substantially Neesima's ordination. His introduction by Prof. J. H. Seelye and Rev. Dr. A. C. Thompson's recounting of his experience in the U.S. were

board members were moved by Neesima's determination and donated a total of $5,000. That sum was the seed money for Doshisha Eigakko, what is now Doshisha University, a Christian university located amidst many Buddhist temples and Shinto shrines in Kyoto, a previous capital of Japan, in 1875.[27] The following year, in 1876, Dr. Dwight Whitney Learned (1848–1943), a Yale graduate, joined the faculty of Doshisha.[28] When it became an official university in 1888 (comprised of schools for English, theology, girls, and nurses' training), 899 students were enrolled.[29] In 1885, just ten years after its founding, the first missionary, Aoki Sin'ichi, a theological student, was sent to Hawai'i by Doshisha.[30]

Neesima returned to his homeland after ten years in the U.S. with a strong ambition to establish a Christian university and to spread Christianity. He believed that Christianity must provide the basis for an education.[31] He wished not only to nurture individuals with diverse skills and abilities, but also "to foster moral character, noble conduct and a lofty spirit; to send out not only talented men of science but men of a sensitive conscience as well . . . [I]t must be founded on faith in God, love of Truth and kindness."[32] In his last days, Neesima said that those who teach students must treat them respectfully.[33] His educational policy of respecting each individual student has been maintained at Doshisha over the years; I grew up in this legacy of Neesima's spirit in Doshisha.

Neesima died in 1890 at the age of forty-six, apparently worn out by itinerant fund raising campaigns. One month before his death, in December, fatigued by such ambitious activity, he observed a branch of winter plum in a garden of the Mukadeya hotel in Oiso, near Tokyo. It was quietly beginning to bloom in the beginning of winter weather. He received a heart warming encouragement as he saw the plum blossoms,

---

reported verbatim. ("Rev. Neesima."; Thompson, "Charge to Mr. Neesima.")

27. Ueno, *Doshisha Hyakunen Shi*, 63–91.

28. Ibid., 704.

29. "Statistics of all Doshisha schools." In 1888, out of 899 students, there were eighty-one theological students.

30. Takenaka, "Doshisha to Hawaii," 79–80.

31. Neesima, "The Aim in Establishing Doshisha University," 22.

32. Ibid., 14. The symbol of Doshisha consists of three white inverted equilateral triangles on a purple background, just like Amherst College's symbol. The design represents the Christian trinity or the cultivation of mind, spirit, and body.

33. Niijima, "Doshisha Soritsu Jusshunen Kinen Enzetsu," 107, "Yuigon," 403.

unpretentious messengers from God of the coming spring. Inspired, he penned the poem "Winter plum blossoms in my garden."[34]

God, too, is watching over us to bring God's word to pass. God's people will stay on course till their eyes have seen the coming of the glory of the Lord. When we see the bud of a plum blossom, we think of all the energy the bud is exerting to bloom even in the cold winter. It is not just the energy of the bud, it is the energy of all creation in which God is vigorously working to cause this flower to bloom. At that moment we feel embraced by the cosmic energy that is an expression of God's love and grace. God's love in this world is a huge power that aims to blossom flowers and commune with humans.

"CONSIDER THE LILIES (AND THE *YUKIWARISOU*)"

In Luke 12:13–48, Jesus teaches God's stewardship of creation with reference to beautiful lilies (12:27) and grass (12:28).[35] "The grass of the field is alive today and tomorrow is thrown into the oven" (Luke 12:28), namely, the grass is transient. God clothes such existence. The Greek word usually translated "lilies" (*krinon*) means simply the more generic "flower." In Palestine, purple anemone bloomed everywhere and is the most likely referent for *krinon*,[36] reminiscent of the color of Solomon's purple robes.[37] Flowers are dressed up much more beautifully than Solomon ever was in all his glorious days. Grasses and flowers are transient, but God clothes them beautifully. Therefore, we should not worry.

---

34. Neesima's poem "Winter plum blossoms in my garden" has remained a conscious part of life at Doshisha University for nearly one and a half centuries, as evidenced by a newly composed *Noh* play, "*Teijo no ume* (Plum blossoms in a garden)." The play was first presented at the 130th commemoration of the founding of Doshisha University on November 26, 2005, in Doshisha's Hardy Hall. Also, Takenaka Masao (1925–2006), a Yale-educated Japanese theologian, expressed appreciation for Neesima's poem. He enjoyed plum blossoms in February not only on the Doshisha campus but also at the Kitano Shinto Shrine, a place famous for plum blossoms in Kyoto. Professor Takenaka sometimes took his Doshisha students to the Kitano Shinto Shrine to enjoy the plum blossoms. He often expressed his Christian faith by drawing plum blossoms in a Japanese ink-painting style.

35. Riley, *Preface to Luke*, 63.

36. Arndt, *The Gospel according to St. Luke*, 318.

37. Marshall, *The Gospel of Luke*, 528; Bock, *Luke*, 1,162.

In Japan there is a long running popular dramatic television series on prime time. The 2009 season presented the saga of Naoe Kanetsugu's life. Naoe Kanetsugu (1560–1620) was a Japanese samurai famed for his service to two generations of the Uesugi daimyo. Naoe was taught by Uesugi Kenshin (1530–78) in his youth that conquering the world is a trifling affair, but what matters is to live one's life with righteousness. In one episode, when faced with very difficult circumstances, Naoe finds a tiny flower in deep snow. Its name is *yukiwarisou*: *yuki* meaning "snow," *wari* "to break," and *sou* "grass." Hence, the *yuki-wari-sou* is a sign that spring wills to come even in such cold, snowy days! Japanese television viewers profoundly understood how hope was afforded Naoe by the discovery of the flower.

Humans meet the beauty of flowers dressed up by God. We simply go outside and walk around gardens or natural areas to find something beautiful attracting our attention. In spite of ourselves, we utter "Ah! What a beautiful flower that is!" At the moment we utter "Ah," we are deeply united with the rest of God's creation by the sight of God's beauty and a sign of divine active presence. Jeremiah and Joseph Hardy Neesima encountered God through the beauty of budding flowers, a hope-inspiring beauty in the midst of a good but wintry created order, a world yearning for the "watching" God to fulfill the promises of his word. Might we make use of *ikebana*—and other proleptic glimpses of Spring in the world—to invite this Japanese generation, and others on this troubled planet, to "consider" those divine promises and the call of God?

WORKS CITED

Alika, Clifford, and Miya Owkaka, "Sho-Chiku-Bai: Japanese-American Congregationalists." In *Hidden Histories in the United Church of Christ*, vol. 1, edited by Barbara Brown Zikmund, 154–71, 191–92. New York: United Church, 1984.

Ames, Roger T., and Henry Rosemont, Jr. *The Analects of Confucius: A Philosophical Translation*. New York: Ballantine, 1998.

Arndt, William F. *The Gospel according to St. Luke*. Saint Louis, MO: Concordia, 1956.

Bock, Darrell L. *Luke*. 2 vols. Baker Exegetical Commentary on the New Testament 3B. Grand Rapids: Baker, 1996.

Bonk, Jonathan. "The Gospel and Ethics." *Evangelical Review of Theology* 33.1 (2009) 47–61.

Chang, Chung-yuan. *Creativity and Taoism: A Study of Chinese Philosophy, Art and Poetry*. New York: Julian, 1963.
Craigie, Peter C., et al. *Jeremiah 1–25*. Word Biblical Commentary Vol. 26. Dallas: Word, 1991.
Davis, Jerome Dean. *A Sketch of the Life of Rev. Joseph Hardy Neesima, L.L.D.: Founder and First President of Doshisha, Kyoto*. 1890. Reprint. Kyoto: Doshisha University, 1936.
"Farewell Address." *The Missionary Herald* 70.11 (1874) 357.
Hardy, Arthur Sherburne. *Life and Letters of Joseph Hardy Neesima*. 1891. Reprint. Kyoto: Doshisha University Press, 1980.
———. "Woodstock, Connecticut, August 29, 1920. To the President and Trustees of the Doshisha University." *Niijima Kenkyu* [Neesima studies] 49 (July 1977) 34.
"Information on the names El Niño and La Niña." In "What is an El Niño?" Accessed May 10, 2011. http://www.pmel.noaa.gov/tao/elnino/el-nino-story.html.
Kato, Nobuo. *Niijima Jo Sensei Ryakuden* [A short biography of Prof. Joseph H. Neesima]. Kyoto: Nihon Kanko Bijutsu Shuppansha, 1969.
King, Philip J. *Jeremiah: An Archaeological Companion*. Louisville, KY: Westminster/John Knox, 1993.
Lundbom, Jack R. *Jeremiah 1–20: A New Translation with Introduction and Commentary*. The Anchor Bible Commentary. New York: Doubleday, 1999.
Marshall, I. Howard. *The Gospel of Luke*. New International Greek Testament Commentary. Exeter: Paternoster, 1978.
Moltmann, Jürgen. "Perichoresis: An Old Magic Word for a New Trinitarian Theology." In *Trinity, Community and Power: Mapping Trajectories in Wesleyan Theology*, edited by M. Douglas Meeks, 111–26. Nashville, TN: Kingswood, 2000.
———. "Response to Megumi Yoshida." *Sino-Christian Studies: An International Journal of Bible, Theology and Philosophy* 3 (2007) 115–22.
Neesima, Joseph H. "The Aim in Establishing Doshisha University." In *The Founding of The Doshisha and Doshisha University: How The Doshisha Was Established, The Aim in Establishing Doshisha University*, 11–24. Kyoto: Doshisha, 1960.
Niijima, Jo. "Doshisha Daigaku Setsuritsu no Shii [The aim in establishing Doshisha University]." In *Doshisha Setsuritsu no Shimatsu* [How the Doshisha was established], *Doshisha Daigaku Setsuritsu no Shii* [The aim in establishing Doshisha University], 21–42. Kyoto: Doshisha, 1973.
———. "Doshisha Soritsu Jusshunen Kinen Enzetsu [The commemorative address at the tenth anniversary of the founding of the Doshisha]." In *Niijima Jo Zenshu* [The complete works of Joseph Hardy Neesima] *Volume 1*, 105–9. Kyoto: Dohosha, 1983.
———. "Yuigon [Neesima's will]." In *Niijima Jo Zenshu* [The complete works of Joseph Hardy Neesima] *Volume 4*, 403–4. Kyoto: Dohosha, 1989.
"Rev. Joseph Neesima." *The Missionary Herald* 70.12 (1874) 381–82.
Riley, Harold. *Preface to Luke*. Macon, GA: Mercer University Press, 1993.
"Statistics of all Doshisha schools." In Niijima, Jo, "Doshisha Daigaku Setsuritsu no Shii [The aim in establishing Doshisha University]," 31–32. Kyoto: Doshisha, 1973.
Takenaka, Masao. *Consider the Flowers: Meditations in Ikebana*. Translated by Masao Takenaka. Tokyo: Kyo Bun Kwan, 1990.
———. "Doshisha to Hawaii: Senzen no Koryu no kiseki wo tazunete." [Doshisha and Hawaii: commemorating the centennial of the contracted Japanese immigration

in Hawaii]. *Doshisha America Kenkyu* (Journal of Doshisha, American Studies) 22 (1986) 79–80.

"The Committee of Nomination . . ." *The Missionary Herald* 70.11 (1874) 345.

Thompson, A. C. "Charge to Mr. Neesima." *The Missionary Herald* 70.12 (1874) 382–85.

Ueno, Naozo. *Doshisha Hyakunen Shi, Tsushi-hen 1* [The history of Doshisha for one hundred years, total history vol. 1]. Kyoto: Doshisha, 1979.

Yeow, Choo Lak. *Minister as Theological Educator*. Singapore: TTC, 1979.

Yoshida, Megumi. "A Consideration on 'Cross-Cultural Matrix' for Mission: A Christian Legacy and the Dao of Tea as Japanese Culture." *The Journal of Theologies and Cultures in Asia* 7 & 8 (2008/2009) 161–79.

———. "Looking at A Continuity in Cultural Heritage: A Case-Study on Chinese Philosophical Influences on Japanese Ikebana." *A Peer-Reviewed Electronic Journal for Asian Studies on the Pacific Coast* (2008/2009). No pages. Online: http://mcel.pacificu.edu/easpac/2008/yoshida.php3.

———. "The Icon Image of 'The Holy Trinity' by Andrei Rublev and Moltmann's Theological Reflection." Paper presented at the one-day seminar "Religion and the Arts" at the Elmfield House, University of Birmingham, UK, 2008.

Part IV
Reports and Conclusion

16

2010Boston from the Student Perspective

Gina A. Bellofatto

2010BOSTON WAS DESCRIBED BY Rodney Petersen, a conference co-chair, as a "student-oriented, academic conference to consider what the 'next wave' of Christian mission will look like."[1] Based on this description, one might ask to what degree 2010Boston actually embodied these two characteristics and achieved this particular purpose, of being (1) student-oriented and (2) academic; while (3) reflecting on the changing contours of world mission and Christianity? The outcomes of the conference could be measured in a variety of ways, but perhaps a particularly revealing method would be to assess the responses of some students who attended. How did these students react to the academic nature of the conference? What did they take away from discussions of the "next wave" of Christian mission?

At the Edinburgh 1910 World Missionary Conference, "technological advance was hailed as the handmaid to the spread of the gospel worldwide."[2] Compared to Edinburgh 1910, 2010Boston had considerably more to offer by way of technology, and students certainly took advantage of it. 2010Boston made use of the Internet, including a website, blog, YouTube videos, and a constant live Twitter feed throughout the four-day event.[3] Increased ease of international travel was marginally

---

1. Petersen, "Next Wave."

2. Johnson and Ross, eds. *Atlas of Global Christianity*, xvi.

3. Eva Pascal (Boston University PhD student) tweeted @2010Boston_Conf (twitter.com/2010Boston_Conf).

important due to the relatively high number of international Christian scholars and students in the Greater Boston area from which the conference drew. The perspectives of students represented in this chapter were shaped largely by their presence at 2010Boston, but also by the media employed by conference coordinators.

COMPARATIVE CHRISTIANITY: THE RISE OF GLOBAL CHRISTIANITY, 1910–2010

One significant source of student involvement in 2010Boston was *The Rise of Global Christianity*, a course taught at the Boston University School of Theology (BUSTH) in the fall of 2010 by Todd Johnson (a co-chair of 2010Boston). The course (for which I was the teaching assistant) provided a survey of the changing status of global Christianity over the past one hundred years, comparing the global context of Christianity in 1910 with that in 2010. Using the *Atlas of Global Christianity* as a textbook, the course analyzed global Christianity by major Christian traditions, United Nations regions, languages, and peoples. Paralleling the 2010Boston conference, the course was intentionally ecumenical in its approach, featuring guest speakers from Protestant, Roman Catholic, Anglican, Orthodox, and Mormon backgrounds.[4] Early in the course we decided to ask students to participate in a blog based on small group reflections on lectures from guest speakers. These sessions were then distilled by the discussion moderators (doctoral students in the class) and posted on the blog.[5] Many of the blog posts directly corresponded to the eight major themes of 2010Boston: Changing Contours of Christian Unity, Mission in Context, Disciples in Mission, Education for Mission, Mission and Post-colonialism, Mission in a Pluralist World, Mission and Post-Modernity, and Salvation Today.

The class sessions helped prepare students for the convening of 2010Boston by bringing to light many—sometimes controversial—is-

---

4. Guest lecturers included Brian Grim (Pew Forum on Religion and Public Life), Rodney Petersen (Director, BTI), Nimi Wariboko (Andover Newton Theological School), Matthew Bowman (Georgetown University), Luke Veronis (Holy Cross Greek Orthodox School of Theology), Ian Douglas (bishop, Diocese of Connecticut), Vincent Machozi (Boston University), Jonathan Bonk (Overseas Ministries Studies Center), Dana Robert (Boston University), and Jay Gary (Regent University).

5. The blog can be found at 2010bostonmission.blogspot.com.

sues of global Christianity and world missions. For example, Rev. Ian Douglas (Bishop of the Diocese of Connecticut within the Episcopal Church USA) delivered a lecture that discussed unity and diversity at both the local and global levels within the Anglican Communion, and how the Communion is struggling to be God's church in the world; this parallels the conference theme "Changing Contours of Christian Unity." Dana Robert's lecture on the history and current status of mission frontiers also addressed several themes of the conference, including "Mission in Context," "Mission and Post-Colonialism," and "Disciples in Mission." Although the Edinburgh 1910 meeting was in many ways influenced by the Christian student movements of its time,[6] attendees of Edinburgh 1910 did not experience this kind of parallel preparation and direct involvement of students, nor was anything like it coordinated with the other centennial celebrations in 2010.

2010Boston, held from 4–7 November, was convened during the progress of the BUSTH course. Following their attendance at the conference, students were required to write short personal reflection papers about their experiences. These papers provide much insight into the question of the conference's impact and to what student attendees gained (in both theory and practice) from the consideration of conference themes. It is primarily these reflections that speak to the three subjects at hand: the value of the student orientation of the conference, its academic nature, and its discourse concerning the "next wave" of Christian mission.[7]

STUDENT-ORIENTED

Dana Robert, in her plenary lecture (the first of the conference), stressed the fact that students have always been an important catalyst for mission. (As a more recent example of this, she highlighted the establishment of Goodwill Industries by a Boston student, a NGO-model of self-support for those in poverty.) College students, seminarians, and Christian missions ought to remain inseparable, she argued, hence the crucial impor-

---

6. Stanley, *World Missionary Conference*, 6, 8, 88, 320.

7. All quotations by and references to students hereafter are drawn from their 2010Boston reflection papers for *Comparative Christianity: The Rise of Global Christianity, 1910–2010*, which were written in the fall of 2010.

tance of bringing Boston-area seminarians together to dialogue about the meaning of missions on the 100th anniversary of the Edinburgh 1910 conference. There were several ways students could be involved in the 2010Boston conference, including student paper presentations and follow-up discussion in workshop sessions moderated by BTI faculty members, as well as the break-out discussion groups (also on the eight conference themes) during the concluding assembly at The Memorial Church at Harvard University.

I spoke with many students who felt that the large plenary sessions were valuable and educational, but lacked space for genuine discussion (and opportunity for disagreement) on important topics. This is one reason why the students who attended 2010Boston were particularly impressed with the student paper presentation workshops. These sessions allowed conference attendees to discuss issues among themselves, and many experienced their most profound moments of the conference under the guidance of fellow students. Boston University student Ryong Jae Jung was impressed that so many student presenters were non-Western, having attended sessions by Taiwanese and Korean students. The student papers included deeply theological and missiological reflection regarding current social and cultural issues such as prostitution, short-term missions, interreligious conflict, and the work of faith-based organizations. Presenters outlined what they saw as issues and concerns in global mission and Christianity today and offered prescriptive measures to these problems (according to many students, measures often missing from the plenary talks).

After Brian Stanley's plenary lecture on the vision and blindness at the Edinburgh 1910 World Missionary Conference, fifty high school students from Lexington Christian Academy (who had attended the Friday morning session at Boston University) met with doctoral students Eva Pascal and Daryl Ireland to debrief.[8] In contrast to the primary focus of Edinburgh 1910, Pascal and Ireland found that these students were focused on showing the good news of Jesus Christ through service and charitable works as opposed to conversion-focused ministry. Pascal commented, "it is evident that a new generation of missionaries was in our midst." The presence of high school students at this lecture was sig-

8. Pascal tweeted this event: "Youth important 4 2010Boston Conference BU's ajD & D.Ireland discuss w 50+ LCA high schoolers re view of mission/service – & we survived :)."

nificant; it symbolized that Christian scholars and laypeople alike should always keep in mind the upcoming generation of ministers in order to help them maneuver through whatever new waves of Christian mission they might encounter in the future. This sentiment was also expressed by student Heetae Kim, who throughout the conference could not help but feel the weight of responsibility as a Christian Korean student for the future of Korea.

ACADEMIC

Student Jeffrey Rickman stated, "that the most exciting part about the conference was being around all of the great minds who attended." Of the four major missions conferences in 2010, the Tokyo and Cape Town meetings consisted largely of active practitioners of mission, while Edinburgh and Boston were geared more towards academic discourse. Indeed, the conveners of 2010Boston aimed to create a truly academic conference; this was evident in many ways, not the least of which was the choice of leading "Christian mission" scholars for plenary speakers: Peter Phan of Georgetown University, Dana Robert of Boston University, and Daniel Jeyaraj of Liverpool Hope University, for example. Despite this, there were many grievances from students that 2010Boston was *overly* academic and theoretical, not providing enough practical information or application points regarding the next wave of Christian missions.

In general, student attendees of 2010Boston desired more hands-on application of the theory presented to them—insight on *how* to engage in the changing contours of world mission and Christianity. For example, ThD student Daryl Ireland stated that "it would have been fascinating to discuss not only *what* mission is, but also *how* mission should be carried out." More particularly, student Jungmin Byon, in response to Peter Phan's lecture on interreligious dialogue, commented that Phan did not discuss "how to foster such dialogue for people who have a different understanding of other religions"—a crucial aspect of Phan's vision of equal footing for mission and interreligious dialogue to be realized.

Boston University lecturer in mission studies Elizabeth Parsons commented that the gap between reflection and mobilization needs to be narrowed in mission studies. This was reiterated by ThD student Gun Cheol Kim: "what is needed is not the dichotomous schism between academia and practice but the re-drawing of mission contours in terms of integrity." Such an objection can only be expected, however; students want to learn and gain knowledge, but also tend to be an activist group. They want to test and apply theories to the world around them. It was suggested by Ireland that the "conference could just as easily [have] revolved around the practice of mission in the twenty-first century as it did the theory of mission." Perhaps a more balanced blend could have been achieved.

Although the plenary lectures were largely theoretical, the desire for application was regularly met in the student-led small group sessions. Eric Lewellen commended BU/GCTS ThD student Travis Myers and his theologically driven prescriptions for more unity, fellowship, and collaboration in evangelism between older established congregations and newer immigrant churches in the United States. In response to Daniel Castiglione's paper on the "Asian-ness" of Jesus in the same session, nearly everyone in attendance was able to contribute to the discussion of how to avoid cultural imposition by missionaries in the Chinese context. This, too, was a strength of the student sessions; in allowing a wide range of strong opinions to be expressed, participants were able to gain practical insights for mission from their peers (many of whom were active practitioners of mission). Thus the conference as a whole, according to Eva Pascal, "faced some of the most difficult challenges of the last 100 years of missions head on, with honesty."

REFLECTIONS ON THE CHANGING CONTOURS OF WORLD MISSION AND CHRISTIANITY

In support of the strong academic and ecumenical nature of the conference, student Samuel Youngs stated that "conferences and inter-Christian dialogue of this nature encourage me greatly, and instill more confidence in me that the issues attending global Christian expansion and the 'changing contours' of mission work stand to be resolved, or at least alleviated, by an interpenetrating and mutually concerned church."

Christian witness to other religious traditions was a recurring theme throughout 2010Boston (as it was at Edinburgh 1910), and many students were compelled to rethink their understanding of and relationship with adherents of other religions. Plenary speakers Peter

Phan (Roman Catholic), Athanasios Papathanasiou (Greek Orthodox), and Brian McLaren (emergent Evangelical) in particular spoke about Christian interactions with "the other" and how those interactions might change in the twenty-first century. ThD student Bruce Yoder picked up on this theme of "other" or "otherness" occurring throughout the conference, noting that "whether with respect to those upon whom mission initiatives focus their efforts or with regard to Christians from other places, traditions, and cultures, Christian mission interactions with the *other* brings new challenges and opportunities." Students were particularly impressed with Peter Phan's plenary session, in which he argued that mission and interreligious dialogue ought to be more like "close friends" than competitors for position. This lecture sparked serious critical thinking among conference attendees as they pondered the relationship and interactions between Christians and non-Christians around the world.

Possibly even more significant than the subject of interreligious dialogue was the ecumenical focus of the conference; according to many students in their reflection papers, this was one of the conference's strengths. Ethnomusicology student Edward Sywulka summarized it well: "Ecumenical gatherings like this provide unique opportunities for Christians to witness to their history with Christ and their understanding of Christ." 2010Boston provided the "rare opportunity" (as one student described it) to interact with members of other Christian traditions, with representatives from Protestant (Evangelical, Mainline, and Pentecostal), Roman Catholic, Orthodox, Anglican/Episcopal, and Independent traditions. The phrase "rare opportunity" is ironic, considering that most of the students at 2010Boston came from one of the ten member schools of the Boston Theological Institute, one of its primary goals being to follow through on its "ecumenical imperative."[9] Perhaps student attendance and participation at 2010Boston will lead to a renewed interest and personal responsibility in the opportunities provided by the BTI throughout the consortium and other ecumenical/interfaith happenings in the Greater Boston area. Other students found that throughout the conference many aspects of their own theology, missional call, and ministries were being called into question. Many were challenged to think about the future generations of Christians as

---

9. Boston Theological Institute, "Ecumenical Imperative."

they reflected on the previous 100 years. What will this generation do to help the next prepare for their "next wave" of Christian mission?

CONCLUSION

Daryl Ireland concluded his reflection paper stating that "the conference was a gift to Boston students and others who gathered together." Judging from the reflections of twenty-four graduate students in two of Greater Boston's Christian institutions, 2010Boston succeeded in embodying its two primary objectives—to be student-oriented and academic-focused—and achieving its chief goal of considering what the "next wave" of Christian mission will look like. Although many criticized the heavily academic nature of the conference, there is no doubt that 2010Boston served both students and non-students alike by stimulating their thinking about global mission and Christianity in the twenty-first century.

The Edinburgh 1910 World Missionary Conference also claimed to be a student-oriented conference, and the impact on students in attendance was substantial. There were a number of students from the Student Christian Movement and the World Student Christian Federation serving at the conference who later became prominent theologians and scholars in the field.[10] It remains to be seen what kind of long-term impact the discussions at 2010Boston will have on seminarians and students in the Boston area. Perhaps those now involved in Christian mission have already heard from future preeminent theologians and scholars—young women, Asians, and Africans—as well as from the next generation of missionaries by way of the students at Lexington Christian Academy. Going forward, student reflections on the 2010Boston conference reveal not only the impact of the gathering, but also unfinished conversations for the next wave of Christian mission.

WORKS CITED

Boston Theological Institute. "The Ecumenical Imperative." No pages. Online: bostontheological.org/ecumenical_imperative.html.

Johnson, Todd M., and Kenneth R. Ross, eds. *Atlas of Global Christianity*. Edinburgh: University of Edinburgh Press, 2009.

10. Stanley, *World Missionary Conference*, 6.

Petersen, Rodney L. "Next Wave: The Changing Contours of World Mission and Christianity." No pages. Online: 2010boston.org/assets/files/Next%20Wave%20 in%20Mission(1).pdf.

Stanley, Brian. *The World Missionary Conference, Edinburgh 1910*. Grand Rapids: Eerdmans, 2009.

Introduction to the Three Conference Reports

THROUGHOUT 2010, VARIOUS PROTESTANT and ecumenical theological and ecclesial communities gathered to reflect on the centenary anniversary of the 1910 Edinburgh World Missionary Conference. Throughout the twentieth century, trajectories from that conference (and a series of others) led, often indirectly, to the beginning of mission movements, the development of ecumenical agencies, the recognition of world Christianity, and increased Christian engagement with peoples of other faiths. Missiologist Ralph Winter singled out four of these centenary conferences as particularly important: Tokyo (May), Edinburgh (June), Cape Town (October), and Boston (November). Of these four conferences, Tokyo and Cape Town were the most clearly evangelical while Edinburgh and Boston most clearly ecumenical; likewise, each had its own particular emphasis. In line with mainstream evangelical thought, Tokyo was unapologetic about "Finishing the Task" of worldwide evangelism; its accent on discipleship, however, added depth to its breadth. The closing "Tokyo Declaration" signaled the conference's explicit affirmation of evangelism and sponsorship by the U.S. Center for World Mission, the Global Network of Mission Structures, and various churches in Korea and Japan. Its planning group consisted of persons representing Evangelical mission agencies. Edinburgh 2010 was carried out by a council representative of many strands of the world church, and was hosted by the University of Edinburgh with endorsement by the World Council of Churches. Its "Common Call" reflects the conference's amazing ecclesiastical and ethnic diversity and its emphasis on the *missio Dei*. Cape Town was a champion of holistic mission, bringing evangelism and social justice together. By far the largest conference with well over 4,000 participants, it was organized by the Lausanne Movement in partnership with the World Evangelical Alliance. The "Cape Town Commitment" expounded biblical, theological, historical, and strategic perspectives on world evangelization. The conference in Boston drew together students, faculty, clergy, and lay persons from over twenty different countries under the auspices of the Boston Theological Institute, the ecumenical (and now interfaith) consortium of theological schools in the Greater Boston area. The Boston conference was largely academic, calling professors and research students to explore missionary history, the emergence of World Christianity, and contemporary missiological issues.

At the 2010Boston conference, representatives who had attended Tokyo, Edinburgh, and Cape Town were invited to present brief reports during a session dedicated to the centenary year. Bishop Ian Douglas (Episcopal Diocese of Connecticut) moderated the session, posing a series of insightful questions and commenting on the ecumenical and theological scope of the three conferences.

17

Tokyo 2010

Global Mission Consultation

Allen Yeh

AT LEAST A DOZEN conferences in 2010 celebrated the centenary of the Edinburgh 1910 World Missionary Conference. Ralph Winter, founder of the U.S. Center for World Mission (USCWM), singled out four of them as being particularly significant: Tokyo, Edinburgh, Cape Town, and Boston.[1] Tokyo led the effort with the first conference of these four from May 11–14, 2010, at Nakano Sun Plaza in western Tokyo. In many ways, it was fitting that Tokyo be the first, because its emphasis was on evangelism of unreached people groups—what is often termed "finishing the task" or "frontier missions." Much as the first European settlers in America had to blaze trails through the wilderness in their expansion westward, the organizers of Tokyo 2010 have the vision of pioneering Christian work in places that have never before heard the gospel. It almost seems anachronistic today to think about "unreached people groups" in our over-globalized world, but there are still almost 7,000 people groups[2] who have never heard the gospel (at the first Lausanne Congress in 1974, Ralph Winter famously redefined "nation," the Greek word *ethne* in, e.g., Matthew 28:19, as ethno-linguistic groups, not po-

---

1. Yeh, "Tokyo 2010 and Edinburgh 2010."

2. According to the Joshua Project (http://www.joshuaproject.net/), out of 16,567 people groups on earth, there are 6,838 who have no gospel access. That is 41.3 percent of all people groups that are unreached. It is important, however, to distinguish between that and the world's population. Some people groups are tiny, so the actual percentage of unreached *people* may be different from the percentage of unreached people *groups*.

litical entities). It was at Lausanne '74 that two streams of evangelical missiology emerged, what might be termed "frontier missions" and "holistic mission."[3] Tokyo 2010 is the former; Cape Town 2010 is the latter. Some people think of frontier missions as being the child or the younger sibling of holistic mission, but really the two are more like twins birthed from the same mother: mid-twentieth-century Neo-evangelicalism[4] (which itself was a reaction against early twentieth-century fundamentalism). Because Winter was the one to single out these four conferences, it is correspondingly appropriate that Tokyo serve as the vanguard, because he was the one who had a vision for all four conferences as serving different purposes in fulfilling the legacy of Edinburgh 1910.[5]

The conference was organized by the USCWM, through local churches in Japan, in partnership with churches in Korea. The reconciliation between these two heretofore bitter East Asian enemies was but one of the intentional outcomes of the conference. Another clearly radical move was having the conference in one of the most resistant mission fields on earth, as many people have regarded Japan as the second-hardest mission field after the Muslim world.[6] As with Edinburgh 1910's continuation committee, which was considered its greatest legacy (the main reason why it was considered the "birthplace of the ecumenical movement," not because of its actual representation at the conference itself), Tokyo 2010 aims to keep its momentum and

---

3. Even the singular/plural distinction is significant, as missiologists like Lesslie Newbigin and David Bosch have pointed out.

4. A name coined by Harold Ockenga, encompassing the thinking and ministry of people like himself, as well as Billy Graham, Harold Lindsell, and Carl F. H. Henry, among others.

5. Not only this present publication, but also other periodicals such as *Christianity Today* ("Spotlight: The Future(s) of Mission," 54.8 [August 2010]) and *Missiology: An International Review* (39.2 [April 2011]) have picked up on this "multiple conference" idea.

6. Edinburgh 1910, in contrast, was held in the most Christian land at the time. The same might be said of Cape Town, as sub-Saharan Africa is one of the heartbeats of world Christianity today, along with China and Korea. So, in this sense, Edinburgh 1910 and Cape Town 2010 might be more kin due to having the conference in the center of gravity of Christianity, whereas Tokyo 2010 and Edinburgh 2010 have the unintentional commonality of holding the conference in lands largely devoid of Christianity. An interesting corollary observation is the relationship between Christianity and wealth, which has been turned on its head. A century ago, Christian nations were wealthy nations. Today, in contrast, wealthy Japan has few Christians, while Africa is one of the most Christian regions.

fulfill its stated goals via the Global Network of Mission Structures (GNMS), much as Cape Town has the Lausanne Movement as an ongoing movement. The planning committee chairman was Yong Cho, a Korean who works for the USCWM. Korean mega-churches such as Onnuri Community Church and Yoido Full Gospel Church provided speakers and financial backing. The chairman of the whole conference was Obed Alvarez from Latin America, the chairman of the Japanese host committee was Minoru Okuyama, and Hisham Kamel from Egypt was the General Coordinator, thus ensuring intercontinental representation within the leadership team.

The theme of the conference was "Making Disciples of Every People in Our Generation," clearly hearkening back to John Mott's famous watchword of 1910, "The Evangelization of the World in This Generation," but with the twist of replacing the word "evangelization" with "discipleship" because the main verb in the Great Commission (Matt 28:18–20) is "make disciples." One of the outcomes of the conference was a major document, the Tokyo Declaration, just as the Lausanne '74 Congress produced the Lausanne Covenant. The Declaration[7] makes its own version of a holistic statement—not in reformulating mission as evangelism + social justice, but as emphasizing depth in mission as discipleship, contrary to the false stereotype of frontier missions as having merely a "shallow" evangelistic emphasis. It also contains a pledge for all the signatories (again, not individual people, but mission organizations) to aim for the completion of the task as set forth in the Great Commission, which requires cooperation for its fulfillment.

Another one of Winter's contributions was to make clear the distinction between modalities and sodalities.[8] He saw the greatest amount of cooperation as coming from sodalities, so that provided the basis for delegates: no individuals were invited, but rather missionary societies and organizations that sent their own representatives. Tokyo 2010 had about 1,000 attendees, larger than Edinburgh 2010 (300 people) but smaller than Cape Town 2010 (4,000 people). The different sizes contributed greatly to the pros and cons of each conference. For example, Edinburgh 2010's small size contributed to intimacy and efficiency—everybody had the opportunity to meet everyone else, and everyone had a voice in formulating policies, strategies, and theologies. Cape Town

---

7. The Tokyo Declaration can be found at: http://gnms.net/declaration.html.
8. The former is ecclesial structures; the latter is para-church organizations.

2010's large size contained perhaps the most diverse representation of Christians in history, and the effectiveness of manpower. Tokyo 2010's size was between the two and had a correspondingly fine balance of both.

If I could highlight the most powerful moment of the entire conference, it would be this: Stefan Gustavsson of Sweden gave a Macedonian call ("come over and help us") lecture about how to evangelize secular Europeans, the "prodigal sons" of Christianity today. It was a good lecture—if a bit academic—but the organizer of the conference, Yong Cho, had a remarkable response. Tearfully, he called for the entire conference to spontaneously pray for Europe to regain its faith, and he invited all the European delegates to come up to the stage. In a remarkable turn, all the Two-Thirds World Christians cried out on behalf of their brothers and sisters in Europe—in particular, two Koreans and two Africans (representing two of the strongest centers of Christianity) led the prayers. The Holy Spirit was moving; that was the most authentic and unforgettable part of the whole conference. I thought, if only the Edinburgh 1910 delegates could have seen this—what a difference a century makes! The Two-Thirds World churches have come of age, while Europe has declined; who would have believed this a century ago? However, a Korean-American delegate said to me after that session, "What a sobering reminder to the Korean church that we should not rest on our laurels—I can already sense that we are going the way of Europe, so we should not become arrogant." Perhaps I, as an American, can also say the same thing of the U.S.

Probably the most glaring omission at Tokyo 2010 was the lack of any mention of social justice. This is surprising considering that Ralph Winter was at the 1974 Lausanne Congress on World Evangelization in Switzerland where he signed the Lausanne Covenant. That Covenant explicitly reconstructed the bond between evangelism and social justice as both equal partners in mission. This reparation was in response to the twentieth century, so often dichotomized by schisms like the fundamentalist-modernist controversy and the creation-evolution debate. Today, Evangelicals have tried to return to a holistic eighteenth- and nineteenth-century Evangelicalism similar to that of John Wesley, Charles Finney, and William Wilberforce. One of the criticisms of the Urbana 2009 missions conference is that it seemed to be all about social justice but included hardly any talk of evangelism. I would say the opposite was true of Tokyo 2010. However, talking to members of the U.S. Center for

World Mission, they said the omission of dialogue about social justice is because Tokyo 2010 is just one piece of the puzzle: the other three conferences of 2010 have made much of social justice, but Tokyo was aiming to do what it does best: namely, evangelism and frontier missions, what is called "finishing the task."

It is obvious that so much of Tokyo 2010 cannot be spoken of apart from the legacy of Ralph Winter who passed away in 2009. He was one of the most significant missiologists of the twentieth and twenty-first centuries. He was a missionary to Guatemala, the founder of the U.S. Center for World Mission, and he started the Perspectives on the World Christian Movement course that has educated laypeople all over the world about world missions. He often thought "outside the box" in profound ways. Tokyo 2010 was meant to be the culmination of his life's work, and unfortunately he died just a year before seeing his vision realized. In a sense, Tokyo 2010 parallels Edinburgh 1910 in that both were the brainchild of one man, one missiological genius. In the case of a proposed Cape Town conference that never happened in 1810, it was William Carey. In 1910, it was John R. Mott. In 2010, it is Ralph Winter. His contributions to frontier missiology were not meant to be divisive, however. He still attended Lausanne conferences and was friends with holistic mission people. A perfect example was the inaugural Ralph Winter lectureship at William Carey International University in March 2010 (a year after his death) when René Padilla, a firm advocate of holistic mission, was invited to deliver the series. Tokyo and Cape Town, as the two major evangelical conferences celebrating Edinburgh 1910, can likewise stand side by side with an expectation of cooperation rather than competition. Winter did not tout Tokyo 2010 as the best successor to Edinburgh 1910, but as one of several contributors to the monumental task of world mission, one which requires the resources of all of God's people.

WORKS CITED

Missiology: An International Review 39.2 (April 2011). Electronic Issue.
"Spotlight: The Future(s) of Mission." *Christianity Today* (August 2010). No pages. Online: http://www.christianitytoday.com/ct/2010/august/17.11.html.
Yeh, Allen. "Tokyo 2010 and Edinburgh 2010: A Comparison of Two Centenary Conferences." *International Journal of Frontier Missions* 27.4 (October–December 2010) 117–25.

Lausanne III

A Success?

LouAnn Stropoli

AT FIRST GLANCE, THE Third Lausanne Congress on World Evangelization, otherwise known as Cape Town 2010, appeared to be an enhanced Urbana Student Missions Conference (held in the USA every three years). Similar to Urbana, Cape Town 2010 was packed with music and video presentations, skits, Bible expositions, and plenary and breakout sessions. Beneath this layer of interactions, however, were found the mechanisms of a working Congress that sought to facilitate global dialogues, renew the call of the Great Commission texts, and ignite the global Evangelical church to humbly bring the "whole gospel" to the "whole world" in unified diversity and in the spirit of the Lausanne Covenant.[1]

Building on the foundation of previous gatherings that include the historic Edinburgh World Missionary Conference of 1910, which elevated mission "to be the central place of the church,"[2] and Lausanne 1974, which gave birth to the Lausanne Movement and the drafting of the Lausanne Covenant, Cape Town 2010 brought together the largest and most diverse gathering of global interdenominational Evangelical leaders in the history of the movement. Those present included pastors,

---

1. The 1974 Lausanne Covenant can be viewed online at www.lausanne.org/covenant.
2. Ross, "Edinburgh 1910," xvi–xvii.

missiologists, lay leaders, missionaries, business associates, and younger ministry leaders from various backgrounds. Participants were assigned to tables of six with the purpose of bringing together people from diverse backgrounds and cultures. On a smaller scale, participants modeled the global conversation as they listened, shared, and strategized in cross-cultural relationships during their table discussions.

The inspirational theme of Cape Town 2010 was "God is on the Move." This theme was fleshed out with plenary sessions focused on Asia, the Middle East, Latin America and the Caribbean, Africa, Eurasia, and the West. Listeners were inspired by testimonies of God's continuous movement throughout times of persecution and hardship. The seats left empty by missing Chinese participants bore witness to one of the most public and blatant examples of religious restriction found across the globe in recent times. Of the over 250 intended Chinese participants and volunteers, only three were permitted out of China to attend the Congress. A few more who were already out of the country for other reasons were also able to attend, but the final count of those present was a small fraction of the intended Chinese representation. The empty chairs voiced a powerful statement and put prayer for these missing participants in the forefront of the minds and hearts of those present.

The main themes of the Congress challenged the global Evangelical church to convey the whole gospel. This holistic gospel includes a faith accompanied by action, as demonstrated by fighting for social justice, feeding the hungry, clothing the poor, responding to HIV/AIDS, and seeking the freedom of the millions of slaves in today's world. While the participants were challenged to live out the gospel with actions of love, they were also reminded not to forsake the proclamation of the gospel with actual words. As Sri Lankan pastor Ajith Fernando stated, St. Francis was "all the time using words," not just actions, as is often mistakenly assumed.[3] Furthermore, the concept of truth itself was reaffirmed, including the truth of the words found in the Bible. In affirmation of this truth, Carver Yu, president of China Graduate School of Theology, encouraged the participants to live with plurality, not pluralism.[4] Additionally, those present were called to reconciliation. They were first called to reconcile

---

3. Fernando, "Ephesians 1." Address can be found at http://conversation.lausanne.org/en/conversations/detail/10963.

4. Yu, "Post-communist China." Address can be found at http://conversation.lausanne.org/en/conversations/detail/11377.

their own personal relationships and then to facilitate reconciliation in the areas of inter-personal, ethnic, and national relations. A powerful example of reconciliation was demonstrated when a Palestinian woman and an Israeli man spoke together of their commitment towards forgiveness and peace.[5] Among the remaining themes of the conference, the prosperity gospel was addressed, men and women were encouraged to work side by side, and a new model of partnership was presented: one in which there are no superstars, but rather equal cross-cultural partners gathering in one another's homes and working together for the sake of global evangelization.

SUCCESSES

One of the most powerful aspects of the Congress was the opportunity to meet and connect with believers from all around the world. It is one experience to read a story about someone one does not know; it is another experience to sit down face to face and hear a testimony from his or her own voice. In a personal meeting, the joy and/or tears found in the eyes of the speaker tell their own significant story. These interpersonal connections are integral in promoting the reality of a unified global church, for it is people who are reconciled to one another who will then bring about the reconciliation of Christians, of ethnic groups, and of the nations. These interpersonal connections were one of the most powerful outcomes of Cape Town 2010. For these reasons, the cross-cultural and cross-national relationships that grow out of the Congress have the potential to influence the church in significant ways in years to come.

This was not a Congress only for those present in Cape Town.[6] Another success was the bringing together of thousands of people who participated not only in person, but also via the Internet and GlobaLink sessions. The themes discussed at the Congress provided a foundation upon which conversations could be expanded through online videos and discussion forums. The influence on the global Evangelical church would be greatly limited if those 4,000–5,000 people present were the

---

5. Qubti and Sered, "Jewish Palestinian Reconciliation." Address can be found at http://conversation.lausanne.org/en/conversations/detail/11418.

6. More information on the GlobaLink sessions can be found at http://www.lausanne.org/cape-town-2010/globalink.html.

only ones "in the know." The increased transparency and wider participation enlarges the opportunity for connectedness and continued growth of the movement.

Another strength of the Congress was its appeal to younger leaders. The style of communication (which included short snippets of information and quick changeovers from speakers to videos), the young leaders' lounge, and various other aspects of the Congress were specifically geared towards reaching the next generation of leaders. They were able to learn by watching and interacting with the more experienced leaders who were gathered around them. Although the style of communication may have been geared too much towards the younger generation, leaving the more experienced generation longing for more depth and length in presentation, the desire to empower the next generation of leaders cast an encouraging light on the future of the Lausanne Movement and the Evangelical church.

CHALLENGES

Along with the many successes of Lausanne III, there were also challenges. Although the Congress was more diverse than any Lausanne gathering in the movement's history—with an increased percentage from the majority world—there were too few women and too few younger leaders, both among the leadership and participants. Furthermore, given that Lausanne is a community of relationships, there are some indigenous church organizations that remain outside the scope of this network. These organizations represent committed Evangelical believers whose leaders have the potential to greatly contribute to the global conversation, yet, they were not present in Cape Town. Continued effort is needed towards a truly connected and global Evangelical representation. Furthermore, if Lausanne were to expand its network and broaden its ecumenical ties, the global Evangelical constituency might be challenged to rethink its definition of the clause "the whole church," which might then broaden its opportunity to reach the whole world.

Another challenge to the success of Cape Town 2010 was an overemphasis on English. In some instances speakers struggled to read a script in English that would have been much more powerfully communicated in their own first languages with the addition of subtitles or a translator. The same principle applied to the musical worship. Although the music was phenomenal, a greater emphasis on indigenous modes of worship—for example, the inclusion of a Hindi Yeshu Bhajan (a devotional song in the traditional Indian style)—would have greatly enhanced the global aspect of the musical worship. There were attempts to sing Western styled songs in many different languages, but singing a translated song is different from experiencing worship in musical heart languages from around the globe. Additionally, the presentations were strictly timed and perhaps too scripted. No doubt preparation and adherence to a schedule are necessary as is an assurance that the messages shared are representative of the movement, but the Congress might have had a greater opportunity to stimulate thinking "outside the box" if more voices had been freely shared.

Finally, one of the greatest challenges of Cape Town 2010 finds expression in the deep desire of participants near and far to engage in significant dialogue. For this dialogue to make a difference it must provide an opportunity for each one to speak and be heard, as well as to listen to and learn from others. The Congress itself was partially successful in this respect, but mostly due to the large number of participants and a tightly packed schedule, significant opportunity for engagement was limited. In the aftermath of the Congress, the implementation of creative and inventive ideas are essential for the message of Lausanne III to be heard and acted upon throughout the local representations of the global Evangelical church.

CONCLUSION

Lausanne III seemed to showcase no superstars; nor was there a voice that paralleled Ralph Winter's inspiring call to rethink the definition of the Greek word *ethne* at the 1974 Lausanne Conference. However, this is not necessarily a negative aspect of the Cape Town 2010. It is possible that for the global Evangelical movement to expand in this next generation, the messages and themes of Lausanne III will need to grow deep roots in the hearts of the local churches. In his opening address, Doug Birdsall, Executive Chairman of Lausanne, expressed his desire that the Congress "be reported upon as the most united expression of the church that the world has ever seen."[7] Perhaps that unified expression will be most evident as one person reconciles to another and justice and unity are sought in homes and local communities. When that unity becomes a local reality and when the vision of Lausanne becomes the lifeblood of local communities of believers, the whole world has a much better chance of hearing the whole gospel. It is then that Lausanne III will be determined to be a success.

WORKS CITED

Fernando, Ajith. "Bible Exposition Ephesians 1." Plenary address, Cape Town 2010, Cape Town, South Africa, October 17–24, 2010.

Qubti, Shadia, and Dan Sered. "Jewish Palestinian Reconciliation." Address, Cape Town 2010, Cape Town, South Africa, October 17–24, 2010.

Ross, Kenneth. "Edinburgh 1910: A Defining Moment." In *Atlas of Global Christianity*, edited by Todd M. Johnson and Kenneth R. Ross, xvi–xvii. Edinburgh: Edinburgh University Press, 2009.

Yu, Carver. "Presenting the Truth in Post-Communist China." Address, Cape Town 2010, Cape Town, South Africa, October 17–24, 2010.

---

7. Doug Birdsall, "Cape Town 2010 Opening Celebration," Address can be found at http://conversation.lausanne.org/en/conversations/detail/11322

19

Witnessing for Christ Today

Christian Mission Beyond Edinburgh 2010

Kapya John Kaoma

As we celebrate the missionary conference of 1910, we should ask, to what will future generations of Christians look back in 2110? Unlike Edinburgh 1910, which viewed the evangelization of the world as imperative to mission, the Edinburgh 2010 conference emphasized "witnessing for Christ today." The conference was a clear testimony of the new contours in mission and world Christianity. Indeed, Christian mission is full of divine surprises! What was unimaginable at Edinburgh 1910 was possible in 2010. It was a humbling experience to share the same space with those who had gathered in 1910. Even more so, it was exhilarating to be among the many Africans at Edinburgh 2010.

EDINBURGH 2010 IN REVIEW

The Edinburgh 2010 conference was held June 2–6, 2010, with 297 delegates in attendance. Among these were Christians of Orthodox, Roman Catholic, and Pentecostal backgrounds. Others came from African Initiated Churches (AICs), while some others were from diverse mainline Protestant churches. Church-related institutions and organizations were also represented.[1]

The mission conference set out to address nine main themes on modern mission.[2] Key priorities "for Christian mission" from 1910 to 2010 were identified by over 100 scholars of various Christian traditions around the globe who began the study process in 2008. Most of their recommendations were published in *Edinburgh 2010: Witnessing to Christ Today*, the text that served as a study guide to the participants. Originally, planners intended 60 percent of delegates to come "from the global south, 50% women, and 20% under the age of 30."[3] However, over 160 delegates were from the global North (with the United States alone having more official delegates than the whole of Africa).[4] Worse still, only 32 percent of the delegates were women and a mere 6 percent were under the age of thirty.[5]

Just as each day began with an ecumenical worship service, the conference also ended with an ecumenical closing celebration service at which the Archbishop of York, John Sentamu, challenged the church to know where "the church of Jesus Christ is going." Arguing that participants in God's mission ought to know, Sentamu regretted that amidst

---

1. About 100 delegates were appointed by the Edinburgh 2010 Study Process Monitoring Group while a further 200 were picked by various churches, organizations, and institutions. "Delegate Information," accessed November 1, 2010.

2. The nine themes were (1) foundations for mission, (2) Christian mission among other faiths, (3) mission and post-modernities, (4) mission and power, (5) forms of missionary engagement, (6) theological education and formation, (7) Christian communities in contemporary contexts, (7) mission and unity—ecclesiology and mission, (8) mission spirituality, and (9) authentic discipleship. Seven transversals included women and mission, youth and mission, healing and reconciliation, Bible and mission/mission in the Bible, contextualization, inculturation and dialogue of worldviews, subaltern voices and ecological perspectives on mission. For a detailed study of the main themes, see Balia and Kim, *Edinburgh 2010*.

3. "Delegate Information," accessed November 1, 2010.

4. Based on the official registration list, the United States was represented by forty-five delegates and the United Kingdom by thirty-five. The entire African continent was represented by forty-one delegates, fifteen of whom are residents of the global North. The country of Zimbabwe, for example, was not represented.

5. According to the conference's official records, ninety-five delegates were women and only nineteen were under thirty years of age. Seventy-seven different nationalities, sixty-five countries of residence, and sixty-two mother tongues were represented. Data received by personal e-mail correspondence with Kirsteen Kim, December 6, 2010.

injustices of our time, "the church's activities and energies appear to be totally irrelevant to the needs of the world today."[6]

The concept of *missio Dei* ran through all nine main study themes and to some extent the transversals.[7] The presence of this concept differentiated Edinburgh 2010 from 1910. Whereas those who gathered in 1910 saw the church as the force behind mission, delegates at Edinburgh 2010 understood God as the source of mission. The ecumenical discussion of *missio Dei* made it possible for diverse Christian traditions to offer reflections on mission.

EDINBURGH 2010 ON THE ISSUES

Almost all speakers raised issues with unjust economic and power structures that demean the poor as issues with which Christian mission should contend. Questions of political and economic power and how they affect both international and church relations were equally discussed. Although ecological issues were raised in passing, socio-political, economic, and ecumenical issues seemed to suggest new contours of mission in global Christianity at Edinburgh 2010.

The occurring ecological crisis is one of the biggest moral challenges that confront Christian mission today. The current ecological crises such as air and water pollution, deforestation, climate change, and many other ecological predicaments are adversely affecting the lives of the poor and the integrity of our planet.

Edinburgh 2010 introduced a number of missiological terms such as "missionary power," "ecumenical charity," "budding ecumenism," and "mission to the North,"[8] as well as correctly recognized that the Christianization of the global South followed the exploitation of natural resources. Sadly, however, the conference did not add eco-mission as a cutting-edge concept for mission and evangelism. Yet the growing numbers of Christians in the global South should be a cause for concern in the face of the ongoing ecological crisis.

---

6. Sentamu, untitled sermon, accessed October 9, 2010. The service was streamed and broadcasted live by the BBC. Prayers were said in different languages and the African choir in Edinburgh attended the occasion.

7. See footnote 2 for list of transversals.

8. Edinburgh 2010, "Key Terms."

Unlike participants at Edinburgh 1910, who were mostly active practitioners of mission, scholars of mission and church officials dominated the 2010 conference deliberations.[9] It is not an overstatement to suggest that while there has been a shift from church-centered to God-centered mission, in reality, God's mission is still imprisoned in the academy, official church institutions, and research institutions. Perhaps this was one of the weaknesses of Edinburgh 2010. Most of the participants were academicians, ordained ministers, or church officials. That said, the project of Christian mission should be informed by listening to the voices of men and women who are participating in God's mission at the grassroots level. Christian mission takes place wherever God's people participate faithfully in the *missio Creator Dei*.

The separation between the economically rich North and poor South influences the perception of mission. In its *Common Call*, the conference noted that the asymmetries and imbalances of power divide and trouble the church and world. Thus, "[w]e are called to find practical ways to live as members of One Body in full awareness . . . [that] Christ welcomes and empowers the poor and afflicted, and the power of the Holy Spirit is manifested in our vulnerability."[10]

In her keynote address, Dana Robert noted that the independence of African and Asian churches in the 1950s and 1960s "added urgency to the conviction that mission [is] a task of the whole church, and not just the West."[11] However, this "multi-directional" nature of Christian mission is still to be realized in our generation.[12] For example, "the asymmetries and imbalances" of power define Christian mission; the title "missionary" is reserved for Western missionaries while "immigrant missionary" is reserved for non-Westerners! Despite the fact that "partnership" remains the most-cited concept in mission, the mutuality of God's people is still to be realized.[13]

---

9. Official records show that about thirty-five participants were professors, fifty-five were holders of some sort of doctorate, and more than fifty-seven were reverend doctors. Over 134 delegates were ordained ministers. In addition, the records show that over 100 participants represented academic and research institutions across the globe.

10. Edinburgh 2010, "Common Call."

11. Robert, "Mission and Unity."

12. Ibid.

13. Responding to Dana Robert's keynote address, Tinyiko Sam Maluleke, Executive Director: Research at the University of South Africa (and president of the South African Council of Churches), observed that while one African represented all Africans in

Edinburgh 2010 acknowledged that churches in the global South ought to respond to the Great Commission (Matt 28:19–20). The conference also highlighted the growing influence of the global South in re-evangelizing the North.[14] The conference's *Common Call* equally celebrated "the renewal experienced through movements of migration and mission in all directions."[15] Amidst such optimism, Fidon R. Mwombeki (general secretary of the United Evangelical Mission based in Wuppertal, Germany) noted that although independent missionaries from the South are founding churches in Europe, "European official churches have not yet known how to deal with this phenomenon."[16]

Edinburgh 2010 addressed the issues of economic inequality, political instability, and worsening world poverty as matters of concern for mission studies. It was argued that these issues have displaced many Christians from their homelands. As many non-Western Christians make the global North their home, integrating them in the mission of God is imperative. Unfortunately, churches with a history in the North are finding it hard to do so. In most cases, these more recent churches are "immigrant churches" for "immigrant Christians" with "immigrant pastors." Yet, for all Christians, any foreign country is motherland, and any motherland is a foreign country.[17]

The realities of globalization should not threaten mission, but propel it into new directions. Just as the world has become global, Christian mission should become inclusive of the other. Unlike politics, God's mission has no territorial boundaries. The call to participate in God's mission is to all Christians regardless of geographic and economic locations. This call is the starting point of understanding Christian mission in our time.

1910, the situation has not changed much. "It has become common for Africa to be presented but not present." His argument was that while Christian mission is taking place in the global South, the global North still sets the agenda. In other words, despite efforts to institute partnership in mission, "African churches feel they are treated as 'junior partners,' and that the situation will not change as long as there is economic inequality." The Anglican Communion and Baptist World Alliance, "Conversations Around the World 2000–2005," 27.

14. See the official list of parallel session presentations, http://www.edinburgh2010.org/en/resources/papersdocuments.html, accessed November 1, 2010.

15. Edinburgh 2010, "Common Call."

16. Edinburgh 2010, "Key terms."

17. "The Epistle to Diognetus," in *Early Christian Writings*, 145.

CONCLUSION

The joys and aspirations of Edinburgh 2010 will only be realized if all believers, wherever they are found, participate in the creator's mission. The value of Edinburgh 2010 for the future of global Christianity lies in how God's people respond to the challenges of our time. There were certainly shortfalls about the conference; however, the ecumenical nature of the conference, the diversity of presenters and participants, and, above all, the fellowship enjoyed among the delegates will all go a long way in forging future mission endeavors.

WORKS CITED

Balia, Daryl, and Kirsteen Kim. *Edinburgh 2010: Witnessing to Christ Today*. Oxford: Regnum, 2010.

Edinburgh 2010. "Common Call." No pages. Online: http://www.edinburgh2010.org/fileadmin/files/edinburgh2010/files/conference_docs/Common_Call_final.pdf.

———. "Delegate Information." No pages. Online. http://www.edinburgh2010.org/en/participate/delegate-information.html.

———. "Key Terms for Mission and Christian Unity in 2010." No pages. Online: http://www.edinburgh2010.org/en/news/en/article/4645/key-terms-for-mission-and.html.

Robert, Dana L. "Mission and Unity in the 'Long View' from 1910 to the 21st Century." Keynote address, Edinburgh 2010. Edinburgh, Scotland, June 2–6, 2010.

Sentamu, John. Untitled sermon. Closing celebration, Edinburgh 2010. Edinburgh, Scotland, June 2–6, 2010.

The Anglican Communion and Baptist World Alliance. "Conversation Around the World 2000–2005." In *The Report of the International Conversations between the Anglican Communion and the Baptist World Alliance*. London: Anglican Communion Office, 2005.

"The Epistle to Diognetus." Translated by Maxwell Staniforth. In *Early Christian Writings: The Apostolic Fathers*. London: Penguin Classics, 1968.

20

The Eight Themes of 2010Boston

Rodney L. Petersen

INTRODUCTION TO THE EIGHT THEMES

IN 1910, THE WORLD Missionary Conference met in Edinburgh to hear the results from eight different commissions that had prepared reports on the status of the global missionary effort.[1] The commissions had conducted two years of research on their assigned topics, each producing a single-volume report that was distributed to all of the delegates before they headed to the conference in Scotland. The Eight Commissions were as follows:

1. Carrying the Gospel to all the World
2. The Native Church and its Workers
3. Education in Relation to the Christianization of National Life
4. The Missionary Message in Relation to the Non-Christian Religions
5. The Preparation of Missionaries
6. The Home Base of Missions
7. Relation of Missions to Governments
8. Co-Operation and the Promotion of Unity

1. Stanley, *World Missionary Conference*, 32–35.

Nothing this systematic or ambitious was attempted by those planning the Edinburgh centennial celebration in Boston, but there was an effort to solicit involvement by students, faculty, and others around eight topics that generally related to the eight themes of Edinburgh 1910.[2] This effort grew out of the identities of the schools of the Boston Theological Institute (BTI), to be ecumenical and academic in nature with a focus on the phenomenon that is missionary history, the expansion of the Church, and the rise of World Christianity. Behind the eight themes developed for the Boston conference were a number of annual consultations on global mission reaching back twenty years, held in ecumenical and interfaith settings within the BTI schools and in memory of missiologist Orlando E. Costas, former Dean of the Faculty, Andover Newton Theological School (1984–87). Some of this work appeared in a volume that posited an *Antioch Agenda* for mission appropriate to the twenty-first century.[3]

The eight Boston themes constituted the Boston conference's recognition of areas for important missiological reflection and theological education. As such, they represent the Boston conference's contribution to the Edinburgh process and wider set of centenary discussions.[4] The eight mission themes were:

1. Changing Contours of Christian Unity
2. Mission in Context
3. Disciples in Mission
4. Education for Mission

---

2. The International Mission and Ecumenism faculty committee of the schools of the Boston Theological Institute, responsible for planning 2010Boston, included Daniel Jeyaraj and Nimi Wariboko (Andover Newton Theological School), Raymond Helmick, S.J. and Catherine Cornille (Boston College, Department of Theology), Margaret Guider, O.S.F. (Boston College, School of Theology and Ministry), Dana Robert and Elizabeth Parsons (Boston University School of Theology), Ian Douglas and Christopher Duraisingh (Episcopal Divinity School), Todd Johnson and Timothy Tennent (Gordon-Conwell Theological Seminary), Susan Abraham (Harvard Divinity School), and Fr. Luke Veronis (Holy Cross Greek Orthodox School of Theology).

3. Jeyaraj, et al, *Antioch Agenda*. Much of this work over the twenty-year period is reflected in articles published during this time in the *BTI Newsletter* and *BTI Magazine*. See Petersen and Simion, *Tracing Contours*.

4. A summary of the conference is offered by Norman Thomas in Thomas, "2010Boston." See additional and related articles in this same edition of the *International Bulletin of Missionary Research*.

5. Mission and Post-Colonialism

6. Mission in a Pluralist World

7. Mission and Post-Modernity

8. Salvation Today

Boston themes 1 (Unity), 4 (Education for Mission) and 8 (Salvation Today) related to Edinburgh themes 8 (Cooperation and Unity), 5 and 3 (Preparation of Missionaries and Education in Relation to the Christianization of National Life) and 1 (Carrying the Gospel . . .) respectively. Boston themes 2, 3, 5, 6, and 7 were only loosely related to Edinburgh themes 2, 3, 7, 4, and 6, respectively. Differences between the two conferences' themes are the result of BTI faculty interests and reflect the contemporary issues of globalization, contextualization, and the evolution of mission studies.

CROSS-CUTTING ISSUES OF POST-MODERNITY AND POST-COLONIALISM

Papers were delivered on the eight Boston themes throughout the course of the conference with a closing plenary session held at The Memorial Church at Harvard University. Before the final reflections on those eight themes, Susan Abraham of Harvard Divinity School reminded us of the requisites of a post-colonial and post-modern world framing the missionary endeavor today. The paragraph put forward by Abraham for response was: "How do we shape a theology of mission in terms of culture and politics? That is, how does a post hermeneutical idea of culture and politics impact a theology of mission? Four issues are relevant to such a theology of mission: liberation, conversion, conflict and reconciliation. Each of these issues in a postcolonial framework demands that a theology of mission articulate an 'ethos of engagement' with contemporary economic structures, religious difference, religious and communal violence and dialogue across complex space and time."

The nine keynote speakers of the conference responded to Abraham's remarks, stressing concerns that relate to the eight Boston themes. Ruth Padilla DeBorst (Latin American Theological Fraternity) responded by drawing attention to the fact that stories frame our lives, as emphasized by Brian McLaren in the course of the conference. Such narratives within which we locate ourselves are massively powerful, she said. However, the discourses, the conversations, and the challenging of our categories are not just for taking us into new discourses and conversations. They are to take us to new patterns of faithful living.

Angelyn Dries, O.S.F. (St. Louis University) drew attention to the concern that while we were "literally pilgrims around the Boston area" during the multisite conference, we must not miss the "contemplative dimension" that underscores mission and that was a part of the worship component of the conference. If we have something to say it comes from a profound sense of who we are individually and before God as human beings and as Christian people. The complexity of this religious identity was emphasized by Daniel Jeyaraj (Liverpool Hope University and Andover Newton Theological School) in his response: "In India itself we have pre-colonial Christianity, colonial Christianity, post-colonial Christianity, neo-colonial Christianity, non-colonial Christianity . . . All are represented." Which one we are and which we want to accept or dismiss must be specified. But, he said, "Without conversion, it seems to me we are stagnant . . . European and American questions need not be questions of people in India and different parts of the world . . ."

Reflecting on Abraham's remarks, Brian McLaren noted that what came to his mind was the text of 2 Corinthians 5:16, that "From now on . . . we regard no one from a human point of view . . . So if anyone is in Christ, there is a new creation . . ." Refusing all dichotomies, McLaren wondered whether if even by classifying others as Christian or non-Christian we are betraying our identity in Christ; whether seeing the world in these bipolar terms of "us" and "them" is just the mere translation from one human point of view (or "as in the flesh") to another. "If that's the case, the central command of Jesus, the great command he said, suddenly has enormous political and cultural and social power: calling us to love God with all our heart, soul, mind, and strength, not our God as opposed to their god, but the God who is above all—the creator of all . . ."

Athanasios Papathanasiou (*Synaxis Greek Orthodox Theological Journal*) added three comments on dialogue: First, this dialogue must not be "encaged" in the illusion that our Christian world must only exist of religious entities and realities; dialogue has to be with people of every persuasion, philosophy, and class. Second, it must be characterized by conversion, but not conversion in terms of colonialism: "Conversion has

... a two-fold basis: political as well as anthropological. A political basis of conversion has to do with religious freedom. [An] anthropological aspect of conversion is that conversion equals the capacity of human beings to change, to repent, to question the world around it, not to be a product of randomness." Third, conflict and reconciliation go together with conversion. Conflict is shaped by religious rivals, one of which is the religion of fanaticism that erodes every religious identity (both conservative and liberal) and theology; the second religious rival to which we owe conflict is the religion of mammon or plutocracy that challenges true conversion.

Proposing that we abandon uni-directional language in mission, Peter Phan (Georgetown University) suggested the image of a missionary as an "unwanted, uninvited guest." As such we bring our gift to a host who may do whatever she or he wants with the gift we have to offer. Furthermore, conversion should not be understood as an effort toward membership in another religion, but as a mutual conversion to truth: "You convert me; I convert you, into truth, not into an organization, not to a religion, but into truth." Phan also reminded us that political realities are not the same the world over: Communism is still a reality in selected regions of Asia. Therefore, not all Christians are living with post-colonialism.

In responding to Abraham's question of how mission might lead to peace and reconciliation, Dana Robert (Boston University) suggested that while there is no easy solution, some aspects of a response might be found in the need for humanization. In the history of mission there is an "underneath" quality that doesn't get told in the history books, that of authentic human relationships. It is out of such that conversion occurs. Mission might best be thought of as the church "breathing." John 20:22 indicates that when the resurrected Lord met with his disciples he breathed on them and said, "I send you the Holy Spirit." Mission as breathing suggests it as a natural life cycle: "If we don't breathe we die, if the church doesn't breathe it dies. We inhale in worship. We inhale in coming together as community, and we breathe outreach so that mission should be seen as this complete cycle . . . Another way of looking at mission as breathing means that hospitality becomes the beginning of the cycle . . . as we come together in community, our first responsibility is inclusion and making others welcome . . . That's part of the inhaling.

The exhaling becomes the sending, the out-breathing of the Spirit that comes out of that fullness."

Brian Stanley (University of Edinburgh) noted the importance of three concepts: post-colonial, secularism, conversion. "It seems to me the central priority for us in thinking about Christian mission is to deal not with an artificially delimited concept of colonialism, but with an ongoing reality of domination where it exists for our human history and always will exist." In addressing secularism, Stanley stated that, "Secularism [in India] was the necessary cement of a nation-state, a way of holding together different religious communities. And in many ways that was true in Europe as well in the Enlightenment; secularism was the necessary price to pay for religious toleration and peace. The way forward in Nigeria is a form of secularism for Christians and Muslims to live together in peace. Christians need to think in more complex ways about secularism and to see that it's not all bad." He lastly addressed the socially destabilizing nature of conversion, that it is an anti-colonial force: "Conversion must be understood by Christians in ways that separate it very clearly from any colonialization of the mind. I do not convert you. The Christian understanding is that conversion is a work of the Spirit."

John Sentamu (Anglican Archbishop of York), responding to the question of "how we shape a theology of mission in the context of culture and of politics" asked, "If you were given the opportunity to start the church from scratch, what would it look like?" Responding to his own question, Sentamu noted that two Greek words, *ecclesia* and *parochois*, would define that reality. The first term, *ecclesia*, implies a people who have been summoned by God. The second, *parochois*, is the word from which we get the word "parish." Under Roman rule, non-citizens (or non-belongers) were given a place to meet, which is what the "church" is all about: providing a home for the homeless who have been summoned by God. Toward this end, Sentamu concluded that, "Christ is at work at all cultures, but is at home in none of them."

These thoughts offer us a theology of mission in the context of culture and politics, one that is grounded in the incarnation, said Sentamu. It has to do with the death and resurrection of Christ. When that is the actual shaping of our theology, culture itself will have to be converted. Sentamu stated that, "For me, Jesus is what humanity means by God and what God means by humanity... The church in the end is a home for the homeless, the non-belongers, for all the pilgrims . . . I agree with professor Brian Stanley, we don't convert, only God converts . . . I can be a signpost pointing somewhere, but please, we don't convert. And if you think you can, then your culture needs to be redeemed and converted as well."

In relation to the challenge of post-modernity and post-colonialism, mission was affirmed by the nine keynotes as something rising out of a deep contemplative and spiritual experience. It is a mission that seeks to overcome polarities in its call for a common search for the truth. It is deeply relational, yet destabilizing to vested establishments, and offers a home to the homeless in its radical ecclesial vision. This engagement with the 2010Boston conference theme, "The Changing Contours of World Mission and Christianity," was made more specific when it came time to report on the eight conference themes. Faculty from the different BTI schools responded by offering summary remarks from their study groups.

EIGHT THEMATIC CONSIDERATIONS AND GROUP OBSERVATIONS FOR CHRISTIAN MISSION

1. Changing Contours of Christian Unity[5]

Unity as a Christian concern has developed through a century of Christian debate since the 1910 Edinburgh World Missionary Conference and the subsequent emergence of the ecumenical movement.[6] At first, distinctions were drawn between *international* and *ecumenical,* the former the political reality of a multiplicity of separate states and the latter connotative of the unity found in Christ. This division is challenged not only by questions related to the separation of religion and state but also by a "wider" ecumenism that finds in all living faiths witness to religious truth. Among the churches issues of doctrinal identity were seen early on to be preeminent. More recently these have receded before

---

5. This group was chaired by Professor Raymond Helmick, S.J. of the Boston College Department of Theology. Professor Helmick was chosen for this from his sustained commitment to Christian unity as well as his fostering of inter-religious relationships and to restorative conflict mediation. On the related Edinburgh Commission VIII, see Stanley, *World Missionary Conference,* 277–302.

6. See the ten models of unity found in church history as given by Thomas, *Missions and Unity,* 85–220.

institutional considerations and divisions in ethics and practice. As much as ecumenism as fostered by Edinburgh, its precipitating movements and subsequent events, was a kind of ecclesial triumph for certain theories of the church,[7] ecumenism has also raised challenges for contemporary Protestant denominationalism, Eastern Orthodoxy, and Roman Catholicism: What is the future of the church to be? Is it to be found in a union of churches, a conciliar arrangement, or some coalition or confessional model? Is the end in view simply some form of mutual recognition? For some, church union has never existed but is best found in some form of "charismatic diversity."[8]

Edinburgh helped to spawn efforts at ecumenical unity through a turbulent century, notably the International Missionary Council (1921), Life and Work movement (1925), Faith and Order movement (1927), as well as other cooperative entities. The discussion of Christian unity was one of an enlarging circle with Orthodox, Roman Catholics (particularly after Vatican II), and Evangelical and Pentecostal defections and additions. War-time (WWII) cooperation, efforts at post-war spiritual renewal, and reactions to the Holocaust and other mass atrocities created both a new "non-denominational" climate that fostered the forms of church union alluded to above and helped to erode boundaries among denominations and even religious groups, but also contributed to new forms of religious fundamentalism. Schools of theology, seminaries and university divinity schools—many dating back to the period of denominational formation—would find themselves increasingly shaped by such divisions. Theological consortia would become breeding grounds for theological cooperation in the midst of such thinking.

Several observations rose to the surface during the study group's discussion of this topic at the Harvard session. First, recognition that Christians no longer emphasize the territorial significance of Christianity as "Christendom" but instead "locate" faith in confessional authenticity lodged in concepts such as the freedom of conscience and religious liberty. This observation is a part of a second one that was raised by the group, that is, an acknowledgment of the difference between the teach-

---

7. A "Branch Theory" of church history, affirming a common source and final reconciliation of church difference, has often shaped a prevailing ecumenical ethos. As developed by Philip Schaff, see Shriver, *Philip Schaff: Christian Scholar and Ecumenical Prophet*.

8. Cullmann, *Unity Through Diversity*.

ings of Christ and the teachings or practices of domination, superiority, and exclusion associated with competing narratives of meaning. This point is a part of a third recognition, that of the inherent dignity of persons as expressed in their central convictions, convictions of faith that cannot be simply dismissed but must be recognized for what they are, a point raised by Edinburgh in Commission III (Education in Relation to the Christianization of National Life).[9] To grant such recognition to the religious other and yet to maintain our own faith commitments deepens the mystery behind the unity we seek as churches and in relation to the whole of humanity and, finally, rules out any unity from a spirit of domination.

2. Mission in Context[10]

The contextual nature of mission is such that it shapes the bearer of the message, the recipient of the message and the message itself. The question of the context for the missionary task was taken up by Commission II at Edinburgh and seen in the contrast drawn between an individualistic view of that task and one that saw in the church not the goal of mission but instrument of mission, a view that would grow in prominence in later mission conferences.[11] With attention given to the nature of the church came the question of the identity of the church. This drew out attention to the "three-self" principle, that the church is to be

---

9. Stanley, *World Missionary Conference*, 193. This point is similar to that raised by Professor Helmick as central to Jesuit identity in the introduction to the *Spiritual Exercises* of St. Ignatius, "saving the proposition of the other"; see Helmick, S.J., *Living Catholic Faith in a Contentious Age*, 48–49.

10. This group was chaired by Margaret Guider, O.S.F. of the Boston College School of Theology and Ministry. Sr. Guider is past-president of the American Society of Missiology and serves as an advisor to missionary societies, religious congregations, and Catholic institutions. She is a member of the Sisters of St. Francis of Mary Immaculate. On the related Edinburgh Commission II, see Stanley, *World Missionary Conference*, 132–66.

11. In 1952 at a conference of the IMC, Wilhelm Anderson proposed that both church and mission should be taken up in the *missio Dei*, the mission of God. The Father sent the Son; the Father and Son sent the Spirit; and now the Spirit sends the church. The church has a missional character (Johannes Blauw, *The Missionary Nature of the Church* [1962]). Following the merger of the IMC into the WCC (1961) and subsequent to Vatican II (1962–65), the term became more popular; "the Church on earth is by its very nature missionary." Flannery, *Ad Gentes Divinitus*, 813. This history is recounted in Van Gelder, *The Essence of the Church*, 32–36. See also Guder, "The Church as Missional Community," 114.

characterized by self-government, self-support, and self-propagation.[12] The Report of Commission II highlighted the growing concern over the inculturation of the churches with special attention given to church leadership, structures and discipline. Each of these concerns related to questions of sexuality, race, and class, issues that continue to confront church discipline and practices today. To be added to the "three-self" principle is a fourth principle of special importance for theological education, "self-theologizing." This point, suggested by South African missiologist David Bosch (1929–92), suggests a need for authentic local expressions of Christian faith that are neither characterized by undue syncretism on the one hand, or by cultural "captivity" on the other, a point suggested by conference keynote Brian McLaren and seen in the incarnational theology of mission advocated by Sr. Guider.[13]

Four observations were prominent in the report from the working group on Mission in Context. It was first recognized that there exists a plurality of contexts, plurality of experiences, multiplicity of belongings, and that people live simultaneously in multiple contexts. Second, it was recognized that such contexts also exist diachronically, that is, through time and, as such, shape the life of faith in the immediate present. We need to recognize what has been lost, what has been made invisible, erased, and suppressed. These things are important for purposes of reconciliation, forgiveness, and for dealing with human frailty and behaviors that have misshaped the life of the gospel. Third, the context of mission also includes the communion of the saints, that great cloud of witnesses cited in Hebrews 12. It involves *conversio*, *conversatio*, and *contemplatio* as a single whole (as articulated by Thomas Merton). Conversion is not simply an initial experience but something that is ongoing; a mindful understanding that the intensification of our particularity is affirmed through our baptism, and as a performative act is eschatologically irreversible. Finally, it involves not so much of a map as a compass such that we can negotiate different contexts as followers of Jesus. In this, the conversation was strongly supportive of the work of

---

12. Attributed to mission strategists Henry Venn (1796–1873) and Rufus Anderson (1796–1880). See Shenk, "Rufus Anderson and Henry Venn." This threefold motto was later adopted by the Three-Self Patriotic Movement in China after missionaries were expelled from the country in 1949.

13. Bosch, *Transforming Mission*, 450–57. Robert Schreiter's project, *Constructing Local Theologies* (1985), also works in this venue. See also Guider, "From the Ends of the Earth," 329–46.

the "translatable" and transformative possibilities of the gospel into all languages and cultures as developed in the work of Scottish and African missiologist Andrew Walls and of his many students.[14]

3. Disciples in Mission[15]

Jesus called disciples, those who would be willing to follow him whatever their background (their nature) or their training (their nurture). His only criterion was "follow me." While not focused on discipleship, or even spirituality, Edinburgh's Commission III (Education in Relation to the Christianization of National Life) was concerned about the edificatory as well as evangelistic and leavening effects of mission, still "Disciples in Mission" was a pervasive concern at Edinburgh with its pattern of daily prayer and worship. Stanley writes that the "ethos of the conference was shaped by the spirituality of the Student Volunteer Movement," its zeal for world mission combined with individual and corporate prayer.[16] Mission was not so much an activist political concern as it was a spiritual call to obedience to Christ as centered on the much debated "watchword"—"the evangelization of the world in this generation"—put forward by John R. Mott,[17] long-serving leader of the YMCA and the World Student Christian Federation (WSCF), who presided over the Edinburgh Conference.

The meaning of discipleship and effective spirituality in shaping that discipleship is again a matter of growing concern.[18] Mission involves the spiritual formation of persons who follow Jesus, "disciples in mission." If spirituality can be defined as "a growing intimacy with God experienced through persons, places, events, and things in everyday life," as put by

---

14. See in particular, Walls, *Cross-Cultural Process*.

15. This group was chaired by Fr. Luke Veronis of Holy Cross Greek Orthodox School of Theology, chosen by virtue of his work in cross-cultural church revitalization and mobilizing Orthodox seminarians for mission and as the school's director of the newly established Missions Institute of Orthodox Christianity. On the related Edinburgh concerns, see Commission III in Stanley, *World Missionary Conference*, 88–90, 167–204 *et passim*.

16. Stanley, *World Missionary Conference*, 88–90.

17. Mott, *The Evangelization of the World*.

18. An example is The Valparaiso Project on the Education and Formation of People in Faith, under the direction of Dorothy C. Bass (www.practicingourfaith.org), a Lilly Endowment project based at Valparaiso University that develops resources to help contemporary people live the Christian faith with vitality and integrity in changing times.

Nicki Vandergrift,[19] it is clear that the spirituality of the followers of Jesus moves toward mission, the "breathing out" of the church as put by keynote speaker Dana Robert. Discipleship is a movement toward self-emancipation with socio-political consequences (Paulo Freire), that is, mission.[20] If the nature of this spirituality at the Boston conference was different from that of Edinburgh a century earlier, it was perhaps more Trinitarian than Christocentric in corporate expression.

Writing with a history of discipleship in mind, Brian McDermott, S.J. adds definition to such spiritual "breathing" by drawing attention to Christian discipleship grounded in the *lectio divina, meditatio, oratio, contemplatio,* and finally *actio,* which we might identify with mission. This characterizes the work of Orthodox mission in many settings around the world.[21] Fr. Veronis has given special attention to disciples in mission in contemporary Albania, a country where Christian faith had been all but exterminated under an atheist government, but is experiencing a vibrant resurrection.[22] This speaks to a renewal of interest in spirituality in our own time, often put as opposed to institutional religion. However, disciples in mission are caught in the tension of a personal discipleship and one that is deeply communal nature. This is a tension found throughout the history of mission but seen most pointedly in sodalities of mission, such as monasticism, but always decided in favor of the value of community. It is seen today in the "New Monasticism," a contemporary movement toward social justice, environmentalism and non-violence that rejects the privatization of Christianity in favor of mission through forms of communal expression.[23]

Several points that are synchronous with this history were highlighted by this group in relation to the idea of "disciples in mission." First was the affirmation that our model in discipleship must be Jesus, the original model in spreading the gospel. We must remember and return to our roots, imitating Christ and how he made and treated disciples. Second is to recall that discipleship is a journey and that disciples on

---

19. Vandergrift, *Organic Spirituality.* She sketches steps of slowing down, sharing our stories, stillness, solitude, surrender, and solidarity.

20. A connection between spirituality and mission is clearly drawn in articles in Währisch-Oblau and Mwombeki, *Mission Continues,* 63–92.

21. See Veronis, *Missionaries, Monks, and Martyrs.*

22. Veronis, *Go Forth.*

23. Wilson-Hartgrove, *New Monasticism.*

a journey welcome others on a similar journey, one that is in the same direction, that is, toward Christ. Third, this journey is one characterized by humility, an aspect of mission in need of recovery. Disciples have a job to do; they are to bear witness to the narrative of salvation through Jesus. They are to share this story in a manner characterized by humility, a spiritual virtue that enables us to continue to learn. Finally, this is a journey we are called to make together and in concert with the best of our missionary forbearers.

4. Education for Mission[24]

Education for mission often takes place "on the street" but moves toward the academy as new techniques and approaches in the general culture are learned and mastered. The Gospel of Mark presents Jesus as a master of the tradition and as a consummate innovator. Over the years this same pattern can be seen in the emergence of new orders and agencies given to mission, characterized as "sodalities" (movements) in distinction from "modalities" (ordered structures) of the church, by missiologist Ralph Winter.[25] The emergence of missiology as an academic field in Europe in the nineteenth century,[26] the development of Andover Seminary in North America as a preparatory institution for Protestant mission,[27] the role played by St. John's Seminary in Roman Catholic mission,[28] and even contemporary church-based mission studies programs now offered throughout the world are evidence of this innovation. Even the small Indian state of Nagaland supports over fifty Christian theological colleges, many of them dedicated to education for mission. Education, often

24. This group was facilitated by Elizabeth Parsons of Boston University School of Theology. She teaches interdisciplinary courses in religion and development with special emphasis on worldview differences and meaning-making in postmodern societies. On the related Edinburgh concerns, see Commissions III and V in Stanley, *World Missionary Conference*, 167-204, 316-317 *et passim*.

25. These terms are from the Presbyterian missiologist Ralph Winter, in "The Two Structures of God's Redemptive Mission."

26. Myklebust, *The Study of Missions in Theological Education*, 67-157. See the work of Karl Graul, director of the Leipzig Mission, and Gustav Warneck, "founder" of Protestant missionary science. Warneck significantly influenced the Catholic missiologist Josef Schmidlin (1876-1944), thereby initiating a history of interaction between Protestantism and Catholicism on mission that continues to this day and is seen in the 2010Boston conference.

27. Bendroth, *A School of the Church*.

28. See the chapter in this volume by Angelyn Dries, O.S.F.

a gift of the church to society, has proliferated in the mode of education for mission in many different regions of the world. Desmond Tutu writes that, "The promotion of ecumenical cooperation in theological education is at the heart of the mission of the church and vital for the future of the ecumenical movement as a whole."[29]

The group came together around the two questions of who is a missionary and how one is to be educated for the task of mission. Four observations came to the surface in light of these twin foci. First, it was felt that there needs to be a stronger relationship between churches and theological schools, or, more broadly, the academy. What is actually happening in the churches, such as cross-cultural short-term mission trips, is not necessarily being carried into the purview of the theological school; and what is going on at the academic level is not necessary being translated to the churches. Second, this training and education should concern not just new imagery of what mission means but new approaches and structures that do not necessarily rely solely on literacy and verbal knowledge within communities where mission would be enacted.[30] Third, there are many non-Christian venues to which we should also be open as loci of the Spirit's work and the enactment of God's mission. Finally, a deeper discussion is needed, not only about what is mission, but also about what is education, the latter also always affected by what we mean by the former.[31]

5. Mission and Post-Colonialism[32]

The world of 1910 was one of racial hierarchy and of Western hegemony. Stanley writes that the missionary movement "absorbed" these theories

---

29. Werner, et al. *Handbook of Theological Education in Global Christianity*. The volume as a whole is a rich compendium of contemporary thought on Education for Mission. The comment by Desmond Tutu is found on p. xxi.

30. In line with the interests of Edinburgh Commission III (Education in Relation to the Christianization of National Life), Education for Mission may need to focus not only upon the preparation and discipleship of individuals, but also on a witness to "new Christian identities for nations in the non-Western world" (Stanley, *World Missionary Conference*, 167). Parsons' own interest includes concerns of meaning-making and social policy in postmodern societies. See her book, *What Price for Privatization?*

31. The question of the nature of theological education was a focus of the thirty-fifth anniversary of the BTI. See Petersen and Rourke, *Theological Literacy for the Twenty-First Century*.

32. This group was facilitated by Professor M. T. Dávila of Andover Newton Theological School. With interests in mission, she is a leader in the BTI Hispanic

without significant adjustment. This is evident in the composition of those who attended the conference.[33] Questions about the nature of Western civilization and of its political hegemony were not generally at issue and would only become more apparent with the increasing approach of World War I. However, to be involved with mission in the twenty-first century is to recognize that Europe and North America are no more the "Christian heartland" than Seoul, Singapore, and São Paulo. The "center of gravity" has shifted from the North Atlantic world to Africa, Latin America, and some parts of Asia.

Andrew Walls argues this demographic shift is similar to what happened to Christianity in the late second century as it moved out of the Jewish and into the Hellenistic world. Walls uses three formative Christian thinkers—Paul, Justin, and Origin—to outline a three-stage model for conceptualizing the way by which Christianity moves into new cultures throughout the world: (1) borrowing from the inheritance (Paul); (2) critiquing the inheritance for purposes of acceptance or rejection (Justin); and (3) reconfiguring and reconciling with the inheritance (Origin).[34] The theological task for the twenty-first century is to continue navigating beyond the European and North Atlantic experience of Christianity and to allow leadership in the cultures of Africa, Latin America, and Asia to step forward. Insights from Africa and elsewhere will enlarge our vision of theology, challenge our conception of individual and social pathology, and deepen our perspective on salvation.[35]

The group discussing mission and post-colonialism made the following observations and recommendations. First, it was noted that we must keep in mind the mixed benefits of Christianity's relationship with colonialism, and the complexity of relationships marked by domination

---

Faculty colloquium and has published in areas of immigration, the use of force and just war theory, as well as on Catholic social teaching and globalization and the Millennium Development Goals. On the related Edinburgh Commission VII, see Stanley, *World Missionary Conference*, 248–76.

33. Stanley, *World Missionary Conference*, 273. On the non-Western presence at Edinburgh, see pp. 91–131.

34. Walls, "Theology and Scholarship in a Global Church," in Jeyaraj et al., 41.

35. *Ministerial Formation*, a publication of the Ecumenical Theological Education Programme, Unit I, Unity and Renewal, is helpful in presenting issues that foster and encourage critical ecumenical consciousness and global reflection. Additional aspects of theological education are taken up by the Oxford Centre for Mission Studies. An example of global Christian theological work is in Spencer and Spencer, *The Global God*. See Evans, et al., *The Globalization of Theological Education*.

that has been brought to light by descriptive tools of post-colonial theory and theology. Second, it was asked, what are the theological tools we have to address and to move beyond the complexities of this relationship in a way that brings life and helps us look forward with hope? We have to go on and ask about the nature of that hope and reconciliation. What do we do with the principles of mercy and love of neighbor, with the ideas of a new creation, a new humanity, and what God may be affecting in us today? Finally, as the question was raised, can we seek reconciliation while keeping the social critique alive so as not to abuse relationships, being careful of what we've learned and of how our relationships with others have often been marked by humiliation and "othering," rather than by forwarding our common Christian heritage and those things that will enable us to be marked in solidarity by life, love, and hope? This question, often asked in contexts of social healing and with respect to political forgiveness, drives the conversation toward restorative justice.[36]

6. Mission in a Pluralist World[37]

The tension over identity, whether that is social, class-oriented, gender-based, or ethnic, takes on greater significance as we move into the area of religious pluralism. This area is one that shapes not only the work of mission, but has had political implications for Christianity throughout history, most notably in the formation of Carolingian and Southern Europe, in the shaping of Northern Europe and the North Atlantic world in the early modern period, and again today.[38] Post-colonial concerns are often issues of religious pluralism as well. Religion, whether universal or particular in its ethnic or cultural associations, has been

---

36. See the articles in Narváez, *Political Culture of Forgiveness and Reconciliation*. Work on restorative justice is in debt to Zehr, *Changing Lenses*. For forgiveness and restorative justice as applied to the American setting, see Shriver, *Honest Patriots*.

37. This group was facilitated by Catherine Cornille, Chair of the Boston College Department of Theology, in recognition not only of her general theological leadership but also of her particular academic and personal interest in this topic area. On the related Edinburgh Commission IV, see Stanley, *World Missionary Conference*, 205–47.

38. The place of religion in shaping the contours of Europe is explored by different authors. See, for example, Hodges, et al., *Mohammed, Charlemagne, and the Origins of Europe*. For early modern Europe, see, for example, Prestwich, *International Calvinism, 1541–1715*; and for early modern Catholicism, O'Malley, *Trent and All That*; and Williams, "Erasmus and the Reformers on Non-Christian Religions and *Salus Extra Ecclesiam*." On Pope John Paul II and the social significance of a European Parliament, see Weigel, *Witness to Hope*. Cf. Huntington, *The Clash of Civilizations*.

central to questions of personal and social identity.³⁹ This has implications for world order and the non-violent resolution of conflict. The religious diversity of the world is present particularly in the United States where recent demographic trends have brought attention to this reality. This religious diversity affects ministries and workplaces and increasingly requires conscious hospitality, a potential theological resource for civility.⁴⁰ It is increasingly a matter of conscious choice to belong to any religion, but it is also a matter of choice to affirm multiple religious identities.⁴¹ It is precisely here, in the area of encouraging informed choice, that education for mission matters most.⁴² In light of the interweaving of religion, identity and issues of alienation, pointed to by Felix Wilfred and others, it might be that "the church's promotion of interreligious dialogue may be one of its greatest missionary services."⁴³

Several important points were made by the group. First, interreligious dialogue teaches that every context for mission is highly particular and specific, something also recognized by the group for "mission in context." A second and equally important challenge is that each context is relational. In the post-conflict situation of Indonesia, where a Christian minority lives among a larger Muslim community, what can

39. Hicks, "Issues of Identity and Protracted Conflict." See the work of Felix Wilfred, who writes on issues of identity and religion, pointedly on whether the engagement of Christianity with the religion and culture of India can ever appear other than conflictual apart from a subaltern approach. See, for example, his book, *The Sling of Utopia*.

40. Yong, *Hospitality and the Other*; and Mouw, *Uncommon Decency*.

41. Cornille, *Many Mansions*? See also Joseph Montville, "Multiple Religious Belonging: Compassion, Life and Death," 4–10; and Cornille, *The Im-Possibility of Interreligious Dialogue*. This is a point made in an autobiographical way by Paul F. Knitter in *Without Buddha I Could Not be a Christian*.

42. The mark of this change in religious identity can be traced from a largely Protestant heritage at the nation's founding to the mid-twentieth century with the appearance of the sociological study by Herberg, *Protestant, Catholic, Jew*, equating these three faiths with establishment status. The work of the Pluralism Project at Harvard University (http://pluralism.org/) illustrates an expanding religious variety in the United States. Philip E. Hammond contends that recent social revolutions have yielded an increased emphasis on personal autonomy and have removed the churches from their traditional role as institutions mediating accepted values in American life; see his *Religion and Personal Autonomy*. To this must be added the effects of recent patterns of immigration. Whatever the validity of Hammond's argument, a growing complexity in religious demography is found across the American landscape that makes a common moral voice more difficult to discern, a fact and theme discerned in Berthrong, *The Divine Deli*.

43. This point is made by Bevans and Schroeder, *Constants in Context*, 385.

mission mean apart from hospitality and forming relationships?[44] Third, we are becoming more aware that the Holy Spirit is at work in mission, perhaps even in other religions beyond the confines of Christian tradition. By what criteria can we discern the presence of the Holy Spirit in other religious traditions? This discussion reminds us of the importance of the Holy Spirit in all missionary activities. It is God (and) the Spirit who converts, not the missionary. So this third point raises a question: How does the Holy Spirit work in our missionary endeavors? Specifically, what is the relationship between mission and inter-religious dialogue? The group felt that it might not always be helpful to distinguish the two, but that we might need a form of interreligious dialogue that is alert to the truth of what we believe. Both participants in the dialogue testify to their faith, recognize that both participants are hoping that the other will understand and be inspired by the truth that is experienced and lived and believed in by the other side. Here is the genesis of engaged comparative theology, an important discipline for theological education in the twenty-first century.[45]

7. Mission and Post-Modernity[46]

If modernity is characterized by a confidence in liberal politics, the use of reason, and work of science/technology, we have entered an age that is often uncertain of these verities for a host of reasons. A post-modern reading of contemporary religious life adds a number of correctives to how we read texts and how that reading shapes practice. We might take note of an *aesthetic* corrective that stresses experiential concreteness and intuitive imagination over rationalist abstraction, a *cultural* corrective that insists on cultural autonomy and tradition as the wisdom of

---

44. Mission as an aspect of a "new" or "wider" ecumenism was pioneered by S. Wesley Ariarajah in 1998. See his book, *Not Without My Neighbor*; see also Dupuis, *Toward a Christian Theology of Religious Pluralism*.

45. Francis X. Clooney, S.J. presents the genealogy of the term "comparative theology" and argues for its usefulness through the work of others as well, such as Raimon Panikkar, Robert Neville, Keith Ward, and others, in *Comparative Theology*.

46. This group was facilitated by Todd Johnson, Director of the Center for the Study of Global Christianity at Gordon-Conwell Theological Seminary. Through his work as co-editor (with Kenneth Ross) of the *Atlas of Global Christianity,* Johnson is alert to the changing face of Christianity in multiple post-modern settings. On the related Edinburgh Commission VI, see Stanley, *World Missionary Conference*, 316–24 *et passim*.

a particular community over against universalizing tendencies, and a *political* corrective that insists that there is no pure reason. The issue of how our identity shapes our reading of a text, whether that might be our gender, social location, or other cultural marker is a concern among missiologists of different ethnicities not only in the academy or in a given political community *per se*, but the local church.[47] Effective mission recognizes such tension.

Criticism that comes from a deconstructionist perspective was seen as a value and opportunity by this group. First, the questions posed by deconstructionist thinking open up the arena of conversation to new voices and new information. Second, such thinking specifically opens up the possibility of new levels of understanding and of trust, particularly important in a post-colonial context. Third, through such fresh efforts at understanding lies the hope that we might discover again the Christ beyond our assumptions. This opportunity of redefinition extends back into the Western world or the global north. The Western world needs such a reintroduction to Christ growing out of the many questions and fresh perspectives that are possible through a deeper relational engagement with others. Fourth, it is precisely this kind of relational engagement that can open the way for youth to find in the church the hope and means necessary for our common future.

8. Salvation Today[48]

Salvation, of course, is the point of mission. Ever since the formation of the modern ecumenical movement in the wake of the 1910 Edinburgh World Missionary Conference there has been a growing consciousness of the interdependent nature of global Christianity. The final group presenting expressed agreement that the meaning and the call of mission is "salvation," though there was not full agreement as to

---

47. As an example of this, Manuel Jesús Mejido makes the point that an increasing Hispanic population in the United States alerts us to he need for greater recruitment of Latino students and faculty and for programs that are more sensitive to he needs of this population, "U.S. Hispanic/Latinos and the Field of Graduate Theological Education."

48. This group was facilitated by Peter Kuzmič, President of the Evangelical Theological Seminary, Osijek, Croatia and Professor of Missions and European Studies at Gordon-Conwell Theological Seminary. Given Kuzmič's leadership in both Evangelical circles and with European ecumenical groups, he was a particularly apt person to lead this group. On the related Edinburgh Commission I, see Stanley, *World Missionary Conference*, 49–72 *et passim*.

the meaning of the term. Different understandings of salvation define different practices of mission. There was, however, a sense that in salvation one finds restoration to the *imago Dei*, or image of God.[49] This second point drew us to find in the word "salvation" a very comprehensive term, seen in the Hebrew *shalom*, that includes regard for common humanity and rescuing humanity from all that dehumanizes. This suggests cooperation with the concerns summarized in the Millennium Development Goals of the United Nations.[50] Third, salvation was also conceived of as the restoration of one's individual relationship with God, evangelism was conceived of as the main mode of mission, and proclamation as the primary means with residual benefits upon the positive outworking of relationships with others.[51] For many, a proper understanding of salvation carries with it a sacramental concept of salvation related to a specific theology of the Church.[52] Finally, "'salvation' today" means restoring right relationships with others and may be found in a variety of social, political and other settings.[53]

49. This is a point of special sensitivity to the Orthodox Christian community, fully present and participatory in the Boston conference. Orthodoxy's emphasis upon anthropology and Trinity in matters of salvation helped to shape the worship opportunities of the conference. For the topics of Trinity and personhood in Orthodoxy, see Zizioulas, *Being as Communion*.

50. Under the auspices of Bread for the World, the BTI together with Episcopal Divinity School had held a series of public lectures and fostered an academic course that drew attention to the MDG's as an aspect of Christian mission. See Douglas and Petersen, "Global Reconciliation."

51. See the theme and papers for the 2005 Conference on Mission and Evangelism of the World Council of Churches with its emphasis upon mission as reconciliation as paradigmatic for mission in the twenty-first century. In work for the Conference on World Mission and Evangelism of the World Council of Churches (Athens 2005), he outlines six aspects of reconciliation and healing: truth, memory, repentance, justice, forgiveness, and love. See Matthey, "Mission as Ministry of Reconciliation"; cf. Lederach, *The Journey Toward Reconciliation*.

52. The tension with understanding salvation as both implicit in the will of God alone and as worked out through a series of sacramental practices is seen most clearly in the theology of the Church in Roman Catholicism. A series of documents draw this out, including Vatican II declarations such as *Nostra Aetate* (Declaration on the Relationship of the Church to Non-Christian Religions) and *Lumen Gentium* (Article 16 of the Dogmatic Constitution of the Church) on the one hand, and more recently encyclicals *Redemptoris Missio* (1990) and *Dominus Iesus* (2000) on the other.

53. Elizabeth V. Spelman reminds us of the human desire to repair, calling humanity *homo reparans*, in *Repair: The Impulse to Restore in a Fragile World*, a point which finds its societal counterpart in the array of articles published in *The Atlantic* (July/

AN ANTIOCH AGENDA FOR TODAY

The formation of narratives to live by and their impact on us was a fundamental point raised by Brian McLaren at the 2010Boston conference. For McLaren, the rejection of stories of Domination (Imperial), Revolution (Revenge), Purification (Scapegoating), Isolation, Accumulation, and Victimization in favor of Jesus' story of the Kingdom of God is paramount in today's world. We catch a glimpse of Jesus' vision for the Kingdom in what we might refer to as the *Antioch Agenda*. In line with Ruth Padilla DeBorst on the need for public confession to replace power, referring to the agenda of God's Kingdom as an *Antioch Agenda* is to underscore the work that Jesus came to do as announced in the Gospel of Luke, citing Isaiah 61:1–2: "The Spirit of the Sovereign LORD is on me, because the LORD has anointed me to proclaim good news to the poor. He has sent me to bind up the brokenhearted, to proclaim freedom for the captives and release from darkness for the prisoners, to proclaim the year of the LORD's favor and the day of vengeance of our God, to comfort all who mourn . . ." (The New International Version).

Our vision for mission as an *Antioch Agenda* draws upon that ancient Roman city of Antioch which played such an important role in the formation of those who identified themselves as followers of Jesus.[54] These were Jews and Gentiles who apparently gave up all other obligations as necessary with the exception of consciously developing a worldview grounded in Jewish monotheism and in the testimony of Jesus as the Christ. As such, they were called Christians ("Christ-bearers," Acts 11:26). They appeared to order their lives in accord with what would be a first council of the church about which Paul later reports in Acts chapter 15 (cf. Gal 2–5). As such we might identify four marks of continuity between that first *Antioch Agenda* and one today.

First, the requirements for free entry into participation in this new community were minimal; a belief in Jewish monotheism and in the testimony of Jesus was all that was required (Acts 15:19–35). Over the last millennium the church has been defined primarily in terms of Matthew 16:16–19, with its language of stability (rock), defensiveness (gates of hell shall not prevail) and exercise of power (control of the keys; binding and loosing). In the new millennium, a Gospel of forgive-

---

August, 2009) on "How to Fix the World."

54. Jeyaraj, "Introduction," xiii; and Petersen, "Section Introduction," 155–62.

ness envisioned in Acts 15 could draw forth new patterns of church and community that might open the way through the division of Orthodoxy and Catholicism, heal the internal split in the Latin Church between Protestants and Roman Catholics, and find the means to move beyond the institutional alienation subsequent to the Enlightenment.[55] In its simplicity the Jerusalem Council lays down the basis of the church with other and later confessional documents worked out in relation to emerging questions in different cultural contexts.

Second, all were welcome. Whether Jew or Gentile in the first century, slave or free in ensuing centuries, or male and female today, this extension of a human rights tradition welcomes all people (Gal 3:28–29). So impressed were Paul and Barnabas in their day with such a new community of people that it was believed that the God whom Jesus Christ revealed was the God for all peoples (Acts 10:34–36).[56] The multicultural and multiethnic context of this first congregation of "Christians" at Antioch further inspires our thoughts about a new *Antioch Agenda* in our times. In this way, the followers of Jesus in Antioch set an example for what would become all future "Christian" assemblies.

Third, the church was the mission and the mission was the church, a point of identity with the contemporary understanding of a *missio Dei*. The story of the first commissioning of missionaries (Acts 13:1) offers insight into this identity of mission and church. The Book of Acts tells how a narrative of the kingdom of God was carried beyond Antioch. Barnabas and Saul (Paul), perceived through the Spirit to be called and set apart for a special mission, were to be sent on a first missionary journey to the dark continent of Europe. Strengthened with spiritual power, the three prophets and teachers remaining in Antioch, Simeon called Niger, Lucius of Cyrene, and Manaen, laid their hands on the two departing ones, their names indicating that at least two of the three may have been African in origin.[57] While the gospel is embedded

---

55. In assessing the historical concerns and ethico-psychological principles of classic liberal theology as inherited from the Enlightenment through the theology of Albrecht Ritschl, and that of the supra-historical concerns of Karl Barth, Paul Lehmann concludes that Protestantism, and in a certain way the Christian movement generally, will prosper to the extent it is able to learn from the dialectic provided by these two theologians in the reaffirmation of the Christian doctrine of forgiveness. See Lehmann, *Forgiveness*, 195.

56. Horrell, "Becoming Christian."

57. Otabil, *Beyond the Rivers of Ethiopia*, 62–63.

in Judaism, this scene and the events portrayed in Acts chapters 13–14 carry us to the first council of the church at which issues of gospel and culture are preeminent. The experience of this mission would shape the church at the Jerusalem Council (Acts 15:1–35), called to consider the early church's first cultural crisis occasioned by the Antioch mission. The decision reached: one did not have to become Jewish before becoming a follower of Jesus. Today we stand on the point of another cultural crisis, a "clash of civilizations"—and we are learning that we do not need to become "Western" before becoming Christian. Antioch pointed the way forward.

The agenda then, as now, is our fourth point of affinity between the first *Antioch Agenda* and ours today. The *Antioch Agenda* is an agenda that involves all peoples in the proclamation of the good news of Jesus Christ. It finds specific focus in the pressing issues of our day. These issues can be said to be the need for human flourishing, the demands of reconciliation in specific settings, an affirmation of religious freedom in the context of a dialogue among religions, and the necessity of freedom from fear.

The eight Millennium Development Goals (MDGs) offer a vision of human flourishing. Defined by the United Nations, they form a template for action. The first goal, for example, may be understood through the lens of Christian missional reflection: the goal of eliminating extreme *poverty and hunger* draws us to consider how all are made in the image of God; or, second, that of reducing *child mortality* calls us to reflect on the incarnation, that the embodiment of Christian hope came into the world as a child. We might similarly find deep theological resonance behind all of the eight "anti-poverty" goals.

Second, mission in the twenty-first century is also about reconciliation. Reconciliation, accompanied by forgiveness, grounded in justice—these all are central to Christian spirituality and open the gates forward to the repair of the world (*tikkun olam*). Robert Schreiter calls attention to the vertical, horizontal, and cosmic aspects of reconciliation.[58] Reconciliation involves, to use the words of Samuel Escobar, "Transforming Service."[59] It is the "liturgy after the liturgy," to adopt the expression of Orthodox theologian Ion Bria.[60]

58. Schreiter, *Reconciliation: Mission & Ministry in a Changing Social Order*.
59. Escobar, *The New Global Mission*, 142–54.
60. Bria, *The Liturgy After the Liturgy*.

Third, Christian mission assumes and promotes religious freedom. There is a growing sense across the globe that rights and obligations arise from the people as embodied in the *Universal Declaration of Human Rights* set forth by the United Nations (1948). This was given further significance for religious consciousness and liberties in the U.N.'s *Declaration on the Elimination of All Forms of Intolerance and of Discrimination Based on Religion or Belief*.[61] The social reality of people migrating around the world, contemporary technology and media—as well as an increasing tendency to standardize national citizenship—have all promoted a sense of global citizenship. With this has come an increasing understanding of the necessity for a dialogue among religions in the context of the freedom of religion.

A fourth goal for mission in the twenty-first century is to promote freedom from fear. This must also be a dimension of mission in the twenty-first century. "Do not fear" is the charge given to Abraham, alike to Joshua, then with resonances through Jesus to John's vision, the Apocalypse. "Be strong and courageous . . . I myself will be with you" (Deut 31:23). The monotheistic faiths tell us that we live in a world of the one God, upon whose goodness we can totally rely. The victory cry of the Lamb who was slain is that, "He will wipe away every tear from their eyes. There will be no more death or mourning or crying or pain, for the old order of things has passed" (Rev 21:4).[62]

This *Antioch Agenda* would become so identified with human liberation that it would be criticized as libertarianism (Gal 5:13), a critique sometimes made of churches today. As Jeyaraj writes: "The Antiochian School of theology highlighted the humanity of Jesus Christ who was deeply interested in the total welfare of all peoples in general and the poor and the marginalized in particular. Antiochian Christians were mission-minded; they sent out missionaries to evangelize their neighbors. They received guests from Jerusalem and other places, and helped them to realize the multicultural reality of Christ's church. Their church remained authentically local and particular, and yet intentionally, multicultural and international. They supported intercultural learning, relational healing and reconciliation."[63]

---

61. United Nations Department of Public Information, 1982.
62. Helmick, *Living Catholic Faith*, 13–23.
63. Jeyaraj, "Introduction," xvi–xvii.

In her remarks at the 2010Boston conference, Angelyn Dries, O.S.F. argued that the, "Boston-influenced Catholic experience" links with many elements of the *Antioch Agenda* as proposed above. She goes on to write in her chapter that the issues raised, "include the establishment of new relationships, a surmounting of deep-seated prejudices through an alternative lifestyle that bridges the gap between insider and outsider, a need for and vision of human flourishing, a review of the Millennium Development Goals of the United Nations, engagement in the demands of reconciliation, and freedom from fear." In terms that underscore the spiritual significance of this mission, she adds: "The *Antioch Agenda* points also seem perfectly matched with the *Our Father*: Establish new relationships (Our Father); overcome deep seated prejudices by an providing alternative lifestyle that bridges the gap between insider and outsider (Your kingdom come); need for and vision of human flourishing: the Millennium Development Goals of the U.N. (Give us this day our daily bread); demands of reconciliation (Forgive us our trespasses, as we forgive those who trespass against us); freedom from fear (Deliver us from all evil)."[64]

What makes the *Antioch Agenda* such an appropriate image for the work of mission in the twenty-first century is the movement of mission beyond geographic considerations. The "new" Antioch is the whole world, the agenda for which is the whole gospel. As we read in the gospel of John, this agenda is good news for the entire world (*cosmos* as in John 3:16). The center of gravity of the church may no longer be in the West, but it is not without the West.[65] Global mission is a global enterprise.

The implications of this demographic shift for theological education—and the training of church leadership—are drawn out by historian Andrew Walls who acknowledges that just "as Christians explored their faith in engagement with the Hellenistic culture, [and] strengthened and established their faith and in the process saved the Greek academy," so "Christian interaction with the cultures of Africa and Asia . . . may cause us to see something more of the fullness of Christ, and in the process see vocation restored and the salvation of scholarship itself."[66] As the churches enter their third millennium, they must take stock of their fundamentally different identity and mission

---

64. See the chapter by Angelyn Dries, O.S.F. in this volume.
65. Jenkins, *The Next Christendom*.
66. Walls, "Theology and Scholarship in a Global Church," in Jeyaraj et al., 48.

from that which was assumed at the beginning of the twentieth century. As the first *Antioch Agenda* was the occasion for the first church council, and consequent redefinition of the church, so mission in the twenty-first century will reshape ecclesiology.

We stand on the edge of something new: With Christianity's projected growth in Asia alone expected to soon outstrip that found in Europe and North America, "the changing contours of world mission and Christianity" are upon us. Each of the traditions represented in the BTI stands at a crossroads in terms of identity and mission. Each finds its ecclesiology challenged by mission. Edinburgh was not able to forestall the ravages of the twentieth century or the violence that has carried us into the twenty-first. An agenda for the next wave of mission will surely include reconciliation as set forth at the World Council of Churches' International Ecumenical Peace Convocation in Jamaica (May 2011). The mission we seek is liberative and graceful. It sees the *imago Dei* in each or sees it not at all. Its end will be forgiveness and reconciliation. And, finally, it will do what religion has always done, offer a sense of identity, give direction to life and provide consolation in the face of loss. With its unique academic mosaic, 2010Boston challenges the future shape of identity and mission with the imaginative image of an *Antioch Agenda*.

WORKS CITED

Amin, Samir. *Eurocentrism: Modernity, Religion, and Democracy: A Critique of Eurocentrism and Culturalism*. Translated by Russell Moore and James Membrez. New York: Monthly Review, 2009.

Ariarajah, S. Wesley. *Not Without My Neighbor*. Geneva: WCC, 1999.

Bendroth, Margaret. *A School of the Church: Andover Newton Across Two Centuries*. Grand Rapids: Eerdmans, 2008.

Berthrong, John. *The Divine Deli: Religious Identity in The North American Cultural Mosaic*. Maryknoll, NY: Orbis, 1999.

Bevans, Stephen B., and Roger P. Schroeder. *Constants in Context: A Theology of Mission for Today*. American Society of Missiology Series 30. Maryknoll, NY: Orbis, 2004.

Blauw, Johannes. *The Missionary Nature of the Church: A Survey of the Biblical Theology of Mission*. New York: McGraw-Hill, 1962.

Bosch, David. *Transforming Mission: Paradigm Shifts in Theology of Mission*. American Society of Missiology Series 16. Maryknoll, NY: Orbis, 1991.

Bria, Ion. *The Liturgy after the Liturgy: Mission and Witness from an Orthodox Perspective*. Geneva: WCC, 1996.

Clooney, Francis X., S.J. *Comparative Theology: Deep Learning across Religious Borders.* Hoboken, NJ: Wiley-Blackwell, 2010.

Cornille, Catherine. *The Im-Possibility of Interreligious Dialogue.* New York: Crossroad, 2008.

———. *Many Mansions? Multiple Religious Belonging and Christian Identity.* Eugene, OR: Wipf and Stock, 2010.

Cullmann, Oscar. *Unity through Diversity: Its Foundation, and a Contribution to the Discussion Concerning the Possibilities of Its Actualization.* Philadelphia, PA: Fortress, 1988.

Douglas, Ian T., and Rodney L. Petersen, eds. "Global Reconciliation: Faith and the Millennium Development Goals." In *Overcoming Violence: Religion, Conflict and Peacebuilding*, edited by Rodney L. Petersen and Marian Gh. Simion, 165–67. Newton, MA: BTI, 2010.

Dupuis, Jacques. *Toward a Christian Theology of Religious Pluralism.* Maryknoll, NY: Orbis, 1999.

Escobar, Samuel. *The New Global Mission: The Gospel from Everywhere to Everyone.* Downers Grove, IL: InterVarsity, 2003.

Evans, Alice Frazer, Robert A. Evans, and David A. Roozen, eds. *The Globalization of Theological Education.* Maryknoll, NY: Orbis, 1993.

Flannery, Austin, ed. *Ad Gentes Divinitus.* Vol 1, *Vatican Council II: The Conciliar & Post Conciliar Documents.* New York: Costello, 1987.

Guder, Darrell. "The Church as Missional Community." In *The Community of the Word: Toward an Evangelical Ecclesiology*, edited by Mark Husbands and Daniel J. Treier, 114–28. Downers Grove, IL: InterVarsity, 2005.

Guder, Darrell L., and Lois Barrett, eds. *Missional Church: A Vision for the Sending of the Church in North America.* Grand Rapids: Eerdmans, 1998.

Guider, Margaret E., O.S.F. "From the Ends of the Earth: 'International Minister' or Missionary? Vocational Identity and the Changing Face of Mission in the USA. A Roman Catholic Perspective." In *Antioch Agenda: Essays on the Restorative Church in Honor of Orlando E. Costas*, edited by Daniel Jeyaraj, Robert W. Pazmiño, and Rodney L. Petersen, 329–46. New Delhi: Indian Society for the Promotion of Christian Knowledge, 2007.

Hammond, Philip E. *Religion and Personal Autonomy: The Third Disestablishment.* Columbia, SC: University of South Carolina Press, 1992.

Helmick, Raymond G., S.J., *Living Catholic Faith in a Contentious Age.* New York: Continuum, 2010.

Herberg, Will. *Protestant, Catholic, Jew.* Garden City, NY: Doubleday, 1955.

Hicks, Donna. "Issues of Identity and Protracted Conflict." In *Forgiveness and Reconciliation: Religion, Public Policy, and Conflict Transformation*, edited by Rodney L. Petersen and Raymond G. Helmick, S. J., 129–49. Philadelphia, PA: Templeton, 2001.

Hodges, Richard, and David Whitehouse. *Mohammed, Charlemagne, & the Origins of Europe: The Pirenne Thesis in the Light of Archeology.* Ithaca: Cornell University Press, 1983.

Horrell, David G. "Becoming Christian: Solidifying Christian Identity and Content." In *Handbook of Early Christianity: Social Science Approaches*, edited by Anthony J. Blasi, Paul-André Turcotte, and Jean Duhaime, 309–36. New York: Altamira, 2002.

Huntington, Samuel P. *The Clash of Civilizations and the Remaking of World Order.* New York: Simon & Schuster, 1996.

Irvin, Dale T., and Scott W. Sunquist, eds. *The History of the World Christian Movement.* Maryknoll, NY: Orbis, 2001.

Jenkins, Philip. *The Next Christendom: The Coming of Global Christianity.* New York: Oxford University Press, 2002.

Jeyaraj, Daniel. "Introduction." In *Antioch Agenda: Essays on the Restorative Church in Honor of Orlando E. Costas,* edited by Daniel Jeyaraj, Roberto W. Pazmiño, and Rodney L. Petersen, xiii–xxi. New Delhi: Indian Society for the Promotion of Christian Knowledge, 2007.

Jeyaraj, Daniel, Robert W. Pazmiño, and Rodney L. Petersen, eds. *Antioch Agenda: Essays on the Restorative Church in Honor of Orlando E. Costas.* New Delhi: Indian Society for the Promotion of Christian Knowledge, 2007.

Johnson, Todd M., and Kenneth R. Ross, eds. *Atlas of Global Christianity.* Edinburgh: University of Edinburgh Press, 2009.

Knitter, Paul F. *Without Buddha I Could Not be a Christian.* New York: Oneworld, 2009.

Lederach, John Paul. *The Journey Toward Reconciliation.* Scottdale, PA: Herald, 1999.

Lehmann, Paul. *Forgiveness: Decisive Issue in Protestant Thought.* New Yorker: Harper, 1940.

Matthey, Jacques, and the Ecumenical Formation Team. "Mission as Ministry of Reconciliation." Preparatory Paper No. 1. Conference on World Mission and Evangelism, Athens, May, 2005.

Mejido, Jesús. "U.S. Hispanic/Latinos and the Field of Graduate Theological Education." *Theological Education* 34.2 (Spring 1998) 51–71.

Montville, Joseph. "Multiple Religious Belonging: Compassion, Life and Death." *BTI Magazine* 9.1 (2009) 4–10

Mott, John R. *The Evangelization of the World in this Generation.* New York: Student Volunteer Movement for Foreign Missions, 1905.

Mouw, Richard. *Uncommon Decency: Christian Civility in an Uncivil World.* Downers Grove, IL: InterVarsity, 2010.

Myklebust, Olav Guttorm. *The Study of Missions in Theological Education,* 2 vols. Egede Instituttet. Oslo: Forlaget Land og Kirke, 1955.

Narváez, Leonel, ed. *Political Culture of Forgiveness and Reconciliation.* Bogotá: Fundación para la Reconciliación, 2010.

O'Malley, John W. *Trent and All That.* Cambridge: Harvard University Press, 2000.

Otabil, Mensa. *Beyond the Rivers of Ethiopia: A Biblical Revelation on God's Purpose for the Black Race.* Accra, Ghana: Alter, 1992.

Parsons, Elizabeth. *What Price for Privatization? Cultural Encounter with Development Policy on the Zambian Copperbelt.* Lanham, MD: Lexington, 2010.

Petersen, Robert L. "Strategies for Holistic Mission. Section Introduction." In *Antioch Agenda: Essays on the Restorative Church in Honor of Orlando E. Costas,* edited by Daniel Jeyaraj, Robert W. Pazmiño, and Rodney L. Petersen, 155–62. New Delhi: Indian Society for the Promotion of Christian Knowledge, 2007.

Petersen, Rodney L., and Nancy M. Rourke, eds. *Theological Literacy for the Twenty-First Century.* Grand Rapids: Eerdmans, 2002.

Petersen, Rodney L., and Marian Gh. Simion, eds. *Tracing Contours: Reflections on World Mission and Christianity. Selected Articles from the* BTI *Newsletter.* Newton, MA: Boston Theological Institute, 2010.

Philip, T. V. *Edinburgh to Salvador: Twentieth Century Ecumenical Missiology.* Kashmere Gate, Delhi, India: Indian Society for the Promotion of Christian Knowledge, 1999.

Prestwich, Menna, ed. *International Calvinism, 1541–1715.* New York: Oxford University Press, 1985.

Schreiter, Robert. *Reconciliation: Mission & Ministry in a Changing Social Order.* New York: Orbis, 1992.

Shenk, Wilbert R. "Rufus Anderson and Henry Venn: A Special Relationship?" In *International Bulletin of Missionary Research* 4 (1981) 168–72.

Shriver, Donald. *Honest Patriots: Loving a Country Enough to Remember its Misdeeds.* New York: Oxford University Press, 2005.

Shriver, George H. *Philip Schaff: Christian Scholar and Ecumenical Prophet. Centennial Biography for the American Society of Church History.* Macon, GA: Mercer University Press, 1987.

Spelman, Elizabeth V. *Repair: The Impulse to Restore in a Fragile World.* Boston: Beacon, 2003.

Spencer, Aída Besançon, and William David Spencer, eds. *The Global God: Multicultural Evangelical Views of God.* Grand Rapids: Baker, 1998.

Stanley, Brian. *The World Missionary Conference, Edinburgh 1910.* Grand Rapids: Eerdmans, 2009.

Thomas, Norman. "2010Boston: The Changing Contours of World Mission and Christianity." *International Bulletin of Missionary Research* 35.1 (January 2011) 10–11.

———. *Missions and Unity. Lessons from History, 1792–2010.* Eugene, OR: Cascade, 2010.

United Nations Department of Public Information, *Declaration on the Elimination of all Forms of Intolerance and of Discrimination Based on Religion or Belief.* United Nations, 1982.

Van Gelder, Craig. *The Essence of the Church: A Community Created by the Spirit.* Grand Rapids: Baker, 2000.

Vandergrift, Nicki Verploegen. *Organic Spirituality: A Sixfold Path for Contemplative Living.* Maryknoll, NY: Orbis, 2000.

Veronis, Luke. *Go Forth: Stories of Missions and Resurrection in Albania.* New York: Conciliar, 2010.

———. *Missionaries, Monks, and Martyrs: Making Disciples of All Nations.* Minneapolis: Light and Life, 1994.

Währisch-Oblau, Claudia, and Fidon Mwombeki, eds. *Mission Continues: Global Impulses for the 21st Century.* Eugene, OR: Wipf and Stock, 2010.

Walls, Andrew. *The Cross-Cultural Process in Christian History: Studies in the Transmission and Appropriation of Faith.* Maryknoll, NY: Orbis, 2002.

———. *The Missionary Movement in Christian History: Studies in the Transmission of Faith.* Maryknoll, NY: Orbis, 1996.

———. "Theology and Scholarship in a Global Church." In *Antioch Agenda: Essays on the Restorative Church in Honor of Orlando E. Costas,* edited by Daniel Jeyaraj, Roberto W. Pazmiño, and Rodney L. Petersen, 41–48. New Delhi: Indian Society for the Promotion of Christian Knowledge, 2007.

Weigel, George. *Witness to Hope.* New York: Cliff Street, 1999.

Werner, Dietrich, David Esterline, Namsoon Kang, and Joshva Raja, eds. *Handbook of Theological Education in Global Christianity: Theological Perspectives, Ecumenical Trends, Regional Surveys.* Oxford: Regnum, 2010.

Wilfred, Felix. *The Sling of Utopia: Struggles for a Different Society.* New Delhi: Indian Society for the Promotion of Christian Knowledge, 2005.

Williams, George H. "Erasmus and the Reformers on Non-Christian Religions and *Salus Extra Ecclesiam.*" In *Action and Conviction in Early Modern Europe*, edited by Theodore K. Rabb and Jerrold E. Seigel, 319–70. Princeton: Princeton University Press, 1969.

Wilson-Hartgrove, Jonathan. *New Monasticism: What it Has to Say to Today's Church.* Grand Rapids: Brazos, 2008.

Winter, Ralph D. "The Two Structures of God's Redemptive Mission." In *Perspectives on the World Christian Movement: A Reader*, edited by Ralph Winter and Steven Hawthorne, 178–90. Pasadena, CA: William Carey Library, 1981.

Yong, Amos. *Hospitality and the Other: Pentecost, Christian Practices, and the Neighbor.* Maryknoll, NY: Orbis, 2008.

Zehr, Howard. *Changing Lenses: A New Focus for Crime and Justice.* Scottdale, PA: Herald, 1990.

Zizioulas, John D. *Being as Communion: Studies in Personhood and the Church.* New York: St. Vladimir's Seminary Press, 1996.

Appendix I

2010Boston Schedule

Centennial Celebration of Edinburgh 1910
"The Changing Contours of World Mission and Christianity"
A Conference of the Boston Theological Institute

PRE-CONFERENCE

Wednesday Afternoon, November 3
(Location: Boston University Photonics Center)
6:30pm Open reception before open lecture
7:30pm Peter Phan (Georgetown University)
"Mission of the Triune God, Mission of the Church, Mission of the World"

Thursday Morning, November 4
(Location: Boston University)
10–12pm *"The Significance of Edinburgh, 1910-2010: An Overview"*
An Edinburgh 2010 debriefing and discussion with professors Dana Robert and Norman Thomas

Appendix I

Thursday Afternoon, November 4
(Locations: Boston University and Andover Newton Theological School)
1:30–4:30 Afternoon options
- 2010Boston/OMSC art exhibit
- Trolley bus tour of historic mission sites in Boston/Newton/Cambridge

Thursday Evening, November 4
(Location: Park Street Church)
5:30pm Campus Ministries Sponsored Dinner
"Challenging Today's Students for Missions"
Welcome and opening prayer: Dr. Gordon Hugenberger (Senior Minister, Park Street Church)
A word from our hosts: John Chung (Minister of Missions, Park Street Church), Chris Nichols (Director, New England InterVarsity Christian Fellowship), Pat McLeod (Director, Boston Campus Crusade for Christ)

2010BOSTON CONFERENCE BEGINS

Thursday Evening, November 4
(Location: Park Street Church)
7:00–8:30pm Musical offering from Park Street Church
Welcome from conference co-chairs and worship coordinator
Introduction: Dennis Hollinger (President, Gordon-Conwell Theological Seminary)
First Keynote: Dana Robert (Boston University)
"Boston, Students, and Missions from 1810 to 2010"
Litany and Worship
8:30pm Reception

Friday Morning, November 5
(Location: Boston University & Holy Cross Greek Orthodox School of Theology)
8:30–9:00 Worship in Marsh Chapel, Boston University

9:00–10:15 Welcome: Mary Elizabeth Moore (Dean, BU School of
    Theology)
Introduction: Dana Robert (Professor of World Christianity and
    History of Mission, Boston University)
Second Keynote: Brian Stanley (University of Edinburgh)
"*Discerning the Future of World Christianity: Vision and Blindness at the
    World Missionary Conference, Edinburgh 1910*"
10:15–10:30 Break
10:30–11:45 *Reports from Edinburgh, Tokyo and Cape Town* (Marsh
    Chapel)
Moderated and with comment/reflection by Episcopal Bishop Ian Douglas (Connecticut)
- Allen Yeh (Biola University) on the Tokyo 2010 Global Missions Consultation
- LouAnn Stropoli (Center for the Study of Global Christianity) on Lausanne III
- Kapya John Kaoma (Anglican Communion) on the Edinburgh 2010 conference

11:45–11:55 Song and Prayer: Tracy Wispelwey

Friday Afternoon, November 5
12:00–2:00 American Society of Missiology, Eastern Fellowship
    Luncheon Meeting
1:00–2:00 Introduction: M.L. Daneel (Professor of African Christianity
    and Missiology, Boston University)
Third Keynote: Daniel Jeyaraj (Liverpool Hope University & Andover
    Newton Theological School)
"*Theological Education and Mission: A Non-Western Reflection*"

2:15–4:15 *Student Paper Workshop with Faculty Chairs (Session I)*
1. Changing Contours of Christian Unity
Fr. Raymond Helmick, SJ (Boston College, Department of Theology)
- Cheryl Rice: Ecological Ecclesiology
- Michael Chadwell: Acts 10
- Jennifer Frazer: Rahner's Embodied Grace

2. Mission in Context
Margaret Guider, O.S.F. (Boston College, School of Theology and Ministry)
- ChaoLuan Kao: Chinese Christian Movements
- Eva Pascal: Faith Based Organizations in Thailand

3. Disciples in Mission
Fr. Luke Veronis (Holy Cross Greek Orthodox School of Theology)
- Nathaniel Samuel: Theological Aesthetics of Mission
- Marcus Mescher: A Theology of Neighbor
- Andrew Thompson: Communities of the Spirit

4. Education for Mission
Elizabeth Parsons (Boston University School of Theology)
- Jared Byas: Primer on Faith and Globalization
- Lisa Beth White: U.M. ARMY
- Frank Lan: Christian Education in China

5. Mission and Post-Colonialism
Nimi Wariboko (Andover Newton Theological School)
- Katie Lazarowicz: Identity and Mission
- Megumi Yoshida: Symbiotic Mission through *Ikebana*

6. Mission in a Pluralist World
Catherine Cornille (Boston College, Department of Theology)
- Travis Myers: Biblical Pneumatology and Theology of Religions
- Cristina Richie: Vegetarianism as Evangelism
- Anne Hillman: Spirit Soteriology and Theology of Religions

7. Mission and Post-Modernity
Christopher Duraisingh (Episcopal Divinity School)
- Jeff Lane: Henry Venn
- Wendy Morrison: Tillich's Existential Doubt

8. Salvation Today
Peter Kuzmič (Gordon-Conwell Theological Seminary)

3:30–4:15 *Mission and the Arts*
Introduction of OMSC artists in residence program: Dwight Baker
    (OMSC)
Presentation (Oxnam Room, BU): Emmanuel Garibay, OMSC artist in
    residence (2010–2011)
Presentation (Room B19, BU): Christopher Gilbert, film producer:
    "Beyond Empires"; the story of Bartholomaus Ziegenbalg
    (1684–1719)

Friday Evening, November 5
(Location: Holy Cross Greek Orthodox School of Theology)
5:30–6:00 Orthodox Vespers (Holy Cross Chapel)
6:10–7:10 Conference Dinner (Maliotis Cultural Center, Holy Cross
    and Hellenic College)
7:15–8:30 Welcome: Fr. Thomas Fitzgerald (Dean, Holy Cross Greek
    Orthodox School of Theology)
Introduction to Holy Cross's Missions Institute of Orthodox
    Christianity: Fr. Luke Veronis (MIOC Executive Director
    and Professor of Mission, Holy Cross)
Introduction: Fr. Emmanuel Clapsis (Professor of Orthodox Theology)
Fourth Keynote: Athanasios N. Papathanasiou (*Synaxis Greek
    Orthodox Theological Journal*)
"*Journey to the Center of Gravity: Christian mission one century after
    Edinburgh 1910*"

Saturday Morning, November 6
(Location: Andover Newton Theological School)
7:30–8:30 Presidential Breakfast

(Location: McGuinn Hall, Boston College)
8:30–8:50 Morning Worship
8:50–9:00 Welcome: Catherine Cornille (Chair, Department of
    Theology, Boston College)
9:00–10:00 Introduction by Peter Kuzmič (Professor of Mission and
    European Studies, Gordon-Conwell Theological Seminary)
Fifth Keynote: Ruth Padilla DeBorst (Latin American Theological
    Fraternity)

"*Wooden boxes and latticed windows: Christian witness and the post-colonizing, post colonized church*"
10:00–10:10 Stretch Break
Introduction: Mark Massa, S.J. (Dean, Boston College School of Theology and Ministry)
Sixth Keynote: Peter Phan (Georgetown University)
Christianity and the Wider Ecumenism: "*Mission and Inter-religious Dialogue: Edinburgh, Vatican II, and Beyond*"
11:10–11:45 Logistics and Break
11:45–12:45 NEMAAR reception with a word from Pres. Grove Harris and Kwok Pui-Lan (Episcopal Divinity School, President, AAR)

Saturday Afternoon, November 6
12:45–2:45 Student Paper Workshop with Faculty Chairs (Session II)
1. Changing Contours of Christian Unity
Fr. Raymond Helmick, SJ (Boston College, Department of Theology)
- Timothy Snyder: Improvising with Tradition
- Derrick Lemons: Evangelical Missional Shifts

2. Mission in Context
Margaret Guider, O.S.F. (Boston College, School of Theology and Ministry)
- Yoknyam Dabale: The Fires Keep Burning
- Yeon-seung Lee: Rural Resurrection in Korea

3. Discipleship and Mission
Fr. Luke Veronis (Holy Cross Greek Orthodox School of Theology)
- Joachim Kwaramba: Discipleship of Rich and Poor
- Yongho Lee: Franciscan Mission in Korea

4. Education for Mission
Elizabeth Parsons (Boston University School of Theology)
- Amelia Koh-Butler: Educating Missionary Communities
- Lisa Beth White: Methodist Border Friendship

5. Mission and Post-Colonialism
Nimi Wariboko (Andover Newton Theological School)

- Travis Myers: US American Ecclesiology of Mission
- Daniel Castiglione: The Asian-ness of Jesus
- Mary Cloutier: From Among Her Own Children

6. Mission in a Pluralist World
Catherine Cornille (Boston College, Department of Theology)

7. Mission and Post-Modernity
Christopher Duraisingh (Episcopal Divinity School)
- Sara Staley: Parabolic Role for Church in Reconciliation
- Glenn Harden: Mission to Prostitutes and its Critics

8. Salvation Today
Peter Kuzmič (Gordon-Conwell Theological School & Evangelical Theological Seminary, Osijek, Croatia)
- Peter Folan: Illich and Christian Service Trips
- Daniel O'Neill: Leaves from the Tree of Life
- Elizabeth Cademartori: LDS Development in Tonga

OMSC scholars in residence: "Our Stories: The World Church in Mission" (moderated by Jonathan Bonk, executive director of OMSC)

1. Kehinde Olabimtan, Nigeria, "Theological Education in West Africa: A Case Study"
2. Ohene Kumi, Ghana, "Church in Ghana: Opportunities and Challenges"
3. Watson Omulokoli, Kenya, "Maseno 1910"
4. Emmanuel Garibay, Philippines, "Proclaiming the Gospel through Art"
5. Sr. Odilia Bulayungan O.S.B., Philippines, "Life among 'the least of these'"
6. Paw Gaw, Myanmar, "Women and Church in Myanmar"
7. Qingxin Jiang, China, "Urban House Churches in China: Challenges and Opportunities"
8. Chee Seng Yip, Malaysia, "Mission to Migrant Workers"

2:45–3:00 Break
3:00–3:30 Presentation of the *Atlas of Global Christianity*, Todd Johnson, ed. (Gordon-Conwell Theological Seminary)
3:30–4:15 Celebration and Worship: Songs of Global Peacemaking
4:15–4:30 Break
Introduction: Margaret Guider, O.S.F. (Professor of Missiology, Boston College)
Seventh Keynote: Angelyn Dries, O.S.F. (St. Louis University)
"From Boston to the Whole World: 20th Century North American Roman Catholic Missions and the 'Antioch Agenda'"

Saturday Evening, November 6
(Location: Heights Room, Corcoran Commons, Boston College)
5:30–7:30 Massachusetts Council of Churches Ecumenical Dinner

(Location: St. Ignatius Church, Boston College)
Introduction: Nick Carter (President, Andover Newton Theological School)
Eighth Keynote: Brian McLaren (Author, *Everything Must Change*)
"Christian Mission and Peace-Making: Discerning our Secret Non-Weapon"
9:00–9:15 Closing Liturgy

Sunday Morning, November 7
(Location: The Memorial Church, Harvard University)
11:00 Morning Service at Memorial Church (Rev. Dr. Peter Gomes presiding)
Ninth Keynote Address & First in the Noble Lecture Series: Archbishop of York John Sentamu, (Harvard University's William Belden Noble Lecturer for 2010)
"Who is Jesus and What Does He Mean to Those Who Put Their Trust in Him?" Part I: *"God's Mission is Performative"*

Sunday Afternoon, November 7
12:30–2:00 Lunch break
2:00–4:00 General Assembly with principals at The Memorial Church, moderated by Rodney Petersen (BTI Executive Director)
2:00–3:00 Introduction of method by Rodney Petersen

Question on the Nature of Mission in the 21st Century, posed by Susan Abraham (Professor of Ministry Studies, Harvard Divinity School)

Keynote speakers respond

3:00–3:30 Break into eight small groups for discussion of conference themes

3:30–4:00 Small group faculty chairs report to assembly; statement of summary points and suggestions for further study

Closing Prayer: Dennis Hollinger, Chair, BTI Board of Trustees (President, Gordon-Conwell Theological Seminary)

4:00–5:00 Closing Reception (Buttrick Room, Memorial Church)

POST-2010BOSTON CONFERENCE EVENT

Anglican Archbishop of York John Sentamu continues 2010Boston reflections in the course of the remaining Harvard University Noble Lectures:

Monday, November 8, 8pm
(Location: The Memorial Church, Harvard University)
Part II: *"God's Mission is Transformative"*

Tuesday, November 9, 8pm
(Location: The Memorial Church, Harvard University)
Part III: *"God's Mission is Restorative Justice"*

Appendix II

2010Boston Worship Guide

NOVEMBER 4, 2010
PARK STREET CHURCH

Litany

Scripture Lessons 2 Timothy 1:3–14, 1 Timothy 4:6–12
A Litany from Timothy

Leader: Creator, Sustainer, Maker of all people, thank you for calling us with a holy calling, and for preparing us in advance to do good work. We are grateful for the ministry You place before us, and we praise You for the enduring gospel of Jesus Christ.

People: Rekindle the gift of God that is in us.

Leader: Rock of Ages, You are sovereign over all people, places, and events. You are timeless, transcending each of our days and moments. Your word, God, declares that with You, one day is like a thousand years, and a thousand years are like one day. We recognize that Your acts are in accordance with Your own holy purpose, and we humbly open ourselves to Your will and plan.

People: Rekindle the gift of God that is in us.

Leader: *God of Strength, forgive us for acting weak and cowardly. Free us from our spirit of timidity and give us victory over the fears, self-doubt, second-guessing, fragile egos, and lack of confidence that hinder us from confidently embarking on the ministry You set before us.*

People: May we rely on Your power, God, and remember that You called us, not according to our works, but according to Your own purpose and grace. Give us a spirit of power and of love and of self-discipline. Make us ready for the tasks You give. Rekindle the gift of God that is in us.

Leader: *Lord, forgive us for questioning Your purpose in our lives and for failing to remember the joy and confidence we experienced when we first put our trust in You. Have mercy on our weakness and build us up in the assurance of Your love. Forgive us for neglecting our fervor for Your gospel and zeal for sharing the good news of Jesus Christ.*

People: Jesus, You abolished death and brought life and immortality to light through the gospel. You gave grace to us before the ages began. Thank you for your mercy and love.

Leader: *Thank you, Lord, for the countless missionaries who first experienced their call to serve and love people in far away places while they were students. Thank you for the legacy of missionaries like E. Stanley Jones, Jim and Elisabeth Elliot, John R. Mott, Samuel Mills, Adoniram and Ann Judson, Henry Opukaha'ia, Mary Josephine Rogers, James Anthony Walsh, Edgar Helms, and Martha Drummer whose single-mindedness and dedication to the gospel of Christ were forged in their youth. God of Power, give us boldness to join in suffering with these servants of Yours, who sacrificed much for the sake of the treasure You entrusted to them. Like these missionaries, may we worship You with a clear conscience, confident that we serve You with a sincere faith.*

People: Let no one despise our youth, but help us to set the believers an example in speech and conduct, in love, in faith, and in purity. Rekindle the gift of God that is in us.

Leader: *Fill the teachers of the BTI with passion and courage to proclaim Your message of grace to students here in Boston and especially to empower people who may be despised by their youth around the world. Lay on our hearts the importance of this juncture in their students' lives as they explore new ideas and life paths. As they shape identities, choose careers and partners, and determine how they want to spend their time, may their teachers walk beside them, as Paul walked beside Timothy, to guide with gentleness, love, and truth. Open doors of opportunity that we may proclaim Your message of hope to those who are searching.*

People: We are grateful to You, Christ Jesus our Lord, who strengthens us, because You judged us faithful and appointed us to Your service. Rekindle the gift of God that is in us.

Leader: *Lord, help us to be constantly prayerful, dependent on You for guidance and strength. Day and night, help us to remember each other in our prayers. O God, You are the one in whom we put our trust. We know You are able to guard until that the end of time what we have entrusted to You. Help us to hold to the faith and love that are in Christ Jesus, by the help of Your Holy Spirit.*

People: Rekindle the gift of God that is in us.

Song: Here I Am, Lord[1]

NOVEMBER 5, 2010
MARSH CHAPEL, BOSTON UNIVERSITY

Morning Prayer

---

1. Written by Daniel L Schutte.

Hymn: "Rise to Greet the Sun"[2]

Prayer: Prayer 5 of St. Basil the Great (5th century)

Leader: O Lord Almighty, God of hosts and of all flesh , Who dwellest on high and lookest down on things that are lowly, Who searchest our hearts and innermost being, and clearly foreknowest the secrets of men; O unoriginate and everlasting Light, in Whom is no variableness, neither shadow of turning; Do Thou, O Immortal King, receive our supplications which we, daring because of the multitude of Thy compassions, offer Thee at the present time from defiled lips; and forgive us out sins, in deed, word, and thought, whether committed by us knowingly or in ignorance, and cleanse us from every defilement of flesh and spirit. And grand us to pass through the night of the whole present life with watchful heart and sober thought, ever expecting the coming of the bright and appointed day of Thine Only-begotten Son, our Lord and God and Saviour, Jesus Christ, whereon the Judge of all shall come with glory to reward each according to his deeds. May we not be found fallen and idle, but watching, and upright in activity, ready to accompany Him into the joy and divine palace of His glory, where there is the ceaseless sound of those that keep festival, and the unspeakable delight of those that behold the ineffable beauty of Thy countenance. For Thou art the true Light that enlightenest and sanctifiest all, and all creation doth hymn Thee unto ages of ages. Amen.

Psalter: Psalm 33[3]

1 Rejoice in the Lord, O you righteous.
    Praise befits the upright.
2 *Praise the Lord with the lyre;*
    make melody to God with the harp of ten strings.
3 Sing to God a new song;
    play skillfully on the strings, with loud shouts.

  2. Words: Chao Tzu-ch'en; trans. by Mildred A. Wiant and Bliss Wiant, 1946; Music: Hu Te-ai; arr. by Bliss Wiant, 1936; Trans. 1965 © Bliss Wiant
  3. Words: Psalm 33:3, 8; Music: Erika K. R. Hirsch, 2006

4 For the word of the Lord is upright,
   and all God's work is done in faithfulness.
5 God loves righteousness and justice;
   the earth is full of the steadfast love of the Lord.
6 By the word of the Lord the heavens were made,
   and all their host by the breath of God's mouth.
7 God gathered the waters of the sea as in a bottle;
   the Lord put the deeps in storehouses.
8 Let all the earth fear the Lord;
   let all the inhabitants of the world stand in awe of God.
9 For God spoke, and it came to be;
   God commanded, and it stood firm.
10 The Lord brings the counsel of the nations to nothing;
   God frustrates the plans of the peoples.
11 The counsel of the Lord stands for ever,
   the thoughts of God's heart to all generations.
12 Happy is the nation whose God is the Lord,
   the people whom God has chosen as God's heritage.
13 The Lord looks down from heaven;
   God sees all humankind.
14 From where God sits enthroned God watches
   all the inhabitants of the earth—
15 The Lord who fashions the hearts of them all,
   and observes all their deeds.
16 A king is not saved by his great army;
   a warrior is not delivered by his great strength.
17 The way horse is a vain hope for victory,
   and by its great might it cannot save.
18 Truly the eye of the Lord is on those who fear him,
   on those who hope in God's steadfast love,
19 to deliver their soul from death,
   and to keep them alive in famine.
20 Our soul waits for the Lord;
   God is our help and shield.
21 Our heart is glad in the Lord,
   because we trust in the Lord's holy name.
22 Let your steadfast love, O Lord, be upon us,
   even as we hope in you.

New Testament: Revelation 21:1–4

Then I saw a new heaven and a new earth. The former heaven and the former earth had passed away, and the sea was no more. I also saw the holy city, a new Jerusalem, coming down out of heaven from God, prepared as a bride adorned for her husband. I heard a lout voice from the throne saying, "Behold, God's dwelling is with the human race. God will dwell with them and they will be God's people and God will always be with them [as their God]. God will wipe every tear from their eyes, and there shall be no more death or mourning, waiting or pain, [for] the old order has passed away. (NAB)

Meditation on Scriptures

We name silently or aloud our hopes for a new heaven and a new earth.

Hymn: "We Wait for New Heavens"[4]

NOVEMBER 5, 2010
HOLY CROSS CHAPEL

Orthodox Vespers Service

Priest: Blessed is our God, now and always, and forever and ever.

Reader: Amen.

Come, let us worship God our King and bow down.
Come, let us worship Christ Goid our King and bow down.
Come, let us worship Christ, our King and our God, and bow down before the Lord.

Psalm 103 (104)

---

4. Christian Tamaela, Indonesia (based on a Central Moluccas traditional melody).

Reader: Bless the Lord, O my soul! O Lord, my God, you are great indeed! Clothed in pomp and brilliance, arrayed with light as with a cloak, stretching out the sky as a tent-cloth, establishing your lofty halls on water. You make the clouds your conveyance, you surge on the wings of the wind. You make the winds your messengers, and flaming fires your attendants.

You settled the earth on its foundation: it shall stand unmoved from age to age. The abyss covered it like a garment; the waters stood above the mountains. At your rebuke, they take to flight, at the peal of your thunder, they flee. They hurdle the hills and run down the dales to the place you have chosen for them. You have set up a boundary not to be passed: they shall never return to cover the earth.

Down in the gullies, you make springs to rise; waters shall flow between the mountains. They shall give drink to the beasts of the field; wild asses will seek them to quench their thirst. The birds of the sky shall abide by them; from among the rocks, they will raise their song. From your lofty halls you refresh the hills; the earth shall be fed with the fruit of your works.

You make green pastures for the cattle and food-plants for the service of men and women, so that bread may be drawn from the earth, and wine that gladdens the human heart; oil to make the face shine, and bread to strengthen the human heart.

The trees of the plain shall be satisfied, the cedars of Lebanon that God planted. Sparrow shall build their nests in them, herons shall call them their home. To the deer belong the high mountains; to rodents, the shelter of the rock. You have made the moon to mark the seasons; the sun knows the time of its setting. You establish darkness, and it is night, wherein the forest creatures prowl. Young lions roar for their prey, and call out to God for their meat. As the sun rises, they will come together, and aly themselves down in their dens. People will go out to their labor, and work until eventide.

How great are your works, O Lord! In wisdom you have wrought them all. The earth is filled with your creatures, even the wide and open sea. Within it are countless creeping things, living beings small and large. Upon it there are ships a-sailing, and the great beast you made to have fun. All of them look to you to give them their food in due season. You provide and they gather up; you open your hands, and they are full. You hide your face, and they cringe; you suspend their breath, and they die and return to their dust. You send forth your breath, and they live; you renew the face of the earth.

May the Lord's glory endure forever, may the Lord rejoice in his works. The Lord looks upon the earth, and makes it quake; touches the mountains, and they smoke. I will sing to the Lord as long as I live, I will praise my God as long as I last. Would that my thoughts be pleasing to God, and I will rejoice in the Lord. May the sinners vanish from the earth, and the wicked be no more. Bless the Lord, O my soul! The sun knows the time of its setting. You establish darkness and it is night.

How great are your works, O Lord! In wisdom you have wrought them all.

Glory to the Father, and to the Son, and to the Holy Spirit, now and always, and forever and ever. Amen.
Alleluia, alleluia, alleluia, glory to You, O God. (2x)
Alleluia, alleluia, alleluia, glory to You, O God. O Lord, our hope, glory to You.

The Litany Of Peace

Priest: In peace, let us pray to the Lord.

People: Lord, have mercy.

Priest: For heavenly peace and for the salvation of our souls, let us pray to the Lord.

People: Lord, have mercy.

Priest: For peace in the whole world, the stability of God's Holy Churches and for the oneness of all, let us pray to the Lord.

People: Lord, have mercy.

Priest: For this holy house, and all who enter it with faith, reverence and godly fear, let us pray to the Lord.

People: Lord, have mercy.

Priest: For our Father and Archbishop Demetrios, the honorable presbyters, the deacons in Christ, for all the clergy and the people, let us pray to the Lord.

People: Lord, have mercy.

Priest: For our country, the President, and all in public service, let us pray to the Lord.

People: Lord, have mercy.

Priest: For this city and this Parish, for every city and land, and for the faithful who live in them, let us pray to the Lord.

People: Lord, have mercy.

Priest: For temperate weather, abundance of the goods of the earth, and for peaceful times, let us pray to the Lord.

People: Lord, have mercy.

Priest: For those who travel, by land, sea and air, for those who are sick or suffering or in captivity, and for their safekeeping, let us pray to the Lord.

People: Lord, have mercy.

Priest: That we may be spared all affliction, wrath, danger and want, let us pray to the Lord.

People: Lord, have mercy.

Priest: Help us, save us, have mercy on us and keep us, O God, in Your grace.

People: Lord, have mercy.

Priest: Remembering our most holy, pure, blessed and glorious lady, the Theotokos and ever-virgin Mary, with all the saints, let us commit ourselves and one another, and our whole life to Christ our God.

People: Lord, have mercy.

Priest: For to you is due all glory, honor and worship, Father, Son and Holy Spirit, now and always, and forever and ever. Amen.

Cantor: Lord, I have cried out to you, hear me, O Lord. Hear me O Lord, Lord I have cried out to you, hear me. Receive the voice of my prayer when I cry out to you, hear me, hear me O Lord.

Let my prayer be set forth as incense before you, and the lifting up of my hand as an evening sacrifice. Hear me, hear me, O Lord.

If you retain sins, Lord, O Lord, who can stand? With you there is forgiveness.

In you, O blessed one, the divine Paul has found an imitator bearing the same name, adorned with the same virtues of purity, spiritual courage, constancy in the midst of perils; for you were enflamed with zeal for the true Faith, a defender of Orthodoxy. Together with him, you too are now glorified in the dwellings of heaven.

For your name's sake, O Lord, I have waited for you. My soul has waited for your promise, my soul has hoped in the Lord.

By the garrote of your solid teachings, you choked off and brought and end to Arius, who denied the divinity of Christ, and the impious Macedonius, O blessed hierarch; and the correctness
of your doctrine strengthened Orthodoxy. Thus, accepting your brilliant confession, the Lover of Mankind made you a sharer in His Kingdom in heaven.

From the morning watch until night, from the morning watch let Israel hope in the Lord.

O blessed father, well-named confessor, protector of those who acclaim you with fervor, O holy Paul: save us from all sin, all dangers, all the storms of the passions and from tyranny. As an acceptable hierarch, as an invincible witness, you can plead freely before Christ our God.

For with the Lord is steadfast love and in him is full redemption, and he will redeem Israel from all their iniquities.

Glory be to the Father and to the Son and to the Holy Spirit.

O venerable father, having been clothed as a bishop, you imitated the zeal of your namesake, the apostle Paul, enduring the same persecutions and dangers as he. You took pains to put an end to the blasphemy of Arius. Suffering for the sake of the eternal and consubstantial Trinity, you overcame the impious Macedonius, the adversary of the Spirit. Then, having explained the true Faith to all, you went to share the dwelling of the bodiless angels; forever with them, now intercede for the salvation of our souls.

Both now and always and forever and ever. Amen.

Who will not call you blessed, All-holy Virgin? Who will not hymn your child-birth without labor? For the only-begotten Son, who shone from the Father beyond time, came forth from you, pure Maiden, ineffably incarnate. By nature he is God, by nature he became man for our sakes, not divided in a duality of persons, but known without confusion in a duality of natures. O honored and all-blessed, implore him to have mercy on our souls.

Priest: Wisdom. Let us be attentive!

Everyone: O Gladsome light of holy glory of the holy, blessed, heavenly, immortal Father, O Jesus Christ: arriving at the hour of sunset and having seen the evening light, we praise the Father, Son, and Holy Spirit, God. It is worthy for You to be praised at all times with happy voices, O Son of God and Giver of life; and therefore the world glorifies You!

Priest: The Evening Prokemenon.

Cantor: You, God, are my fortress; your steadfast love will meet me. (2x) Deliver me from my enemies, my God; protect me from those who rise up against me. You, God, are my fortress; your steadfast love will meet me.

Reader: Grant, Lord to keep us this evening without sin, Blessed are You, Lord, God of our fathers and praised and glorified is Your name forever. Amen. Lord, let Your mercy come upon us, for we have trusted in You. Blessed are You, Lord; teach me Your commandments. Blessed are You, Master; make me to understand Your commandments. Blessed are You, Holy One; enlighten me with Your commandments. Lord, Your love endures forever; do not turn away from the work of Your hands. To You belong praise, song, and glory, to the Father and the Son and the Holy Spirit, now and forever and to the ages of ages. Amen.

Appendix II

The Completion Litany

Deacon: Let us complete our evening prayer to the Lord.

Cantor: Lord, have mercy.

Deacon: Help us, save us, have mercy on us, and keep us, O God, in Your grace.

Cantor: Lord, have mercy.

Deacon: That this whole evening may be perfect, holy, peaceful and without sin, let us ask of the lord.

Cantor: Grant this, O Lord.

Deacon: An angel of peace, a faithful guide, a guardian of our souls and bodies, let us ask of the lord.

Deacon: Forgiveness and remission of our sins and offenses, let us ask of the Lord.

Cantor: Grant this, O Lord.

Deacon: All that is good and profitable for our souls, and peace in the world, let us ask of the Lord.

Cantor: Grant this, O Lord.

Deacon: That we may live out our lives in peace and repentance, let us ask of the Lord.

Cantor: Grant this, O Lord.

Deacon: A Christian end to our life, peaceful, free of suffering or shame, and a good defense before the dread judgment seat of Christ, let us ask of the Lord.

Cantor: Grant this, O Lord.

Deacon: Remembering our most holy, pure, most blessed and glorious lady, the Theotokos and ever-virgin Mary, with all the saints, let us commend ourselves, and one another, and our whole life to Christ our God.

Cantor: To You, O Lord.

Priest: For You are a good and loving God and to You we give the glory: to the Father and to the Son and to the Holy Spirit, now and always, and forever and ever.

Cantor: Amen.

Priest: Peace be to all.

Cantor: And to your spirit.

Deacon: Let us bow our heads to the Lord.

Cantor: To You O Lord.

Priest: May the might of Your Kingdom be blessed and glorified, of the Father and the Son and the Holy Spirit, now and forever and to the ages of ages. Amen.

The Aposticha

Your Martyrs did not renounce You, O Lord, nor did they deviate from Your commandments. Through their intercessions, have mercy on us.

Blessed are they whom You have chosen and taken to yourself, O Lord. Your creative command was my beginning and real existence. For wishing to construct me as a living creature from both invisible and visible natures, from earth You fashioned my body, and You gave me a soul through Your divine and vivifying insufflation. Therefore, O Savior, repose Your servants in the land of the living where the righteous dwell.

Their Souls will dwell among good things. The tasting of the tree of old became the cause of pain unto Adam in Eden when the serpent discharged his poison. For through him entered death which devoured man and with him the entire species. But the Master came and threw down the dragon and gave us resurrection. So to Him let us cry aloud: O Savior, be merciful, and with the righteous repose those whom You have taken unto yourself.

Priest: Lord, now let Your servants depart in peace, for my eyes have seen Your salvation. A light of revelation to the nations, and glory to Your people Israel.

People: Holy God, holy mighty, holy immortal, have mercy on us. (3x)

Glory to the Father and the Son and the Holy Spirit, now and forever and to the ages of ages. Amen.

All Holy Trinity, have mercy on us. Lord, forgive our sins. Master, pardon our transgressions. Holy One, visit and heal our infirmities for Your name's sake.

Lord have mercy. Lord have mercy. Lord have mercy. Glory to the Father and the Son and the Holy Spirit, now and forever and to the ages of ages. Amen.

Our Father, who art in heaven. Hallowed be Thy name. Thy kingdom come. Thy will be done. On earth as it is in heaven. Give us this day our daily bread, and forgive us our trespasses, as we forgive those who trespass against us. And lead us not into temptation, but deliver us from evil.

For Yours is the Kingdom, and the power and the glory, of the Father and the Son and the Holy Spirit, now and forever and to the ages of ages. Amen.

The Apolytikion

Your confession of the divine Faith established you in the Church as another Paul, full of zeal, among the hierarchs. Your innocent blood cries out to the Lord with that of Abel and Zechariah.

Virgin mother of God, we praise you as the means of the salvation of our race; for your Son and our God, who through the Cross accepted suffering in the flesh he had taken from you, has redeemed us from corruption, for he loves mankind.

Glory to the Father and the Son and the Holy Spirit.

Having crossed the sea of asceticism, driven by the breeze of abstinence, you escaped the storm of the passions. O venerable father, namesake of holy Paul, you endured persecutions, dangers, and mistreatment by heretical babblers; but you overthrew the doctrine of Arius and put to flight the heresy of Nestorius in your zeal for the Church of Christ. Intercede before Him, O blessed hierarch, for the savation of our souls.

Now and forever and ever Amen.

I have recourse to your holy protection as to a haror of salvation, O spotless Virgin Mary, and I ask you to take pity: do not reject your servant, but save him from present affliction, O you who have compassion by nature. O mother of the Most High God, by your constant prayer, save your faithful servants from adversity.

When you saw hanging on the cross the ripe cluster of grapes which you had produced without labor, O Virgin, you cried out, mourning and weeping: "My Son, pour forth the sweet nectar that takes away the drunkenness of the passions. For my sake, who gave birth to you, O Benefactor, manifest Your mercy, O Lord!"

Priest: Wisdom. Blessed is the One who is Christ, our God, always now and forever and to the ages of ages.

Cantor: Amen. Make firm O Lord our God the holy Orthodox faith in this city and community.

Priest: Most Holy Theotokos save us.

Cantor: You are honored more than the cherubim, and you have more glory when compared to the seraphim. Without corruption you gave birth to God the Word. We magnify you the true Theotokos.

Priest: Glory be to You, O Lord our God, glory be to You. May Christ our true God, have mercy on us and save us, through the prayers of His most holy mother, our lady the Theotokos and ever-Virgin Mary, by the power of the precious and life-giving Cross, through the intercessions of the holy prophet, forerunner and Baptist John, of the holy, glorious and all praiseworthy apostles, of the holy glorious and triumphant martyrs, of the holy ancestors of God Joachim and Anna, and of all the saints, have mercy on us and save us, for You are a good and loving God.

Through the prayers of our holy fathers and mothers, Lord Jesus Christ, have mercy on us and save us.

NOVEMBER 6, 2010
BOSTON COLLEGE

Morning Prayer

Leader: In the beginning, when darkness was on the face of the deep and the Spirit of God brooded over the waters, God said, "Let there be light."

People: And there was light.

Leader: In the beginning, when it was very quiet, God spoke.

People: And what God was, the Word was.

Leader: When the time was right, God sent the Son. He came among us.

People: He was one of us.

Leader: Jesus said: "I am the light of the world. Whoever follows me will have the light of life and will never walk in darkness."

People: He is our light.

Leader: Jesus said: "The water that I will give will become a life-giving spring within and give eternal life."

People: He is the water of life.

Leader: Glory to God, who gives us light, glory to God in the highest, and on earth may peace reign among people of faith.

People: Amen.

A Reading from the Gospel of Matthew 5:1–9

1 Now when Jesus saw the crowds, he went up on a mountainside and sat down. His disciples came to him, 2 and he began to teach them. He said: 3 "Blessed are the poor in spirit, for theirs is the kingdom of heaven. 4 Blessed are those who mourn, for they will be comforted. 5 Blessed are the meek, for they will inherit the earth. 6 Blessed are those who hunger and thirst for righteousness, for they will be filled. 7 Blessed are the merciful, for they will be shown mercy. 8 Blessed are the pure in heart, for they will see God. 9 Blessed are the peacemakers, for they will be called children of God.

People: We hear you Lord Jesus. Transform us in love.

Song: To See You[5]

God of Earth and Time, Music, Beauty
God of every child, citizen, immigrant
Purify our minds, soften judgment
Bring us into light, open our eyes
To see You

---

5. Words and music by Tracy Wispelwey.

Intercession

Leader: Where ignorance, self-love and insensitivity have fractured life in community,
People: Give us your light, O God of love.
Leader: Where injustice and oppression have broken the spirit of peoples,
People: Give your light, O God who frees.
Leader: Where hunger and poverty, illness and death have made life an enbearable burden,
People: Give your light, O God of grace.

Worship and Celebration – Music and Peacemaking[6]

Come Together in Love

Come, people come, your spirits will be filled
In the dreams of God, your spirits will be filled

Reconciler Jesus, the Holy Spirit Comfort
Creator God of all, hold us together in Peace

East, West, North, South, here us as we sing
From any creed or language, come together in love

Peacemaker

We follow the Reconciler,
We bear His name and give you what he gave to us
Peacemaker and healer,
Jesus taught us and leads us in the world now
Peace

---

6. All songs written by Tracy Wispelwey, copyright The Restoration Project, except "With Kindness," written by Brian McLaren, copyright Brian McLaren, and based off of a prayer by Teresa of Avila. All songs will be released on an upcoming album, February 2011, except "With Kindness," which can be found on the CD *Songs For a Revolution of Hope*. To find out more about this project and when it will be available to buy and download, or listen to other songs written by Tracy, please visit RestorationVilliage.com.

Amahoro

Amahoro (5x)
Love, love, love, show us the way (4)
Peace show us the way (2x)
Hope (9x) show us the way

Sunrise

Sunrise
The Son rises for me to be peace
Peace breaks the fear
And it is for all
So everyone can know
It is for all
A way of peace and love

Jesus
He is a way of peace and love

He is a home for everything refugee
A place to rest when we are running away
He washes us when our eyes have seen death
He is our love when we have none left to give

Mercy Blessed

Only goodness flows from God
Blessed is God's Mercy
Forgiving debt and redeeming wrongs
Blessed is God's Mercy
This is why we stand in love
Blessed is God's Mercy

Call to Nonviolence

We withdraw our hands, from things that destroy,
systems that oppress, from selfishness
We will walk the earth in nonviolence,

the strength of peace and truth, imagination
Lifting up your love, transforming our lives
Walking in the dreams of God

Las manos retiramos, de cosas que destruyen,
los sistemas que oprimen, de la avaricia
Andaremos por la tierra sin la violencia,
en la fuerza de la paz y la imaginación
Levantando tu amor, transformándose nuestras vidas
Caminamos en los sueños de Dios

Arise

Arise, arise
Your light, your light has come
Nations will come, all will come, all will come (2x)

For your love has turned me around
For your love has turned me around
Nations will come, all will come, all will come (2x)

With Kindness

Christ has no body, here but ours
No hands no feet, here on earth but ours
Ours are the eyes through which He looks
On this world with kindness

Ours are the hands through which He works
Ours are the feet on which He moves
Ours are the voices through which he speaks
To this world in kindness

Through our touch, our smile, our listening ear
Embodied in us, Jesus is living here
Let us go now, filled with the Spirit
Into the world, with kindness

NOVEMBER 6, 2010
ST. IGNATIUS CHURCH, BOSTON COLLEGE

Worship Evening Service

Call to worship: "Christ the Light of the Universe"

Hymn: "Phos Hilaron"

Stay with us, O God, this night, so that by your strength we may rise with the new day to rejoice in the resurrection of your Son, Jesus Christ our Savior. Amen.
(Collect for Saturday Night Prayer from Celebrating Common Prayer)

Psalm 96 (NRSV)

1 O sing to the LORD a new song; sing to the LORD, all the earth. 2 Sing to the LORD, bless God's name; tell of God's salvation from day to day. 3 Declare God's glory among the nations, the LORD's marvelous works among all the peoples. 4 for great is the LORD, and greatly to be praised; God is to be revered above all gods. 5 *for all the gods of the peoples are idols, but the LORD made the heavens.* 6 Honor and majesty are before the LORD; strength and beauty are in the LORD's sanctuary. 7 *Ascribe to the LORD, O families of the peoples, ascribe to the LORD glory and strength.* 8 Ascribe to the LORD the glory due God's name; bring an offering, and come into God's courts. 9 *Worship the LORD in holy splendor; tremble before the LORD, all the earth.* 10 Say among the nations, "The LORD is king! The world is firmly established; it shall never be moved. God will judge the peoples with equity." 11 *Let the heavens be glad, and let the earth rejoice; let the sea roar, and all that fills it;* 12 let the field exult, and everything in it. Then shall all the trees of the forest sing for joy 13 *before the LORD; for God is coming, for God is coming to judge the earth. God will judge the world with righteousness, and the peoples with his truth.*

Litany[7]

In Peace, let us pray to the Lord,
Lord, have mercy.
For the Peace of God and for our salvation, let us pray to the Lord,
Lord, have mercy.
For the Peace of the whole world and for the Church, let us pray to the Lord,
That we may reach out to meet one another and rejoice to find that we are brothers and sisters in Christ,
Lord, hear our prayer.
That we may all be one, worshipping God as beloved sons and daughters, in spirit and truth, *Lord, hear our prayer.*
That we may end the sin of our division so that we may declare God's glory among the nations,
Lord, hear our prayer.
That we may commit ourselves to the non-violent way of Jesus and transform the world through offering forgiveness and radiating the Peace of God,
Lord, hear our prayer.
Let us begin by offering one another a sign of that forgiveness and reconciliation.

Trisagion

The Lord be with you,
And also with you.
Let us pray (*in unison*):
Holy God, Holy and Mighty, Holy and Immortal, have mercy on us.
Holy God, Holy and Mighty, Holy and Immortal, have mercy on us.
Holy God, Holy and Mighty, Holy and Immortal, have mercy on us.
Glory be to the Father, and to the Son, and to the Holy Spirit, both now and ever and to the ages of ages. Amen.
Let us pray the prayer that our Lord taught his disciples to pray. I invite each of you to pray in your mother tongue:

---

7. Thank you to Teva Regule, Benjamin Durheim, and Matthew Sigler for this liturgy.

The Lord's Prayer

Hymn: "All Praise to Thee My God This Night" (Tallis' Canon)

Closing Prayer (in unison)[8]
O Jesus Christ, our Lord and Savior. You promised to always be with us. Kindle our hearts with the fire of the Holy Spirit. Give us the spirit of Wisdom and faith, of daring and of patience of humility and firmness, of love and of repentance, through the prayers of this
community. Amen

NOVEMBER 7, 2010
MEMORIAL CHURCH, HARVARD

Final Blessing

Leader: Let us open our hands and receive the Lord's blessing.

May the love of the cross,
The power of the resurrection,
And the presence of the Living Lord,
Be with you always.
And the blessing of the Eternal God,
Creator and Sustainer,
Risen Lord and Savior,
Giver of justice and love,
Be upon you now and evermore.

People: Amen.

---

8. Sergius Bulgakov, excerpted from a *Prayer for Unity*.

Appendix II

Sending Hymn: "Sing Together on Our Journey: A Hymn for the Boston Theological Institute"[9]

Sing together on our journey! Sing with joy, Alleluia!
Share, as we proceed, canticle and creed, and with faith and fervour strong
spin our stories into song; sing with joy, Alleluia!

Pray together on our journey! Pray in love, Alleluia!
Say the Name you praise not in hurtful ways as a hammer or a sword
but as life for all outpoured; pray in love, Alleluia!

Seek together on our journey! Seek the truth, Alleluia!
In the Spirit grow, trusting we will know, where to look and when to leap
reaching high and digging deep; seek the truth, Alleluia!

Walk together on our journey! Walk in peace, Alleluia!
With the Crucified risen at our side, let us listen and befriend,
quick to mediate and mend; walk in peace, Alleluia!

Dance together on our journey! Dance with hope, Alleluia!
Follow with your feet freedom's thrilling beat, with endurance amply shod,
doing justice, knowing God; Dance with hope, Alleluia!

Sing together on our journey! Sing with joy, Alleluia!
Stewards of the earth, given second birth, to our Maker we belong,
praise the Source of every song; sing with joy, Alleluia!

---

9. Lyrics: Brian A. Wren; Music: Peter Cutts

Index of Proper Names

Abraham (patriarch), 68–69, 75, 81, 296
Abraham, Susan, 274–77
Achomota, Ghana, 88
Ackerman, Eloisa, 215
Acts, 112–13, 294–95
Ad Gentes (*AG*), 42, 85, 91–92, 95, 114
Adventist Development and Relief Agency (ADRA), 201
Afghanistan, 7, 9, 11, 209
Africa, 4, 7, 9–11, 17, 49, 54–59, 61, 88–89, 114, 119, 134, 136, 158, 163–71, 174–75, 177, 198, 209, 257, 262, 268, 271, 287, 297
African(s), 54, 63, 158, 166, 168, 252, 259, 267, 270–71
African American(s), 17, 158, 163–77
African Christianity, 60
African Initiated Churches (AIC), 61, 267
African Islam, 60
African Mission School Society, 163
Afro-American Religious Studies, 165
Agape Home, 203–4, 206–7
AIDS, 198, 200, 204–6, 209, 262
Albania, 284
All-Slum Savings and Loan Program, 204

Allen, Roland, 120
Alpha Course, 139
Alvarez, Obed, 258
Ambedkar, B. R., 52
America, *see* United States of America
American(s), 15–16, 19, 36–37, 133, 158, 163–65, 167–68, 171, 259
American Baptist Convention, 165
American Bible Society, 16, 18
American Board of Commissioners for Foreign Missions (ABCFM), 16, 29, 133, 156, 161, 234, 236
American Catholic Congress, Second, 29
American Colonization Society, 17–18
American English, 144
American Indians, 16, 19 (see also Indians (American); Native American(s); Plains Indian)
American Missionary Association, 165
American Society of Missiology, 281
Americanism, 30, 87
Americas, the, 58, 134
Amherst College, 161, 236–37
Amistad Reservoir, 213
Amnesty International, 197
Amsterdam, Netherlands, 47
Anansi stories, 35

Index of Proper Names

Anderson, Rufus, 282
Anderson, Wilhelm, 281
Andover Newton Theological School, 246, 274, 276, 286
Andover Theological Seminary, 15–18, 20–22, 156, 161, 236, 285
Andover, Massachusetts, 236
Andrade, Esperanza "Hope", 217
André, Gabriel, 30
Anglican(s), 23, 62, 155, 246, 251
Anglican Communion, 24, 247
Anglo(s), 214–16
Anglo-Saxon, 167
Angola, 21
Ann Arbor University, 175
Antigonish Movement, 40
Antioch, Syria, 113, 293–95; metaphorically, 297
Antioch Agenda, 29, 41–42, 44, 79, 274, 292–98
Antiochian Christians, 296
Apocalypse, the, 296 (*see also* Revelation, Book of)
Aquinas, Thomas, 38, 190
Arabic, 14, 145
Aramaic (culture), 136
Aramaic (language), 147
Archbishop of Canterbury, 43
Archdiocese of Boston, Roman Catholic, 22, 28, 32, 36–39
Archdiocese of New York, Roman Catholic, 32
Argentina, 116
Ariarajah, S. Wesley, 290
Arkansas, 177
Arroyo Colorado (Texas river), 214
Asbury Theological Seminary, 156
Asia, 10–11, 24, 30, 39, 49–50, 52–55, 57–62, 88, 105, 114, 200–202, 262, 277, 287, 297–98
Asian(s), 250, 252
Asian Christianity, 60

Assisi, Italy, 102
Atlanta, Georgia, 21
Atlas of Global Christianity, 3, 11–12, 56–57, 246, 290
Augustine (of Hippo), 75, 183
Azariah, V. S., 62
Aztec, 135
Baha'i, 90
Baja California, 43
Balia, Daryl, 75
Balthasar, Hans Urs von, 99
Bangkok, Thailand, 114, 200, 202, 204–5
Bantu, 89
Baptist Missionary Magazine, 165
Baptist Missionary Society, 195
Baptist(s), 17, 149
Barnabas, 294
Barrett, Lois, 114
Barth, Karl, 98–99, 294
Bass, Dorothy C., 283
Batanga, Cameroon, 175
Beacon Hill, Boston, Massachusetts, 36
Bellamy, Joseph, 16
Bellofatto, Gina, 157
Benedict XVI, Pope, 101, 103, 24 (*see also* Ratzinger, Josef)
Benga, 175
Berman, Guillermo "Willie", 219, 225
Betania Elementary School, 221
Bible(s), 10, 18, 21, 52, 76, 126, 136–40, 142–45, 147–49, 170, 182, 191, 203, 221, 233, 235, 261–62, 268
Bible study, 8, 14, 17, 139, 223
Bible women, 60
Birdsall, Doug, 265
Birmingham, England, 59
Bolenda School, The, 172
Bolivia, 39
Bolondo Girls' School, 173

Bolondo Mission Station, 172
Bombay, India, 49
Bonaventure, 184
Boniface, 43
Bonino, José Miguez, 115
Bonk, Jonathan, 225, 246
Bonomelli, Geremia, 87, 95
Booth, William, 20
Bosch, David, 78–79, 196, 257, 282
Boston, Massachusetts, 13, 20–27, 28–30 32–37, 39, 41, 43–44, 63, 88, 133, 141, 161, 235, 246, 251–52, 255, 274–76
Boston College (BC), 22, 28, 32, 35, 159, 274, 279, 281, 288
Boston College Department of Theology, 79, 288
Boston College School of Theology and Ministry, 159, 274, 280
Boston Deaconess Training School, 21 (*see also* New England Deaconess Training School)
Boston Harbor, 36, 43
Boston Missionary Training School, 21
Boston Seaman's Friend Society, 30
Boston Theological Institute (BTI), 13, 26, 155–57, 246–48, 251, 255, 274–75, 279, 286, 292, 298
Boston University, 20–21, 155, 159–60, 245–46, 248–49, 274, 277, 285
Boston University School of Theology, 20–21, 160, 246–47, 274, 285
Bowersock, Glen, 80
Bowman, Matthew, 246
Braaten, Carl, 102
Bradford Academy, 15–16, 18
Brainerd, David, 14–15
Branch Theory, 280
Brazil, 9

Brazilians, 43
Bria, Ion, 295
Bridgman, Elijah Coleman, 235
Brighton, Massachusetts, 28, 30
Britain, 57–58 (*see also* Great Britain; United Kingdom)
British Broadcasting Corporation (BBC), 269
British Empire, 19, 58, 114, 128
British English, 144
Brookline, Massachusetts, 25
Brown, Altha, 168, 170
Brownsville, Texas, 213–14, 222
Bruges, Belgium, 92
Bruneau, Joseph, 30–31, 33
BTI Magazine, 274
BTI Newsletter, 274
Buchanan, Cornelius, 15
Buddha, 105
Buddhism, 52, 89, 94, 136, 200–201, 231
Buddhist(s), 11, 129, 145, 201
Buenos Aires, Argentina, 118
Burkina Faso, 7, 158
Burma (Myanmar), 17, 19, 201, 203
Burmese (language), 17, 19
Burns, John J., 38
Burns Library, 35
Burrows, William R., 79
Burundi, 7
Buthelezi, Manas, 115
Butler, Jon, 30
Byon, Jungmin, 249

Cabasilas, Nicholas, 75–76
Caesarea (Caesarea Maritime), 112
Cairns, David S., 48–50, 52–53, 59–62, 89
California, 62
Call for Forty Thousand, 38
Cambodia, 7, 200–201

Cambridge, Massachusetts, 22, 32, 34, 43, 209
Cambridge, University of, 56
Cameron County, Texas, 214–16, 218
Cameroon, 175
Campbell, Laura Kreis, 174
Canaan, 234
Canada, 88, 175
Canadians (French), 43
Canterbury, Archbishop of, 199
Cape Town Commitment, 255
Cape Town, South Africa, 63, 98, 110, 116, 121, 260
Cape Town 2010 ("Cape Town"), 63, 157, 249, 254–58, 260–65
Cape Verdeans, 43
Cardijn, Joseph-Léon, 37
Carey, George, 199
Carey, Lott, 163
Carey, William, 15, 17, 149, 195, 260
Caribbean (region), 35, 58, 262
Caritas International Thailand, 201
Castiglione, Daniel, 250
Castoriadis, Cornelius, 80
Catholic(s), 22–24, 30, 36–43, 32, 93, 96, 196 (*see also* Roman Catholic(s))
Catholic Action, 37
Catholic Church, 84, 92–96, 101–3, 117, 195, 198 (*see also* Roman Catholic Church)
Catholic Church Extension Society, 29
Catholic Foreign Mission Board, 32
Catholic Foreign Mission Seminary (Maryknoll), 34
Catholic Foreign Mission Society of America (Maryknoll Fathers and Brothers), 23, 32–33
Catholic Hour Radio, 34
Catholic Mission in Human Development Centre, 201
Catholic Office for Emergency Relief and Refugees, 201
"Catholic Radio Hour", 34
Catholic Students Mission Crusade, 34
Catholic University of America, 31, 36
Catholicism, 23, 30, 42, 285, 288, 294 (*see also* Roman Catholicism)
Caucasian, 214
Census Bureau, United States, 214
Center for the Study of Global Christianity, 290
Chad, 7
Chaldean (language), 14
Challoner, Richard, 29
Chandler, Letitia Grace, 175
Chandler, Zachariah, 175
Charismatic(s), 8, 99
Charybdis, 102
Chennai, India, 139, 148
Cheverus, Jean-Louis, 29
Chiang Kai-shek, 52
Chiang Mai, Thailand, 159, 200, 202–3
Chile, 39–40
China, 4, 9, 11, 18, 22, 24, 31, 38–39, 43, 47, 49–55, 57, 78, 89, 94, 114, 155–56, 201, 235, 257, 262, 282
China Graduate School of Theology, 262
China Inland Mission, 55, 57
China Inland Society, 196
Chinese (language), 135, 145, 235
Chinese (people), 51, 54
Chinese Bible, 235
Chinese Communism, 38
Chloe (early church), 122
Cho, Yong, 258–59

Christ Church, Hartford, Connecticut, 163
Christendom, 49, 72, 89, 114, 133, 280
Christian and Missionary Alliance, 158
Christian Connections for International Health, 209
Christianization, 88, 128, 269, 273, 275, 281, 283
Christmas, 69
Christology, 73, 76–77, 90, 104, 108, 184
Christomonism, 74
Chronicles (books of), 139
Chrysostom, John, 70
Church of South India, 47
Churchman, 87
City-WideOpen Studies (CWOS), 230
Clapsis, Emmanuel, 76
Clarendon Street Baptist Church, Boston, 21
Clark College, Atlanta, 21
Clark, Ida, 122
Clarke, G., 194
Clooney, Francis X., 290
Cloutier, Mary, 158
Coady, Moses M., 40
Coahuila, 217
Cold War, 160, 197
Colombia, 115, 155
Columbia, Pennsylvania, 175
Combes, Texas, 215
Commission (of 1910 World Missionary Conference), I, 49–55, 57, 60, 88, 94, 291; II, 281–82; III, 59, 281, 283; IV, 48, 85, 89–90, 288; VI, 290; VII, 287; VIII, 86–87, 279
Commission for Mission and Evangelism (World Council of Churches), 71
"Common Call", 254, 270–71
Communism, 25, 37–40, 277
Community Health Development Centre, 205
Conference of Major Superiors of Men, 40
Confucianism, 89
Congregation for the Doctrine of the Faith (CDF), 101–2
Congregation for the Evangelization of Peoples, 100
Congregational Church (denomination), 236
Connecticut, 15, 17, 156, 161, 163, 230
Connecticut, Diocese of (Episcopal), 246–47, 255
Considine, John J., 38–42
Convention of Kanagawa, 235
Conversion of the Pagan World, The, 34
Copp Hill, Revere, Massachusetts, 36
Corisco Mission, 172–73
Cornelius (book of Acts), 112
Cornille, Catherine, 274, 288
Cornwall, Connecticut, 17
Costa Rica, 116
Costas, Orlando E., 274
Council of Florence, 95–96
Cracknell, Kenneth, 90
Cremona, Italy, 87
Croatia, 291
Crummell, Alex, 169–70
Crusades, 128
Currents in World Christianity Project, 48
Cushing, Richard James, 28, 34, 36–39, 42
Cuzco, Peru, 39

Index of Proper Names

CWME (Commission on World Mission and Evangelism, World Council of Churches), 114
Cyril (the philosopher), 43

d'Escoto, Miguel, 40
Dalits, 52
Danville, Kentucky, 172
Dao, 231-33
Daoism, 90
"Dark Continent" (Africa), 49, 54
Davis, Albert, 143
De Activitate Missionali Ecclesiae, 85
Deaconess Hospital (Boston), 20
DeBorst, Ruth Padilla, 275, 293
Deerfield, Illinois, 156
Dejima, Japan, 235
Del Rio, Texas, 213
Delaney, Emma, 170
Denmark, 58
Detroit, Michigan, 175
Dialogue and Proclamation (DP), 100-101, 106
Development Dialogue on Values and Ethics (DDVE), 199
Dindigul, India, 140
Dishman Elementary School, 215
District Six (Cape Town), 110, 111
District Six Museum, 110, 118
Distrito Fronterizo (Methodist Church of Mexico), 219
Distrito San Pablo (Methodist Church of Mexico), 219
Divine Liturgy, 70
Doane Hall (Overseas Ministries Study Center), 230
Dodge City, Kansas, 183
Dogmatic Constitution, 91, 102, 292
Dominus Iesus, 101-2, 292
Donovan, Vincent, 131
Doshisha Eigakko, 237

Doshisha University, 161, 234-35, 237-38
Doshisha University School of Theology, 161
Douglas, Ian, 246-47, 255, 274
Dries, Angelyn, 276, 285, 297
Drummer, Martha, 21
Dunbar, Charles B., 169
Dunwoodie Seminary, 30
Dupuis, Jacques, 100-102
Duraisingh, Christopher, 274

Eaglesrest, 201
East Asia, 49-50, 5720
Eastern Conference of the Methodist Church of Mexico, 219
Eastern Europe, 198
Eastern Orthodox Churches, 5
Eastern Orthodoxy, 280
Ecuador, 39, 116
Edinburgh, Scotland, 4, 13, 63, 273
Edinburgh, University of, 254, 278
Edinburgh 2010, 26, 48, 63, 88, 132, 157, 249, 254-58, 267-72
Edinburgh World Missionary Conference (Edinburgh 1910, "Edinburgh Conference"), 3, 6, 9, 19-20, 23, 28-29, 39, 43, 47-50, 54-56, 58-63, 67, 71-72, 75, 77, 84-98, 102-3, 137, 157, 195, 245, 247-48, 250, 252, 254, 256-57, 259-61, 267, 270, 214-15, 279-81, 283-88, 290-91, 298 (*see also* World Missionary Conference)
Edo, Japan, 235
Edwards, Jonathan, 16
Egypt, 258
El Salvador, 116
Eleazar Kindergarten, 221
England, 155

English (language), 87, 135, 144, 182–83, 214–15, 219, 234, 236–37, 264
Enlightenment, 10, 278, 294
Episcopal Church, 247, 251
Episcopal Divinity School, 274, 292
Episcopal Theological School, 20
Equatorial Guinea, 172
Escobar, Samuel, 295
Essenes, 127
Eucharist, 70–71, 101
Eurasia, 262
Europe, 4, 23–24, 43, 47, 51, 58, 60, 88, 133, 167, 198, 236, 259, 271, 278, 285, 287–88, 294, 298
European(s), 60, 171, 176, 259
European Parliament, 288
Evangelical(s) (evangelical(s)), 59, 102, 119–20, 259
Evangelical Theological Seminary, 291
Evangelicalism (evangelicalism), 24, 102, 120, 195, 259
Evangelii Nuntiandi, 93, 99, 181
Ewing, J. Franklin, 36
Exodus, Book of, 130, 140

Fabella, Virginia, 41
Falcon Reservoir, 213
Fang (people), 176
Farquhar, John Nicol, 90
Father Jim Hennessey Mission Club, 37
Federation of Asian Bishops' Conferences (FABC), 86
Felicity (early church), 122
Fernando, Ajith, 102, 262
Field Afar, The, 23, 33–34
FIFA (Fédération Internationale de Football Association), 110
Finney, Charles, 259

First United Methodist Church (McAllen, Texas), 219
First World War, 57 (*see also* World War I)
Fisk University, 170
Fleming, Louise, 170
Fordham Mission Institute, 36
Fordham University, 36
Foreign Mission School, 17
Foreign Mission Sisters of St. Dominic, 33 (*see also* Maryknoll Sisters of St. Dominic)
Fort Hill, Roxbury, Massachusetts, 36
Fourth Inter-American Conference on Religions, 40
France, 22, 32
Francis of Assisi, 116, 138, 262
Francis, William Cushing, 39
Francke, August Hermann, 148
Frederick University, 148
Free Burma Rangers (FBR), 203, 206–7
Freire, Paulo, 284
French (language), 33, 135
French-Canadians, 43
Friedrich the Wise, 148
Friends of the Samaritans, 201
Fuller Theological Seminary, 156
Funk, Robert, 184

Gabon, 158, 168, 172, 174–77
Gaboon, 174
Galilee, 127
Gallicanists, 30
Gandhi, Mohandas, 52, 129
Garden of Hope, The (GOH), 200, 202–3, 206–7
Garden of the Soul, The, 29
Gardner, Gary, 208
Gary, Jay, 246
Gates Foundation, 198

Gatu, John, 114
Gaudium of Spec (GS), 91
Gayraud, Wilmore, 165
General Association of Congregational Churches, 16
General Board of Global Ministries (GBGM), United Methodist Church, 219
Genesis, book of, 17, 130
Gensichen, Laurentius, 143
Gentile(s), 112, 293-94
Georgetown University, 246, 249, 277
Georgia, 21
German (language), 135, 219
German(s) (people), 43
German Pietism, 141
Germany, 88, 148, 156, 271
Ghana, 88
Gigot, Francis, 31
Gittins, Anthony, 224
Glaucha, Germany, 148
Global Fund, 198
Global Network of Mission Structures (ONMS), 254, 258
GlobaLink, 263
Good Samaritan, 159, 180-87, 189, 191
Good, Adolphus, 176
Goodwill Industries, 20, 247
Gordon, A. J., 21
Gordon-Conwell Theological Seminary (GCTS), 250, 274, 290-91
Gore, Charles, 59
Gospels (books of the Bible), 126, 128, 182, 285, 293, 297
Grace Congregational United Church of Christ (Rutland, Vermont), 236
Graham, Billy, 98, 257
Great Awakening, 14

Great Britain, 139, 169 (*see also* United Kingdom)
Great Commission, 108, 171, 258, 261, 271
Greater Boston, 30, 141, 246, 251-52, 255
Greek (language), 21, 135, 144, 147-48
Greek Orthodox, 251
Greeley, Horace, 169
Green Point Common (Cape Town), 110
Grim, Brian, 246
Griswold, Benjamin, 165
Gründler, Johann Ernest, 149
Guadalupe Hidalgo, Treaty of, 216
Guatemala, 260
Guider, Margaret, 274, 281-82
Gulf Of Mexico, 213
Gustavsson, Stefan, 259
Gutiérrez, Gustavo, 41, 159, 181, 184, 187

Habermas, Jürgen, 80
Haight, Roger, 102
Haitians, 43
Halle (Saale), Germany, 148
Halle Mission, *see* Royal Danish-Halle Mission
Hanley, Roger (family), 29
Harding, Mary Lucy, 168, 175-77
Hardy, Alpheus, 235-36
Hardy, Arthur Sherburne, 235
Hardy, Mrs. Alpheus (Susan), 235-36
Hardy Hall (Doshisha University), 238
Harlingen, Texas, 215
Harmony of the Gospels, 31
Hartford, Connecticut, 163
Harvard Divinity School, 32, 274-75
Harvard University, 32, 43, 207, 248, 275, 280, 289

Hasseltine, John, 15
Hasseltine (Judson), Ann, 15–19
Hawaii, 15, 17–18, 62, 237
Hawaiian (language), 17
Haystack Prayer Meeting, 15, 156
Hebrew, 14, 17, 21, 144, 147–48, 234, 292
Hebrew(s) (people), 165
Hebrew Bible, 148, 182, 191
Hebrews, Letter to the 149, 165, 282
"Hebrewisms", 35
Heian period, 231
Heim, Mark, 77, 102
Heinz, John, 149
Hellums, Susan, 219
Helmick, Raymond, 274, 279, 281
Help for Pastors, 201
Helms, Edgar, 20
Henderson, Chas., 172
Hennessey, Jim, 37
Henry, Carl F. H., 257
Herodians, 126
Hesselgrave, David, 102
Heuertz, Christopher, 188–90
Hick, John, 73
Hidalgo County, Texas, 214, 216, 218
Hidden, Mary E., 236
Hindi, 135, 145
Hindu(s), 11, 52, 129, 145
Hinduism, 90, 94, 136, 146, 200
Hispanic, 214, 291
Hispanic Faculty Colloquium (Boston Theological Institute), 286–87
HIV, 198, 200, 204–6, 209, 262
Hoekendijk, J. C., 72
Hogan, John, 30, 33
Holiness Club, 156 (see also Holy Club)
Holiness revivals, 196
Holland (Netherlands), 58, 235
Hollywood, 84

Holocaust, 118, 280
Holy Club, 14 (see also Holiness Club)
Holy Cross Greek Orthodox School of Theology, 25, 246, 274, 283
Holy Roman Empire, 128 (see also Roman Empire)
Hopkins, Samuel, 16
Hoste, D. E., 55
Houston, Texas, 224
Huber, Douglas, 209
Human Development Center (HDC), 204–5, 207
Hunan, China, 43
Hunton, William A., 166

Iglesia Metodista de México (Methodist Church of Mexico), 160, 213, 219–21, 225
Ignatius of Loyola, 14, 35
Illich, Ivan, 129
Illinois, 156
Independent tradition, 8, 251
India, 4, 11, 15–18, 34, 47, 49–50, 52, 54, 56, 88–89, 98, 133, 136, 140, 143, 148, 156, 169, 198, 200, 276, 278, 289
Indian Missionary Society of Tirunelveli, 62
Indian sub-continent, 57–58
Indians (American), 14 (see also American Indian; Plains Indians)
Indonesia, 98, 156, 200, 289
Inquisition, 118
Inter-American Conference on Religious, Fourth, 40
Inter-Varsity Christian Fellowship, 20
International Ecumenical Peace Convocation, 298

International Mission and Ecumenism Faculty Committee (Boston Theological Institute), 274
International Missionary Council (IMC), 88, 98, 280–81
Internet, 24, 135, 137, 140, 245, 263
Interreligious Council (Uganda), 209
Ireland, Daryl, 248–50, 252
Irish (people), 22, 43
Irish-American, 22
Isaiah (book of), 130
Isaiah (prophet), 117
Islam, 26, 49, 54–56, 60, 62, 95, 136, 200
Israel, 112, 117
Israelites, 182–83
Italian(s), 22, 43
Ithaca, Greece, 75

Jamaica, 35, 298
Jamaica Plain, Massachusetts, 33
Jamaican(s), 35
James (apostle), 39, 122
Japan, 4, 30, 49–51, 54, 57, 68, 90, 94, 156, 161, 229–31, 234–37, 239, 254, 257
Japan Mission (ABCFM), 236
Japanese (language), 234
Japanese (people), 54, 236, 239
Jeju (Quelpart) Island, South Korea, 62
Jeremiah (prophet), 233–34, 239
Jerusalem, 27, 88, 98, 112–13, 296
Jerusalem Council, 294–95
Jesuit(s), 14, 35, 43, 99
Jesuit Refugee Service (JRS), 201
Jewish (people), 112
Jewish (religion), 295
Jew(s), 94–95, 112, 129, 145, 182–83, 293–94

Jeyaraj, Daniel, 5–6, 8, 10, 41, 249, 274, 276, 296
Jinan, China, 53
Jinyu, 11
John (apostle), 296
John J. Burns Library, 35
John (Gospel of), 182, 297
John XXIII, Pope, 85, 87
John Paul II, Pope, 97, 99–100, 102, 288
Johnson, Todd, 246, 274, 290
Jonah, 79
Joshua, 296
Joshua Project, 256
Judaism, 35, 91, 95, 102, 191, 295
Judeans, 127
Judson, Adoniram, 15–18
Judson, Ann Hasseltine, 15–19
Jung, Ryong Jae, 248
Justin (Martyr), 287

Kamel, Hisham, 258
Kanagawa, Convention of, 235
Kanetsugu, Naoe, 239
Kärkkäinen, Veli-Matti, 102
Kasatkin, Nicolas, 67
Kauffman, Christopher, 32
Keesmaat, Sylvia, 115
Kelley, Francis C., 29
Kenshin, Uesugi, 239
Kentucky, 156, 172
Khandeshi, 11
Kim, Gun Cheol, 249
Kim, Heetae, 249
Kim, Kirsteen, 75
King, Martin Luther Jr., 112, 129
Kings (books of), 139
Kingdom (of God), 23, 27, 41, 70–72, 74, 76–78, 99, 120, 122, 127, 130, 143, 195, 293–94, 297
Kinney County, Texas, 216
Kirk, Andrew, 102, 194

Kitano Shinto Shrine, 238
Korea, 24, 50, 54, 62, 156, 231, 249, 254, 257
Korea, South, 40
Korean peninsula, 54
Korean Protestants, 54, 62
Korean(s), 54, 62, 258–59
Kraemer, Hendrik, 98
Kreider, Alan, 79, 113
Krishna, 105
Kristof, Nicholas, 208
Kuhn, Thomas, 78
Kuzmič, Peter, 291
Kwan, Simon Shui-Man, 79
Kyoto, Japan, 161, 234, 237–38
Kärkkäinen, Veli-Matti, 102

La Niña, 228
Lambarene, Gabon, 176
Landeskirchliche Gemeinschaften, 142
Lange, Joachim, 143
Laos, 9, 201
Latin, 85, 91, 101, 135, 138, 144
Latin America, 5, 7, 11, 38–39, 41, 58–59, 61, 114, 135, 258, 262, 287
Latin America Bureau, 38–39
Latin American Theological Fraternity, 275
Latin Americans, 7
Latin Church, 294
Latino(s), 291
Latourette, Kenneth Scott, 39
Lausanne, Switzerland, 98
Lausanne Committee for World Evangelization (LCWE), 98, 265
Lausanne conferences, 260, 264
Lausanne Congress on World Evangelization, First (Lausanne 1974), 256–59, 261, 265

Lausanne Congress on World Evangelization, Third (Cape Town 2010, Lausanne 2010, Lausanne III), 20, 116, 119, 121, 261, 264–66
Lausanne Covenant, 258–59, 261
Lausanne Movement, 254, 258, 261, 264, 266
Lausanne Special Interest Group on Reconciliation, 121
Leadership Conference of Women Religious, 40
Learned, Dwight Whitney, 237
Lee, Moonjang, 5, 8–10
Lefebvre, Marcel-François, 102
Lehmann, Paul, 294
Leninism, 53
Leo XII, Pope, 30
Leucorea University, 148
Levinas, Emmanuel, 69
Lewellen, Eric, 250
Lewis, Marilyn, 170–71
Lexington Christian Academy, 248, 252
Liberia, 17, 168, 172, 174
Lilly Endowment, 283
Linden, Ian, 197
Lindsell, Harold, 257
Lithuanians, 43
Liverpool Hope University, 249, 276
Logos, 90
Lohse, Eduard, 185
Loisy, Alfred, 31
London Missionary Society (LMS), 15
London, England, 87
Louisiana Purchase, 15
Love Line Family Centre, The, 201
Lower Rio Grande Valley, 160, 213
Loyola, Ignatius of, 14
Lucius of Cyrene, 294
Luke (evangelist), 182, 184

348 Index of Proper Names

Luke, Gospel of, 184, 293
Lumen Gentium (*LG*), 91, 93, 95, 100, 102, 292
Luther Theological Seminary (St. Paul, Minnesota), 156
Luther, Martin, 116, 148, 236
Lütkens, Franz Julius, 143
Luzbetak, Louis, 36
Lydia House, 201
Lysisus, Johann, 143

Macedonian Call, 259
Machozi, Vincent, 246
Madagascar, 57
Madrid, Spain, 6
Magadhi Bihari, 11
Maier, Joseph, 204
Maine, 19
Maitili, 11
Malayan peninsula, 55
Malaysia, 145, 200
Malden, Massachusetts, 15, 18
Mali, 6
Malley, John, 92
Maluleke, Tinyiko Sam, 270
Manaen, 294
Management Sciences for Health, 209
Manchuria, 49, 62
Mandarin, 20
Manila, Philippines, 98
Manna, Paolo, 34
Marine Bible Society, 17
Mark, Gospel of, 182, 285
Marquette University, 159
Marshall, Katherine, 199
Martin Luther University, Halle-Wittenberg, 148
Marxist-Leninism, 53
Mary, Virgin, 145, 216
Maryknoll, New York, 23

Maryknoll Fathers and Brothers (Catholic Foreign Mission Society of America), 23, 32–33, 38, 40
Maryknoll Sisters of St. Dominic, 23, 28, 33
Maryknoll Society, 30, 39
Maryknoller(s), 34, 39–40
Masao, Takenaka, 238
Mass, 29
Massachusetts, 14–15, 17–19, 23, 25, 39, 43, 236
Massachusetts Bay, 36
Massachusetts Home Mission Society, 29
Matamoros, Mexico, 213, 218
Matthew, Gospel of, 181–82
Matthey, Jacques, 76–77
Maurice, Frederick Denison, 90
Mauritius, 57
Maverick County, Texas, 216
Maximus the Confessor, 75–76
Mayan, 135
Mayling, Soon, 52
McAllen Conference (United Methodist Church), 219
McBee, Silas, 86–87, 95
McBrien, Richard, 92
McCarthy, Joseph, 38
McDermott, Brian, 284
McGilvary School of Divinity, 159
McGlinchey, Henry, 34, 43
McGlinchey, Joseph, 34
McLaren, Brian, 251, 275–76, 282, 293
McWorld, 115
Mejido, Manuel Jesús, 291
Melanchthon, Philip, 148
Memorial Church, The (Harvard University), 248, 275
Menaul, Harriet, 173
Menkel, Charity Sneed, 168, 172–74

Menkel, Peter, 172–74
Mercy Centre, 205
Merton, Thomas, 282
Methodism, 14, 156, 223, 225
Methodist(s), 48, 52, 149
Methodist Border Friendship Commission (MBFC), 160, 188, 190, 213, 216–26
Methodist Church of Mexico (Iglesia Metodista de México), 168, 213, 219–21, 225
Methodius, 43
Mexican Methodist Border Mission, 219
Mexican Revolution, 216
Mexicans, 216, 219, 222
Mexico, 160, 215–16, 218–22, 224–25
Mexico City, Mexico, 118
Michaelis, Johann Heinrich, 148
Michigan, 175
Middle East, 262
Millennium Development Declaration, 200
Millennium Development Goals (MDGs), 41, 199, 220, 287, 292, 295, 297
Mills, Samuel, 15–18
Missio Creator Dei, 270
Mission Enacted course, 209–10
Mission Frontiers, 170
Mission Institute, Fordham, 36
Mission Institute of Orthodox Christianity, 25, 36
Missionary Society of Saint James the Apostle, 39
Mississippi Valley, 17
Modern Challenge of the Missions, The, 37
Mohammedan, 54
Moltmann, Jürgen, 72, 232–33
Mongolia, 7

Monrovia, Liberia, 172–73
Moody, Dwight, 19, 23
Moore, George, 170
Moravian Church, 149
Mormon, 246
Mother-Baby Unit, 204
Mott, John R., 23, 48–53, 55–56, 59–62, 85, 88, 157, 258, 260, 283
Mt. Hermon One Hundred, 19, 23
Mukadeya hotel, 237
Mulherin, Mary Gabriella, 40
Müller, Friedrich Max, 146
Muslim(s), 11, 56, 94–95, 129, 145, 257, 278, 289
Mwombeki, Fidon R., 271
My Ogowe, 168, 176
Myanmar (Burma), 201–3
Myers, Travis, 250
Myklebust, Olav G., 132

Nagaland, India, 285
Nagasaki Bay, Japan, 235
Nakano Sun Plaza, 256
Namibia, 114
Nassau, Isabella, 168, 172–73, 175–76
Nassau, Mary, 173
Nassau, Robert Hamill, 168, 174, 176
National Catholic Commission on Migration (NCC), 201
National Missionary Society of India, 62
Native American(s), 35, 43, 216 (*see also* American Indians; Indians (American); Plains Indians)
Nazareth Manifesto, 140
Neesima, Joseph Hardy (Niijima Jo), 161, 234–39
Negro, 164, 166–68, 170, 176
Neo-evangelicalism, 257
Nepal, 7, 200
Netherlands (Holland), 58, 235

Index of Proper Names

Netland, Harold, 102
Neville, Robert, 290
New Age, 77
New Bedford, Massachusetts, 39
New Delhi, India, 98
New England, 15, 18, 29
New England Deaconess Training School, 20 (see also Boston Deaconess Training School)
New Englander(s), 15, 17
New Haven, Connecticut, 17, 156, 161, 230
New Light Foundation, The, 201
New Mexico, 219
New Monasticism, 284
New Testament, 32, 59, 77, 130, 134, 136, 148, 184, 235
New World, 43
New York, Roman Catholic Archdiocese of, 32
New York State, 23, 30, 32-34, 87
New York City, New York, 17, 32, 87
New York Review, 30
New York Theological Seminary, 165
Newbigin, Lesslie, 257
Newell, Harriet, 17
Nicholas M. Williams special collection, 35
Nigeria, 11, 278
Nissiotis, Nikos, 73
Noh theatre, 231
Nolan, Albert, 185-88, 190
Nomads On a Mission Active in Divine Service (NOMADS), 224
Non-Christians, 94-96, 100-101, 103-5, 107, 129, 136, 145, 195, 229, 251, 276
Non-Westerners, 270
North(ern) America, 4-5, 15, 18-19, 24, 40, 47, 57, 60, 88, 218, 285, 287, 298

North American Free Trade Agreement (NAFTA), 217-18, 222
North Carolina, 33, 156
Northern Africa, 10
Northern Europe, 288
Northfield, Massachusetts, 19
Nostra Aetate (NA), 85, 91, 94-95, 102, 292
Nouwen, Henri, 188
Nuevo Laredo, Mexico, 214

Oceania, 58
Ockenga, Harold, 257
O'Connell, William, 30, 34, 36, 43
Oduyoye, Mercy, 41
Odysseus (Ulysses), 68
Odyssey, The, 68
Ogden, Phoebe, 172
Ogden, Thomas Spencer, 172
Oiso, Japan, 237
Oklahoma, 43
Okuyama, Minoru, 258
Oldham, J. H., 39
OMF International, 196 (see also China Inland Mission)
Onnuri Community Church, 258
On the Permanent Validity of the Church's Missionary Mandate Redemptoris Missio (RM), 97
"Onward Christian Soldiers", 22
Opukaha'ia, Henry, 15-18, 26
Orbis Books, 40
Orient, 49, 54
Oriental (Orthodox), 58
Orientalist, 31
Origen, 75
Orthodox Christianity, 5, 24, 58, 70, 246, 251-52, 267, 280, 294
Osijek, Croatia, 291
Ottaviani, Alfredo, 91-92
Our Father, 41, 297

Index of Proper Names   351

Overseas Ministries Study Center (OMSC), 161, 229-30, 246
Oxfam, 197
Oxford Centre for Mission Studies, 287
Oxford, England, 14, 156

Pacific Islands, 88
Pacific rim, 57
Pacific Islands, 88
Padilla, René, 260
Paganism, 54, 136
Palestine, 238
Palestinian, 263
Palmer Theological Seminary, 156
Panama Congress on Christian Work in Latin America, 59
Panikkar, Raimon (Raimundo), 74, 290
Papathanasiou, Athanasios, 251, 276
Paris, France, 14, 31-32
Paris, University of, 14
Park Street Church, Boston, 17
Parks, Rosa, 122
Parravicino Revel, Sabina, 87
Parsons, Elizabeth, 249, 274, 285-86
Pasadena, California, 156
Pascal, Eva, 159-60, 208, 245, 248, 250
Pastors' Children Scholarship, 220
Patna, India, 34
Pattaya, Thailand, 98
Paul, apostle (Saul), 76, 106, 149, 287, 293-94
Paul VI, Pope, 85, 92, 99, 181
Paulist Fathers, 32
Penelope, 68
Pentecostal/Charismatic renewal, 8
Pentecostal Christianity, 8-9, 61, 216, 251, 267
Pentecostals, 61

President's Emergency Plan for AIDS Relief (PEPFAR), 198
Perry, Matthew, 235
Persia, 50
Perspectives on the World Christian Movement, 260
Peru, 39
Peter, apostle, 79, 112, 116, 120, 149
Petersen, Rodney, 41, 245-46
Pew Forum on Religion and Public Life, 246
Phan, Peter, 80, 249, 250-51, 277
Pharisee(s), 127
Philadelphia, Pennsylvania, 148-49, 156, 175
Philippines, 9, 98
Phillips Academy, 236
Pia Desideria, 142
Pieris, Aloysius, 74
Pietism, 141-43, 148
Pinnock, Clark, 102
Pittsburgh Theological Seminary, 156
Pittsburgh, Pennsylvania, 149
Plains Indian, 183
Pluralism Project at Harvard University, 289
Pohl, Christine, 188-90
Polish, 43
Pontifical Council for Inter-Religious Dialogue, 100
Pontifical Council for the Pastoral Care of Migrants and Iterant People, 43
Poor Man's Catechism, The, 29
Portland, Maine, 19
Portuguese, 7
Post-World War II era, 37
Premnath, D. N., 41
Presbyterian Church, 49, 62, 172, 216
Presbyterian, The, 165

Presbyterian Corisco Mission, 172
Presbyterian Freedmen's Bureau, 177
Presbyterian Mission, 175
Presidential Palace, El Salvador, 121
Price, Thomas F., 23, 33, 39
Project Lek, 204
Protestant, Catholic, Jew, 289
Protestantism, 13, 15, 18–19, 25, 29–30, 36, 38, 42, 47, 53, 56–59, 85, 87–88, 133, 143, 285, 289
Protestant(s), 8, 22, 24, 29, 33, 39, 43, 47–48, 50, 54, 58, 62, 84, 86, 95, 98–99, 103, 117, 130, 160–61, 196, 204, 236, 246, 251, 254, 268, 280, 294
Punjab, India, 11
Pure Land Buddhism, 231
Puritan, 236

Qi, He, 12
Qur'an, 105, 145

Rahab Beauty Shop, The, 201
Rahner, Karl, 99
Ralph Winter Lectureship, 260
Randolph, Massachusetts, 43
Rangiah, John, 62
Ratzinger, Josef, 101 (*see also* Benedict XVI, Pope)
Recreational Vehicle (RV), 215, 224
Redemptoris Missio (*RM*), 97, 99–100, 292
Reed, Jeff, 79
Regent University, 246
Rejoice Urban Development Project, 201
Revelation, Book of, 59, 77 (*see also* Apocalypse)
Revere, Massachusetts, 36
Reynosa, Mexico, 218
Ricci, Matteo, 78
Rickman, Jeffrey, 249

Rieger, Joerg, 186
Rio Grande (river), 213–14, 216, 218
Rio Grande Mission Conference of the United Methodist Church, 219
Rio Grande Valley, Lower, 160, 213–14, 223
Rise of Global Christianity, The (Boston University course), 246
Rist, Gilbert, 208
Ritschl, Albrecht, 294
Robert, Dana L., 133, 156, 246–47, 249, 270, 274, 277, 284
Roddan, Celestine, 43
Rogers, Mary Josephine "Mollie", 22–23, 28, 33–34
Roman Catholic(s), 29, 86, 91, 251 (*see also* Catholics)
Roman Catholic Church, 5, 29, 86, 91 (*see also* Catholic Church)
Roman Catholicism, 36, 84, 280, 292 (*see also* Catholicism)
Roman Empire, 111, 114, 128 (*see also* Holy Roman Empire)
Romans (people), 126
Romero, Oscar, 122, 141
Roncalli, Giuseppe, 87
Rooney, Paul F., 43
Ross, Kenneth, 4, 290
Roxbury, Massachusetts, 32–33, 36
Royal Danish-Halle Mission, 133, 143
Ruiz, Ramón Eduardo, 218
Russia, 38, 67–68, 149
Russian-Japanese War, 67
Russian Orthodox, 67
Russian(s), 68
Rutland, Vermont, 236
Rwanda, 7

Sabbath, 18
Sacks, Jonathan, 191

Sadducee(s), 126
Saint Pius X Society, 102
Salem Harbor, Massachusetts, 16
Salvation Army, 20
Samaritan(s), 127, 182 (*see also* Good Samaritan)
Samartha, Stanley J., 98
Samurai, 161, 235, 239
San Antonio, Texas, 71
San Juan, Texas, 216
San Luis Potosi, Mexico, 220
San Salvador, El Salvador, 121
Sanders, Ethan R., 56
Sanneh, Lamin, 164, 166
Sanskrit, 20
Santiago, Chile, 40
São Paulo, Brazil, 287
Sarah (wife of Abraham), 68
Saxony, Germany, 148
Schaff, Philip, 280
Schreiter, Robert, 41, 282, 295
Schultze, Benjamin, 149
Scotland, 48, 50, 60, 89, 273
Scripture Union, 137
Scylla, 102
Second American Catholic Congress, 29
Second World War, 57, 98 (*see also* World War II)
Second Vatican Council, 42 (*see also* Vatican II)
Seelye, J. H., 236
Senator John Heinz History Center, 149
Senegal, 209
Sentamu, John, 268, 278
Seoul, South Korea, 287
Seven Virgin Spirits, 140
Shandong Christian University, 53
Shanghai, China, 47, 235
Sheppard, William, 170
Shinto, 90, 231, 237–38
Shriver, Donald, 117
Shema, 182
Siberia, Russia 62
Sierra Leone, 169
Simeon, 294
Sin'ichi, Aoki, 237
Sine, Tom, 115
Singapore, 287
Sioux Falls, South Dakota, 37
Sisters of St. Francis of Mary Immaculate, 281
Slater, Thomas Ebenezer, 90
Smedt, Joseph De, 92
Smith College, 22, 33
Smith, Amanda, 169
Smith, Gerrit, 169
Smith, Stephen, 175
Sneed (Menkel), Charity, 168, 172–74
Sneed, James, 172
Sneed, Lavinia, 172–75
Sobrino, Jon, 102, 187
Society for the Propagation of the Faith (SPF), 22, 28, 32–34, 42
Society of the Divine Word, 36
Solomon, 238
South Africa, 9, 61, 110–11, 120
South Africa, University of, 270
South African Council of Churches, 270
South America, 88
South Asia, 57
South Boston, Massachusetts, 34
South Korea, 40
South Pacific, 15, 18
South Padre Island, Texas, 215–16
Southeast Asia, 30, 57, 201–2
Southern Baptist Convention, 216
Southern Pathan, 11
Southwest Texas Annual Conference, United Methodist Church, 218–19

Spain, 216
Speer, Robert E., 53, 89
Spelman, Elizabeth V., 292
Spener, Philip Jacob, 141–43, 148
Spirit in Education Movement (SEM), 201
St. James Society, 39
St. John's Seminary, 22, 28, 30–34, 285
St. Louis University, 276
St. Paul, Minnesota, 156
St. Paul's Church, Cambridge, 32, 34, 43
St. Petersburg, Russia, 149
Stanley, Brian, 67, 72, 157, 248, 278–79, 282–84, 286
Starr County, Texas, 216
Statement of Lament for Evangelicals and the Legacy of Apartheid, 120–21
Statistical Atlas of Christian Missions, 57
Stephen (biblical), 122
Stockbridge, Massachusetts, 14
Strieby, Michael E., 164–65, 167
Student Christian Movement, 48, 252
Student Volunteer Convention, 170
Student Volunteer Movement for Foreign Mission (SVM), 20–22, 57, 88, 168, 283
Study Process Monitoring Group (Edinburgh 2010), 268
Sub-Saharan Africa, 7, 136, 198, 257
Sulpician(s), 22, 28, 30–34
Sun Yat-sen, 52
Sumatra, Indonesia, 55
Swahili, 135, 145
Sweden, 259
Switzerland, 99, 259
Synaxis Greek Orthodox Journal, 276
Sywulka, Edward, 251

Table Mountain, South Africa, 110
Taiwan, 156
Taiwanese, 248
Tamaulipas, Mexico, 217–18
Tambaram, India, 88, 98
Tamil (language), 149
Tamil (people), 133, 150
Tamil Nadu, India, 140
Taylor, Horace S., 235–36
Taylor, James Hudson, 196
Taylor, William, 20
Telegu Baptist Natal Mission, 62
Telugu (language), 149
Tennent, Timothy, 102, 274
Testem Benevolentiae, 30
Texas, 213–14, 216–19, 221, 223–24
Texas Environmental Almanac, 217
Thailand (Siam), 19, 160, 193, 200–202, 210
Thecla (early church), 122
Theological Commission (Second Vatican Council), 91
Theology House, St. John's Seminary, 32
Theravada Buddhism, 201
Third World, 41, 67, 72
Thompson, A. C., 236
Three-Self Patriotic Movement, 282
Timbuktu, Mali, 6
Timor, 7
Timothy (biblical), 149
Tirukkural, 150
Tiruvalluvar, 150
Titus, 149
Tokyo 2010, 26, 63, 157, 249, 254–60
Tokyo Declaration, 254, 258
Tokyo, Japan, 51, 235, 237
Torres, Camilo, 115
Torringford, Connecticut, 15
Tracy, Joseph V., 32
Tranquebar Mission, 143, 149

Index of Proper Names 355

Tranquebar, India, 133, 148
Treaty of Guadalupe, Hidalgo, 216
Trinity, 70, 74–75, 77, 93, 292
Trinity Evangelical Divinity School, 156, 158
Turkey, 25, 50
Tutu, Desmond, 286
Twitter, 245

Uganda, 60, 209
Ultramontanist, 30
Ulysses (Odysseus), 68
Underground Railroad, 175
United Church of Christ, America, 236
United Evangelical Lutheran Church of South Africa, 115
United Evangelical Mission, 271
United Friedrich University, 148
United Kingdom, 23, 268
United Methodist, 216
United Methodist Action Reach-Out Mission by Youth (U.M. ARMY), 220, 224
United Methodist Church, 160, 213–16, 219–21, 224
United Nations, 41, 197, 199, 220, 292, 295–97
United States of America (US, USA), 9, 14–20, 22–24, 26, 30, 32, 38, 42–44, 51, 93, 105, 133, 135, 138–39, 149, 158, 160–61, 163–64, 166–67, 169, 172–75, 196–97, 213, 215, 216, 218, 200, 222, 229, 235–37, 247, 250, 256, 259, 261, 268, 289, 291
University of Edinburgh, 254, 278
University of Paris, 14
University of South Africa, 270
Uraga Harbor, Japan, 235
Urbana Student Missions Conferences, 20, 259, 261

United States Agency for International Development (USAID), 198
U.S. Center for World Mission (USCWM), 254, 256–60

Vacation Bible Schools, 221
Val Verde County, Texas, 216
Valparaiso Project on the Education and Formation of People in Faith, The, 283
Valparaiso University, 283
Vandergrift, Nicki, 284
Van Engen, Charles E., 102
Vatican, the, 30–31, 38, 40, 101
Vatican II, 42, 84–88, 91–99, 101–3, 108, 280–81, 292 (*see also* Second Vatican Council)
Vatican Splendors: A Journey through Faith and Art, 149
Vega, Mario, 122
Vénard, Theophane, 30
Venn, Henry, 282
Vermont, 236
Veronis, Luke, 246, 274, 283–84
Vietnam, 114, 201
Vietnam War, 118
Vietnamese, 43, 106
Virgen de San Juan del Valle Shrine, 216
Virgin Mary, 145, 216
Volf, Miroslav, 69
Volunteer Pledge, 20

Wainwright, J. M., 163
Wake Forest University, 156
Walls, Andrew, 85, 147, 283, 287, 297
Walsh, James Anthony, 22–23, 30–34, 39, 43, 115
Ward, Keith, 290
Wariboko, Nimi, 246, 274
Warren, Max, 116

Washington D.C., 34, 140
WCC, 47, 71, 119, 229, 281 (see also World Council of Churches)
Webb County, Texas, 216
Werner, Dietrich, 132
Wesley, Charles, 14
Wesley, John, 14, 116, 149, 156, 259
West Africa, 61, 167, 174
West Asian, 136
West Indians, 169
West Indies, 169
West Virginia, 172
Western Europe, 133
Westminster Theological Seminary, 156
Whitby, Canada, 88
White, Lisa Beth, 160
Whitefield, George, 14
Whitewright, J. S., 53
Whitewright Institute and Museum, 53
Whitney, Larry, 155
With Passion and Compassion: Third World Women Doing Theology, 41
Wilberforce, William, 259
Wild Rover, 235
Wilfred, Felix, 289
Willacy County, Texas, 214
William Carey International University, 260
Williams, John J., 33
Williams, Joseph J., 28, 34–36, 42
Williams, Nicholas M., 35
Williams College, 15, 156
Williams Special Collection, 35
Wilson, John Leighton, 168
Winston-Salem, North Carolina, 156
Winter Lectureship, 260
Winter Texans, 215
Winter, Ralph, 254, 256–60, 265, 285
Wolfensohn, James, 199

Women's Board of the Northwest, The (Presbyterian Mission), 175
Woman's Home Missionary Association, 30
Women's Mission Society, 172
Woodstock Theological Center at Georgetown University, 35
Workers are Few, The, 34
World Bank (WB) 197, 199
World Christian Database, 8, 11
World Christianity, 40
World Conference on Mission and Evangelism, 71
World Council of Churches (WCC), 47, 71, 77, 88, 98, 119, 199, 228–29, 254, 281, 292, 298
World Council of Churches' International Ecumenical Peace Convocation, 298
World Council of Churches (WCC) Vancouver Assembly, 229
World Cup, FIFA (football/soccer), 110
World Birding Center, 214
World Evangelical Alliance, 255
World Faith Development Dialog, 199
World in Boston Exposition, 29
World Missionary Conference (WMC), 4, 13, 23–24, 47–48, 50, 61–62, 84–89, 92, 94–96, 98, 108, 273 (see also Edinburgh World Missionary Conference)
World Student Christian Federation, 252, 283
World Vision, 194, 199
World War I, 43, 287 (see also First World War)
World War II (WWII), 6, 36, 160, 197, 200, 219, 280 (see also Second World War)
Wright, Chris, 116

Wuppertal, Germany, 271
Wuthnow, Robert, 180, 198, 200
WWII, 200, 280 (*see also* Second World War; World War II)

Xaverian Brothers, 37

Yale Divinity School, 40, 156, 161
Yale University, 14–15, 17, 40, 156, 161, 237–38
Yeshu Bhajan, 165
Yoder, Bruce, 251
Yoido Full Gospel Church, 258
Yong, Amos, 102
York, England, 268, 278
Yoruba, 135
Yorubaland, 60

Yoshida, Megumi, 161
Young Christian Students, 37
Young Men's Christian Association (YMCA), 19, 22, 52, 166, 283
Youngs, Samuel, 250
YouTube, 245
Yu, Carver, 262

Zapata County, Texas, 216
Zealots (first-century Jewish), 127
Ziegenbalg, Bartholomäus, 58, 133, 143, 149
Zimbabwe, 268
Zinzendorf, Nicholas von, 149
Zizioulas, John, 76
Zwemer, Samuel, 56